the link between animal abuse and human violence

the link between ANIMAL ABUSE and HUMAN VIOLENCE

EDITED BY ANDREW LINZEY

sussex
ACADEMIC
PRESS
BRIGHTON • PORTLAND

2 4 6 8 10 9 7 5 3 1

First published in 2009 by
SUSSEX ACADEMIC PRESS
PO Box 139
Eastbourne BN24 9BP

and in the United States of America by
SUSSEX ACADEMIC PRESS
920 NE 58th Ave   Suite 300
Portland, Oregon 97213-3786

British Library Cataloguing in Publication Data
A CIP catalogue record for this book is available from the British Library.

Library of Congress Cataloging-in-Publication Data
The link between animal abuse and human violence / edited by Andrew Linzey.
  p. cm.
  Includes bibliographical references and index.
  ISBN 978-1-84519-324-9 (h/c : alk. paper) —
  ISBN 978-1-84519-325-6 (p/b : alk. paper)
  1. Animal welfare—Psychological aspects. 2. Violence—Forecasting.
  I. Linzey, Andrew.
  HV4708.L54 2009
  616.85′82—dc22

                                                        2009013830

MIX
Paper from
responsible sources
FSC® C013056

Typeset and designed by SAP, Brighton & Eastbourne.
Printed by TJ International, Padstow, Cornwall.
This book is printed on acid-free paper.

Contents

About the Editor and Contributors   x

Introduction   1
Does Animal Abuse Really Benefit Us?
Andrew Linzey

Part I   Overviews of Existing Research   11
Introduction *by Andrew Linzey*

1   Measuring Animal Cruelty and Case Histories   13
    Marie Louise Petersen and David P. Farrington

2   Types of Cruelty: Animals and Childhood Cruelty,   24
    Domestic Violence, Child and Elder Abuse
    Marie Louise Petersen and David P. Farrington

3   A Lifespan Perspective on Human Aggression and Animal Abuse   38
    Eleonora Gullone

Part II   Emotional Development and Emotional Abuse   61
Introduction *by Andrew Linzey*

4   Empathy as an Indicator of Emotional Development   63
    Andrea M. Beetz

5   Emotional Abuse of Children and Animals   75
    Franklin D. McMillan

Part III   Children, Family Violence, and Animals   93
Introduction *by Andrew Linzey*

6   Cruelty, Children, and Animals: Historically One,   95
    Not Two, Causes
    Sabrina Tonutti

7 Examining Children's Exposure to Violence in the Context   106
   of Animal Abuse
   Frank R. Ascione

8 Women-Battering, Pet Abuse, and Human–Animal   116
   Relationships
   Clifton P. Flynn

9 The Role of Animals in Public Child Welfare Work   126
   Christina Risley-Curtiss

Part IV   Animal Abuse and Serial Murder   143
Introduction *by Andrew Linzey*

10 Developmental Animal Cruelty and its Correlates in Sexual   145
    Homicide Offenders and Sex Offenders
    Llian Alys, J. Clare Wilson, John Clarke and Peter Toman

11 Reducing the Link's False Positive Problem   163
    Jack Levin and Arnold Arluke

Part V   Ethical Perspectives on Human–Animal Relations   173
Introduction *by Andrew Linzey*

12 Is Human Rights Speciesist?   175
    Conor Gearty

13 Responding Ethically to Animal Abuse   184
    Mark H. Bernstein

14 The New Canaries in the Mine: The Priority of Human   190
    Welfare in Animal Abuse Prosecution
    Elizabeth Clawson

15 The Structure of Evil   201
    Mark Rowlands

16 'Vile attentions': On the Limits of Sympathetic Imagination   206
    Daniel B. Williams

Part VI   Law Enforcement, Offenders, and Sentencing Policy   221
Introduction *by Andrew Linzey*

17 An FBI Perspective on Animal Cruelty   223
    Alan C. Brantley interviewed by Randall Lockwood and Ann W. Church

18 Laws and Policy to Address the Link of Family Violence   228
   Joan E. Schaffner

19 Dealing with Animal Offenders   238
   Angus Nurse

20 Implications for Criminal Law, Sentencing Policy and Practice   250
   Martin Wasik

Part VII   Prevention and Professional Obligations   **261**
Introduction *by Andrew Linzey*

21 A Legal Duty to Report Suspected Animal Abuse – Are   263
   Veterinarians Ready?
   Ian Robertson

22 The Role of Veterinarians and Other Animal Welfare   273
   Workers in the Reporting of Suspected Child Abuse
   Corey C. Montoya and Catherine A. Miller

23 Animal Cruelty and Child Welfare – The Health Visitor's   281
   Perspective
   Dawn Hawksworth and Rachel Balen

Part VIII   The Abuse of Wild Animals   **295**
Introduction *by Andrew Linzey*

24 Overview of Research   297
   Nicola Taylor and Tania Signal

25 Hunting as an Abusive Sub-culture   302
   John Cooper

26 Hunting as a Morally Suspect Activity   317
   Priscilla N. Cohn and Andrew Linzey

27 Dolphin Drive Hunts and the Socratic Dictum: 'Vice harms   329
   the doer'
   Thomas I. White

Index   341

About the Editor and Contributors

Andrew Linzey (editor) is Director of the Oxford Centre for Animal Ethics (www.oxfordanimalethics.com) and a member of the Faculty of Theology in the University of Oxford. He was previously Senior Research Fellow in Ethics, Theology and Animal Welfare at Mansfield College, Oxford, from 1992–2000 and at Blackfriars Hall, Oxford, 2000–2006. From 1987 to 1992, he was Director of Studies of the Centre for the Study of Theology in the University of Essex, and from 1992 to 1996, he was Special Professor in Theology at the University of Nottingham. In 1998, he was Visiting Professor at the Koret School of Veterinary Medicine at the Hebrew University of Jerusalem. He was Honorary Professor at the University of Birmingham from 1996–2007, and is currently Honorary Professor at the University of Winchester, and Special Professor at Saint Xavier University, Chicago. He also holds the first Professorship in Animal Ethics at the Graduate Theological Foundation, Indiana.

Professor Linzey has written more than one hundred and fifty articles and authored or edited twenty books on theology and ethics, including seminal works on animals: *Animal Theology* (SCM Press and University of Illinois Press, 1994 and 1996); (co-edited with Dorothy Yamamoto) *Animals on the Agenda: Questions about Animals for Theology and Ethics* (SCM Press and University of Illinois Press, 1998 and 1999); *Animal Gospel: Christian Faith as If Animals Mattered* (Hodder and Stoughton and Westminster/John Knox Press, 1999 and 2000); *Animal Rites: Liturgies of Animal Care* (SCM Press and The Pilgrim Press, 1999 and 2001); (co-edited with P. A. B. Clarke) *Animal Rights: A Historical Anthology* (Columbia University Press, 2005), (co-edited with Tom Regan) *Animals and Christianity: A Book of Readings* (Wipf and Stock, 2008), and *Creatures of the Same God* (Winchester University Press, 2007). He is also co-editor (with P. A. B. Clarke) of the *Dictionary of Ethics, Theology, and Society* (Routledge, 1995). Professor Linzey's work has been translated into Italian, French, Spanish, German, Chinese, Taiwanese, and Japanese. In 2001, he was awarded a DD (Doctor of Divinity) degree by the Archbishop of Canterbury in recognition of his 'unique and massive pioneering work at a scholarly level in the area of the theology of creation with particular reference to the rights and welfare of God's sentient creatures'.

Llian Alys received her bachelor's degree in Psychology from the University of Wales, Swansea, her master's degree in Forensic Psychology from the University of Kent at Canterbury, and her PhD from the University of Portsmouth. Her doctoral dissertation was titled: 'How do they live with themselves? The roles of moral disengagement and thought suppression in maintaining morally abhorrent behaviour'. She has worked as a Social Emotional and Behavioural Support Assistant (SEBSA) with Ceredigion County Council, and is now a Crime Analyst with the National Policing Improvement Agency, UK.

Arnold Arluke is Professor of Sociology and Anthropology at Northeastern University and Senior Scholar at Tufts University Center for Animals and Public Policy. His research examines conflicts and contradictions in human–animal relationships. He has published over eighty articles and nine books, including *Regarding Animals* (Temple University Press, 1996), *Brute Force: Animal Police and the Challenge of Cruelty* (Purdue University Press, 2004), *Just a Dog: Understanding Animal Cruelty and Ourselves* (Temple University Press, 2006) and *The Sacrifice: How Scientific Experiments Transform Animals and People* (Purdue University Press, 2006). He has received the Human Hero award from the MSPCA, the Distinguished Scholar Award from the International Association of Human–Animal Organizations, and the Charles Horton Cooley Award from the Society for the Study of Symbolic Interaction. He also edits, with Clinton Sanders, the Animals, Culture, and Society series for Temple University Press.

Frank R. Ascione received his bachelor's degree in Psychology from Georgetown University in 1969 and his doctoral degree in Developmental Psychology from the University of North Carolina at Chapel Hill in 1973. He is a Professor in the Department of Psychology and Adjunct Professor in Family and Human Development at Utah State University (USU). Dr Ascione has published: *Cruelty to Animals and Interpersonal Violence: Readings in Research and Application* (1998), *Child Abuse, Domestic Violence, and Animal Abuse: Linking the Circles of Compassion for Prevention and Intervention* (1998); *Children and Animals: Exploring the Roots of Kindness and Cruelty* (2005), and *The International Handbook of Theory, Research, and Application on Animal Abuse and Cruelty* – all published by Purdue University Press. He has also authored *Safe Havens for Pets: Guidelines for Programs Sheltering Pets for Women who are Battered* (Utah State University, 2000). Dr Ascione was selected to receive the 2001 Distinguished Scholar Award from the International Association of Human–Animal Interaction Organizations and the International Society for Anthrozoology. He serves on the editorial boards of *Anthrozoös* and *Aggression and Violent Behaviour*, and is an adjunct faculty member with the American Humane Association.

Rachel Balen is Principal Lecturer in Social Work in the Centre for Applied Childhood Studies at the University of Huddersfield. She is course leader of the MA in Child Welfare and Protection, and has research interests in the psychosocial interests of children with cancer and their families, research with children, and social work education.

Andrea M. Beetz received her master's degree in Psychology and her PhD from the Friedrich-Alexander-University Erlangen-Nuremberg, Germany. As a post-doctoral researcher, she spent several years in the USA, at the University of California at Davis and Utah State University at Logan, where she conducted research on human–animal interactions, animal cruelty, zoophilia, and attachment. At the University of Cambridge, she further investigated attachment to humans and animals and emotional intelligence. In 2006, she founded the research group called 'Humans and Animals' at the Department of Education at the University of Erlangen, and coordinates research on the evaluation of animal assisted therapy/education projects. Other current areas of research in association with the Department of Psychology at the University of Erlangen include connections among attachment, emotion regulation, and motives.

Mark H. Bernstein holds the Joyce and Edward E. Brewer Chair in Applied Ethics at Purdue University. He specializes in animal ethics, more specifically in their legitimate moral status and the extent, scope, and content of human obligations to non-human animals. In addition to working on papers in these areas, Professor Bernstein is in the process of writing a book on partiality. This work examines the grounding and justification of extending special consideration to the interests of some groups based on particular relationships that obtain among the members of that specific group (e.g., family, nationality, religion, and species). Part of the argument will show that species membership, in and of itself, holds no moral significance. Professor Bernstein's books include *Fatalism* (University of Nebraska Press, 1992), *On Moral Considerability* (Oxford University Press, 1998), and *Without A Tear* (University of Illinois Press, 2004). Professor Bernstein is a Founding Fellow of the Oxford Centre for Animal Ethics.

Alan C. Brantley, former FBI Supervisory Special Agent (retired), is currently the owner of a behavioural science oriented forensic consulting firm. Prior to his retirement from the FBI, Mr Brantley was assigned to the National Center for the Analysis of Violent Crime and the Behavioral Analysis/Behavioral Science Units, FBI Academy, Quantico, Virginia, USA. In addition to specialization in criminal investigative analysis and the assessment of dangerousness/threats, he was responsible for providing training in criminal psychology to law enforcement officers from all over the world who attended the FBI's National Academy. Mr Brantley has provided expert testimony in criminal and civil proceedings nationally and internationally, and he has testified before congressional committees in the United States House of Representatives regarding interpersonal violence. He has lectured extensively and taught courses in the United States and in many other countries on a wide array of topics dealing with criminal psychology, violent crime scene analysis, assessment of dangerousness/threats, and profiling.

Ann W. Church is an expert in legislative affairs and politics. A graduate of the Ohio State School of Social Work, she worked for a year in the Ohio State legislature, five years in The US Senate, nearly twenty years handling government affairs for the Humane Society of the United States, on both a presidential and a senate campaign, and as director of a political action committee. She has been directly involved in gaining enactment of animal protection laws in a number of states, and is currently Director of the Eastern Mountain Region of the Humane Society of the United States.

John Clarke completed his PhD in Psychology at the University of Sydney. He has done extensive research looking at psychopaths in the workplace, criminal profiling, serial killers, serial rape, animal cruelty offenders, and sexual homicide crime scene analysis. Dr Clarke consults widely for corporations and government departments experiencing problems with a suspected workplace psychopath, as well as working with victims of workplace psychopaths. He has conducted lectures on psychopaths in the workplace, criminal profiling, and criminal psychology at the University of Sydney and to members of various government departments, charities, corporations, professional bodies, and training organizations. He is also the author of three books: (with Andy Shea) *Touched by the Devil* (Simon and Schuster and John Blake Publishers, 2001 and 2003); *Working with Monsters* (Random House, 2005), and *Pocket Psycho* (Random House, 2007).

Elizabeth Clawson is currently pursuing a Master of Science degree at George Mason University's Institute for Conflict Analysis and Resolution in Arlington, Virginia, USA. She holds a Bachelor of Arts degree in politics with honours from Whitman College, Walla Walla, Washington, USA, and was recently a visiting member of Christ Church in the University of Oxford, where she studied international security and ethical analyses of violence. Her academic interests include ethical philosophies of animal treatment, roles of violence in human conflict, and two-level negotiation processes.

Priscilla N. Cohn began teaching Philosophy at Bryn Mawr College where she gained her PhD on the work of Heidegger. She has taught Philosophy for more than thirty-five years, and has written on animals, environmental issues, and ethical problems, as well as on contemporary philosophers and the history of philosophy, publishing in both English and Spanish. She was made full Professor in Philosophy at Pennsylvania State University in 1982, and was made Professor Emerita at Abington College at Pennsylvania State University

in 2001. She has pioneered courses in animal ethics and lectured on five conti-
nents. For three years, 1990–1993, she was Director of the Summer School
Course in animal rights at Complutense University (Madrid) at El Escorial –
which were the first courses of their kind in Spain. She also taught at the
Graduate School Course on Applied Ethics at the University of Santiago de
Compostela in 1991. She has published seven books, including: *Contraception
in Wildlife*, Book I, edited with E. D. Plotka and U. S. Seal (1996) and *Ethics
and Wildlife* (1999), both published by The Edwin Mellen Press. Professor
Cohn is Associate Director of the Oxford Centre for Animal Ethics.

John Cooper was called to the Bar of England and Wales in 1983 and to the
Australian Bar in 1989. He is a member of the Bar Council, and the Bar Human
Rights Committee, and is editor of the *Criminal Bar Quarterly*. John Cooper is
an academic advisor to University College London's *Jurisprudence Review*. His
publications include: 'Whistle Blowers in the National Health Service' (*British
Medical Journal*, 1998); *Abuse of Process* (Sweet & Maxwell, 2000); *Judicial
Review in Summary Hearings* (Sweet & Maxwell, 2000); 'In Defence of
Tradition: Similarities Between Those Who Apologise for the Slave Trade and
Those Who Would Retain Hunting' (League Against Cruel Sports, 2000); 'A
Bill of Rights for Nepal' (International Conference in Kathmandu, 2001); 'The
Developing Law of Privacy' (Law Society, 2005); 'The Rule of Law' (*London
Law Review* – Royal Courts of Justice, London, 2006), 'Intercepting
Communications – An Analysis on RIPA 2000' (International Covert Police
Conference, London, 2007); 'Article 3 – The Road to Ultra Violence'
(*Jurisprudence Review*, 2007), and 'The Future of Torture' (Kurdish Human
Rights Project, 2007). His textbooks include: *Cruelty: An Analysis of Article 3*
(Sweet & Maxwell, 2002), and *The Encyclopaedia on Data Protection and
Privacy* (Sweet & Maxwell, 2006). His Appellate work has led to influential
changes in the law, including *R v. Whitewind*, referred to by the Law
Commission (No. 304) as the 'Whitewind Dilemma' on Infanticide; *R v. Baker
& Ward*, on the legal defence of duress; *Arthur v. Anker*, on blackmail; and *R v.
Bahador*, on sexual bad character. John Cooper has been Chairman of the
League Against Cruel Sports for fourteen years and has advised them on all
legal aspects of their campaigns, including the Hunting Act and the merits of
prosecutions under legislation.

David P. Farrington received BA, MA, and PhD degrees in Psychology from
the University of Cambridge. He is Professor of Psychological Criminology in
the Institute of Criminology, University of Cambridge. He has been President
of the American Society of Criminology, the British Society of Criminology,
the European Association of Psychology and Law, and the Academy of
Experimental Criminology. He has received the Sellin-Glueck and Edwin
Sutherland awards of the American Society of Criminology, the Senior Prize
of the British Psychological Society Division of Forensic Psychology, the Joan
McCord award of the Academy of Experimental Criminology, the

Distinguished Scholarship Prize of the American Sociological Association Criminology Section, and the Beccaria Gold Medal of the Criminology Society of German-Speaking Countries. He has published over fifty books and monographs and over four hundred and forty articles on criminological and psychological topics. His latest books are *Saving Children from a Life of Crime* (Oxford University Press, 2007) and *Key Issues in Criminal Career Research* (Cambridge University Press, 2007).

Clifton P. Flynn is Professor of Sociology at the University of South Carolina Upstate where he has taught since 1988. He is the past Chair and current Secretary/Treasurer of the Section on Animals and Society of the American Sociological Association. Dr Flynn serves on the editorial boards of both *Society & Animals* and *Anthrozoös*. In 2001, his Animals and Society course was chosen as the 'Best New Animals and Society Course' (2001) by the Humane Society of the United States, and was featured on 'The Osgood File' on CBS radio. He has written numerous articles on animal abuse and its relationship to family violence, including a new chapter that analyzes animal abuse from a sociological perspective in the *International Handbook of Theory, Research and Application on Animal Abuse and Cruelty* (Purdue University Press, 2007). He has edited *Social Creatures: A Human and Animal Studies Reader* (Lantern Books, 2008).

Conor Gearty is Professor of Human Rights Law and Director of the Centre for the Study of Human Rights at the London School of Economics (LSE). His books include *Can Human Rights Survive?* (Cambridge University Press, 2006) and *Civil Liberties* (Oxford University Press, 2007). He has written extensively on human rights and terrorism. He is also a barrister and founding member of Matrix Chambers, from where he continues to practice.

Eleonora Gullone is Associate Professor of Psychology at Monash University, Victoria, Australia. She is a research developmental psychologist and a Fellow of the Australian Psychological Society. Professor Gullone's research has focused upon the emotional development of children and adolescents, including empathy development. She has published over eighty articles in internationally renowned journals in addition to several invited chapters, and has co-edited a book on quality of life. In addition to her focus on human well-being, over the past decade Professor Gullone's work has extended to an examination of humans' relationships with non-human animals. In particular, she has focused on the increasingly recognized link between human violence and animal abuse. Related to this, Professor Gullone has been involved in the only Australian study existing to date to demonstrate the significant link that exists between animal cruelty and family human violence. She has also completed several works examining the underlying commonalities between children's relationships with other children and animals. She is also the founder and convenor of the Australian Psychological Society Interest Group on the

Promotion of Animal Welfare. Professor Gullone is a Fellow of the Oxford Centre for Animal Ethics.

Dawn Hawksworth is a Registered General Nurse, Paediatric Nurse, and Community Specialist Practitioner working as a Health Visitor in a socially deprived area of Huddersfield. In 2007, she was awarded an MA in Child Welfare and Protection with distinction from the University of Huddersfield, with specialist interests in multi-agency practice. She is currently employed by Kirklees Primary Care Trust as a Health Visitor and Practice Teacher. Her specialist interest, underpinned by experience in practice, is the relationship between animal cruelty, child abuse, and family violence. With the broad aim of raising awareness within health and social care, she has presented literature review findings at local multi-agency workshops, and she is currently working with Kirklees Safeguarding Children Board in the development of training material for frontline staff. In 2007, she became a member of the Links Group, which pioneers an understanding of the interrelationship between child abuse, animal abuse, and family violence. She is an Associate Fellow of the Oxford Centre for Animal Ethics.

Jack Levin is the Brudnick Professor of Sociology and Criminology at Northeastern University in Boston, where he directs the Centre on Violence and Conflict and teaches courses in the sociology of violence and hate. He has authored or co-authored twenty-eight books and more than one hundred and fifty articles, including a number on murder and other forms of violence (including animal cruelty). Dr Levin was honoured by the Massachusetts Council for Advancement and Support of Education as its 'Professor of the Year'. He has spoken to a wide variety of community, academic, and professional groups, including the White House Conference on Hate Crimes, the United States Department of Justice, OSCE's (Organization for Security and Cooperation in Europe) Office for Democratic Institutions and Human Rights (a membership of fifty-nine countries), and the International Association of Chiefs of Police.

Randall Lockwood joined the ASPCA in 2005 as the Senior Vice-President for Anti-Cruelty and Legislative Initiatives. Previously, he was Vice-President at the Humane Society of the United States, a post he held from 1984 to 2005. Dr Lockwood has a doctorate in Psychology from Washington University in St. Louis, and was Assistant Professor in the Psychology Departments of the State University of New York at Stony Brook and Washington University in St. Louis. For more than thirty years, Dr Lockwood has worked with humane societies and law-enforcement agencies, serving as an expert on the interactions between people and animals. He has testified in numerous trials involving cruelty to animals or the treatment of animals in the context of other crimes, including dog fighting, child abuse, domestic violence, and homicide. His efforts to increase public and professional awareness of the connection between animal abuse and other forms of violence were profiled in an award-winning 1999 British Broadcast Corporation/Arts and Entertainment Network documentary entitled 'The Cruelty Connection'. Dr Lockwood is a Fellow of the American College of Forensic Examiners and has served as a faculty member of the 'Jumpstart' program established by the American Prosecutors Research Institute since its inception. He frequently provides training for law-enforcement, social service, mental health, and veterinary professionals. His latest book, co-authored with Leslie Sinclair and Melinda Merck, is *Forensic Investigation of Animal Cruelty: A Guide for Veterinary and Law Enforcement Professionals* (Humane Society Press, 2006).

Franklin D. McMillan received his veterinary degree at Ohio State University and is currently Clinical Professor of Medicine at Western University of Health Sciences College of Veterinary Medicine. He is also a private practice veterinary internist, and veterinary consultant for Best Friends Animal Society. He is the editor and co-author of *Mental Health and Well-being in Animals* (Wiley Blackwell, 2005), and the author of *Unlocking the Animal Mind* (Rodale Press, 2005).

Catherine Miller is a licensed Clinical Psychologist in the state of Oregon and an Associate Professor and Director of Academic Issues with the School of Professional Psychology at Pacific University in Oregon. She supervises graduate students in the in-house training clinic and teaches courses in ethics and juvenile forensics. Her research interests include childhood animal cruelty, animal hoarding, and adolescent and young adult stalking.

Corey C. Montoya received her BA in Psychology from Fort Lewis College in 2003. She received her MS in Clinical Psychology from Pacific University in 2006. She is currently pursuing a doctoral degree in Clinical Psychology at Pacific University in Forest Grove, Oregon. Her major areas of research are child maltreatment and filicide.

Angus Nurse is an Associate Lecturer in Social Sciences with the Open University (East of England Region), a PhD student at the Faculty of Law, Humanities, Development and Society at Birmingham City University (formerly UCE) and a Research Fellow at the University of Lincoln. He is a graduate of the University of Leicester with a master's degree in Criminal Justice Studies and has lectured in sociology, public policy, and pressure group politics at Birmingham City University (UCE) and (as a guest lecturer) at Anglia Ruskin University. Current research interests include: the enforcement of wildlife crime in the UK, the nature of criminality and reasons why people commit wildlife and animal crimes, wildlife legislation in the UK, green and environmental criminology, representations of criminal justice policy in media, cinema and television, the application of privacy legislation, and compensation culture and alternate dispute resolution within the contemporary UK. Past research includes: commercial and internet crime, and annual reports on wild bird crime for the Royal Society for the Protection of Birds (RSPB). Publications include: *The Forgotten Children: Young People in Prison* (assistant editor) for the Institute for the Study and Treatment of Delinquency at King's College, London (1998); *The Thin Green Line* (Enforcing Wildlife Crime in the UK), a Faculty Working Paper for the (then) University of Central England (2000); and numerous articles on wildlife crime and environmental legislation.

Marie Louise Petersen, originally from Denmark, received her bachelor's degree in Criminology and Criminal Justice from the University of Glamorgan in 2003, and completed her MPhil in Criminology at the University of Cambridge in 2004. Her MPhil dissertation, 'Animal Cruelty: Criminological Issues', addressed the largely neglected links between animal cruelty and criminal behaviour in the UK. In particular, her focus on child abuse, domestic violence, and elder abuse showed that the cycle of abuse often begins with violence against animals. She argues that animal cruelty can be a predictor of concurrent and future violence, but that there is a need for prospective longitudinal studies in order to determine whether animal cruelty is a risk factor for adult violence. An earlier version of Marie's research, with David P. Farrington, appeared in the journal *Victims & Offenders* (2007). Marie has been commissioned to provide a definition of cruelty to animals for the forthcoming *Dictionary of Forensic Psychology 2008*. Her ongoing research interests are animal abuse and cruelty, violence and psychopathology.

Christina Risley-Curtiss is an Associate Professor of Social Work at Arizona State University and has over twenty years of practice and management experience in a combination of public health and child welfare. She has authored/co-authored many publications and presented numerous scholarly papers and workshops to various state and national groups. Her primary areas of research are the animal–human bond and child welfare. Her course – Animal–Human Connections – was awarded the Animals and Society 'Distinguished New Course Award' (2004) by the Humane Society of the United States. She has a grant-funded national study of social work practitioners' knowledge of the animal–human bond, and a grant-funded field internship with an animal welfare agency. She chairs The Arizona Humane LINK, a coalition of animal welfare and human service agencies in Maricopa County, Arizona, which sponsors an 'Investigating and Treating Animal Cruelty: Creating A Humane Community' conference annually. Most recently she has been appointed an Adviser and Fellow of the new Oxford Centre for Animal Ethics. She grew up on a farm in Connecticut, where her father and grandfather practiced veterinary medicine. She does hands-on rescue work including volunteering at the Best Friends Katrina shelter in Tylertown, Mississippi, and helped found a TNR feral cat program at Arizona State University. She currently lives in a trans-species cultural home with more than fourteen other animals.

Ian Robertson has the unusual distinction of being both a qualified veterinarian and a barrister (Barrister and Solicitor of the High Court of New Zealand) who specializes in the area of animals and the law. He originally trained as a veterinarian, and ran a successful chain of five veterinary practices in New Zealand. His transition from being a veterinarian to an animal law legal specialist was inspired through working as a television presenter of endangered species from around the world for Fox Television (USA). Dr Robertson founded Animal-Law, a specialist consultancy which provides legal advice, education and assistance in respect of legal issues involving animals. He has appeared and presented on public television and radio, penned magazine columns, and published three books. He developed New Zealand's first course on animal law taught at Canterbury University Law School. In addition to teaching in New Zealand, Dr Robertson also lectures the subject of Animal Law at Leeds Law School in England. He is currently co-authoring two books on animal law, planning and teaching animal law modules for veterinary universities, and is engaged with key institutions in England and the USA establishing an international programme to provide secondary and tertiary education on animal law.

Mark Rowlands is Professor of Philosophy at the University of Miami, Florida. He received a DPhil from the University of Oxford, and over the past two decades has worked at several universities in the UK, USA, and Ireland, and has held visiting fellowships at universities in Iceland, Finland and Australia. Professor Rowlands' research has primarily focused on issues in the philosophy of mind and moral philosophy. In the former area, his published work includes *Supervenience and Materialism* (Ashgate, 1995), *The Body in Mind* (Cambridge University Press, 1999), *The Nature of Consciousness* (Cambridge University Press, 2001), *Externalism* (Acumen, 2003), *Body Language* (MIT Press, 2006), and *The New Science of the Mind: From Extended Mind to Embodied Phenomenology* (MIT Press, 2008). In the area of moral philosophy, he has written extensively on the moral status of non-human animals and the natural environment. Here, his publications include *Animal Rights: A Philosophical Defence* (Macmillan, 1998), *The Environmental Crisis* (Macmillan, 2000), and *Animals Like Us* (Verso, 2002). He has also put a not inconsiderable amount of effort into convincing the general public of the wonders of philosophy. The resulting books were *The Philosopher at the End of the Universe* (Ebury, 2003), and *Everything I Know I Learned from TV* (Ebury, 2005). His books have been translated into more than ten languages. His autobiography, *The Philosopher and the Wolf* was published by Granta in 2008. Professor Rowlands is a Founding Fellow of the Oxford Centre for Animal Ethics.

Joan E. Schaffner is an Associate Professor of Law at the George Washington University Law School. She received her BS in mechanical engineering (magna cum laude) and JD (Order of the Coif) from the University of

Southern California and her MS in mechanical engineering from the Massachusetts Institute of Technology. She worked at the law firm of Irell & Manella in Los Angeles California and clerked for the Honorable Marianna Pfaelzer in the Central District of California before coming to George Washington University. During that time she also served as convener of the Advisory Group on Federal Benefits to the Gender Bias Task Force of the Ninth Circuit. Professor Schaffner teaches Civil Procedure, Remedies, Sexuality and the Law, and Animal Law Lawyering, and writes in these areas as well. She is the faculty adviser to Lambda Law, the GLBT student organization at George Washington, and is faculty adviser and editor-in-chief of the *American Intellectual Property Law Association Quarterly Journal*. Professor Schaffner directs the George Washington Animal Law Program which consists of the George Washington Animal Welfare Project (AWP), a pro bono effort of faculty and students devoted to researching and improving animal welfare laws in the District of Columbia; the Animal Law Litigation Project, a partnership with the Humane Society of the United States, designed to provide clinical litigation opportunities to George Washington law students on Humane Society of the United States projects; seminars in animal law; and a student chapter of the Animal Legal Defense Fund (SALDF) to which she is faculty adviser. Professor Schaffner has testified on behalf of non-breed-specific dangerous dog laws and the DC Animal Protection Amendment Act of 2007, spoke on the first Animal Law panel as part of the SALT Cover Public Interest Retreat, and is Vice Chair, Publications Chair, and Editor of the newsletter of the ABA TIPS Animal Law Committee. Professor Schaffner is a Fellow of the Oxford Centre for Animal Ethics.

Tania Signal received her PhD in Psychology from the University of Waikato, New Zealand. While at Waikato she was a member of the Animal Behaviour and Welfare Research Centre and was involved in behavioural assessments of animal needs and abilities. A move to Australia in 2003 to take up a teaching position at Central Queensland University necessitated a change in research focus. A long-held interest in the connection between attitudes towards, and treatment of, animals, aspects of personality (i.e., empathy), and individual potential for interpersonal violence led to collaboration with Dr Nicola Taylor (Sociology); a number of articles concerning attitudes towards animals and empathy, human–animal interaction generally, and interpersonal violence and harm to companion animals specifically have been published, enhanced by a cross-disciplinary psychology/sociology approach. Dr Signal is on the editorial board of *Society & Animals* and acts as a reviewer for a number of international journals.

Nicola Taylor received her graduate degree in Sociology at Manchester Metropolitan University, where she addressed the sociology of human–animal interaction and argued that sociology could, and should, take account of human–animal relations. Following posts at the Universities of Edinburgh and

Oxford, Dr Taylor moved to Australia to a post at Central Queensland University. She is now a Lecturer in Sociology at Flinders University in South Australia where she continues to research human–animal relations. Dr Taylor has published a number of articles concerning human–animal interaction, domestic violence and harm to companion animals and has been highlighting the importance of studying these areas to sociologists, policy makers, and practitioners alike since 1997. She is an honorary member of the New Zealand Centre for Human–Animal Studies, Executive Director of the Centre for Animal Liberation Affairs, and acts as reviewer for a number of international journals dedicated to human–animal studies, such as *Society & Animals* and the *Journal of Critical Animal Studies*.

Peter Toman is a therapist in South Australia and is in the process of completing a master's degree in Clinical Psychology at the University of South Australia. He has worked in a community-based sex offender treatment programme for ten years. During that time he has presented papers on the treatment of sex offenders both in Australia and overseas. He has also presented seminars and training sessions on sex offender treatment and management to a wide range of groups, including child protection workers, youth workers, community correctional officers, correctional officers, police, and church groups.

Sabrina Tonutti is Lecturer and Researcher in Cultural Anthropology at the University of Udine, Italy. After a degree in Humanities at the University of Trieste, Italy, in 1996, she specialized in Social and Cultural Anthropology at the University of Padua, and received her PhD in 2006 for a dissertation on the anthropology of the animal rights movement. Her work was published in 2007 as *Diritti Animali: Storia e antropologia di un movimento* (Forum Ed.). Dr Tonutti is currently working at the Department of Economics, Society and Territory (University of Udine, Italy) and has carried out ethnographic research in Italy, Switzerland, and the UK. Her studies focus on human–animal relationships, new social movements (and particularly animal advocacy as a social and cultural phenomenon), biodiversity and local knowledge, anthropology of food, and epistemological reflections on the human–animal divide in anthropology. She is the author of more than thirty articles and several books, including: *Water and Anthropology* (EMI, 2007); (with R. Marchesini) *Manuale di zooantropologia* (Meltemi, 2007); and (with R. Marchesini) *Animali magici* (De Vecchi, 2000). Dr Tonutti is a Fellow of the Oxford Centre for Animal Ethics.

Martin Wasik is Professor of Criminal Justice at Keele University, and formerly Professor of Law at Manchester University. He is a barrister and sits part-time as a Crown Court judge on the Midland Circuit, dealing with criminal trials and sentencing matters. Until the end of June 2007 he was also Chairman of the Sentencing Advisory Panel and member of the Sentencing

Guidelines Council, independent bodies established by statute which together develop and issue sentencing guidelines for the criminal courts. He teaches criminal law, evidence and sentencing, and is one of the authors of *Blackstone's Criminal Practice*, which is authoritative and widely used by practitioners.

Thomas I. White is the Conrad N. Hilton Professor in Business Ethics and Director of the Centre for Ethics and Business at Loyola Marymount University in Los Angeles, California. Professor White received his doctorate in philosophy from Columbia University and taught at Upsala College and Rider University in New Jersey before moving to California in 1994. His publications include five books: *Right and Wrong* (Prentice-Hall, 1988), *Discovering Philosophy* (Prentice Hall, 1990), *Business Ethics* (Prentice-Hall, 1993), *Men and Women at Work* (Career Press, 1994) and *In Defense of Dolphins*, as well as numerous articles on topics ranging from sixteenth-century Renaissance humanism to business ethics. His most recent research has focused on the philosophical implications – especially the ethical implications – of the scientific research on dolphins. His book on this topic, *In Defense of Dolphins: The New Moral Frontier* (Blackwell, 2007) addresses the ethical issues connected with human–dolphin interaction – for example, the deaths and injuries of dolphins in connection with the human fishing industry and the captivity of dolphins in the entertainment industry. Professor White is a Scientific Adviser to the Wild Dolphin Project, a research organization studying a community of Atlantic spotted dolphins in the Bahamas. He is an Adviser to, and a Fellow of, the Oxford Centre for Animal Ethics.

Daniel B. Williams graduated from Harvard College in 2006, with a degree in English and American Literature and Language, and Romance Languages and Literatures. His senior thesis on animals in the novels of J. M. Coetzee won a Thomas T. Temple Hoopes Prize, the Le Baron Russell Briggs Thesis and Travelling Prizes, and the Bowdoin Prize for Undergraduate Essays in the English Language. He is currently reading for the MPhil in Criticism and Culture at the University of Cambridge, where he is a Gates Scholar and member of Magdalene College.

J. Clare Wilson is a Reader in Forensic Psychology at the University of Portsmouth, and a chartered forensic psychologist. Her main research areas include children's eyewitness memory, investigative interviewing of children, assessing children's 'wishes' for the Family Court, delinquency and children's understanding of secrets, criminal processes and criminal intent. In addition to her many published articles, she has written, with Martine Powell, *A Guide to Interviewing Children: Essential Skills for Counsellors, Police, Lawyers and Social Workers* (Allen & Unwin, 2001). Dr Wilson has been a trainer in investigative interviewing with children with police, social workers, lawyers, and psychologists in both the UK and Australia.

the link
between ANIMAL
ABUSE **and** HUMAN
VIOLENCE

Does Animal Abuse Really Benefit Us?

ANDREW LINZEY

It is quite clear that in abusing animals we abuse our relationship with animals, and that we abuse ourselves. We become less human to the extent that we treat any living beings as things.

R. D. LAING

I

Philosophers and thinkers have long accepted that there is a connection between the abuse of animals and the abuse of weaker human beings. A roster of illustrious names can be garnered in this regard, including Pythagoras, St Thomas Aquinas, John Locke, Alexander Pope, Arthur Schopenhauer, and Jeremy Bentham, as well as modern ones like Albert Schweitzer and Mohandas K. Gandhi. Immanuel Kant, regarded as one of the most influential thinkers of Europe and the late Enlightenment, was typical in that regard. In his lectures on ethics, given between 1775 and 1780, he expostulated: 'If he is not to stifle his human feelings, he must practice kindness towards animals, for he who is cruel to animals becomes hard in his dealings with men'.[1] Although Kant did not believe that we had direct duties to animals, he clearly held that human interests were sufficient in seeking to limit cruel behaviour to animals.

Historically, this view manifested itself in the passing of a range of animal protection measures in the nineteenth century. Cruel behaviour to animals, it was thought, needed to be legally curbed in order to prevent cruelty to human subjects. It found its classic expression in the preamble to Lord Erskine's Cruelty to Animals Bill in 1809: 'The abuse of that [human] dominion by cruel and oppressive treatment of such animals, is not only highly unjust and immoral, but most pernicious in its example, having an evident tendency to harden the heart against the natural feelings of humanity'.[2] Notice how cruelty is deemed not only unjust but also injurious to ourselves.

The logic, then, seemed inescapable: people who are cruel to animals will be cruel to human subjects. Indeed, such a thought was so established that Kant himself referred to how in 'England butchers and doctors do not sit on a jury because they are accustomed to the sight of death and hardened'.[3] People thought that there must be such a connection, and assumed that it was so. There was very little strictly empirical evidence, other than pure observation, to support such a link.

Over the last forty years, however, the link has been the subject of sustained enquiry and research. Psychological, sociological, and medical connections have been made by a variety of researchers, and a considerable volume of empirical evidence has been amassed. While some of the research is clearly at a pioneering stage, the case for thinking that there is a link is now stronger than ever. Consider, for example, some of the findings reviewed in the chapter by Marie Louise Petersen and David P. Farrington (*Measuring Animal Cruelty and Case Histories*):

- Of 429 adult inpatient admissions to psychiatric hospital divided into aggressive and non-aggressive samples: 23% killed dogs and cats purposely and 18% tortured them (aggressive sample), and 10% killed and 5% tortured dogs and cats (non-aggressive sample). (1979)
- Of 152 males, divided into aggressive and non-aggressive samples: 25% of aggressive criminals reported five or more acts of cruelty to animals, 6% of non-aggressive, and none of the non-criminals. (1985)
- Of 64 inmates: 48% of those convicted of rape and 30% convicted of child molestation had histories of animal cruelty. (1986)
- Of 28 sexual homicide perpetrators: 36% committed acts of animal cruelty in childhood, and 46% in adolescence. (1988)
- Of 117 inmates, divided into violent and non-violent criminals: 63% of violent criminals committed animal cruelty versus 11% of non-violent criminals. (1999)
- Of 45 violent offenders versus 45 non-violent offenders: cruelty to animals greater in the violent sample, 56% versus 20%. (2001)
- Of 164 battered women and 199 control women: animal cruelty predicted official and self-reported violence in children. (2004)
- Of 261 incarcerated male inmates: 43% had engaged in animal cruelty. Of these, 63% reported that they had hurt or killed dogs and 55% had abused cats. (2005)

All such statistical correlations need to be interpreted with care, of course, but these and many other findings indicate an impressive degree of convergent research. That is not to say that they are themselves conclusive. It needs to be frankly admitted that there are ongoing problems of methodology, control, and definition that need to be addressed: how should one define 'cruelty', 'abuse', or 'harm'? How does one set up control groups as an adequate measurement, and for how long? How can one devise the much-needed longitudinal studies that explore whether abuse is a factor over a significant period of time?

More fundamentally still, how can one detect *one* factor as a cause, or a probable cause, among so many variables at work within abusive relations? Animal cruelty is one of the diagnostic tests employed by the FBI in assessing dangerousness – will we ever be able to go further than that? These and other questions are variously addressed in the pages that follow.

II

Apart from questions of methodology and interpretation, there are wider issues about how we should view the findings themselves. The case for wider recognition of the link still faces two sets of objections – one from the 'human' side; the other from the 'animal' side.

The first is from some concerned for child welfare especially, who judge that they must keep their work separate from concerns for animals lest their special focus is obscured, or their work mired in wider controversies about the treatment of animals. 'Including concerns about animal abuse weakens our strategic thrust', as one child protection officer said to me recently. And this position is buttressed by a number of misconceptions that still, sadly, find a voice. To take just one example, one medical commentator recently discussing the tragic case of a five-year-old savaged to death by her uncle's pit bull terrier, maintains: 'It seems to me that the UK remains a proud nation of dog lovers and child haters'.

In fact, it is implausible to think that those who keep dangerous dogs are dog lovers, or do so from motives relating to animal kindness. Many dangerous dogs are kept for purposes of guarding property, where dogs are taught to attack or to fight (illegal dog-fighting is on the increase in the United Kingdom). Even fighting dogs must be trained or at the very least encouraged to fight, which is often achieved by treating them in a cruel manner. And pit bulls themselves were originally bred and reared for the purposes of bull-baiting, hardly an animal-friendly practice.

Our commentator continues: 'Contrary to the conventional assumption of a direct link between the abuse of animals and that of children, the lesson of history is that it is quite possible for a society to combine concern for animal welfare with indifference towards the welfare of children',[4] and he cites Victorian society – and how the SPCA was founded before the NSPCC – as an example. But, as Sabrina Tonutti shows in Chapter 6 (*Cruelty, Children, and Animals: Historically One, Not Two, Causes*), that overlooks the fact that the pioneering anti-cruelty movement in Britain (and in other countries) encompassed both children and animals, and that many luminaries for animal welfare, such as Lord Shaftesbury, William Wilberforce, and Fowell Buxton – to take only three examples – were also involved in campaigns for the alleviation of human misery, including help for the poor and child protection. Moreover, members of the SPCA helped found and finance the NSPCC.

But there is another reason for thinking that animal abuse must be taken seriously and that is because it so heavily implicated in cases of family violence and child abuse in particular. Again, Petersen and Farrington review some of the evidence:

- Of 53 children (who met criteria for child abuse or neglect): 60% of these families abused/neglected their pets. In 88% of families displaying child physical abuse, cruelty to animals was also present. (1983)
- Of 23 families with history of animal cruelty: 35% involved children on the risk register of Social Services. (1998)
- Of 300 children who sexually abuse other children and commit other violent offences: 20% of children who sexually abuse other children and commit violent offences had a history of sexually abusing animals. Many of these children had been severely abused themselves. (1998)
- Of 38 women at a domestic violence shelter: 71% of those who owned a pet reported that the male partners had threatened or harmed the animals. 18% delayed entering a shelter because of fear of what would happen to their pet. (1998)
- Of 72 women at domestic violence shelters: 88% (of 68% that had pets) indicated animal cruelty committed in their presence. In 76% of the cases, children had witnessed the abuse. 54% of the children who witnessed the cruelty copied this behaviour. (1999)
- Of 7,264 women at domestic violence shelters: 16% had animals hurt or killed by partner. (1999)
- Of 107 women at a domestic violence shelter: (of 40% who owned pets) 47% reported that their pet was either threatened or harmed. 40% of these had delayed entering a shelter because they feared for their pet. (2000)
- Of 61 women in shelters: (of 82% who owned pets) 49% reported that the partner had threatened their pet, 46% that their pet had been harmed, and 27% reported that concern for the welfare of their pet had affected their decision to leave. (2003)
- Of 481 sexually abused children, 412 psychiatric outpatient children, and 540 normal children: 18% of sexually abused children were cruel to animals, compared with 3% of normal children. (2003)
- Of 164 battered women and 199 control women: children from violent homes were more likely to be cruel to animals (11% versus 5%). (2004)

These and other findings indicate a common pattern of abuse in which battered women, children, and animals are all victims. With the possible exception of the link between animal abuse and serial murder, the case is the strongest in the literature.

The second concern is from some animal advocates who fear that the focus on the link obscures the moral case for animals. Animal abuse should be regarded as wrong in itself, they claim, regardless of its adverse effects on human beings. Mark Bernstein in chapter 13 (*Responding Ethically to Animal Abuse*) rightly stresses how animals should not be regarded as having only instrumentalist value but intrinsic value because they are sentient beings that can suffer in analogous ways to human subjects. The danger is that we treat animals in an instrumentalist way as 'canaries in the mine', as Elizabeth

Clawson indicates in Chapter 14 (*The New Canaries in the Mine: The Priority of Human Welfare in Animal Abuse Prosecution*). In short, the issue is injustice to the victims, not the humanity of the abusers.

But this is surely a one-sided view of 'liberation' (for want of a better word). For example, the emancipation of women involves (as many feminists have pointed out) not only the liberation of women from unjust or abusive relationships, but also the liberation of men themselves. Men need to be liberated from their own machismo and their own complicity (and more) in the abuses and injustices meted out to women. No one, it might be said, is truly free until they are free from being both perpetrators as well as victims.

Viewed from that more holistic perspective, it can be seen that exploring and discovering how animals suffer from common patterns of abuse, far from weakening the case for their respectful treatment, only strengthens it. There is empirical evidence in that regard also. One of the saddest features of 'abuse literature', concerning both humans and animals, is reading accounts of how those who abuse have themselves been abused. The pattern is now so familiar to welfare agencies that it almost passes without comment, but it indicates, at the deepest level, how we are witnessing a common pattern of dehumanization which urgently requires action at all levels. It would be folly, even if acting out of the highest motives, to fail to see how animal abuse is intricately related to our own.

While some child and animal advocates may be wary of stressing the link, for more than two decades the Humane Society of the United States has pioneered collaborative programmes for many professionals in the US. In the UK it is heartening to note the existence of 'The Links Group', formed in 2001, which commands the support of mainstream charitable organizations in the fields of human and animal welfare (including the NSPCC, RSPCA, British Veterinary Nursing Association, The Buster Foundation, Paws for Kids, Refuge, Wood Green Animal Shelter, and the PDSA). Since its inception, the group has successfully worked together to promote an understanding of the links between child abuse, animal abuse, and domestic violence.

III

A holistic perspective, as put forward here, requires also that we challenge abuse, even and especially when there are apparent 'benefits' (what is often called 'necessary cruelty'). And that issue arises most directly in relation to our treatment of animals than anywhere else. We now give scant attention to those who seek to justify child labour in terms of economics or inferior status for women on the basis of cultural homogeneity, so why should we find ourselves so vulnerable to the argument that animal abuse is justifiable if humans benefit?

Well, of course, the simple answer is that our estimate of human advantage is such that we automatically suppose that almost anything that 'benefits us' is morally right. But that moral calculus should at least be questioned, and we should go further and ask the most basic question of all: can any practice that involves animal cruelty or abuse benefit humans? For it is certainly true that the unquestioning assumption in almost all debates about animals is that benefits justify abuse. And the implications are that we know what these benefits are and they are almost all in favour of abuse. We accept justifications for abuse of animals that we would never (or rather seldom) accept in relation to human subjects, especially infants and children. And the means through which we do this is by reference to anthropocentric utilitarian calculations in which we count ourselves as all-important and animals as totally unimportant.

Not all utilitarianism is the same, of course. Classical utilitarianism or modern philosophical utilitarianism has, in most forms, been sympathetic to animals. Rather the problem lies with a kind of speciesism or egoist-speciesism, defined as the *arbitrary* favouring of one species over another. It is a kind that still predominates in the media. The sort that questions: 'how can you be concerned about the suffering of a few animals when children are starving?' Or 'how can you oppose such and such development if it is of benefit to human beings?' The assumption is that human advantage – no matter how indirect, undefined, hypothetical, or incoherently argued – always trumps animal suffering no matter how severe.

But this appeal to 'benefits' can and should be challenged on its own terms. The problem, or rather one of many problems, with utilitarianism is: who determines the calculation or calculus – by which we balance the utilities or benefits? And of course how is the calculus to be determined?

Consider the ways in which animal abuse might harm us through, for example, de-sensitization, loss of empathy, habituation, and denial. Let us briefly address these factors.

Desensitization refers, *inter alia*, to loss of feeling. We kill but feel nothing. We inflict suffering but feel nothing. Perhaps there are very few that feel absolutely nothing, but some appear to do so. More likely, they are socialized to discount such feelings, or to submerge them, or disregard them through 'emotional political correctness'. My concern here is the form of social authoritarianism regularly practised by parents on children: 'It's only an animal for heaven's sake!' 'You must grow up', 'This is just childish'.

In contrast, of course, our feelings at human killing or human suffering are put in an entirely different category. Consider, for example, the weight placed by judges and others who pass sentence on offenders. Lack of remorse in these contexts is invariably, and surely correctly, construed as a form of pathology. But is it possible to be desensitized about animals and not about humans? Moreover, why should we assume that this bifurcation is not morally suspect?

The same is true of loss of empathy, the loss of the ability to empathize and to relate to others who suffer. As Andrea Beetz shows in Chapter 4 (*Empathy as an Indicator of Emotional Development*), empathy is an essential component in our emotional development. Empathy or sympathy deserves more theological and philosophical attention: without sympathy it is difficult to have any moral imagination of the lives of others, as is also shown in Daniel B. William's Chapter 16 (*'Vile attentions': On the Limits of Sympathetic Imagination*) which illustrates its pivotal role in the remarkable novels of J. M. Coetzee.

What is worse is that we acclimatize ourselves to such losses of feeling through habituation. George Bernard Shaw famously wrote that 'Custom will reconcile people to any atrocity; and fashion will drive them to acquire any custom'. Again he says of people who are cruel: 'Far from enjoying it, they have simply overcome their natural repugnance and become indifferent to it, as men become indifferent enough to anything they do often enough'.[5] Familiarity thus breeds consent. Violence or abusive treatment is regarded as normal. And such abuse is buttressed by a range of institutions (corporations, industry, peer groups, families) that variously benefit from the institutionalization of abuse. Perhaps it is that sense of habituation that most concerned our forbears as shown, for example, by Hogarth's famous engravings of four stages of cruelty in 1751, which begins with cruelty to dogs and ends up with murder and public dissection. Habituation may hurt us because it means that cruelty has become routine.

And then there is the phenomenon of 'denial', which functions as a way of pushing aside uncomfortable moral reality. What might be called a mechanism of 'willed ignorance', of looking the other way, of moral pretence. As T. S. Eliot once remarked: 'Mankind can bear little reality'. Most of us are animal abuse deniers in that sense; we have some inkling that – for example – the products we buy and our food preferences have some costs to the animals involved, but we push such reality aside.

None of this means, of course, that humans who are cruel to animals will automatically be cruel to other humans. There is no simple cause and effect. But these mechanisms are uncomfortably familiar to those whose job it is to combat abuse of weaker human beings. We do not yet know – at least with any degree of certainty – whether the same people who abuse animals will also abuse weaker humans; some may, some may not. Just because the same excuse is given does not, by itself, show the link. The phenomenon of bifurcation is much more subtle. If someone acts violently towards another who is weaker in order to rob him, this only shows that he has no compassion for the person he has robbed, but it does not establish that he lost his compassion for his fellow humans through his previous ill treatment of animals. If half the number of violent criminals abused animals, what does this say of the other half? Does this mean that half of them loved animals and simply hated their fellow humans? We are far from having anything like a complete answer to these, and many other, questions.

Despite these necessary qualifiers, it must at least be right to pose the question of whether these mechanisms (as well as other factors) only harm us in relation to the abuse inflicted on human subjects. Ought not a 'cost/benefit' analysis – which is now regularly employed in ethical evaluation – mean that we should also logically explore the debit side of our abuse of animals? Since

we often appeal to a range of benefits, including those that are purely hypothetical or indirect, in justifying the abuse of animals, are we not also right to
count in a range of costs, or at least risks, when it comes to animals? We need
a full moral audit whenever it is claimed that abuse 'benefits' us. By doing so,
we may at last begin to challenge the terms of public debate.

IV

The issue of violence and abuse has become more and more prominent as we
begin to wrestle with the complexity of abusive relations and recognize their
many, hitherto largely unfamiliar, aspects. It may not be too much to say that
there is now a new consciousness of abuse that is spurring on a much deeper,
more diligent searching of our consciences than ever before.

The value of this volume is in bringing to light one strand in this complexity
– one that has often been misunderstood or insufficiently recognized. No one
is claiming that this aspect holds the key or, by itself, answers all the problems,
but it is surely one aspect that deserves a great deal more careful attention than
it has received so far.

This book is for all those who have a stake in this debate, either because their
academic work relates to the issues involved, or because their professional role
involves contact with the abused or the abusers, both human and animal. The
list includes, but is not limited to: child care officers, community carers, law
enforcement officers, health visitors, veterinarians, anti-cruelty inspectors,
animal protection officers, social scientists, lawyers, psychologists, and criminologists. It comprises a remarkable range of contributions: variously they
provide critical reviews of existing research in the field, examine the latest
evidence, and consider the implications for legal policy as well as the role of
key professionals. There is also a large section that addresses the underlying
philosophical and ethical issues.

The chapters that follow will also be of interest to the growing number of
students who take university and college courses in Animal Ethics, Animal
Law, Animals in Philosophy, as well as the large number of well-established
courses in Human–Animal Studies. After many years of apparent neglect, it is
a delight to see the emergence of such university courses in which students are
encouraged to ask normative questions about the ethics of our treatment of
animals.

The eight sections of the book are gathered around the most important
issues in the debate. Short introductions are supplied by the editor for each
part which briefly outline the central arguments of each chapter. As might be
expected, almost all the contributions concern animal abuse or cruelty that is
illegal in most of the countries under discussion, relating for the most part to
domestic or companion animals. But that leaves, of course, the important issue
of abuse or cruelty that is perfectly legal. Legal abuse in factory farming, in
puppy mills, in entertainment, in research labs, in teaching seminars, in the fur

industry, are some examples of institutionalized abuse that is often not considered abuse. We have not, even within this lengthy work, been able to deal adequately with all the multifarious problems thrown up by the *legal* abuse of animals. However, **Part VIII** tries to grapple with the abuse of wild, free-ranging animals, which in many forms, especially hunting, is still legal throughout the world. These four chapters at least raises the important question of whether socially and legally sanctioned abuse – in this one area alone – might be harmful to human participants as well as the animals concerned.

Quite deliberately, the book has an international flavour. It comprises contributors from seven countries, including a major focus on work in the UK and the US. Abuse, after all, is international in scope, as are the various attempts – both academic and professional – to understand and prevent it. The collection gives prominence both to those who are accomplished researchers in the field, as well as up-and-coming scholars who are likely to be major players in the generations to come.

Most of the contributory chapters began their life as presentations to the International Conference on the Relationship between Animal Abuse and Human Violence held under the auspices of the Oxford Centre for Animal Ethics at Keble College, University of Oxford, in 2007. As the collection developed, some papers were included which arrived too late for presentation at the conference, but which were important in adding to the range of the book and making it as comprehensive as possible.

The conference was the first major academic gathering on this topic in the UK and built on the previous work begun in 2001 by the Links Group. The Centre is grateful to the many sponsoring bodies, including the Links Group, Learning about Animals, One Voice, Women's Aid, Paws for Kids, and especially to the League Trust, the charitable arm of the League Against Cruel Sports. Only the foresight and generosity of the League Trust, together with the many other supporting bodies, made the groundbreaking conference possible.

Although the League, like the other sponsors, is hardly a neutral bystander on the issue of abuse, it is much to its credit that it offered to be the major sponsor of an academic conference where papers were selected by the Centre solely on the basis of their academic merit. A 'Call for Papers' was issued and circulated to all relevant departments in universities throughout the world, and the selection of speakers was based on the scholarly promise of their submitted abstract. As a small recompense for the League's work, the royalties from the book will be divided equally between the League Trust and the Oxford Centre for Animal Ethics.

On a more personal note, my thanks are due to my wife, Jo, who has helped share the burdens of editing and proofing; to Professor Priscilla Cohn for her immense and invaluable assistance at all stages of the preparation of the manuscript; to Kate Kirkpatrick, who has copy-edited the manuscript from start to finish with great skill and forbearance, and to Daniel B. Williams whose generosity and dexterity in copy-editing and proofing immeasurably improved the final text. Finally, special thanks are due to Alastair and Sarah Harden who compiled the index.

ANDREW LINZEY
Oxford Centre for Animal Ethics
June 2008

Notes

1   Immanuel Kant, 'Duties towards animals and spirits', in *Lectures on ethics*, trans. Louis Infield (Indianapolis and Cambridge: Hackett Publishing Company, 1963), p. 240.
2   Lord Erskine, Second Reading of the Bill for Preventing Malicious and Wanton Cruelty to Animals, *Hansard*, House of Lords, 15 May 1809, p. 277.
3   Kant, *Lectures on ethics*, p. 240.
4   Michael Fitzpatrick, 'Our desire to put dogs before children leaves a Nazi taste', http://www.communitycare.co.uk/Articles/2007/07/25/105259/our-desire-to-put-dogs-before-children-leaves-a-nazi-taste.html.
5   George Bernard Shaw, 'Killing for sport' and 'The doctor's dilemma', in *Prefaces to the plays of George Bernard Shaw* (London: Constable and Co., 1934), pp. 144, 258–9.

PART

I

Overviews of Existing Research

Part I comprises three overviews of existing research that provide excellent introductions to the field. In their first essay, Marie Louise Petersen and David P. Farrington (*Measuring Animal Cruelty and Case Histories*) begin by addressing the empirical evidence of a link. After offering a definition of 'cruelty', they then outline the six most widely used instruments for measuring animal cruelty. This is followed by a consideration of some selected case histories of child murderers, mass murderers, and serial killers who had a history of animal cruelty.

In their second essay, Petersen and Farrington (*Types of Cruelty: Animals and Childhood Cruelty, Domestic Violence, Child and Elder Abuse*) detail the main types of cruelty with which animal abuse seems most related: childhood cruelty, domestic violence, child and elder abuse. They then usefully outline the main explanations of cruelty based on ideas of strain, social learning, and the graduation hypothesis, as well as taking a brief look at the major prevention programmes in the UK and the US. They argue that the research does indeed indicate a link between animal cruelty and human violence, but that the research so far is 'methodologically poor'. They conclude that the 'time is ripe for a major research programme to advance knowledge about the causes and prevention of animal cruelty and its implications for criminology'.

Eleonora Gullone's paper (*A Lifespan Perspective on Human*

Aggression and Animal Abuse) amplifies and develops many of the points in Petersen's and Farrington's work, but also stresses the need for a 'lifespan perspective' that demonstrates the 'conceptual and empirical overlap in human aggression and animal abuse'. She utilizes the term 'abuse' – a wider term than 'cruelty'. While she accepts that previous research has various limitations including 'problematic methodologies' such as retrospective reporting, restricted samples, lack of adequate control, and employment of different definitions, she nevertheless concludes that 'across very different respondent groups . . . and methods . . . the co-occurrence between human-directed and animal-directed aggression and violence continues to emerge'. In short, there is 'substantial theoretical and empirical evidence support-ing a link'. In her view, 'substantial evidence' points to the important role that a 'pattern of abusive behaviour toward animals can play in raising alarm that other criminal behaviours are likely occurring in the same environment'.

1

Measuring Animal Cruelty and Case Histories[1]

MARY LOUISE PETERSEN AND DAVID P. FARRINGTON

How convincing is the empirical evidence on the link between cruelty to animals and violence to people? The aim of this chapter is to review the research literature and ask the following questions:

1 To what extent does cruelty to animals in childhood predict violence in adulthood? Is cruelty to animals one of the earliest predictors of later violence? How important is cruelty to animals in comparison with other childhood risk factors for adult violence?
2 Is there any causal link between childhood cruelty to animals and adult violence? What theories explain the link?
3 What are the early risk factors for cruelty to animals? How, and to what extent, can cruelty to animals be prevented? To what extent might adult violence be reduced by preventing cruelty to animals in childhood?
4 To what extent is cruelty to animals in a family associated with partner abuse, child abuse, or elder abuse? Does cruelty to animals precede, follow, or accompany partner abuse, child abuse, or elder abuse? To what extent might cruelty to animals in a family cause partner abuse, child abuse, or elder abuse?
5 To what extent could partner abuse, child abuse, or elder abuse be reduced by preventing cruelty to animals?

These questions have been largely neglected by criminological researchers. As argued by Beirne,[2] it was not until 1997 that a paper about animal abuse was published in a criminological journal: 'Scholarly studies of animal abuse remain virtually non-existent, and the topic is completely ignored in criminology text-books'.[3] Literature on this topic is very limited in most countries; for example, in the United Kingdom only a handful of researchers have published articles relevant to the study of animal cruelty: 'No area of human–animal behaviour is more neglected than animal-related crime and deviance'.[4] Likewise, the study of animal cruelty and abuse as a form of crime in itself remains very limited.[5] One of the main reasons might be that society values animals less than people.[6]

In order to answer the above questions, an extensive search of the literature was conducted including online databases, all available online journals, and newspaper searches. All articles were obtained through interlibrary loan. Keywords used included animal(s) cruelty/abuse, cruel, violence, family, linking, domestic, child, neglect, elder, sexual, serial, killers, and homicide. Unfortunately, we found many methodological problems with the existing research literature on these topics, and hence conclude (see the following Chapter) by laying out a research agenda for the future.

Definition and Types of Animal Cruelty

There are many different types of animal cruelty. In 2002 the inspectorate of the Royal Society for the Prevention of Cruelty to Animals (RSPCA) investigated 114,000 complaints of cruelty in the United Kingdom and obtained over 2,000 convictions.[7] One recent case from London concerned a forty-seven-year-old bartender who was jailed for making so-called 'squish' films. The video in question was labelled by police as one of the most disturbing ever seen. Filmed in a pornographic manner, it showed scenes of extreme cruelty to animals involving mice, guinea pigs, and most sickeningly an eight-week-old kitten, glued to the floor, being crushed to death underfoot.[8] An RSPCA inspector who witnessed scenes from the movies said that these films were the most sickening he had seen in his six years as an animal protection officer. He stated that 'this video is one of the most abhorrent instances of cruelty that our unit has ever come across. The animals involved forcibly endured a long and traumatic ordeal, which ultimately led to a painful death'.

Defining animal cruelty is problematic, because of the existence of socially and culturally sanctioned activities which harm animals, differing attitudes toward different species, and a continuum of severity that can range from teasing to torture.[9] The importance of motive and precise definition cannot be overstated, because what is not clearly defined cannot be reliably measured.[10] In 1999, the Humane Society of the United States defined animal cruelty as 'a set of behaviors that are harmful to animals, from unintentional neglect to intentional killing'.[11]

Ascione defined cruelty to animals as 'socially unacceptable behavior that intentionally causes unnecessary pain, suffering or distress to and/or death of an animal'.[12] This definition excludes socially accepted practices, such as the humane killing of farm animals, hunting, and the use of animals in research. Rowan distinguished between cruelty, abuse, neglect, and use of animals.[13] In cruelty, the offender usually enjoyed observing the animal's suffering; an example would be where a cat's tail was set on fire so that the person could enjoy the sight of the animal fleeing in pain. Abuse involved inappropriate levels of force; for example, where a person kicked a cat who rubbed against his or her leg. This article is concerned with cruelty, including beating, choking, stabbing, kicking, burning, hanging, drowning, shooting, fighting, and throwing. The animals concerned are usually domesticated; cruelty to other species (insects, fish, etc.) is excluded.

Perceptions of what is humane treatment to both children and animals have varied, and continue to vary, both historically and culturally.[14] Also, people have different hierarchies of value for different types of animals. For example, Ascione reported a case where two teenage boys caught a six-month-old kitten in a leg trap, shot arrows into it, and stomped it to death.[15] The boys thought that they were having a great time, filming the event on video. The tape was later confiscated, and when the juvenile court judge was asked if he would recommend further evaluation or counselling for these two boys, his answer was 'no, not just for killing a cat'.

Ascione and Lockwood suggested a threefold typology of animal cruelty among children:

1 *Exploratory/curiosity-based animal cruelty.* The children in this category are likely to be preschoolers, poorly supervised and lacking training in the physical care and humane treatment of a variety of animals, especially family pets.
2 *Pathological animal cruelty.* These children tend to be older than those in the above category. Psychological malfunction may be the basis of their animal cruelty, which may be linked to childhood histories of physical abuse, sexual abuse, and exposure to domestic violence.
3 *Delinquent animal cruelty.* These children are most likely to be adolescents whose animal cruelty may be one symptom of an antisocial personality.[16]

Measuring Animal Cruelty

In the United Kingdom, Piper, Johnson, Myers, and Pritchard analyzed 841 questionnaires from schoolchildren, in research commissioned by the RSPCA, to explore harmful behaviour to animals by children.[17] Some children reported very violent acts toward animals, such as tying cats' legs together and tying them to a railway line in order to watch them die when a train passed. Some children had specific likes and dislikes. For example, some expressed an extreme hatred for black cats, and described them as sneaky and sly. At the same time, some children stated that dogs were 'friends', and said that they would kill anyone who harmed a dog.

Assessing animal cruelty and abuse is important for the early detection of maladjustment and for the prevention of further violence.[18] Cruelty to animals may be a particularly pernicious aspect of problematic child development. Progress in understanding the development of the problem is limited because of the complex nature of cruelty as a construct and the limitations of current assessment measures.[19] Previous research into cruelty to animals has been limited in methods of assessing cruelty. Many studies have used the single item 'cruel to animals' from the Child Behavior Checklist (CBCL)[20] and others have used structured interviewing.[21] Both of these methods have limitations. Assessing cruelty based upon a single item can lack scope and detail, and structured interviewing can be labour-intensive and lengthy.[22] The most widely used instruments for measuring animal cruelty are the six following measures.

1. Interview for Antisocial Behaviour (IAB)[23]

An instrument for measuring a variety of forms of antisocial, aggressive, and destructive behaviours, including animal cruelty. Kazdin and Esveldt-Dawson reported that their measure had acceptable levels of internal consistency. The limitation of this interview is that it relies solely on parental reports of overt behaviour, which limits the assessment of covert behaviours.[24]

2. Children and Animals Assessment Instrument (CAAI)[25]

This was the first extensive instrument developed to measure animal cruelty. It was used to gather data on people's experience with animals, including cruelty to animals either committed or observed. CAAI is a paper-and-pencil, self- and parent-report inventory that produces a total score based on Ascione's nine aspects of cruel behaviour: severity (degree of intentional pain/injury caused); frequency (number of separate acts); duration (period of time over which cruelty occurred); recency (most current acts); diversity across and within categories (number of types and number of animals within a type that were abused); level of concern for the abused animal (termed 'sentience'); covert (related to child's attempts to conceal cruelty); isolated (individual versus group cruelty); and empathy (indications of remorse or concern for the injured animal). Dadds *et al.* found that these nine aspects of cruelty could be reliably measured using a questionnaire format. However, due to the long time required for the completion of this instrument, it may be more suitable for research settings where multiple constructs need to be assessed than for clinical settings.[26] Nevertheless, because this child and parent assessment has good interrater reliability and extensive qualitative information, the CAAI is an important method of assessment of childhood animal cruelty.[27]

3. Boat Inventory on Animal-Related Experiences (BIARE)[28]

This is a semi-structured inventory that includes a set of questions that help children disclose animal abuse in the home, whether they have been abused, and whether they have abused an animal. It can be used as a screening and information-gathering instrument. It was developed to elicit information about a wide range of events to determine whether animal-related trauma, cruelty, or support is part of the history of a child, adolescent, or adult. However, this measure has not been standardized or normed.

4. Children's Attitudes and Behaviours Toward Animals (CABTA)[29]

This is a screening instrument which distinguishes between types of animal cruelty. It examines typical and malicious cruelty to animals. According to Ascione, the CABTA 'holds real promise as a reliable, relatively quickly administered, and valid assessment of childhood animal abuse'.[30] However, no quantitative measures of reliability and validity seem to have been published. Also, the CABTA lacks the kind of qualitative information provided, for example, by the CAAI instrument.

5. Physical and Emotional Tormenting against Animals (P.E.T. Scale)[31]

This is a new self-administered scale which measures physical and emotional abuse against animals by adolescents and preadolescents. It was developed to assess the prevalence and frequency of different types of animal abuse. The scale measures direct animal abuse and exposure to animal abuse. Baldry made the first attempt to establish its reliability and validity in her study of 1,356 Italian adolescents.

6. The Clinical Assessment of Juvenile Animal Cruelty[32]

This clinical manual serves as a guide in assessing the severity of juvenile animal cruelty and is intended to lead the mental health clinician toward the most effective treatment approach for the child and family. It includes ready-to-use interview and assessment protocols which contribute to a simple and pragmatic clinical assessment. According to Haden and Scarpa this measure is possibly the most comprehensive measure of juvenile animal cruelty so far developed. Unfortunately, these instruments generally lack widely-accepted psychometric measures of reliability or validity.

Case Histories of Child Murderers, Mass Murderers, and Serial Killers

According to Federal Bureau of Investigation (FBI) criteria, a mass murderer is someone who kills at least three persons on the same day, while a serial killer 'is the premeditated murderer of three or more victims committed over time in separate incidents'.[33] As stated by Schechter and Everitt, the most apt image for a serial killer is the 'hunter of humans', while the appropriate analogy for a mass murderer is the 'human time bomb'.[34] Case histories of murderers often suggest that they were cruel to animals in their childhoods.

One of Australia's most terrible acts of mass violence occurred in April

1996, when Martin Bryant killed thirty-five people in a nineteen-hour rampage in Port Arthur, Tasmania.[35] It was later found that Bryant had first been referred to mental health officials when he was only seven years old, and again at age eleven when it was found that he had tortured and harassed animals and tormented his baby sister.[36]

In the United States, high school killers Kip Kinkel and Luke Woodham both tortured animals before embarking on their separate killing sprees. Kip Kinkel, fifteen, walked into his high school cafeteria and opened fire on his classmates. Two were killed and twenty-two others were injured, four critically. Later that day police found his parents shot dead in their home. Friends and family said that Kinkel had a history of animal abuse and torture, having boasted about blowing up a cow and killing cats, chipmunks, and squirrels by putting lit firecrackers in their mouths.[37]

Five months before Luke Woodham, sixteen, embarked on his high school killing spree, he killed his dog.[38] In his diary, Woodham gave grotesque details of how he and a friend had tied his 'loved one' up in a plastic bag, had taken her into the woods, and hit her while they listened to her howls. He then covered the plastic bag with lighter fluid and put a match to it. Woodham stated in his diary 'I'll never forget the sound of her breaking under my might . . . I will never forget the howl she made . . . It sounded almost human. We laughed and hit her some more'.[39] His killing spree included stabbing his mother to death and shooting dead his former girlfriend and a second girl.

Notorious Columbine High School students Eric Harris and Dylan Klebold shot and killed twelve classmates and a teacher and injured more than twenty others before killing themselves in one of the worst and most talked-about high school shootings in the United States. These two young juveniles used to brag about mutilating animals to their friends.[40]

There are many examples of serial killers who were cruel to animals. Albert De Salvo, known as the 'Boston Strangler', killed thirteen women. In his youth, he trapped dogs and cats in orange crates and shot arrows through the boxes. One of his favourite pastimes was placing a starving cat in one of his orange crates with a puppy and watching the cat scratch the dog's eyes out.[41]

Edmund Kemper killed eight women, including his mother. He revealed in his trial that he had a history of abusing cats and dogs. For example, at the age of ten he chopped up a cat with a machete and stashed the dismembered parts in his closet. Later he buried a cat alive, dug it up when it had died, then chopped its head off and proudly displayed it in his bedroom.[42] Kemper's mother was concerned with his sadistic behaviour toward cats, and she warned that his grandparents could be in danger.[43]

Carroll Cole, one of the most prolific killers in the United States, was executed in 1985 for five of the thirty-five murders of which he was accused. Cole stated that his first act of violence as a child was strangling a puppy.[44] In the United Kingdom the serial killer Ian Brady, one of the Moors Murderers, frequently enjoyed tossing alley cats out of apartment windows and watching them splat onto the pavement.[45]

A final example is the serial killer Henry Lee Lucas, who has been named as one of the most depraved in history. He grew up with an abusive mother, who made him watch while she had sex with strangers. His mother would also beat him unmercifully and she took pleasure in killing his pets. Later he engaged in sexual activities with his half-brother, who introduced him to bestiality and animal torture. One of their favourite pastimes was slitting the throats of small animals and then sexually violating the corpses.[46]

Of course, it is not only serial killers who have progressed from animal cruelty to murder. In the United Kingdom, as mentioned earlier, Mary Bell was an eleven-year-old girl who was convicted of killing two boys, one aged three and the other aged four. No one had ever paid any attention to the warning signs of Mary's odd behaviour, which included kicking, scratching, and nipping other children. Later she put her hands around the throat of a newborn baby in a pram and pushed her cousin off an air-raid shelter onto the hard concrete floor seven feet below, but no one reported this.[47] Her final act of violence before the murders included the attempted strangling of three school-girls. After her conviction, many people claimed to have seen Mary committing all kinds of violent acts before the murders, including strangling cats and birds.[48] Mary's behaviour might have been caused by her upbringing, since her mother was sexually abusive and tried to kill her four times. When Mary was aged four her mother involved her in sadomasochistic prostitution.[49]

Another famous case in the United Kingdom was the James Bulger murder. Robert Thompson, the more assertive of the two ten-year-olds who killed two-year-old toddler James Bulger, not only bullied children but also tortured and killed stray cats and pigeons. He shot pigeons with his air gun and laughed as he pulled off their heads.[50] Both boys came from abusive family backgrounds that seemed likely to encourage a child to become extremely violent.[51] It appears that Thompson was sexually abused, which could possibly explain why he sexually abused baby James. In addition, Ian Huntley, who was responsible for the killing of two young British schoolgirls in 2003, had a history of animal cruelty.[52] These case studies have many methodological problems, including reliance on second-hand sources, retrospective questioning, and the absence of comparison samples. There have been surprisingly few academic studies of animal cruelty in the childhoods of mass or serial murderers.[53]

MacDonald's Triad

MacDonald was a pioneering figure in identifying animal cruelty as a 'red flag' behaviour for human violence.[54] He was the first to report a clinical impression that the triad of enuresis, fire-setting, and cruelty to animals was an unfavourable prognostic sign characteristic of those who threaten or commit homicide.

Hellman and Blackman were the first to assess (retrospectively) whether this triad of behaviours in childhood was empirically related to aggressive violent crimes in adulthood. They studied violent inmates and concluded that 'the presence of the triad in the child may be of pathognomonic importance in predicting violent antisocial behaviour'.[55] Of their sample of eighty-four violent inmates, seventy-five per cent had an early record of cruelty to animals, fire-setting, and bedwetting, compared to only twenty-eight per cent of non-aggressive criminals.

Wax and Haddox studied the triad in a sample of forty-six male adults who had been referred for psychiatric evaluations by juvenile authorities. They concluded that, of the forty-six offenders, 'six demonstrated the triad of enuresis, fire-setting, and excessive cruelty to animals'.[56] They further argued that 'evidence of the triad or any such documented pattern in childhood should serve as an early warning device for clinicians'.[57]

Heath, Hardesty, and Goldfine argued that many of the early studies of animal cruelty and triad behaviour were methodologically poor.[58] They investigated the relationship between fire-setting, animal cruelty, and enuresis by examining two hundred and four cases of children admitted to an outpatient psychiatric clinic. They found that, while enuresis and animal cruelty were not related to fire-setting, there was a significant association between enuresis and non-cruel fire-setters and also between cruelty to animals and non-enuretic fire-setters.

While some studies report a relationship between the triad and later violent behaviour, the triad is not commonly present in the histories of adolescents or adults who are aggressive or commit criminal acts. In addition, few children who demonstrate the triad remain or become violent later in life.[59] Perhaps because of the conflicting evidence regarding the triad behaviours more recent studies have focused on single behaviours rather than the combination of all three.[60]

Notes

1. This chapter is a revised version of M. L. Petersen and D. P. Farrington, 'Cruelty to animals and violence to people', *Victims and Offenders* 2 (2007): 21–43.

2. Piers Beirne, 'For a non-speciesist criminology: Animal abuse as an object of study', *Criminology* 37, 1 (1999): 117–147.

3. Piers Beirne, 'The use and abuse of animals in criminology: A brief history and current review', *Social Justice* 22, 1 (1995): 5–31.

4. Clifton D. Bryant and William E. Snizek, 'On the trail of the centaur', *Society* 30, 3 (1993), p. 23.

5. Scott Vollum, Jacqueline Buffington-Vollum, and Dennis R. Longmire, 'Moral disengagement and attitudes about violence toward animals', *Society & Animals* 12, 3 (2004): 209–235.

6. Sara C. Haden and Angela Scarpa, 'Childhood animal cruelty: A review of research, assessment, and therapeutic issues', *The Forensic Examiner* (Summer 2005): 23–32.

7. RSPCA Policies on Animal Welfare (Horsham: RSPCA, 2003).

8. Metropolitan Police (2002), 'Animals tortured for "crush fetish" video', http://www.pet_abuse.com/cases/596/EN/UK/20.

9. Fiona Becker, *The links between child abuse and animal abuse*, NSPCC Information Briefings (London: NSPCC, 2001).

10 Linda Merz-Perez and Kathleen Heide, *Animal cruelty: Pathway to violence against people* (Oxford: AltaMira Press, 2004).

11 Anna C. Baldry, 'The development of the P. E.T. Scale for the measurement of physical and emotional tormenting against animals in adolescents', *Society & Animals* 12, 1 (2004): 1–17.

12 F. R. Ascione, 'Children who are cruel to animals: A review of research and implications for developmental psychology', *Anthrozoös* 6, 4 (1993), p. 228.

13 A. N. Rowan, 'Cruelty and abuse to animals: A typology', in F. R. Ascione and P. Arkow (eds), *Child abuse, domestic violence, and animal abuse: Linking the circles of compassion for prevention and intervention* (West Lafayette, IN: Purdue University Press, 1999), pp. 328–334.

14 Barbara Boat, 'Abuse of children and abuse of animals: Using the links to inform child assessment and protection', in F. R. Ascione and P. Arkow (eds), *Child abuse, domestic violence, and animal abuse: Linking the circles of compassion for prevention and intervention* (West Lafayette, IN: Purdue University Press, 1999), pp. 83–100.

15 F. R. Ascione, cited in Barbara Boat, 'Abuse of children and abuse of animals'.

16 F. R. Ascione and R. Lockwood, 'Cruelty to animals: Changing psychological, social, and legislative perspectives', in Humane Society of the United States (ed.), *The state of animals* (Gaithersburg, MD: Humane Society Press, 2001), pp. 39–54.

17 H. Piper, M. Johnson, S. Myers, and J. Pritchard, 'Children and young people harming animals: Intervention through PSHE?' *Research Papers in Education* 18, 2 (2003): 197–213.

18 Baldry, 'The development of the P.E.T. scale'.

19 M. R. Dadds *et al.*, 'Measurement of cruelty in children: The cruelty to animals inventory', *Journal of Abnormal Child Psychology* 32, 3 (2004): 321–334.

20 T. M. Achenbach, *Manual for the child behavior checklist and 1991 profile* (Burlington, VT: University of Vermont, 1991).

21 See Barbara Boat, 'The relationship between violence to children and violence to animals: An ignored link?' *Journal of Interpersonal Violence* 10, 2 (1995): 228–235; S. R. Kellert and A. R. Felthous, 'Childhood cruelty toward animals among criminals and noncriminals', *Human Relations* 38 (1985): 1113–1129.

22 Dadds *et al.*, 'Measurement of cruelty in children'.

23 A. E. Kazdin and K. Esveldt-Dawson, 'The interview for antisocial behavior: Psychometric characteristics and concurrent validity with child psychiatric inpatients', *Journal of Psychopathology and Behavioral Assessment*, 8, 4 (1986): 289–303.

24 S. C. Haden and A. Scarpa, 'Childhood animal cruelty: A review of research, assessment, and therapeutic issues', *The Forensic Examiner* (Summer 2005): 23–32.

25 F. R. Ascione, 'Children who are cruel to animals'; F. R. Ascione, T. M. Thompson, and T. Black, 'Childhood cruelty to animals: Assessing cruelty dimensions and motivations', *Anthrozoös* 10, 4 (1997): 170–177.

26 Boat, 'The relationship between violence to children and violence to animals'; Dadds *et al.*, 'Measurement of cruelty in children'.

27 Haden and Scarpa, 'Childhood animal cruelty'.

28 Boat, 'Abuse of children and abuse of animals'.

29 E. C. Guymer, D. Mellor, E. S. L. Luk, and V. Pearse, 'The development of a screening questionnaire for childhood cruelty to animals', *Journal of Child Psychology and Psychiatry* 42, 8 (2001): 1057–1063.

30 F. R. Ascione, *Children and animals: Exploring the roots of kindness and cruelty* (West Lafayette, IN: Purdue University Press, 2005), p. 100.

31 Baldry, 'The development of the P.E.T. scale'.

32 E. Zimmerman and S. Lewchanin, *Clinician assessment of juvenile animal cruelty* (Brunswick, ME: Biddle Publishing, 2000).

33 B. T. Keeney and K. M. Heide, 'Serial murder: A more accurate and inclusive definition', *International Journal of Offender Therapy and Comparative Criminology* 39, 4 (1995), p. 304.

34 H. Schechter and D. Everitt, *The A to Z encyclopedia of serial killers* (New York: Pocket Books, 1996), p. 179.

35 P. Wilson and G. Norris, 'Relationship between criminal behavior and mental illness in young adults: Conduct disorder, cruelty to animals and young adult serious violence', *Psychiatry, Psychology and Law* 10, 1 (2003): 239–243.

36 P. Mullen, *Martin Bryant – Psychiatric report* (1996), http://massmurder.zyns.com/martin_b ryant_06.htm.

37 People for the Ethical Treatment of Animals (PETA), 'Animal abuse and human abuse: Partners in crime' (2003), http://www.peta.org/mc/factsheet _display.asp?ID=132.

38 A. Neustatter, 'Killers' animal instincts: The sadistic fantasies that drive serial killers have their roots in childhood – There is a compelling link with cruelty to animals', *The Independent*, 13 October 1998, p. 8.

39 F. R. Ascione, 'The abuse of animals and human interpersonal violence: Making the connection', in F. R. Ascione and P. Arkow (eds), *Child abuse, domestic violence, and animal abuse: Linking the circles of compassion for prevention and intervention* (West Lafayette, IN: Purdue University Press, 1999), p. 50.

40 PETA, 'Animal abuse and human abuse'.

41 R. Lockwood and G. H. Hodge, 'The tangled web of animal abuse: The links between cruelty to animals and human violence', in R. Lockwood and F. R. Ascione (eds), *Cruelty to animals and interpersonal violence* (West Lafayette, IN: Purdue University Press, 1998); Schecter and Everitt, *The A to Z encyclopedia*.

42 Schecter and Everitt, *The A to Z encyclopedia*.

43 J. Wright and C. Hensley, 'From animal cruelty to serial murder: Applying the graduation hypothesis', *International Journal of Offender Therapy and Comparative Criminology* 47, 1 (2003): 71–88.

44 Lockwood and Hodge, 'The tangled web of animal abuse'.

45 Schecter and Everitt, *The A to Z encyclopedia*.

46 *Ibid*.

47 G. Sereny, *The case of Mary Bell: A portrait of a child who murdered* (London: Pimlico, 1972).

48 G. Sereny, *Cries unheard: The story of Mary Bell* (London: Macmillan, 1998).

49 H. Wilce, 'What happens when parents set the tone', *Times Educational Supplement*, 4 February 2003, p. 28.

50 Stephen Glover, 'A story devoid of mercy and hope: Stephen Glover, who observed the trial in Preston and researched the James Bulger case, describes the background to a murder that shook the world', *Evening Standard*, 25 November 1993, p. 18; Neustatter, 'Killers' Animal Instincts'.

51 C. A. Davis, *Children who kill: Profiles of pre-teen and teenage killers* (London: Allison & Busby, 2003).

52 F. Becker and L. French, 'Making the links: Child abuse, animal cruelty and domestic violence', *Child Abuse Review* 13, 6 (2004): 399–414.

53 Wright and Hensley, 'From animal cruelty to serial murder'.

54 J. M. MacDonald, 'The threat to kill', *American Journal of Psychiatry* 120 (1963): 124–130.

55 D. S. Hellman and N. Blackman, 'Enuresis, fire-setting and cruelty to animals: A triad predictive of adult crime', *American Journal of Psychiatry* 122 (1966), p. 1435.

56 D. E. Wax and V. G. Haddox, 'Sexual aberrance in male adolescents manifesting a behavioral triad considered predictive of extreme violence', *Journal of Forensic Sciences* 19, 1 (1974), p. 103.

57 D. E. Wax, and V. G. Haddox, 'Enuresis, fire-setting, and animal cruelty: A useful danger signal in predicting vulnerability of adolescent males to assaultive behavior', *Child Psychiatry and Human Development* 4 (1974), p. 155.

58 G. A. Heath, V. A. Hardesty, and P. E. Goldfine, 'Fire-setting, enuresis, and animal cruelty', *Journal of Child and Adolescent Psychotherapy* 1 (1984): 97–100.

59 P. Nelson, *A survey of psychologists' attitudes, opinions, and clinical experiences with animal abuse*, unpublished doctoral dissertation, The Wright Institute Graduate School of Clinical Psychology, 2001.

60 C. Miller, 'Childhood animal cruelty and interpersonal violence', *Clinical Psychology Review* 21, 5 (2001): 735–749.

Types of Cruelty: Animals and Childhood Cruelty, Domestic Violence, Child and Elder Abuse[1]

MARY LOUISE PETERSEN AND DAVID P. FARRINGTON

Childhood Animal Cruelty and Adult Violence

Most previous studies of the link between childhood animal cruelty and adult violence have been retrospective. Table 2.1 summarizes the samples and findings of the eleven main studies, listed chronologically according to publication date. All except one concluded that there was a link between childhood animal cruelty and later violence toward people. However, five of the studies had no comparison samples.[2]

Of the other six, three compared violent and non-violent offenders.[3] As an example, Merz-Perez *et al.* investigated whether violent offenders were more likely than non-violent offenders to have committed animal cruelty. They found that fifty-six per cent of violent offenders, compared with twenty per cent of non-violent offenders, admitted cruelty to animals in childhood, a statistically significant difference (X2 = 10.6, 1 df, p = .001).

Kellert and Felthous compared aggressive offenders, non-aggressive offenders, and non-offenders.[4] They found that twenty-five per cent of aggressive offenders, six per cent of non-aggressive offenders, and none of the non-offenders reported five or more acts of cruelty to animals. The aggressive offenders were significantly different from the other two groups (X2 = 14.4, 1 df, p < .001). However, prospective probabilities are unknown (e.g., the percentage of children who are cruel to animals who later become violent offenders), and retrospective studies may be subject to retrospective bias in reporting.

Becker, Stuewig, Herrera, and McCloskey carried out the first prospective longitudinal study of the link between childhood animal cruelty and adolescent violence.[5] They initially interviewed one hundred and sixty-four mothers who had been abused by a partner and one hundred and ninety-nine control mothers, and asked them about animal cruelty by their children. They found that twenty-six per cent of cruel children were referred to the juvenile court for violence, compared to fourteen per cent of non-cruel children (not quite significantly different). Animal cruelty significantly predicted self-reported violence.

The Miller and Knutson study did not report a link between animal cruelty and adult violence.[6] They compared three hundred and fourteen prison inmates with three hundred and eight undergraduate students in order to assess their abusive childhood environments and 'exposure' to animal cruelty. Using self-reports, they did not find a substantial association between past experiences of animal abuse and the physical punitiveness of their parents. They found that animal cruelty was more prevalent in their incarcerated sample (sixty-six per cent) than in their sample of students (forty-eight per cent). However, whereas the incarcerated sample was eighty-four per cent male, the student sample was only fifty-seven per cent female.

In the student sample, sixty-nine per cent of males and thirty-three per cent of females had been exposed to animal cruelty. If the student sample had been eighty-four per cent male, an estimated sixty-three per cent would have been exposed to animal cruelty. Miller and Knutson concluded that their data were 'not consistent with the hypothesis that exposure to animal cruelty is importantly related to antisocial behavior or child maltreatment'.[7] However, their variable – 'childhood exposure to animal cruelty' – combined both observed and perpetrated animal cruelty. Hence they did not disentangle and investigate persons who committed animal cruelty.

Animal Cruelty and Domestic Violence

It is widely believed among researchers in the field of animal cruelty that when animals are abused, people are often at risk, and vice versa.[8] Several studies have documented that animal cruelty is frequently a risk factor for the presence of human violence in the home environment.[9] It is argued that the cycle of violent behaviour often begins with violence against animals. For example, as argued by Ascione, although animal abuse does not cause violence to people, it may make violence more likely as animal abuse may desensitize the perpetrator to suffering in general. There is a growing recognition that domestic violence, child abuse, and animal cruelty often occur in the same households because they are all committed by the same person, an adult male.[10]

Table 2.1 summarizes six key empirical studies linking animal cruelty and domestic violence. Unfortunately, five of these studies merely report retrospective information about the extent to which female victims have suffered cruelty to their pets, with no comparable figures from control samples. For example, in a large study conducted by Jorgenson and Maloney,[11] information was gathered from 7,264 women in domestic violence shelters over a three-year period. In the advocacy component, which served battered women who were still living with their abusers, twelve per cent of the women reported that their animals had been threatened, abused, or killed by their batterers. In the shelters, sixteen per cent of women entering a shelter reported that their pets had been hurt or killed by their partners. However, in the component designed to treat the abusers, only one per cent of 1,354 men acknowledged that they had committed any form of animal cruelty, suggesting that most men deny that they are abusers.

Becker *et al.* studied battered women and control women and found that children from violent homes were significantly more likely to be cruel to animals than those from non-violent homes (eleven per cent compared with five per cent).[12]

The other four studies reported the proportion of women with pets who had suffered animal cruelty. The proportions were high: eighty-eight per cent in Quinlisk, seventy-one per cent in Ascione, forty-seven per cent in Flynn, and forty-six per cent in Faver and Strand.[13] Unfortunately, the definition of animal cruelty varied in these studies, sometimes including threatened as well as actual harm. These percentages may have been higher than in the Jorgenson and Maloney study because, with smaller samples, the questioning could have been more detailed and sensitive, leading to more valid reporting.

Animal Cruelty and Child Abuse

The increasing numbers of studies that show that adults who are abusing animals are also likely to abuse their children and that children who abuse animals are also more likely to be victims of abuse suggest that cruelty to animals within a family might be a significant risk factor. Therefore, practitioners should be alerted to the possibility that animal cruelty in a family might be an indicator of child abuse and also an indicator of domestic violence.[14]

Quinlisk suggested a possible link between witnessing a parent being cruel to animals and childhood animal cruelty in her survey, which included seventy-two women at a domestic shelter.[15] According to Flynn, children may learn to abuse animals partly because their socialization experience has included violence in the family.[16] Children sometimes report that parents threaten to kill or dispose of their pet if the child tells an outsider of the abuse in the home.[17] Furthermore, Loar's theoretical findings state that 'being forced to participate in the abuse of a pet is sometimes a parental requirement, one that may put the child on the road to becoming a perpetrator'.[18] Hensley and Tallichet also reported in their study that those who witnessed animal cruelty were more likely to abuse animals frequently.[19]

The first (and only) study to investigate the relationship between child abuse and animal cruelty in the United Kingdom was conducted by Hutton, who reviewed all the cases of animal cruelty that came to the notice of the

RSPCA in one Social Services area in 1980 (Table 2.2).[20] Out of twenty-three families participating in the study, 35 per cent had children who were on the at-risk register of Social Services. An ironic example of the current situation in the United Kingdom is that, while a person may be banned from keeping animals for ten years, no questions are necessarily asked about their risk of abusing their children.[21]

Ascione, Friedrich, Heath, and Hayashi found that the prevalence of cruelty to animals was six times greater for sexually abused children than for normal children (18 per cent compared with 3 per cent).[22] DeViney *et al.* studied fifty-three families who met the New Jersey state criteria for child abuse or neglect and who also had companion animals in their home.[23] Observations during home interviews revealed that pets were abused or neglected in 60 per cent of these families. The most remarkable finding was that in 88 per cent of families displaying child physical abuse, cruelty to animals was also present. Two-thirds of animals were abused by fathers and one-third by children. Finally, Duffield, Hassiotis, and Vizard found that 20 per cent of children who had sexually abused other children and committed other violent offences had a history of sexually abusing animals.[24] However, once again, these studies are retrospective and lack control group information.

Animal Cruelty and Elder Abuse

The link between animal cruelty and elder abuse has not received as much empirical study as the links with child abuse or domestic violence. However, Rosen emphasized the connection between animal cruelty and elder abuse. She reported one humane officer as saying that 'elder and animal abuses go together so often that when I see one I automatically look for the other'.[25]

As with other forms of family violence, recognition of the association between elder abuse and animal cruelty often occurs first in dramatic case histories. A California humane investigator reported responding to a call about a number of abandoned dogs left to starve in an empty apartment. After removing the animals, the humane officer heard whimpering from a closet. Expecting to find more dogs, she was horrified to find an emaciated old man who had also been left behind by his caretakers.[26]

Clinical experience suggests that there are several different situations where elder abuse may be linked to animal cruelty. In some cases the elder person and their pet may live with an adult child or grandchild. The elder person may have lost their spouse and turned to the pet for love and companionship. The adult child or grandchild may be the elder person's caregiver and may neglect or abuse the elder person due to alcohol or drug use, ignorance, immaturity, or frustration.[27]

The abuser may intimidate the elder person by threatening or actually abusing the pet if the elder person does not sign over assets or property to the abuser. There may be financial dependence of the abuser on the elder person.

The elder person may be ashamed or embarrassed to report this kind of treatment because the abuser is a family member. Longitudinal studies are needed to establish the time ordering of animal cruelty, domestic violence, child abuse, and elder abuse.

Causes of Childhood Cruelty to Animals

It has often been suggested that cruelty to animals might be a symptom of or caused by lack of empathy.[28] Kellert and Felthous identified nine different possible motivations for animal cruelty in their study of aggressive criminals, non-aggressive criminals, and non-criminals. Some men admitted snapping the necks of animals, or exploding cats in microwaves. When asked why, they said 'for kicks or fun'.[29] Based on statements from these men, the nine motivations were: (1) to control an animal; (2) to retaliate against an animal; (3) to satisfy a prejudice against a species or breed; (4) to express aggression through an animal; (5) to enhance one's own aggressiveness; (6) to shock people for amusement; (7) to retaliate against another person; (8) to displace hostility from a person to an animal; and (9) non-specific sadism.

It is unclear whether a specific theory of animal cruelty is needed, or whether animal cruelty is merely one symptom of a more general underlying antisocial personality. There are many specific theories – for example, displaced aggression theory, sadistic theory, and sexually polymorphous theory.[30] Several theories suggest that animal cruelty is encouraged by growing up in an abusive environment where violence is witnessed.[31] Some of the most important explanations of animal cruelty are based on ideas of strain, social learning, and the graduation hypothesis.

Strain Theory

Agnew proposed a theory of animal abuse based on strain theory, which was the first attempt to explain the causes of animal cruelty in criminology. He suggested that strain and stress may indirectly or directly lead to animal abuse. Animals may interfere with the achievement of valued goals or engage in other annoying behaviours. As a result some individuals will engage in animal abuse, feeling that the abuse is deserved or necessary for some higher end. Some people may engage in animal cruelty for revenge or personal gain, justifying their behaviour in the process.[32] With this justification, it is important to remember that 'as long as we as a society condone, allow or excuse any type of violence, we give the perpetrators leeway to justify all types of violence'.[33] Strained individuals may engage in animal abuse to reduce strain, to seek revenge against those who have placed them under strain, or to manage the negative emotions associated with strain. For example, 'they may kill or threaten the companion animals of those who have wronged them in an effort to change their "negative" behaviour or to obtain revenge'.[34] Strained individuals may use animals as scapegoats; animals may provide a safe target for the discharge of aggressive feelings.

Social Learning Theory

This theory suggests that the main features of the socialization process are the models to whom children are exposed, the reinforcements and punishments they receive, and the beliefs they are taught and learn.[35] It is argued that those who abuse animals are frustrated individuals who transfer their anger onto animals who cannot retaliate.[36] Many researchers have found evidence linking child-rearing environment with later animal cruelty.[37] Hensley and Tallichet, in their study of two hundred and sixty-one inmates, concluded that animal cruelty was in part a learned behaviour. Also, many serial killers and child and adolescent killers grew up in families where daily beatings and sexually abusive behaviour were part of their life. In a hostile environment, children often mimic their parents' abusive behaviour, and through imitation and reinforcement they become abusive to others – including animals.[38] Aggression then escalates against humans and is passed on to the next generation.

The Graduation Hypothesis

According to this hypothesis, animal abusers will later graduate to more serious acts of violence against humans.[39] In other words, individuals will progress from harming animals to harming humans.[40] However, tests of the graduation hypothesis have produced conflicting findings. Some researchers have found evidence in favour of it.[41] According to Wright and Hensley, 'A possible link between childhood cruelty to animals and later serial murder exists. Each serial murderer . . . seemed to transfer the frustration they received from their mothers or other adults toward weaker animals'.[42] On the other hand, other researchers have found no evidence to support the graduation hypothesis. For example, Beirne argued that this theory lacks coherent empirical evidence, mainly because of insufficient attention to the main concepts such as 'animal abuse' and 'animal cruelty'.[43]

Prevention Programmes

The Humane Society of the United States has recently presented a wide range of programmes that address prevention of human violence and animal cruelty.[44] These programmes aim to teach children to nurture, care for, and interact with animals in order to reduce their tendencies to act violently.[45] One example is the People and Animal Learning programme (PAL). PAL is a nationally recognized violence prevention programme developed by the Wisconsin Humane Society (WHS) in 1993. At-risk Milwaukee area youth are nominated by their teachers and social workers to participate in the programme. Under the supervision of WHS experts, each child works in a team to train a shelter dog to become a well-mannered companion for an adopting family. The children gain an increased sense of self-worth, develop compassion, and learn the importance of success through positive means. Even though the programme was not designed as an intervention programme for juveniles who are cruel to animals, it teaches the children respect, responsibility, and accountability.[46]

In the United Kingdom, animal, child, and domestic violence agencies are beginning to utilize the growing body of knowledge about animal cruelty. Cross-reporting schemes – where issues of concern are shared between the police, animal organizations, and Social Services – are currently being piloted. However, no data is available to evaluate their progress to date. Likewise, the NSPCC has reported that some Area Child Protection Committees are beginning to consider the importance of the link between animal cruelty and child abuse.[47] As a result, in 2001 the NSPCC and RSPCA jointly organized a conference to increase awareness of the link between animal cruelty and violence in the family and to discuss the implications for policy and practice. Cross-reporting and multi-agency communication is designed to counter the best protection available to perpetrators of animal and human abuse – silence and fear.

The core assumption of many of the efforts to prevent violence is that early detection of a predisposition toward violence will provide the best opportunity for meaningful intervention. Farrington and Welsh have described some of the most effective programmes for preventing delinquency.[48] Some of these might similarly be successful in preventing future animal cruelty among children and adolescents. These programmes include general parent education, parent management training, child skills training, preschool intellectual enrichment programmes, and anti-bullying programmes in schools.

Conclusions

Existing research suggests that there are links between animal cruelty and human violence; children who are cruel to animals are at higher risk of growing up into violent adults, and adults who are cruel to animals are at higher risk of committing domestic violence, child abuse, and elder abuse. However, the existing research is methodologically poor. Also, the importance of cruelty to animals compared with other childhood risk factors for adult violence is unclear.

The existing research tends to be based on small, unrepresentative samples, with no or poor control samples, and it relies on retrospective accounts which may be biased by knowledge of more recent events. Prospective longitudinal studies are needed with large representative samples of the population to investigate the prevalence and frequency of animal cruelty at different ages, the importance of animal cruelty as a risk factor for later violence, the prospective probability of adult violence following animal cruelty, the causes of animal cruelty, and the processes by which animal cruelty may lead to adult violence.

These studies face many challenges. First, a clear definition of animal cruelty must be specified. Second, the validity of different methods of measuring animal cruelty must be assessed, for example by comparing self-reports with external criteria such as records or observation. Psychometric measures of reliability are required. A widely accepted standardized instrument is needed that inquires about different types of animals and different types and levels of cruelty. Prevalence and incidence data are needed (for example, within the last year, within a lifetime). Third, while it is important to document developmental sequences including both animal cruelty and other kinds of violence, it is also crucial to investigate what causes what.

Research is needed to specify the probabilities linking animal cruelty, domestic violence, child abuse, and elder abuse in families. For example, is the probability of domestic violence given animal cruelty greater or less than the probability of animal cruelty given domestic violence? Research is also needed to establish the time ordering of these different events, and the effects on children (e.g., of witnessing animal cruelty compared with domestic violence). Theories of the links between these events need to be tested. For example, one possibility is that they are all related because they are all symptoms of the presence of an antisocial adult male in the family, rather than there being any causal links between them. More research is needed on the links between animal cruelty and Conduct Disorder (CD) and Antisocial Personality Disorder (APD). For example, is animal cruelty related to juvenile psychopathy?[49]

Another research priority is to evaluate the effectiveness of methods of preventing animal cruelty and the long-term effects of such prevention (if effective) on later violence. Prevention methods must be based on knowledge about risk factors or causes. Ideally, experimental evaluations are needed and the costs and benefits of prevention programmes should be measured. If indeed there are causal links between animal cruelty and other kinds of violence, preventing animal cruelty may have long-term and wide-ranging benefits. The time is ripe for a major research programme to advance knowledge about the causes and prevention of animal cruelty and its implications for criminology.

Table 2.1 Studies of Animal Cruelty and Violence

Researcher(s): Felthous (1979)

Sample/size: 429 adult impatient admissions to psychiatric hospital. Divided into aggressive and non-aggressive samples.

Main findings: Aggressive sample: 23% killed dogs and cats purposely, 18% tortured them. Non-aggressive sample: 10% killed, 5% tortured dogs and cats. Aggressive adults significantly more cruel.

Researcher(s): Kellert & Felthous (1985)

Sample/size: 152 males, divided into aggressive and non-aggressive criminals and non-criminals.
Main findings: 25% of aggressive criminals reported five or more acts of cruelty to animals, 6% of non-aggressive criminals and none of the non-criminals. Aggressive criminals significantly more cruel.

Researcher(s): Tingle *et al.* (1986)
Sample/size: 64 inmates.
Main findings: 48% of those convicted of rape and 30% convicted of child molestation had histories of animal cruelty.

Researcher(s): Ressler *et al.* (1988)
Sample/size: 28 sexual homicide perpetrators.
Main findings: 36% committed acts of animal cruelty in childhood, 46% in adolescence.

Researcher(s): Miller & Knutson (1997)
Sample/size: 314 inmates vs. 308 undergraduate students.
Main findings: 66% of inmates reported some exposure* to animal cruelty, compared to 63% of a student sample matched for gender.

Researcher(s): Schiff *et al.* (1999)
Sample/size: 117 inmates, divided into violent and non-violent criminals.
Main findings: 63% of violent criminals committed animal cruelty vs. 11% of non-violent criminals (significantly different).

Researcher(s): Merz-Perez *et al.* (2001)
Sample/size: 45 violent offenders vs. 45 non-violent offenders.
Main findings: Cruelty to animals greater in the violent sample, 56% vs. 20% (significantly different).

Researcher(s): Becker *et al.* (2004)
Sample/size: 164 battered women and 199 control women.
Main findings: Animal cruelty predicted official and self-reported violence in children.

Researcher(s): Baldry (2004)
Sample/size: 1,356 Italian adolescents.
Main findings: 51% had abused animals at least once; 67% were boys.

Researcher(s): Baldry (2005)
Sample/size: 268 girls and 264 boys (Italian preadolescents).
Main findings: 46% of boys and 36% of girls admitted at least one type of animal abuse.

Researcher(s): Tallichet *et al.* (2005)
Sample/size: 261 incarcerated male inmates.
Main findings: 43% had engaged in animal cruelty. Of these, 63% reported that they had hurt or killed dogs and 55% had abused cats.

* Some exposure covered many different types of abuse, including witnessing animal cruelty and personally torturing, hurting or killing an animal for fun.

Table 2.2 Studies Relating Animal Cruelty, Domestic Violence, and Child Abuse

Animal cruelty and domestic violence
Researcher(s): Ascione (1998)
Sample/size: 38 women at a domestic violence shelter.
Main findings: 71% of those who owned a pet reported that the male partners had threatened or harmed the animal. 18% delayed entering a shelter because of fear or what would happen to the pet.

Researcher(s): Quinlisk (1999)
Sample/size: 72 women at a domestic violence shelter.
Main findings: Of 68% who had pets, 88% indicated animal cruelty committed in their presence. In 76% of the cases, children had witnessed the abuse. 54% of the children who witnessed the cruelty copied this behaviour.

Researcher(s): Jorgensen & Maloney (1999)
Sample/size: 7,264 women at domestic violence shelters.
Main findings: 16% had animals hurt or killed by partner.

Researcher(s): Flynn (2000)
Sample/size: 107 women at a domestic violence shelter.
Main findings: Of 40% who owned pets. 47% reported that their pet was either threatened or harmed. 40% of these had delayed entering a shelter because they feared for their pet.

Researcher(s): Faver & Strand (2003)
Sample/size: 61 women in shelters.
Main findings: 82% owned a pet. Of these 49% reported that the partner had threatened their pet, 46% that their pet had been harmed, and 27% reported that concern for the welfare for their pet had affected their decision to leave.

Researcher(s): Becker et al. (2004)
Sample/size: 164 battered women and 199 control women.
Main findings: Children from violent homes were more likely to be cruel to animals (11% vs. 5%).

Child abuse and animal cruelty
Researcher(s): DeViney et al. (1983)
Sample/size: 53 children (who met criteria for child abuse or neglect).
Main findings: 60% of these families abused/neglected their pets. In 88% of families displaying child physical abuse, cruelty to animals was also present.

Researcher(s): Hutton (1998)
Sample/size: 23 families with animal cruelty.
Main findings: 35% involved children on the risk register of Social Services.

Researcher(s): Duffield *et al.* (1998)
Sample/size: 300 children who sexually abuse other children and commit other violent offences.
Main findings: 20% of children who sexually abuse other children and commit violent offences had history of sexually abusing animals. Many of these children had been severely abused themselves.

Researcher(s): Ascione *et al.* (2003)
Sample/size: 481 sexually abused children, 412 psychiatric outpatient children, 540 normal children.
Main findings: 18% of sexually abused children were cruel to animals, compared with 3% of normal children.

Notes

1   This chapter is a revised version of M. L. Petersen and D. P. Farrington, 'Cruelty to animals and violence to people', *Victims and Offenders* 2 (2007): 21–43.

2   Anna C. Baldry, 'The development of the P.E.T. Scale for the measurement of physical and emotional tormenting against animals in adolescents', *Society & Animals* 12, 1 (2004): 1–17; Baldry, 'Animal abuse among preadolescents directly and indirectly victimized at school and at home', *Criminal Behaviour and Mental Health* 15, 2 (2005): 97–110; R. K. Ressler, A. W. Burgess, and J. E. Douglas, *Sexual homicide: Patterns and motives* (Lexington, MA: Lexington Books, 1988); S. E. Tallichet, C. Hensley, A. O'Bryan, and H. Hassel, 'Targets for cruelty: Demographic and situational factors affecting the type of animal abused', *Criminal Justice Studies* 18, 2 (2005): 173–182; D. Tingle, G. W. Barnard, G. Robbins, G. Newman, and D. Hutchinson, 'Childhood and adolescent characteristics of paedophiles and rapists', *International Journal of Law and Psychiatry* 9 (1986): 103–116.

3   A. R. Felthous, 'Childhood antecedents of aggressive behavior in male psychiatric patients', *Bulletin of the American Academy of Psychiatry and Law* 8 (1979): 104–110; L. Merz-Perez, K. Heide, and I. Silverman, 'Childhood cruelty to animals and subsequent violence against humans', *International Journal of Offender Therapy and Comparative Criminology* 45, 5 (2001): 556–573; K. Schiff, D. Louwe, and F. R. Ascione, 'Animal relations in childhood and later violent behavior against humans', *Acta Criminologica* 12, 3 (1999): 77–86.

4   S. R. Kellert and A. R. Felthous, 'Childhood cruelty toward animals among criminals and noncriminals', *Human Relations* 38 (1985): 1113–1129.

5   K. D. Becker, J. Stuewig, V. M. Herrera, and L. A. McCloskey, 'A study of fire-setting and animal cruelty in children: Family influences and adolescent outcomes', *Journal of the American Academy of Child and Adolescent Psychiatry* 43, 7 (2004): 905–912.

6   K. S. Miller and J. F. Knutson, 'Reports of severe physical punishment and exposure to animal cruelty by inmates convicted of felonies and by university students', *Child Abuse and Neglect* 21, 1 (1997): 59–82.

7   Miller and Knutson, 'Reports', p. 59.

8   P. Arkow, 'The relationships between animal abuse and other forms of family violence', *Family Violence and Sexual Assault Bulletin* 12, 1–2 (1996): 29–34; F. R. Ascione, 'Battered women's reports of their partners' and their children's cruelty to animals', *Journal of Emotional Abuse* 1, 1 (1998): 119–133.

9 E. DeViney, J. Dickert, and R. Lockwood, 'The care of pets within child abusing families', *International Journal for the Study of Animal Problems* 4 (1983): 321–329; C. A. Faver and E. B. Strand, 'To leave or to stay? Battered women's concern for vulnerable pets', *Journal of Interpersonal Violence* 18, 12 (2003): 1367–1377.

10 L. R. Kogan, S. McConnell, R. Schoenfield-Tacher, and P. Jansen-Lock, 'Crosstrails: A unique foster program to provide safety for pets of women in safe-houses', *Violence against Women* 10, 4 (2004), p. 418.

11 S. Jorgenson and L. Maloney, 'Animal abuse and the victims of domestic violence', in F. R. Ascione and P. Arkow (eds), *Child abuse, domestic violence, and animal abuse: Linking the circles of compassion for prevention and intervention* (West Lafayette, IN: Purdue University Press, 1999), pp. 143–158.

12 Becker *et al.*, 'A study of fire-setting'.

13 J. A. Quinlisk, 'Animal abuse and family violence', in F. R. Ascione and P. Arkow (eds), *Child abuse, domestic violence, and animal abuse: Linking the circles of compassion for prevention and intervention* (West Lafayette, IN: Purdue University Press, 1999), pp. 168–175; F. R. Ascione, 'Battered women's reports of their partners' and their children's cruelty to animals', *Journal of Emotional Abuse* 1, 1 (1998): 119–133; C. P. Flynn, 'Woman's best friend: Pet abuse and the role of companion animals in the lives of battered women', *Violence against Women* 6, 2 (2000): 162–177; Faver and Strand, 'To leave or to stay?'.

14 L. Bell, 'Abusing children – Abusing animals', *Journal of Social Work* 1, 1 (2001): 232–233.

15 Quinlisk, 'Animal abuse and family violence'.

16 Flynn, 'Woman's best friend'.

17 L. Loar, '"I'll only help you if you have two legs," or, Why human services professionals should pay attention to cases involving cruelty to animals', in F. R. Ascione and P. Arkow (eds), *Child abuse, domestic violence, and animal abuse: Linking the circles of compassion for prevention and intervention* (West Lafayette, IN: Purdue University Press, 1999), pp. 120–136.

18 *Ibid.*, p. 125.

19 C. Hensley and S. E. Tallichet, 'Learning to be cruel? Exploring the onset and frequency of animal cruelty', *International Journal of Offender Therapy and Comparative Criminology* 49, 1 (2005): 37–47.

20 J. S. Hutton, 'Animal abuse as a diagnostic approach in social work: A pilot study', in R. Lockwood and F. R. Ascione (eds), *Cruelty to animals and interpersonal violence* (West Lafayette, IN: Purdue University Press, 1998).

21 F. Becker and L. French, 'Making the links: Child abuse, animal cruelty and domestic violence', *Child Abuse Review* 13, 6 (2004): 399–414.

22 F. R. Ascione, W. N. Friedrich, J. Heath, and K. Hayashi, 'Cruelty to animals in normative, sexually abused, and outpatient psychiatric samples of 6- to 12-year-old children: Relations to maltreatment and exposure to domestic violence', *Anthrozoös* 16, 3 (2003): 194–212.

23 DeViney *et al.*, 'The Care of Pets'.

24 G. Duffield, A. Hassiotis, and E. Vizard, 'Zoophilia in young sexual abusers', *Journal of Forensic Psychiatry* 9, 2 (1998): 294–304.

25 B. Rosen, 'Watch for pet abuse – It might save your client's life', in R. Lockwood and F. R. Ascione (eds), *Cruelty to animals and interpersonal violence* (West Lafayette, IN: Purdue University Press, 1998), p. 340.

26 R. Lockwood, 'Making the connection between animal cruelty and abuse and

neglect of vulnerable adults', *The Latham Letter* 23, 1 (2002): 1–24.

27 Community Coalition on Family Violence, 'Animal abuse' (2003), http://www.ccfv.org/elder.htm.

28 C. Miller, 'Childhood animal cruelty and interpersonal violence', *Clinical Psychology Review* 21, 5 (2001), 735–749.

29 Kellert and Felthous, 'Childhood cruelty', p. 1122.

30 L. Merz-Perez and K. Heide, *Animal cruelty: Pathway to violence against people* (Oxford: AltaMira Press, 2004), chapters 3 and 6.

31 S. C. Haden and A. Scarpa, 'Childhood animal cruelty: A review of research, assessment, and therapeutic issues', *The Forensic Examiner* (Summer 2005): 23–32.

32 R. Agnew, 'The causes of animal abuse: A social-psychological analysis', *Theoretical Criminology* 12, 2 (1998): 177–209.

33 M. Fox, 'Treating serious animal abuse as a serious crime', in F. R. Ascione and P. Arkow (eds), *Child abuse, domestic violence, and animal abuse: Linking the circles of compassion for prevention and intervention* (West Lafayette, IN: Purdue University Press, 1999), p. 314.

34 Agnew, 'The causes of animal abuse', p. 197.

35 *Ibid.*

36 J. Wright and C. Hensley, 'From animal cruelty to serial murder: Applying the graduation hypothesis', *International Journal of Offender Therapy and Comparative Criminology* 47, 1 (2003): 71–88.

37 Becker *et al.*, 'A study of fire-setting'; Felthous, 'Childhood antecedents of aggressive behavior'; A. R. Felthous, 'Aggression against cats, dogs and people', *Child Psychiatry and Human Development* 10 (1980): 169–177; A. R. Felthous and B. Yudowitz, 'Approaching a comparative typology of assaultive female offenders', *Psychiatry* 40 (1977): 270–276; Hensley and Tallichet, 'Learning to be cruel?'; Kellert and Felthous, 'Childhood cruelty'; J. D. Rigdon and F. Tapia, 'Children who are cruel to animals: A follow-up study', *Journal of Operational Psychiatry* 8, 1 (1977): 27–36; F. Tapia, 'Children who are cruel to animals', *Child Psychiatry and Human Development* 2, 2 (1971): 70–77; D. E. Wax and V. G. Haddox, 'Enuresis, fire-setting, and animal cruelty: A useful danger signal in predicting vulnerability of adolescent males to assaultive behavior', *Child Psychiatry and Human Development* 4 (1974): 151–157.

38 W. S. Cohen, 'A congressional view of the cycle of violence', in F. R. Ascione and P. Arkow (eds), *Child abuse, domestic violence, and animal abuse: Linking the circles of compassion for prevention and intervention* (West Lafayette, IN: Purdue University Press, 1999).

39 Wright and Hensley, 'From animal cruelty to serial murder'.

40 A. Arluke, C. Luke, and F. R. Ascione, 'The relationship of animal abuse to violence and other forms of antisocial behavior', *Journal of Interpersonal Violence* 14, 9 (1999): 963–975.

41. Felthous, 'Aggression against cats'; Felthous and Yudowitz, 'Approaching a comparative typology'; Kellert and Felthous, 'Childhood cruelty'; Wright and Hensley, 'From animal cruelty to serial murder'.

42 Wright and Hensley, 'From animal cruelty to serial murder', p. 85.

43 P. Beirne, 'From animal abuse to interhuman violence? A critical review of the progression thesis', *Society & Animals* 12, 1 (2004): 39–65.

44 D. K. Duel, *Violence prevention and intervention: A directory of animal-related programs* (Washington, DC: Humane Society of the United States, 2004).

45 F. R. Ascione, *Children and animals: exploring the roots of kindness and cruelty* (West Lafayette, IN: Purdue University Press, 2005).

46 Haden and Scarpa, 'Childhood animal cruelty'.

47 F. Becker, *The links between child abuse and animal abuse*, NSPCC Information Briefings (London: NSPCC, 2001).

48 D. P. Farrington and B. C. Welsh, *Saving children from a life of crime: Early risk factors and effective interventions* (Oxford: Oxford University Press, 2006).

49 D. P. Farrington, 'The importance of child and adolescent psychopathy', *Journal of Abnormal Child Psychology* 33, 4 (2005): 489–497.

A Lifespan Perspective on Human Aggression and Animal Abuse

ELEONORA GULLONE

This chapter aims to review major recent findings documented in the human aggression literature and those documented in the animal abuse literature, in addition to highlighting important findings related to research examining the co-occurrence of animal abuse and human violence. A major purpose of this combined review is to highlight both the conceptual and empirical overlap in human aggression and animal abuse. It is proposed that, given the relatively more sophisticated understanding of human aggression and its perpetrators when compared to animal abuse and its perpetrators, examining the latter within a human aggression framework is likely to lead to significant conceptual advances and to better informed preventative and intervention efforts.

Human Aggression

Human Aggression Defined

Human aggression has been defined as behaviour performed by a person (the aggressor) with the deliberate intention of harming another person (the victim) who is believed by the aggressor to be motivated to avoid that harm. Within this context, 'harm' refers both to physical harm (e.g., punching someone) and to psychological harm (e.g., verbal abuse). Indirect harm is also included within the definition and refers to, for example, damaging or destroying the victim's property. It is also noteworthy that violence is conceptualized as a particularly extreme sub-type of aggression (e.g., murder, rape, assault).[1]

In relation to the multidimensional nature of aggressive behaviour, Anderson and Huesmann have argued that, rather than refer to sub-types of aggression, it is more useful to characterize aggressive behaviour along identified dimensions.[2] In this way, aggressive behaviour can be considered along dimensions including (i) the degree of hostile affect versus agitated affect that is present; (ii) the underlying motive along the dimension of the degree to which the primary or ultimate goal is to cause harm to the victim versus the instrumental goal of the perpetrator deriving a profit or reward through the aggressive behaviour; and (iii) the degree to which the likely consequences were considered, reflecting whether the aggressive behaviour was premeditated (thoughtful, deliberate, slow, and instrumental) or impulsive (automatic, fast, affect-laden). Anderson and Huesmann have also stated that regardless of where the aggressive behaviour falls on the above dimensions, the intention to harm is still a *necessary* goal. This last point is important within the present context since if we are to draw useful conceptual parallels between human aggression and harm perpetrated against animals, given the broad-ranging utilitarian attitudes toward non-human animals (e.g., farming and husbandry practices), conceptualizing behaviours serving a purely instrumental goal in the absence of intention-to-harm as examples of aggression would clearly be problematic.

Developmental Pathways of Aggression

LEARNING PATHWAYS Of particular relevance to environmental and psychological aetiological factors of human aggression is Bandura's social learning theory of aggression.[3] Proposals regarding acquisition pathways of aggression that have developed from Bandura's theory include those yielded from the work of Patterson, DeBaryshe, and Ramsey.[4] These researchers proposed that maladaptive learning processes can be found in families of aggressive children with central factors including poor parental disciplinary strategies and inadequate monitoring of children's activities. Also of relevance are child-rearing characteristics proposed to create bullies.[5] Such characteristics include parental attitudes of indifference toward the child, permissiveness of aggressive behaviour by the child, the use of physical punishment (i.e., the modelling of aggression), and power-assertive disciplinary strategies.

CROSS-GENERATIONAL STABILITY At more extreme levels are child abuse and child neglect, which are now commonly accepted to be factors that place abused or neglected children at increased risk of themselves becoming abusing or neglecting parents.[6] Also, as noted by Repetti, Taylor, and Seeman, 'Risky families are characterized by conflict, anger, and aggression, by relationships that lack warmth and support, and by neglect of the needs of offspring'.[7] Cross-sectional and prospective research overwhelmingly documents that overt conflict and aggression in the family are associated with increased risk of emotional and behavioural problems in children, including aggression, conduct disorder, delinquency and antisocial behaviour, anxiety, depression, and suicide.[8] Although cross-generational stability in aggressive behaviours can be explained by learning processes, it remains likely that there exists an interaction in such stability with genetic/heritable factors.[9] Cognitive processing of information is yet another identified pathway of acquisition.

COGNITIVE VARIABLES According to a cognitive psychology paradigm, throughout our lifetime, as a consequence of our learning experiences, humans develop individual ways of seeing the world. We learn 'how to perceive, interpret, judge and respond to events in the physical and social environment'.[10] We therefore develop perceptual schemata which are stored in memory and subsequently retrieved to guide our perceptions and behaviour. These scripts are otherwise referred to as cognitive scripts and strategies[11] or 'knowledge structures',[12] and are believed to continue to develop, in varying degrees, over time and across the lifespan.

Knowledge structures are argued to influence our perception at multiple levels from the very basic perception of visual patterns to more complex behavioural sequences. Importantly, knowledge structures do not always function at a conscious level. Rather, they become automatized with increased use and over time, and increasingly function outside of conscious awareness.[13] They also incorporate affective states, behavioural repertoire, and belief systems. Importantly, these structures become much more rigid and resistant to change over time. As described by Anderson,

> Developing knowledge structures are like slowly hardening clay. Environmental experiences shape the clay. Changes are relatively easy to make at first, when the clay is soft, but later on changes become increasingly difficult.[14]

In relation to aggression-related knowledge structures, it is generally agreed upon that the hardening begins to take place at around the age of eight or nine.

> People learn specific aggressive behaviours, the likely outcome of such behaviours, and how and when to apply these behaviours. They learn hostile perception, attribution, and expectation biases, callous attitudes, and how to disengage or ignore normal empathic reactions that might serve as aggression inhibitors.[15]

Of concern, children who witness or directly experience violence have been documented to develop a range of problems.[16] Such problems include an increased likelihood of developing beliefs and scripts that support aggression[17] and a tendency to behave violently.[18]

Other important cognitive aetiological factors for aggression include variables that are present in the immediate environment or situation. These include *hostile perception biases*, which refer to a tendency by individuals who are more aggression-prone to be more likely to perceive hostility compared to someone who is not aggression-prone. In other words, such individuals are biased toward perceiving hostility in situations that they find themselves in and have a related tendency to expect that others will behave aggressively or with hostile intentions toward them. Such a bias inevitably compromises problem-solving and ultimately leads to aggressive responses.[19]

An additional set of predictive variables is *attitudes and beliefs*. Individuals who are aggression-prone demonstrate a tendency to hold positive attitudes toward aggressive or violent behaviour. These positive attitudes prepare aggressive-prone individuals to behave in aggressive ways and they also strengthen the aggressive tendency such that aggression-prone individuals are more likely to adopt aggressive problem-solving strategies.

Further highlighting the importance of family environment and parenting experiences on the development of aggression, this micro-environment has been strongly implicated in the cultivation of aggressive beliefs and attitudes. Other important micro-environments include the neighbourhood and the child's school. Thus, children who observe significant adults in their lives behaving aggressively, not only learn those behaviours, as described by Bandura's learning theory, they also learn the belief or attitude that such ways of behaving are normal and acceptable. This has been referred to as *normative belief*. Supporting this pathway of acquisition of normative beliefs, children's beliefs about aggression have been shown to be correlated with those of their parents[20] as well as those of their peers.[21]

According to Eron, there are three ways in which normative beliefs about aggression can influence an individual's perceptions.[22] First, the stronger the normative belief in behaving aggressively, the more likely the individual (adult or child) will be to perceive hostility in others' behaviour. Second, normative beliefs about the acceptability of aggression are likely to enhance the retrieval of aggressive scripts and third, once aggressive scripts for behaviour have been retrieved, they are more likely to be acted upon if acceptable attitudes toward aggression are held.

SELF-ESTEEM   Individual difference variables such as self-esteem have also been documented to play an important role in the acquisition of aggressive beliefs and behaviours. Although it was once believed that people who behave aggressively are more likely to have low self-esteem, it has since been demon-strated that it is not low levels of self-esteem that constitute a risk factor but rather inflated and unstable levels of self-esteem. Research has shown that certain individuals who have high self-esteem are most likely to behave aggres-sively when their self-esteem is threatened.[23] 'In other words, narcissists are the dangerous people, not those with low self esteem or those who are confident in their high self esteem'.[24]

BIOLOGICAL VARIABLES   Other important variables include sex, age, and base-line arousal levels. Specifically, males outnumber females in aggressive tendencies by a ratio of about ten to one. Indeed, males are much more likely to behave aggressively at any age regardless of sex. The effect of age is dramatic with the highest incidence of violence occurring between the ages of fifteen to thirty-five years but particularly between fifteen and twenty-four years.[25]

Regarding baseline levels of arousal, individuals with lower than average baseline levels of arousal seem to be at greater risk of behaving aggressively. Conduct disordered children have been found to have lower baseline heart rates and blood pressure.[26] Similarly children and adolescents with higher levels of antisocial behaviours have been found to have lower resting heart rates.[27] The same has been found for adults, with those displaying psychopathic behaviour also showing lower arousal as measured by EEG[28] or skin conductance.[29] Such outcomes may be due to individuals with lower levels of arousal being more likely to seek situations that will provide them with more stimulation, which may also lead to greater opportunities for aggression. Alternatively, they may be less likely to avoid situations in which aggression is more likely. Learning is also argued to play a role here since research has consistently demonstrated that people habituate rather quickly to repeated exposure to aggression or violence.[30]

It is important to note, however, that although some biological factors appear to be important (e.g., sex), many biological factors such as testosterone have not shown strong effects on aggression. It seems that interaction with environmental factors provides a more powerful explanation (e.g., gender-role learning may be more important than biological sex). Acknowledging the importance of such interaction, Anderson and Huesmann state that severe aggressive and violent acts rarely occur unless multiple precipitating situational and individual difference factors co-occur. Any one precipitating factor alone will only explain a small portion of the variance in aggressive behaviour. Adding to a comprehensive examination of aetiological factors are situational factors.

SITUATIONAL FACTORS   Included among situational factors is the construct of *displaced aggression*, which has been proposed to be a robust phenomenon and constitutes a form of aggression against others (human or non-human animal) who did not play a direct role in the precipitating event.[31] It has been demonstrated that displaced aggression increases if the target of such aggression provides even a minor trigger or the slightest of provocations (e.g., a dog barking). Displaced aggression also increases if the target can be perceived to be a member of a disliked out-group or as having less social value (e.g., a non-human animal).[32] In such instances, certain cognitive mechanisms (see below) are more easily activated.

Opportunity can also be an important situational factor since some situations provide good opportunities to aggress whilst others restrict such opportunities. There are, however, situations wherein opportunity is not relevant, as is the case where the *removal of self-regulatory inhibitions* applies. Indeed, research has shown that normal inhibitory mechanisms that apply for most people seem to be overridden in people who have aggressive tendencies.[33] As is evidenced by statistics of violence, the majority of people do not commit violent acts and would not likely do so, even if they had the opportunity or there was little risk of being discovered or punished. Maintenance of moral standards including self-image, self-standards and a sense of self-worth are all important factors in this regard. As pertinently stated by Anderson and Huesmann, most people do not aggress because they 'cannot escape the consequences that they apply to themselves'.[34]

Nevertheless, as identified by Bandura in his moral disengagement theory, certain mechanisms can explain why and when even people who otherwise have normal or even high moral standards sometimes do behave in ways that could be considered reprehensible.[35] Two particularly well-researched mechanisms are: (i) the cognitive construction of moral justification and (ii) dehumanizing the victim (in the case of animals, this could be conceived of as minimizing the worth/sentience of an animal). Examples of justification include: 'It is important for the well-being of our society' – as could apply to soldiers fighting at war; or 'It is for their own good' – as could apply after beating a child in the name of discipline; or for *personal honour* – as could apply particularly in the case of high self-esteem threats (e.g., beating up the wife to show her who's boss!).

Regarding the mechanisms related to dehumanizing the victim, these essentially ensure that the redefinition of the victim is such that personal moral standards no longer apply. War propaganda is considered a common vehicle for achieving this aim. Politicians throughout history have made use of such a mechanism. For example, a former Australian politician, in his attempts to dehumanize or even demonize asylum seekers, was implicated as playing some part in disseminating the story that the asylum seekers were seen throwing their children overboard.

In sum, the above section has provided a review of pertinent aspects of the rich and vast literature on human aggression with the aim of demonstrating the relevance of such knowledge to animal abuse. It is argued herein that application of such knowledge to the area of animal abuse and to our attempts to understand the links between human violence, criminality, and animal abuse, is likely to lead to considerable conceptual advances in animal abuse understanding. A first step in such a process is to consider definitions of animal abuse within the context of the human aggression literature, and in particular within the context of accepted conceptualizations of human aggression itself.

Animal Abuse

Animal Abuse Defined

Perhaps the most often-cited definition in the animal abuse literature is that put forth by one of the pioneers in the area, Frank Ascione. He has defined animal abuse as 'socially unacceptable behaviour that intentionally causes unnecessary pain, suffering, or distress to and/or the death of an animal'.[36] This and most other definitions – for example Kellert and Felthous's 'the wilful infliction of harm, injury, and intended pain on a nonhuman animal'[37] – include acts of abuse that are *intended* to cause either physical or psychological suffering. This is consistent with understandings of human aggression generally and, as defined above, 'harm' includes both physical and psychological harm.

Following a detailed consideration of a number of definitions of animal abuse, including Ascione's, Dadds, Turner, and McAloon have noted that most definitions comprise a behavioural dimension including both acts of omission (e.g., neglect) and acts of commission (e.g., beating).[38] Thus, it seems to be agreed by authors within the animal abuse literature that an important dimension of animal abuse is some indication that the behaviour occurred purposely, that is, with deliberateness and without ignorance. The requirement of *deliberate intention to cause harm* excludes behaviours that cause pain, suffering, or distress to animals as a consequence of, for example, veterinary procedures or practices that are part of animal husbandry (e.g., tail docking without an anaesthetic in factory-farmed pigs) and general farming practices, even though the end result is the killing of animals, often with measurable suffering involved.

Thus, it is proposed herein that animal abuse be defined as behaviour performed by an individual with the deliberate intention of causing harm (i.e., pain, suffering, distress, and/or death) to an animal with the understanding that the animal is motivated to avoid that harm. Included in this definition are both physical harm and psychological harm. As per the literature on human aggression, animal abuse at the more extreme end of the aggression dimension (e.g., kicking, or stabbing, versus teasing, hitting, tormenting) should be considered to be a violent sub-type of animal abuse, and consequently one that should be of particular concern to officials and legislators. Indeed, more consideration needs to be given to the severity of acts of animal abuse than is currently the case. In this regard, the classification of the underlying motivations of animal abuse is likely to be most useful.[39]

Animal Abuse Motivations

A number of authors have emphasized the importance of determining the motivations underlying animal abuse in order better to understand the behaviour, and particularly its relationship with human violence and aggression.[40] To this end, Kellert and Felthous's nine motivations have been referred to. The nine motivations include: (i) attempts to control an animal (e.g., hitting a dog to stop it barking); (ii) retaliation (e.g., use of extreme punishment for a perceived transgression on the part of the animal such as throwing a cat against a wall for vomiting in the house); (iii) acting out of prejudice against a particular species or breed. Such a motivation is accompanied by the belief that the particular animal is not worthy of moral consideration;[41] (iv) the expression of aggression through an animal (e.g., organizing dog fights); (v) acting out of the motivation to enhance one's own aggression (e.g., using animals for target practice or to impress others) (likely predicted by unstable high self-esteem); (vi) to shock people for amusement (abuse that is very overt and observed by others); (vii) to retaliate against another person or as revenge (e.g., killing or maiming the companion animal of a disliked neighbour); or (viii) displacement of aggression from a person to an animal (e.g., an abused child repeats the abuse they experience on an animal). This motivation typically involves frustrated aggression. Many of the aggressive participants in Kellert and Felthous's study reported being physically abused as children. Participants' self-reports were supportive of displaced aggression, typically involving authority figures who they reported hating or towards whom fear prevented them from expressing aggression directly. Their abuse of animals reportedly served as a displaced expression of the violence they experienced. As stated by Kellert and Felthous, 'It is often easier in childhood to be violent toward an animal than against a parent, sibling, or adult'.[42] Lastly, there is (ix) non-specific sadism, which refers to the desire to inflict suffering, injury or death in the absence of any particular or hostile feelings toward an animal. A primary goal expressed within this motivation was to derive pleasure from causing the suffering. This motive was explained by Kellert and Felthous as sometimes being related to a desire to exercise power and control over an animal as a way of compensating for feelings of weakness or vulnerability.

The above classification scheme was offered by Kellert and Felthous as a first classification attempt. They also noted that despite the ability to list nine separate motivations, their data highlighted the multidimensionality of animal abuse where one motivation alone rarely applied. What is clear from the above classification of motivations is substantial overlap with the characteristics documented in the human aggression literature as predicting/explaining aggressive behaviour toward humans, as reviewed in the previous section. The multidimensionality highlighted by Kellert and Felthous is also a predominant characteristic of aggression toward humans.

The application of the literature regarding human aggression to enhance our understanding of animal abuse may be criticized as not appropriate for a number of reasons, the primary one being that the status occupied by non-human animals in society is different to that applied to humans. This is particularly the case with animals who are classified as 'stock' or 'produce', 'game', or 'vermin'. It is significantly less true, however, for animals afforded 'companion' status, many of who are, in today's society, commonly regarded to be members of the family and who are often lavished with the care and nurturance provided to human family members, so much so that legal custody battles in instances of divorce in the family are not unheard-of. Indeed, in their review of the relationships between childhood cruelty to animals and later aggression against people, Felthous and Kellert argue that 'repeated acts of serious cruelty to socially valued animals (e.g., dogs) are more apt to be associated with violence toward people than are isolated acts of cruelty, minor abuses, and victimization of less socially valuable species (e.g., rats)'.[43]

Such an argument is consistent with moral disengagement theory and its relevance is supported by findings reported by Felthous and Kellert. They investigated psychosocial factors in animal abuse based on reports of twenty-three participants with a history of substantial animal abuse and found that participant reports indicated attitudes toward the animals they had abused as being 'worthless objects, hated objects, or narcissistic objects'.[44] Thus, it can be argued that processes of moral disengagement (including the mechanisms of moral justification and dehumanizing the victim) applied in the human aggression literature are, to some degree, normative in relation to non-human animals, albeit less so in relation to companion animals. Despite such differences, however, the deliberate infliction of animal suffering is considered to be a criminal behaviour in most countries around the world, reflecting community attitudes that such behaviour is abhorrent and by definition deviant. As such, with regard to behaviours that have the intentional suffering of an animal or animals as a goal, as opposed to some other utilitarian end (e.g., food), it is reasonable to argue that the application of conceptualizations and understandings documented in the human aggression literature to animal abuse is logically defensible.

In addition to understanding animal abusers' motivations for their aggressive behaviour, Hensley and Tallichet point out that understanding perpetrators' characteristics and situational circumstances is of importance. Here too, application of knowledge gained from the human aggression literature is likely to lead to conceptual advances. Such knowledge includes that individual difference variables, environmental experiences, and their interaction, are key to gaining a more comprehensive understanding of the fabric of abuse. Supportive of such a position is the fact that studies into animal abuse have documented similar predictors and developmental pathways of animal abuse when compared to interpersonal aggression and violence. The discussion will now turn to this literature.

Predictors and Pathways of Animal Abuse

The research investigating developmental experiences or factors that are associated or co-occur with children's, youths', and adults' abuse of animals can be classified into four main areas, including: experiences of abuse in childhood; the witnessing of abuse directed at humans or animals; and the co-occurrence of animal abuse and human-directed violence or other criminal behaviours in childhood, adolescence, and adulthood. These literatures are reviewed below.

CHILDHOOD EXPERIENCES OF ABUSE AND ENGAGEMENT IN ANIMAL ABUSE
In one of the earliest existing studies showing a relationship between animal abuse and human aggression, Tapia reported that among boys with a history of animal abuse, parental abuse was the most common explaining factor.[45] Similarly, in their work comparing criminal (aggressive versus non-aggressive) and non-criminal retrospective reports of childhood experiences and abuse behaviours, Kellert and Felthous reported that domestic violence and particularly paternal abuse and alcoholism were factors that were common among aggressive criminals with a history of childhood abuse of animals.[46]

Specifically, Kellert and Felthous reported that the family and childhood experiences of many of the aggressive criminals were particularly violent.[47] The domestic violence in the families of the aggressive criminals was most strongly characterized by paternal violence. Of note, three-quarters of the aggressive criminals reported repeated and excessive child abuse compared to

31 per cent of the non-aggressive criminals and 10 per cent of the non-criminals. Among the non-aggressive criminals and non-criminals who were cruel to animals, reports of being physically abused as children were more common. As many as 75 per cent of non-criminals who reported experiences of parental abuse also reported being cruel to animals.

Whilst the research by Felthous and Kellert can be criticized on the basis of its methodology (i.e., retrospective reports), a more recent study by Duncan, Thomas, and Miller found converging findings through the assessment of charts of boys (aged eight to seventeen) with conduct problems.[48] Among these children, histories of physical child abuse, sexual child abuse, paternal alcoholism, paternal unavailability, and domestic violence were assessed. Children were grouped according to whether they had been abusive toward animals or whether they had not. It was found that children in the abusive group were twice as likely to have been physically and/or sexually abused or to have been exposed to domestic violence compared to the non-abusive group. No differences were found on the other variables assessed; however, the findings are limited by the fact that the method of data collection used has traditionally been documented as being a gross method of assessment and thus as having compromised reliability. Other group-relevant differences may therefore have been missed.

The abuse of animals has been proposed to constitute, in part, the displacement of aggression from humans to animals that occurs through the child's identification with their abuser. As previously noted, displaced aggression has been included as one of the nine motivations for animal abuse reported by Kellert and Felthous.[49] By identifying with their abuser, children's sense of powerlessness can be transformed into a sense of control or empowerment. This relates to another of Kellert and Felthous' motivations for abuse, wherein a sense of control over an animal is gained through the abuse and may be motivated by a desire to compensate for feelings of weakness or vulnerability. Such an explanation is consistent with several pathways of acquisition that have been proposed by theorists in the human aggression literature. As noted above, these include Bandura's social learning theory of aggression, which argues that caregiver modelling of aggressive behaviours and power-assertive disciplinary strategies are predictive of the development of aggressive behaviours.[50] Cognitive theories are also useful in explaining the processes of acquisition of animal abuse behaviours, through the construct referred to as 'knowledge structures'. Given that knowledge structures are proposed to develop largely as a consequence of learning experiences, on the basis of theory it would be expected that individuals who experience abuse in their formative years learn specific aggressive behaviours and hostile perceptions, attributions, and expectation biases. They also learn callous attitudes and how to disengage normative empathic reactions that would otherwise serve as aggression inhibitors (and/or otherwise normative development of empathy is suppressed).[51] Indeed such processes have been implicated in the development of conduct problems and disorders in children.[52]

CO-OCCURRENCE OF CONDUCT PROBLEM BEHAVIOUR AND ANIMAL ABUSE

Conduct Disorder (CD) has been defined in the DSM-IV as 'a repetitive and persistent pattern of behaviour in which the basic rights of others or major age-appropriate societal norms or rules are violated'.[53] The onset of Conduct Disorder (CD) may occur as early as five to six years of age but more commonly occurs in late childhood or early adolescence. Although as many as 50 per cent of childhood cases of CD remit by adolescence, adolescent cases of CD rarely begin without warning signs in childhood.[54]

Reported statistics indicate that CD is one of the most frequently diagnosed childhood conditions, in both outpatient and inpatient mental health facilities, particularly in urban areas. Consistent with the general conceptualization of externalizing behaviours, CD comprises a cluster of oppositional and antisocial behaviours including excessive noncompliance, stealing, lying, running away, physical violence, cruelty (to humans and animals), and sexually coercive behaviours.[55] These behaviours are clearly diverse. However, they all share the common characteristic that they violate major social rules and expectations.[56] The disorder is also characterized by constant conflict with others (specifically parents, teachers, and the peer group), and CD in childhood is predictive of other psychological disorders including delinquency, drug abuse, school dropout, suicide, and criminality in adolescence or adulthood. Indeed, cases of CD beginning in childhood account for almost half of all adolescent crime[57] and as many as 75 per cent of youth with CD progress to antisocial personality disorder in adulthood.[58] Further supportive of the continuity, longitudinal studies have found that antisocial behaviour in adulthood begins in childhood.[59]

Diagnostic criteria for CD in the DSM-III and subsequent revised versions include abuse of animals as one criterion. Of particular significance, in their meta-analysis of child conduct problem behaviours, Frick et al. reported a median age of 6.5 years for the occurrence of the first incident of animal abuse along with other aggressive behaviours including fighting (six years), bullying (seven years), and assaulting (7.5 years).[60] Therefore, animal abuse has been found to be one of the earliest indicators of CD, and is listed as such in the DSM-IV-TR version. Further, as many as 25 per cent of children diagnosed with Conduct Disorder display cruelty to animals. In their analysis of the National Epidemiological Survey data set including a nationally representative sample of 43,093 respondents in the United States, Gelhorn et al. found that cruelty to animals (assessed with the item 'Hurt or be cruel to an animal or pet on purpose?') significantly discriminated between those with clinical and sub-clinical conduct problem behaviours. Specifically, 5.5 per cent of males in the sub-clinical group compared to 18 per cent of males in the CD group endorsed the item of animal cruelty. The comparative statistics for females were lower but equally discriminating (i.e., 2.2 per cent versus 6.2 per cent).

Consistent findings have been reported by Luk, Staiger, Wong, and Mathai in their comparison study of one hundred and forty-one clinic-referred children presenting with at least one definite CD symptom apart from animal abuse, and a community sample of thirty-six children, all aged between five and twelve years.[61] Forty children in the clinic-referred group (out of one hundred and forty-one: 28 per cent) compared to one child from the community sample (3 per cent) were rated as sometimes or definitely being cruel to animals (CTA). The findings revealed a trend for the CTA group to be characterized by poorer family functioning. It was also found that those in the CTA group were reported to have more severe conduct problems and to be more likely to be male. An additional finding reported by the authors was that the older children in the CTA group appeared to have a highly elevated self-perception. Luk and colleagues proposed that the elevated self-worth of their CTA sample may be suggestive of the callous and unemotional (CU) trait in children identified in the work by Frick, O'Brien, Wootton, and McBurnett.[62] This trait has been found to manifest as behaviour characterized by lack of guilt and empathy, and superficial charm. Of note, such a cluster of characteristics is similar to the concept of psychopathy in adulthood, and is consistent with findings related to the precipitants of aggression in the form of threats to an unstable and inflated sense of self.[63]

As noted by Frick *et al.*, clinical reports spanning several decades document descriptions of the psychopathic personality as being characterized by egocentricity, absence of empathy and guilt, superficial charm, shallow emotions, and absence of anxiety, in addition to deviant social relationships. Although at one time psychopathic traits and antisocial personality disorder (APD) were considered to be analogous, later work indicated that the antisocial behaviours associated with APD and the motivational and interpersonal processes associated with psychopathy are distinct.[64] In addition, the correlates of the two types of disorder differ. Correlates of APD include adverse family background factors, such as low socioeconomic status, and low intelligence. In contrast, correlates of psychopathic traits include narcissism and low anxiety. Moreover, those individuals who present with both APD and psychopathy features show a more severe and chronic pattern of antisocial behaviour.[65]

BULLYING AND ANIMAL ABUSE IN YOUTH AND THE IMPORTANCE OF WITNESSING AGGRESSION In addition to being linked with CD, animal abuse has been shown to co-occur with bullying behaviours. Further, both animal abuse and bullying have been related to later antisocial behaviours and antisocial personality disorder.[66] Conceptually, animal abuse and bullying behaviours in youth are analogous. Similarities are apparent in the definitions of animal abuse and bullying. A recent definition of bullying indicates that the behaviour involves a desire to hurt, a power imbalance, an unjust use of power, enjoyment by the aggressor, and a general sense of being oppressed on the part of the victim.[67] It is generally agreed that a definition of bullying needs to include an intention to inflict verbal, physical, or psychological harm; a victim who does not provoke the bullying behaviours; and occurrences in familiar social groups.[68]

While explicit in definitions of bullying but not in definitions of animal abuse, there is a clear power imbalance where the perpetrator is more powerful than the victim and uses this power to inflict physical, emotional, or psychological harm on the victim. Also, both animal abuse and bullying behaviours are predominantly observed in male populations. Research has indicated that males have rates of animal abuse that are four times higher than those of females,[69] and that males are more likely than females to engage in bullying behaviours.[70] These sex differences appear to be confined to overt aggressive behaviours, as sex differences have not been consistently reported when bullying measures include indirect forms of bullying.[71] Further suggesting potentially overlapping processes between animal abuse and bullying is their appearance within a close developmental time frame. However, despite the strong conceptual overlap, and with few exceptions, animal abuse and bullying behaviours have traditionally been researched separately.

The exceptions include a study by Baldry,[72] who examined the prevalence of animal abuse, bullying behaviours, and being a victim of bullying in an Italian sample of children and adolescents aged nine to twelve. Supporting the premise that exposure to violence and victimization experiences are related to animal abuse,[73] Baldry found that youth who witnessed violence between family members, or who witnessed harm to animals, were three times more likely to have abused animals themselves, compared to peers without such experiences.

Baldry's results indicated that girls and boys who had engaged in direct bullying behaviours were twice as likely to have abused animals compared with their non-bullying peers. Engagement in animal abuse by boys was predicted by their direct victimization at school and indirect bullying, while engagement in animal abuse by girls was predicted by their exposure to animal abuse and experiences of verbal abuse by their fathers.

In relation to the witnessing of family or domestic violence, Baldry[74] found that children who engaged in bullying behaviours were 1.8 times more likely to have been exposed to domestic violence than those who were not. Exposure to adult aggression and conflict has also been shown to be associated with increased engagement in bullying behaviours.[75] Schwartz et al. also indicated that environments characterized by exposure to adult aggression and conflict are associated with increased engagement in bullying behaviours.[76]

In a second study, Robertson and Gullone investigated relationships between self-reported animal abuse and bullying behaviours in a school-based sample of two hundred and forty-nine adolescents (one hundred and five males, one hundred and forty-four females) ranging in age from twelve to sixteen years.[77] Significant positive relationships were found between bullying and animal abuse. Both behaviours were also found to correlate significantly with bullying victimization, witnessing of animal abuse, and family conflict. Confirming previous findings regarding sex differences in animal abuse, boys were found to score significantly higher than girls.

When examining possible pathways of acquisition for each of animal abuse and bullying behaviours, it was found that each type of behaviour was significantly predicted by the witnessing of animal abuse. Thus, not only did Robertson and Gullone provide empirical support for the co-existence of animal-directed aggression and human-directed aggression in youth, as with Baldry's 2005 results, they also demonstrated support for the important pathway of observational learning in the development of aggressive behaviour, as predicted by Bandura's social learning theory of aggression.

In a study specifically examining the relationship between the witnessing of animal abuse and engaging in the behaviour, Thompson and Gullone surveyed a total of two hundred and eighty-one (one hundred and thirteen males; one hundred and sixty-eight females) school-based adolescents ranging in age between twelve and eighteen years.[78] They found that those who reported having witnessed animal abuse on at least one occasion reported significantly higher levels of animal abuse when compared to those youth who reported never having witnessed such abuse. Of particular note is the finding that youth who reported witnessing a stranger abuse an animal reported significantly *lower* levels of animal abuse. This contrasted with the finding that witnessing of animal abuse by a friend, relative, parent, or sibling related to higher levels of abuse when compared to not witnessing abuse by someone in these categories. These findings support vicarious learning theory – that observation of behaviour is more likely to have an impact on the acquisition of the observed behaviour if the model has a meaningful relationship with the observer. An additional important finding was related to the frequency of witnessing abuse, such that as witnessing frequency increased, rates of animal abuse also increased.

While several studies have demonstrated a relationship between witnessing of abuse and engaging in such behaviour via youth self-report,[79] others have demonstrated the relationship by asking undergraduate students or imprisoned males about their childhood experiences and behaviours, albeit through retrospective reports.[80] Currie also reported a significant relationship between the witnessing of aggressive behaviour (domestic violence) and animal abuse via parent-report.[81] Mother reports regarding their children's animal abuse were compared for a group of ninety-four children (forty-seven mothers) with a history of domestic violence and ninety children (forty-five mothers) without a history of domestic violence. Exposed children, according to their mothers, were more likely to abuse animals compared to children who were not exposed to violence. All of the above studies point to the witnessing of animal abuse (i.e., an aggressive behaviour) as being an important predictor of the learning of, and engagement in, aggressive behaviour. As noted earlier, children who witness or directly experience violence or aggression have been documented to be more likely to develop beliefs and scripts that support aggression[82] and a tendency to behave aggressively.[83] On the basis of these findings, it can be concluded that animal abuse is a marker of other potentially sinister experiences in children's lives.

DOMESTIC VIOLENCE STUDIES One of the most consistently replicated findings supporting a link between human violence and animal abuse is that of significant co-occurrence between family or domestic violence and animal abuse. Recent studies have indicated that more than one half of all abused women have companion animals, that many of these companion animals (in as many as 50 per cent of cases) are abused by the perpetrators of the domestic violence as a means of hurting and/or controlling the women or their children, and that concerns for the safety of their companion animals keep many women (and their children) from leaving or staying separated from their abusers.

Ascione has recently reviewed the literature of the relation between animal abuse and the violence experienced by women by their intimate adult partners within the family environment.[84] Several such studies have now been conducted across several countries, including the United States, Canada, and Australia, and several findings have been yielded with remarkable consistency despite study differences (e.g., country, sample size, methodology).[85] Findings include that between 11.8 and 39.4 per cent of women have reported that the perpetrator *threatened to* hurt or kill their companion animals. Between 25.6[86] and 79.3 per cent[87] of women reported that the perpetrator had *actually* hurt or killed their companion animal(s).

A major limitation of all but two of these studies (i.e., Ascione *et al.* and Volant *et al.*) is that they did not include a comparison group of women who were not in a violent family situation. In the Ascione *et al.* study, 5 per cent of non-abused women reported pet abuse and in the study by Volant *et al.*, zero per cent reported pet abuse. The study by Volant *et al.* involved a group of one hundred and two women recruited through twenty-four domestic violence services in the state of Victoria, and a non-domestic violence comparison group (one hundred and two women) recruited from the community. These researchers also found that 46 per cent of women in the domestic violence sample reported that their partner had *threatened to* hurt or kill their pet, compared with 6 per cent of women in the community sample.

Data have also been obtained relating to the children's witnessing of the animal abuse and the children's abuse of animals. Studies have reported that between 29 and 75 per cent of children in violent families have witnessed the animal abuse and between 10 and 57 per cent of children in these homes have been reported to engage in animal abuse. As noted by Ascione, parental reports of animal abuse in normative samples of children are typically around 10 per cent or lower.[88] Not surprisingly, these results are consistent with other studies reporting that children exposed to domestic violence are more likely to engage in acts of animal abuse than children who have not been exposed to domestic violence.[89]

An additional finding derived from studies investigating the co-occurrence of domestic violence and pet abuse is that between 18 per cent[90] and 48 per cent[91] of women have reported delaying leaving their violent situation out of fear that their companion animal(s) would be harmed or killed in their absence.

CO-OCCURRENCE OF ANIMAL ABUSE AND OTHER CRIMINAL BEHAVIOURS   In addition to domestic violence, research has shown that animal abuse is predictive of other types of criminal behaviours. Arluke, Levin, Luke, and Ascione obtained their data from official records of criminality. Their study also included a comparison group. The researchers identified people who had been prosecuted for at least one form of animal cruelty from the records of the Massachusetts Society for the Prevention of Cruelty to Animals (MSPCA) between 1975 and 1986. They defined animal abuse as cases 'where an animal has been intentionally harmed physically (e.g., beaten, stabbed, shot, hanged, drowned, stoned, burned, strangled, driven over, or thrown)'.[92] Their sample comprised of one hundred and fifty-three participants of whom one hundred and forty-six were male. The comparison group was constituted from individuals matched to the abuse group on variables including gender, socioeconomic status, and age. The study results indicated that animal abusers were significantly more likely than the comparison group participants to be involved in some form of criminal behaviour, including violent offences. Specifically, 70 per cent of those who abused animals also committed at least one other offence compared with 22 per cent of the control group participants. The differences ranged from 11 per cent for the control group and 44 per cent for the abusive group on property-related crimes to 12 per cent for the control group and 37 per cent for the abusive group on public disorder related crimes. For violent crimes, the two groups differed substantially (7 per cent and 37 per cent for the control and abusive groups, respectively). Based on their findings, the authors concluded that a single known act of animal abuse was significantly predictive of increased participation in other criminal offences when compared to a matched sample of adults who did not abuse animals.

Australian Victoria Police data provide support for the findings reported above. Data were obtained from the Statistical Services Division of Victoria Police for all recorded offences in Victoria, Australia for the years 1994 to 2001 (inclusive). Out of four categories of offence (Offences against the person, Offences against property, Drug offences, Other offences), for all alleged offenders, the data clearly showed that the largest proportion of offences was consistently found to be that against property, ranging between 79.52 per cent (n = 344,905) of total offences in 1998, and 80.85 per cent (number = 354,785) in 1999. Over the eight-year period, offences against property constituted 80.8 per cent of the total of 3,364,078 crimes committed in Victoria. Drug offences consistently constituted the smallest proportion and ranged between 2.84 per cent (n = 12,838) in 2001 and 4.23 per cent (n = 18,354) of total offences in 1998. Of note, [Q9] offences against the person also constituted a relatively small proportion of the total number of crimes at an average of 7.71 per cent of all crimes over the eight-year period with the lowest percentage of 7.98 recorded in 2000 and the highest percentage of 8.01 recorded in 2001.

The equivalent statistics relating to criminal offences, classified into the same four categories nominated above, but for alleged animal abuse offenders only, revealed that, for animal abuse offenders, the average percentage of offences committed against the person was substantially higher compared to the percentage for all alleged offenders (25 per cent compared to 8 per cent). The category of offences against the person included such crimes as homicide, rape, assault, abduction/kidnapping, and harassment. Importantly, these statistics are remarkably similar to those reported by Arluke *et al.*, as described above. Thus, there appears to be a greater likelihood that people alleged to have abused animals will engage in offences against the person, including violent crimes, when compared to all alleged offenders.

Of note, when broken down by age and sex, the data showed that, across crime categories, alleged offenders (all alleged offenders, not only animal abuse offenders) were characteristically male. Also, in general, for the Victorian population, the prevalence of alleged offences during the documented time was highest between the ages of twelve and thirty-five years for both males and females with a peak between the ages of eighteen and twenty-five years. When examining age and sex trends for alleged animal abuse offenders and animal abuse offences only, males were over-represented across all age categories for both general alleged offences and specifically for animal abuse offences, with very few exceptions. Further, a peak of offending was observed between the ages of eighteen and twenty-five that decreased steadily beyond these years. The particular importance of these statistics is that human aggression and criminal behaviour is demographically parallel along age and sex lines with animal abuse behaviour. This provides additional support for a link between human aggression and animal abuse and strengthens the argument that animal abuse can be most usefully conceptualized within a human aggression framework.

Conclusions

Studies examining animal abuse have been criticized as having a number of limitations, including problematic methodologies such as retrospective reporting, restricted generalizability of samples (e.g., incarcerated adults), lack of adequate control or comparison groups, and application of different definitions of animal abuse. However, despite these identified limitations, across very different respondent groups (e.g., school-based youth, women from violent homes, incarcerated adults, undergraduate students) and methods (e.g., self-reports, third-party reports, analysis of criminal records), the co-occurrence between human-directed and animal-directed aggression and violence continues to emerge. Evidence is also accumulating to support shared pathways of acquisition of these aggressive behaviours – including, most significantly, the important role played by the direct experiencing of the aggressive or violent behaviour particularly in the form of child abuse, and that played by exposure to, or witnessing of, aggression. There has for some time now been strong acceptance of these pathways of acquisition for human-directed aggression. Given the clear conceptual overlap of human-directed aggression and animal abuse and given the increasingly strong empirical evidence for the co-occurrence of these behaviours beginning in childhood through to adulthood, it should come as no surprise that the two share acquisition pathways.

In concluding, I would like to echo the words of a highly esteemed colleague in drawing upon the researcher-practitioner model and emphasize that in this area of 'the link' – as in several others, such as in the area of youth mental health – the 'difference between what we know and what we do is greater than the difference between what we know and don't know'. Therefore, our need for action is currently greater than our need for more research. In this chapter, I have attempted to demonstrate that there is substantial theoretical and empirical evidence supporting a link between human violence and animal abuse. In other words, there is substantial evidence pointing to the very important role that a pattern of abusive behaviour toward animals can play in raising the alarm that other criminal behaviours are likely occurring in the same environment. In the case of children's abuse of animals, in addition to being concerned for the animals, we should be concerned for the welfare of the children as we have sufficient reason to suspect that their home environments may not be safe. In the case of older children and adolescents, we should be concerned both for the welfare of the youth themselves given the dangers they likely face in their home environments, and for their peers, since they too may be at risk in the form of bullying or related aggressive behaviours. And in the case of adults, if they are abusing animals, there is sufficient evidence to suggest that they are likely also to be engaging in other criminal behaviours, particularly human-directed aggressive behaviours. Last but not least, aggressive and abusive behaviours against animals are alarming in themselves. They are criminal behaviours that deviate from the moral and humane attitudes held by the vast majority of people worldwide and they cause unspeakable levels of suffering to our fellow sentient beings.

Notes

1   C. A. Anderson, 'Aggression', in E. Borgatta and R. Montgomery (eds), *The encyclopedia of sociology*, 2nd edn (New York: Macmillan, 2002).

2   C. A. Anderson and L. R. Huesmann, 'Human aggression: A social-cognitive view', in M. A. Hogg and J. Cooper (eds), *The Sage handbook of social psychology* (Thousand Oaks, CA: Sage Publications Inc., 2003).

3   A. Bandura, *Aggression: A social learning theory analysis* (Englewood Cliffs, NJ: Prentice-Hall, 1973).

4   G. R. Patterson, B. D. DeBaryshe, and E. Ramsey, 'A developmental perspective on antisocial behaviour', *American Psychologist* 44 (1989): 3299–3335.

5   C. R. Olweus, 'Bullying or peer abuse at school: Facts and intervention', *Current Directions in Psychological Science* 4 (1995): 196–200.

6   D. A. Black, R. E. Heyman, and A. M. Smith Slep, 'Risk factors for child physical abuse', *Aggression and Violent Behavior* 6 (2001): 121–188; L. D. Eron, 'The development of aggressive behaviour from the perspective of a developing behaviorist', *American Psychologist* 42 (1987): 435–442; L. Peterson, S. Gable, C. Doyle, and B. Ewugman, 'Beyond parenting skills: Battling barriers and building bonds to prevent

child abuse and neglect', *Cognitive and Behavioral Practice* 4 (1998): 53–74; C. S. Widom, 'Does violence beget violence? A critical examination of the literature', *Psychological Bulletin* 106 (1989): 3–28.

7 R. L. Repetti, S. E. Taylor, and T. E. Seeman, 'Risky families: Family social environments and the mental and physical health of offspring', *Psychological Bulletin* 128 (2002), p. 356.

8 *Ibid.*

9 C. R. Cloniger and A. Gottesman, 'Genetic and environmental factors in antisocial behaviour disorders', in S. A. Mednick, T. E., Moffitt, and S. A. Stack (eds), *The causes of crime: New biological approaches* (New York: Cambridge University Press, 1987).

10 Anderson, 'Aggression', p. 70.

11 L. R. Huesmann, 'An information processing model for the development of aggression', *Aggressive Behavior*, 14 (1988): 13–24.

12 *Ibid.*

13 W. Schneider and R. M. Shiffrin, 'Controlled and automatic human information processing: I. Detection, search and attention', *Psychological Review* 84 (1977): 1–66; A. Todorov and J. A. Bargh, 'Automatic sources of aggression', *Aggression and Violent Behavior* 7 (2002): 53–68.

14 Anderson, 'Aggression', p. 70.

15 *Ibid.*

16 J. D. Osofsky, 'The effects of exposure to violence on young children', *American Psychologist* 50 (1995): 782–788.

17 N. G. Guerra, L. R. Huesmann, and A. J. Spindler, *Community violence exposure, social cognition and aggression among urban elementary-school children* (Ann Arbor, MI: Institute for Social Research, University of Michigan, 2002).

18 Anderson and Huesmann, 'Human aggression'.

19 N. R. Crick and K. A. Dodge, 'A review and reformulation of social information processing mechanisms in children's adjustment', *Psychological Bulletin* 115 (1994): 74–101; K. A. Dodge and A. Tomlin, 'Utilization of self-schemas as a mechanism of attributional bias in aggressive children', *Social Cognition* 5 (1987): 280–300.

20 L. R. Huesmann, L. D. Eton, M. M. Lefkowitz, and L. O. Walder, 'Stability of aggression over time and generation', *Developmental Psychology* 20 (1984): 1120–1134.

21 Anderson and Huesmann, 'Human aggression'.

22 L. D. Eron, 'Seeing is believing: How viewing violence alters attitudes and aggressive behaviour', in A. C. Bohart and D. J. Stipek (eds), *Constructive and destructive behaviour: Implications for family, school and society* (Washington, DC: American Psychological Association, 2001).

23 R. F. Baumeister, L. Smart, and J. M. Boden, 'Relation of threatened egotism to violence and aggression: The dark side of high self-esteem', *Psychological Review* 103 (1996): 5–33; B. J. Bushman and R. F. Baumeister, 'Threatened egotism, narcissism, self-esteem and direct and displaced aggression: Does self-love or self-hate lead to violence?' *Journal of Personality and Social Psychology* 75 (1998): 219–229; M. H. Kernis, B. D. Grannemann, and L. C. Barclay, 'Stability and level of self-esteem as predictors of anger arousal and hostility', *Journal of Personality and Social Psychology* 56 (1989): 1013–1022.

24 Anderson, 'Aggression', p. 72.

25 Anderson and Huesmann, 'Human aggression'.
26 G. A. Rogeness, C. Cepeda, C. A. Macedo, C. Fischer, and W. R. Harris, 'Differences in heart rate and blood pressure in children with conduct disorder, major depression and separation anxiety', *Psychiatry Research* 33 (1990): 199–206.
27 A. Raine, *The psychopathology of crime: Criminal behavior as a clinical disorder* (San Diego, CA: Academic Press, 1993).
28 R. C. Howard, 'The clinical EEG and personality in mental abnormal offenders', *Psychological Medicine* 14 (1984): 569–580.
29 R. D. Hare, 'Electrodermal and cardiovascular correlates of psychopathy', in R. D. Hare and D. Schalling (eds), *Psychopathic behaviour: Approaches to research* (New York: Wiley, 1978).
30 Anderson and Huesmann, 'Human aggression'.
31 A. Marcus-Newhall, W. C. Pederson, M. Carlson, and N. Miller, 'Displaced aggression is alive and well: A meta-analytic review', *Journal of Personality and Social Psychology* 78 (2000): 670–689; W. C. Pederson, C. Gonzales, and N. Miller, 'The moderating effect of trivial triggering provocation on displaced aggression', *Journal of Personality and Social Psychology* 78 (2000): 913–927.
32 Anderson and Huesmann, 'Human aggression'.
33 D. Keltner and R. J. Robinson, 'Extremism, power, and the imagined basis of social conflict', *Current Directions in Psychological Science* 5 (1996): 101–105; E. Staub, *The roots of evil: The origins of genocide and other group violence* (New York: Cambridge University Press, 1989); E. Staub, 'Breaking the cycle of genocidal violence: Healing and reconciliation', in J. Harvey (ed.), *Perspectives on loss: A sourcebook* (Philadelphia, PA: Taylor & Francis, 1998).
34 Anderson and Huesmann, 'Human aggression', p. 309.
35 A. Bandura, 'Selective activation and disengagement of moral control', *Journal of Social Issues* 46 (1990): 27–46; A. Bandura, 'Moral disengagement in the perpetration of inhumanities', *Personality and Social Psychology Review* 3 (1999): 27–46.
36 F. R. Ascione, 'The abuse of animals and human interpersonal violence', in F. R. Ascione and P. Arkow (eds), *Child abuse, domestic violence, and animal abuse: Linking the circles of compassion for prevention and intervention* (West Lafayette, IN, Purdue University Press, 1999), p. 51.
37 S. R. Kellert and A. R. Felthous, 'Childhood cruelty toward animals among criminals and non-criminals', *Human Relations* 38 (1985), p. 1114.
38 M. R. Dadds, C. M. Turner, and J. McAloon, 'Developmental links between cruelty to animals and human violence', *Australian and New Zealand Journal of Criminology* 35 (2002): 363–382.
39 Kellert and Felthous, 'Childhood cruelty'.
40 Dadds *et al.*, 'Developmental links'; C. Hensley and S. E. Tallichet, 'Learning to be cruel?: Exploring the onset and frequency of animal cruelty', *International Journal of Offender Therapy and Comparative Criminology* 49 (2005): 37–47; L. Merz-Perez, K. M. Heide, and I. J. Silverman, 'Childhood cruelty to animals and subsequent violence against humans', *International Journal of Offender Therapy and Comparative Criminology* 45 (2001): 556–573.
41 See Bandura's moral disengagement theory.
42 Kellert and Felthous, 'Childhood cruelty', p. 1124.
43 A. R. Felthous and S. R. Kellert, 'Childhood cruelty to animals and later aggression against people: A review', *American Journal of Psychiatry* 144 (1987), p. 714.
44 A. R. Felthous and S. R. Kellert, 'Psychosocial aspects of selecting animal species for physical abuse', *Journal of Forensic Sciences* 32 (1987), p. 1720.

45 F. Tapia, 'Children who are cruel to animals', *Child Psychiatry and Human Development* 2 (1971): 70–77.

46 A. R. Felthous, 'Aggression against cats, dogs, and people', *Child Psychiatry and Human Development* 10 (1980): 169–177; A. R. Felthous and S. R. Kellert, 'Violence against animals and people: Is aggression against living creatures generalised?' *Bulletin of the American Academy of Psychiatry and Law* 14 (1986): 55–69; Kellert and Felthous, 'Childhood cruelty'.

47 Kellert and Felthous, 'Childhood cruelty'.

48 A. Duncan, J. C. Thomas, and C. Miller, 'Significance of family risk factors in development of childhood animal cruelty in adolescent boys with conduct problems', *Journal of Family Violence* 20 (2005): 235–239.

49 Kellert and Felthous, 'Childhood cruelty'.

50 Bandura, *Aggression*.

51 C. A. Anderson and B. J. Bushman, 'Human aggression', *Annual Review of Psychology* 53 (2002): 27–51.

52 Repetti *et al.*, 'Risky families'.

53 American Psychiatric Association, *Diagnostic and statistical manual of mental disorders: DSM-IV-TR*, 4th edn (Washington DC: American Psychiatric Association, 2000), p. 98.

54 Conduct Problems Prevention Research Group, 'A developmental and clinical model for the prevention of conduct disorder: The FAST Track Program', *Development and Psychopathology* 4 (1992): 509–527.

55 *Ibid.*

56 A. E. Kazdin, 'Conduct disorder in childhood', in M. Hersen and C. G. Last (eds), *Handbook of child and adolescent psychopathology: A longitudinal perspective* (New York: Pergamon, 1990).

57 J. D. Coie and C. L. Bagwell, 'School-based social predictors of serious adolescent psychopathology and dysfunction: Implications for prevention', in D. Cicchetti and S. L. Toth (eds), *Developmental approaches to prevention and intervention* (New York: University of Rochester Press, 1999).

58 H. L. Gelhorn, J. T. Sakai, R. K. Price, and T. J. Crowley, 'DSM-IV conduct disorder criteria as predictors of antisocial personality disorder', *Comprehensive Psychiatry* (in press).

59 Gelhorn *et al.*, 'DSM-IV conduct disorder criteria'; R. Loeber, 'The stability of antisocial and delinquent child behaviour: A review', *Child Development* 53 (1982): 1421–1446.

60 P. J. Frick, Y. Van Horn, B. B. Lahey, M. A. G. Christ, R. Loeber, E. A. Hart, L. Tannenbaum, and K. Hansen, 'Oppositional defiant disorder and conduct disorder: A meta-analytic review of factor analyses and cross-validation in a clinic sample', *Clinical Psychology Review* 13 (1993): 319–340.

61 E. S. L. Luk, P. K. Staiger, L. Wong, and J. Mathai, 'Children who are cruel to animals: A revisit', *Australian and New Zealand Journal of Psychiatry* 33 (1998): 29–36.

62 P. Frick, B. S. O'Brien, J. M. Wootten, and K. McBurnett, 'Psychopathy and conduct problems in children', *Journal of Abnormal Psychology* 103 (1994): 700–707.

63 Baumeister *et al.*, 'Relation of threatened egotism'; Bushman and Baumeister, 'Threatened egotism'; Kernis *et al.*, 'Stability and level of self-esteem'.

64 For example, R. D. Hare, S. D. Hart, and T. J. Harpur, 'Psychopathy and DSM-IV criteria for antisocial personality disorder', *Journal of Abnormal Psychology* 100

(1991): 391–398; T. J. Harpur, R. D. Hare, and A. R. Hakstian, 'Two factor conceptualization of psychopathy: Construct validity and assessment implications', *Psychological Assessment* 1 (1989): 6–17.

65　Frick *et al.*, 'Psychopathy and conduct problems'.

66　Gelhorn *et al.*, 'DSM-IV conduct disorder'.

67　K. Rigby, *New perspectives on bullying* (London: Jessica Kingsley Publishers, 2002).

68　A. C. Baldry, 'Bullying among Italian middle school students: Combining methods to understand aggressive behaviours and victimization', *School Psychology International* 19, 4 (1998): 361–374; A. C. Baldry and D. P. Farrington, 'Bullies and delinquents: Personal characteristics and parental styles', *Journal of Community and Applied Social Psychology* 10 (2000): 17–31; R. S. Griffin and A. M. Gross, 'Childhood bullying: Current empirical findings and future directions for research', *Aggression and Violent Behaviour* 9 (2004): 379–400; T. P. Gumpel and H. Meadan, 'Children's perceptions of school-based violence', *British Journal of Educational Psychology* 70 (2000): 391–404.

69　C. P. Flynn, 'Exploring the link between corporal punishment and children's cruelty to animals', *Journal of Marriage and the Family* 61, 4 (1999): 971–981.

70　Baldry, 'Bullying among Italian middle school students'; K. Bosworth, D. L. Espelage, and T. R. Simon, 'Factors associated with bullying behavior in middle school students', *Journal of Early Adolescence* 19, 3 (1999): 341–362; P. K. Smith and R. Myron-Wilson, 'Parenting and school bullying', *Clinical Child Psychology and Psychiatry* 3, 3 (1998): 405–417; R. Veenstra, S. Lindenberg, A. J. Oldehinkel, A. F. De Winter, F. C. Verhulst, and J. Ormel, 'Bullying and victimization in elementary schools: A comparison of bullies, victims, bully/victims, and uninvolved preadolescents', *Developmental Psychology* 41, 4 (2005): 672–682.

71　Griffin and Gross, 'Childhood bullying'.

72　A. C. Baldry, 'Animal abuse among preadolescents directly and indirectly victimized at school and at home', *Criminal Behaviour and Mental Health*, 15 (2005): 97–110.

73　C. P. Flynn, 'Why family professionals can no longer ignore violence toward animals', *Family Relations* 49 (2000): 87–95; Hensley and Tallichet, 'Learning to be cruel?'

74　A. C. Baldry, 'Bullying in schools and exposure to domestic violence', *Child Abuse and Neglect*, 27, 7 (2003): 713–732.

75　D. Schwartz, K. A. Dodge, G. S. Pettit, and J. E. Bates, 'The early socialization of aggressive victims of bullying', *Child Development* 68, 4 (1997): 665–675.

76　*Ibid.*

77　N. Robertson and E. Gullone, 'The relationship between bullying and animal cruelty behaviours in Australian adolescents', *Journal of Applied Developmental Psychology* (in press).

78　K. L. Thompson and E. Gullone, 'An investigation into the association between the witnessing of animal abuse and adolescents' behavior toward animals', *Society & Animals* 14 (2006): 223–243.

79　Baldry, 'Animal abuse and exposure to interparental violence'; Baldry, 'Animal abuse among preadolescents'; Robinson and Gullone, 'The relationship between bullying and animal cruelty'; Thompson and Gullone, 'An investigation into the association'.

80　Flynn, 'Exploring the link'; Flynn, 'Why family professionals'; B. C. Henry, 'The relationship between animal cruelty, delinquency, and attitudes toward the treatment of animals', *Society & Animals* 12 (2004): 185–207; Hensley and Tallichet, 'Learning to be cruel?'

81 C. L. Currie, 'Animal cruelty by children exposed to domestic violence', *Child Abuse and Neglect* 30 (2006): 425–435.

82 Guerra *et al.*, *Community violence exposure.*

83 Anderson and Huesmann, 'Human aggression'.

84 F. R. Ascione, 'Emerging research on animal abuse as a risk factor for intimate partner violence', in K. Kendall-Tackett and S. Giacomoni (eds), *Intimate partner violence* (Kingston, NJ: Civic Research Institute, in press).

85 F. R. Ascione, 'Battered women's reports of their partners' and their children's cruelty to animals', *Journal of Emotional Abuse* 1 (1998): 119–133; F. R. Ascione, C. V. Weber, T. M. Thompson, J. Heath, M. Maruyama, and K. Hayashi, 'Battered pets and domestic violence: Animal abuse reported by women experiencing intimate violence and by nonabused women', *Violence Against Women* 13 (2007): 354–373; C. Daniell, 'Ontario SPCA's women's shelter survey shows staggering results', *The Latham Letter* (Spring 2001): 16–17; Flynn, 'Why family professionals'; J. A. Quinlisk, 'Animal abuse and family violence', in F. R. Ascione and P. Arkow (eds), *Child abuse, domestic violence, and animal abuse: Linking the circles of compassion for prevention and intervention* (West Lafayette, IN: Purdue University Press, 1999), pp. 168–175; A. Volant, J. Johnson, E. Gullone, and G. Coleman, 'The relationship between family violence and animal abuse', *Journal of Interpersonal Violence* (in press).

86 Flynn, 'Why family professionals'.

87 Quinlisk, 'Animal abuse and family violence'.

88 Ascione, 'Emerging research on animal abuse'.

89 Baldry, 'Animal abuse among preadolescents'; F. Becker, J. Stuewig, V. M. Herrera, and L. A. McCloskey, 'A study of fire-setting and animal cruelty in children: Family influences and adolescent outcomes', *Journal of the American Academy of Child and Adolescent Psychiatry* 43, 7 (2004): 905–912; Currie, 'Animal cruelty by children'.

90 Ascione, 'Battered women's reports'.

91 P. Carlisle-Frank, J. M. Frank, and L. Nielsen, 'Selective battering of the family pet', *Anthrozoös* 17, 1 (2004), 26–42.

92 A. Arluke, J. Levin, C. Luke, and F. Ascione, 'The relationship of animal abuse to violence and other forms of antisocial behavior', *Journal of Interpersonal Violence* 14 (1999), p. 966.

PART

II

Emotional Development and Emotional Abuse

Part II brings together two papers which both address, in different ways, the issue of appropriate emotional relationships with both humans and animals. Andrea M. Beetz (*Empathy as an Indicator of Emotional Development*) argues that the capacity to empathize is critical to the proper emotional development of children. She isolates a neurological basis of empathy – what she terms 'mirror neurons' – as the key factor that enables such development. When this factor is adversely affected by, for example, violence within the home or violence directed toward companion animals – our capacity to empathize is severely hampered, and our emotional growth stilted. Given this shared underlying mechanism, it follows that enhancing one kind of empathy – for either humans or animals – is likely to be reflected in another. Thus there is a correlation between our ability to establish empathetic caring relations with animals and with other humans.

Franklin D. McMillan (*Emotional Abuse of Children and Animals*), on the other hand, is concerned to explore the emotional abuse of children and animals, and maintains that many of our traditional categories of harm are insufficient for both. That children can be emotionally harmed is now well-accepted, but there is also evidence, despite obvious dissimilarities, that animals can also suffer from emotional maltreatment. Ironically, tests on animals, for example in relation to maternal deprivation or sudden induced stress, have shown how they are susceptible *inter alia* to long-lasting anxiety-like behaviour. McMillan maintains that there is a critical need for public education (as well as modification of animal cruelty statutes in the US) to prevent emotional maltreatment both of children and animals, including awareness of those factors (ignorance, frustration, lack of resources) that help fuel abuse in both cases. McMillan concludes that, 'Unpleasant emotions harm the child or animal by way of the distress and suffering they cause, by adverse health effects with which they are associated, and often in a pattern of ongoing emotional suffering that can persist for one's lifetime', making a plea for the recognition of this emotional harm in relation to all sentient species.

4

Empathy as an Indicator of Emotional Development

ANDREA M. BEETZ

Empathy – or rather a lack thereof – is closely linked to the abuse of animals as well as interpersonal violence. On the other side of the spectrum, good empathic skills are a vital and basic factor of socially competent behaviour and correspond with a healthy emotional development in childhood. Also, in adults, empathy towards humans and animals can be seen as both an indicator and an important part of mental and emotional health. This chapter will address the link between empathy towards animals and empathy towards humans, attachment relationships in childhood as basis for emotion regulation and empathy with other living beings, and mirror neurons as the neuronal basis for empathic abilities. Furthermore, the influence of familial animal abuse on the development of empathy in children and the assessment of empathy in cases of animal abuse and interpersonal violence are addressed.

Definitions of Empathy

While empathy is commonly understood etymologically as 'feeling *with* another person', in the academic field, several somewhat differing definitions of empathy exist.

Heinz Kohut defines empathy as the capacity to think and feel oneself into the inner life of another person.[1] Decety and Jackson describe it as a sense of similarity in feelings experienced by the self and the other, without confusion between the two individuals.[2] Most definitions share some basic components and more recent definitions refer to a multidimensional empathy construct.[3] According to Ekman, empathy is a reaction of a person to the emotions of another person. While *cognitive empathy* describes the recognition and understanding of what another person feels, *emotional empathy* causes a person to feel what another person feels. In contrast to this, s*ympathy* induces a wish to help another person to cope with a situation or feelings.[4] Seidel understands empathy as an ability that allows us to know what another person feels; however, it does not necessarily cause us automatically to feel what others feel.[5] Similarly, Eisenberg and Strayer distinguish the understanding/cognitive and the sharing/affective component.[6] The dualistic approach, as described by Eisenberg and Strayer and Ekman, seems the most useful for the comprehension of empathy towards humans as well as animals, particularly with regard to animal abuse and interpersonal violence.

All of the above-cited definitions refer exclusively to empathy towards humans. However, humans also have the capacity to empathize with animals and research shows a link between empathy directed towards humans and towards animals in children[7] as well as adults.[8] A humane education programme designed to enhance empathy towards animals also proved to increase empathy towards humans.[9] The studies previously conducted to investigate this topic document only a correlational link – a clear influence has not yet been reported. Furthermore, an underlying factor that influences the degree of empathy towards both humans and animals has not yet been clearly identified. Empathy towards animals could be expected to be better developed in children who have pets, but research showed that pet ownership *per se* does not make a difference. Rather the emotional closeness in the relationship between child and pet is connected to empathy with animals – only children who report a close relationship to their animal show better developed empathy towards animals.[10]

Empathy, irrespective of its definition as trait or ability, is frequently cited in connection with constructs such as social/emotional competence or intelligence. Mayer and Salovey define emotional intelligence as the ability to perceive emotions, to access and generate emotions as well as to understand and regulate emotions in oneself and others.[11] Thus both the cognitive as well as the affective component of empathy are closely linked to emotional intelligence. Similarly, for the most part, definitions of related constructs like social competence include reference to this ability to empathize with other humans in the way of understanding what other persons feel. Thus, emotion-related processes represent the basis of those competences.

Attachment and Emotional Development

The basis for the development of these emotion-related abilities can be found in attachment theory and research. The concept of attachment is frequently employed with regard to the relationship between humans and animals. Bowlby had observed children's behaviour towards their parents after a separation as well as interactions of mother-child dyads at home.[12] He also drew on research by Harlow and Zimmermann who investigated separation from the mother in infant rhesus monkeys.[13] Bowlby emphasizes that independent from age, the ability to form an attachment to another person is a basic characteristic of an effectively functioning personality and mental health.[14] Therefore, since the

1990s science further expanded the concept of attachment to adult relation-ships and attachment between partners.[15] Around the same time, research on human–animal interactions started to use the term *attachment* when referring to a close bond between pets and their owners. Bowlby further points out that attachment has its own function and is not just a behaviour or motivation that aims at the child's protection from danger, nutrition, or learning from a care-giver.[16]

During the first year of life, children develop an emotional bond with their main caregiver – in most cases the mother – who reacts to the child's attach-ment signals, such as crying, screaming, or other ways of actively seeking closeness, with care-giving behaviour. After the first six months, a child already differentiates between an attachment person and other persons. The child seeks to stay close to the attachment figure,[17] because she serves as a secure base and helps the child to regulate his or her emotions (i.e., external or interpsychic emotion regulation). If a child is in a stressful situation, for example separated from the mother, and reacts with fear, anger, or other negative emotions, the closeness of the returning caregiver in a secure attachment relationship calms the child and regulates his emotions. In childhood, the attachment patterns *secure, insecure-avoidant*, and *insecure-ambivalent* are distinguished.[18] Securely attached children can trust in the availability of their attachment figure and thus can tolerate separations better, for example when they explore or play, and are more open to their surroundings. In contrast, insecurely attached children have no stable mental representation of their attachment figure as caring and reliable and show signs either of hyperactivation or de-activation. The devel-opment of these attachment patterns or styles is influenced by the child's characteristics – some of which might be genetically based – as well as by maternal sensitivity, that is the correct identification and the prompt and adequate reaction to the attachment signals.[19] In the course of attachment-relevant experiences, the child forms an inner representation – an internal working model – of the relationship between himself and his attachment figure. This internal working model enables the child to anticipate attachment-rele-vant events and to plan, regulate, and organize his behaviour according to his expectations.[20] It facilitates the access to emotions, appraisals, and memories relevant to attachment and regulates the emotional communication within the child but also with other persons.[21]

In adulthood, usually three main attachment styles are distinguished: *secure, insecure-dismissing*, and *insecure-preoccupied*.[22] Secure persons find it easy to form close relationships to other persons and feel comfortable depending on others and having them depend on them. Trust, seeking closeness, and valuing close relationships are main characteristics. Persons with a secure attachment style can more easily access their own emotions and are better able to integrate also negative experiences in their internal working model than insecurely attached persons.

Beside these basic attachment styles, the presence of disorganization or an unresolved attachment trauma is also assessed in children as well as adults.

Such disorganization with regard to attachment is linked to a higher prevalence of psychiatric disorders.[23] Disorganization in attachment can be based
on the loss of an attachment figure or experiences of abuse, among other
things.[24] The highest prevalence of disorganized attachment (approximately
80 per cent) is found in maltreatment samples.[25] In contrast, only 15 per cent
of infants in middle-class samples are classified as disorganized.[26] Further
factors promoting disorganization in the child are depression and alcoholism
of the mother as well as marital conflict, since those correlate with parental
rejection and threats to abandon the child.[27] Main and Hesse propose that
disorganization in a child reflects frightened or frightening parental behaviour.[28]

Attachment to Companion Animals

Before proceeding to discuss the detrimental influence of animal abuse in the
family, some critical thoughts about the transfer of attachment theory to the
human–animal relationship are advisable. The following criteria, which distinguish an attachment relationship from other social relationships, have to be met
by the human–animal relationship in order to qualify as an attachment relationship: the attachment figure (in this case the animal) serves as a secure base
for exploration of the environment and is sought out for reassurance during
phases of exploration; in a stressful or dangerous situation the attachment
figure represents a haven of safety and helps the person to regulate his or her
emotions via interaction or just closeness; the attachment figure or the internal
working model of one's relationship to the attachment figure is the source of a
feeling of security. A relationship to a pet can meet these criteria even if the
positive effects of such an attachment have to be attributed rather to an internal
working model – the mental representation of this human–pet relationship –
than to the actual behaviour of the animal itself. Clearly, animals cannot
comfort and give care like a human caregiver can. Nonetheless, humans can
perceive the presence of their pet as consoling, as helping regulate emotions,
and as a haven of safety, a secure base.

It is obvious that not every human–animal relationship meets these criteria
and that only close and trusting relationships can qualify as attachments. This
further explains the link of empathy with close human–pet relationships, but
not mere animal ownership. Additionally, with regard to pets, the care-giving
system – the corresponding system that is activated in the attachment
figure/caregiver, but that is already present in children – plays an important
role. With pets, humans are always in the role of a caregiver, but might also turn
to the animal in stressful times as a haven of safety, for feelings of security and
emotion regulation.

Attachment and Emotional Competences

Research showed that early attachment experiences with parents and parents' ways of dealing with emotions influence the development of the child's ability for adequate emotion regulation and emotional intelligence.[29] Only a few studies have directly investigated the link between attachment, emotional intelligence, and emotion regulation in adulthood.[30] However, those studies also showed a positive relation between secure attachment and emotional intelligence. Steele *et al.* documented a positive relation between attachment security and the interpretation of emotions, one basic factor of empathy, and Suess *et al.* documented its connection to a more functional social perception.[31] Securely attached children can integrate emotions and cognition in stressful situations and they allow themselves to perceive their own negative emotions and to use them for self-regulation.

With regard to attachment to animals, Beetz found that young adults who report a close relationship to animals show higher scores in emotional intelligence than those who did not describe an internal working model that points to attachment security with regard to pets. Furthermore, a secure attachment relationship to pets correlates positively with empathy towards animals.[32]

The Neurological Basis of Empathy – Mirror Neurons

The detection of the existence of mirror neurons by Rizzolatti *et al.* provides a neuronal basis for the explanation of differences in empathy, its cognitive and affective components, and its development.[33] More precisely, mirror neurons can explain the resonance phenomena encountered on a daily basis in interpersonal interactions.[34]

The existence of resonance phenomena – such as contagious laughter or yawning or scratching that causes others to yawn or scratch themselves – is known by scientists and the public. Also, the fact that most mentally healthy adults immediately begin playing imitation games at the sight of a baby falls into this category, as does the adaptation of similar postures and gestures of two persons in a conversation. Another example is 'joint attention', meaning that if one person directs his attention abruptly to something, other persons will also spontaneously look in the same direction, or listen carefully for the sounds the other person might have heard. Resonance is also at work with regard to a person's emotional state – it usually elicits the same emotion in the other person within a social interaction, a phenomenon also known as 'emotional contagion'. Dimberg *et al.* showed in an experiment that even if persons try to keep a neutral facial expression towards emotional stimuli presented to them as photographs of persons with a different emotional expression, they involuntarily react with imitation measured as activity in the facial muscles.[35]

The neuronal basis for all these phenomena are mirror neurons, which function independently of conscious perception or analytic reasoning. Rizzolatti *et al.* investigated neurons specialized in controlling hand actions in monkeys. During each experiment, they recorded data from a single neuron in the monkey's brain while the monkey was reaching for pieces of food. They found a kind of neuron that not only reacted when the monkey performed a certain action himself, but also when someone else performed the same action (e.g., reaching for a peanut on a tray). That this neuron reacted with resonance to the experience of a certain action performed not by the monkey itself but by another living being, was sensational and previously unheard-of. Recently, evidence from experiments with the use of functional magnetic resonance imaging (fMRI), transcranial magnetic stimulation (TMS), and electroencephalography (EEG) strongly supports the existence of the presence of a similar system of mirror neurons in humans. Human brain regions respond during both action and the observation of action performed by another person. The same is true for emotions or perceptions such as pain. In humans, certain brain regions are activated when a person experiences an emotion like sadness, disgust, or happiness, as well as when they see another person experience this emotion or perception.[36] For this reason, mirror neurons can be linked to empathy – they represent the basis of feeling with another person, knowing what they experience. Further support for a link between the mirror system and empathy is given by research that has shown that persons who are more empathic according to self-report questionnaires have stronger activations both in the mirror system for hand actions and the mirror system for emotions.[37] Furthermore, persons with autism, who display obvious difficulties in emphasizing with other persons, show an impairment in the functioning of the mirror neuron system.[38]

Development of the Mirror Neuron System

Research on human infants suggests that the mirror neuron system develops before twelve months of age, and that this system helps babies understand other people's actions.[39] However, the development of optimal mirror neuron functioning requires social interactions, according to the 'use it or lose it' principle.[40] Infants need to experience empathy towards their own emotions and actions by caregivers who respond to them via mirroring and show resonance with the child's perceptions and emotional states. Only then can infants train their mirror neurons, with the help of a sensitively responsive caregiver. This condition is most likely met in an attachment relationship that also fosters a secure inner working model of attachment in a child. Sensitive caregivers who spontaneously and adequately react to the expressed emotions or perceptions of the infant are more frequently found in cases of organized and in particular secure attachment classifications of children.

Mirroring Perceptions and Emotions of Animals?

At this juncture, the mechanism of mirroring has only been investigated and proven for resonance phenomena between human actors, and it is known that persons do not react with mirror neurons to artificial actors, for example. Similarly monkeys and some birds were shown to possess mirror neuron systems; however, the mirroring has again only been documented for observations of actors of their own species.[41]

Nonetheless, it seems not unlikely that humans may react with an activation of the mirror neuron system to animals' expressions of emotion or pain. Common experience shows that many people, especially those who know the animal species or the individual animal, immediately and spontaneously react empathetically to observations or hearing the animal's expression of its adverse emotional state. Taking the example of a dog screaming in pain because someone hurt it, nearly all dog owners – but also many non-owners – display a startled reaction (flinching) and just know that the animal is in pain. Many people also choose not to watch reports or even look at static pictures depicting animal abuse cases, because they cannot stand their own 'feelings' when doing so. Even though this is not evidence comparable to imaging techniques (fMRI, etc.), these day-to-day experiences and observations suggest that humans may react with an activation of their mirror neuron system to the actions and emotions of animals.

Consequences of Animal Abuse and Violence within the Family

Taking the above connections between attachment, the mirror neuron system, and empathy into account, it becomes obvious how detrimental family violence is to the development of emotional abilities – in particular empathy – in a child. If the above-stated assumptions are correct, the following scenarios of how animal abuse, child abuse, and spousal abuse affect child development with regard to emotional abilities are conceivable.

On the one hand, children in violent homes – with spousal abuse, for example – suffer by co-experiencing the pain of the abused mother via their mirror neuron system. To adapt to this, in most cases of longer-lasting spousal abuse, a child needs to develop defensive mechanisms to control the burden of negative sensations and emotions laid upon him by his own mirror neuron system. On the other hand, it is likely that those mirror neurons might not have developed to the same degree as in children in non-violent homes, since the main caregiver is permanently under the threat of violence and extreme stress and hence she will probably not be able to react adequately to her child's attachment signals. As mentioned previously, children who experience abuse themselves, but also those who experience abuse perpetrated by an adult towards their mother, show a higher likelihood for insecure and disorganized attachments. The child needs to suppress his affects permanently to be able to function. Thus, the child cannot develop empathy, at least in its affective component, and other competencies that are subsumed in the concept of emotional intelligence and abilities.

The same applies in cases of repeated child abuse. Here, the direct experience necessitates the development of self-regulation strategies and defensive mechanisms that counteract the activation of the mirror neuron system or the perception of its effects. The development of a secure attachment in this situation seems highly unlikely, except where the mother or another important caregiver besides the abusive parent is serving as a secure base and haven of safety. But even then the conditions for optimal development and the training of mirror neurons in the child are usually not fulfilled.

With regard to the abuse of pets in a home with domestic violence, it is known by practitioners who work with abused children that they do suffer when their pets are threatened or abused. Whether this is transmitted via the activation of mirror neurons has not yet been proven in studies. However, even if only empathy is taken into account, a permanent threat or abuse of the pet requires the development of special emotion regulation strategies and defensive processes in order to protect oneself from permanent suffering through empathizing. While those strategies, such as impaired perception of the feelings of others (humans or animals), are adaptive in a situation of ongoing abuse, they are usually not in a normal surrounding and consequently deficits in adaptive emotion regulation, emotional intelligence, and empathy in normal social interactions will become evident over time.

Both animal abuse and interpersonal violence are frequently linked to a deficit in emotional competencies, be they adequate emotion regulation strategies, emotional intelligence with factors like correct perception of another person's emotions and intentions, or empathy with its affective and cognitive components. Animal abuse and interpersonal violence are, among others, diagnostic criteria for psychiatric disorders such as conduct disorder and antisocial personality disorders – both types of disorder are frequently characterized by a lack of empathic abilities. The questions now are whether the mirror system is not developed appropriately in those perpetrators; whether they really do not have the capacity anymore to spontaneously react to the emotions of others on a neuronal level; or whether other mechanisms down-regulate the perception of the according emotions. It is probably rare – only in cases of mental disabilities – that a mere lack of the cognitive ability component of empathy may be responsible for perpetrating animal abuse or interpersonal violence.

Conclusion

On account of its shared underlying mechanisms being based on secure attachment, emotional intelligence, and perspective-taking, empathy is likely to correlate with more general emotional and social abilities. Thus, it can be taken as an indicator of healthy emotional development in children and adults.

Regarding the explanation of the found correlation between empathy towards animals and empathy towards humans it seems more likely from the mechanisms described above that those factors do not influence each other but are based rather on similar developmental prerequisites like attachment and the training of the mirror neuron system. This does further provide an answer to the question of why enhancing one – empathy towards humans or animals – is reflected in the other. Both are very likely based on and fostered by the same underlying mechanisms of attachment and the training of mirror neurons via the experience of emotional resonance.

Therefore, enabling children to experience trusting and close relationships not only to humans but also to animals provides them with the possibility to further train their mirror neurons, if interactions with a sensitive caregiver have established the basis within the first year of life. The positive correlation of trusting relationships to animals and empathy, however, may in large part be explained by secure attachment figures who give their child the opportunity to own a pet, and who nurture a positive relationship between that pet and their child. Overall, close and trusting relationships with animals, but even more so with a sensitive human caregiver, support the development of emotional abilities.

Notes

1 Heinz Kohut, *How does analysis cure?* (Chicago: The University of Chicago Press, 1984).

2 Jean Decety and Philip L. Jackson, 'The functional architecture of human empathy', *Behavioral and Cognitive Neuroscience Reviews* 3 (2004): 71–100.

3 For example M. H. Davis, 'A multidimensional approach to individual differences in empathy', *JSAS Catalogue of Selected Documents in Psychology* 10 (1980), p. 85; D. Cohen and J. Strayer, 'Empathy in conduct-disordered and comparison youth', *Developmental Psychology* 32, 6 (1996): 988–998; A. I. Alterman, P. A. McDermott, J. S. Cacciola, and M. J. Rutherford, 'Latent structure of the Davis Interpersonal Reactivity Index in methadone maintenance patients', *Journal of Psychopathology and Behavioral Assessment* 25, 4 (2003): 257–265.

4 P. Ekman, *Emotions revealed: Understanding faces and feelings* (London: Weidenfeld & Nicolson, 2003).

5 W. Seidel, *Emotionale Kompetenz: Gehirnforschung und Lebenskunst* (Munich: Elsevier, 2004).

6 Nancy Eisenberg and Janet Strayer, *Empathy and its development* (Cambridge: Cambridge University Press, 1987).

7 F. R. Ascione, 'Enhancing children's attitudes about the humane treatment of animals: Generalization to human-directed empathy', *Anthrozoös* 5, 3 (1992): 176–191; F. R. Ascione and C. V. Weber, 'Children's attitudes about the humane treatment of animals and empathy: One-year follow up of a school-based intervention', *Anthrozoös*, 9, 4 (1996): 188–195; G. F. Melson, 'Children's attachment to their pets: Links to socio-emotional development', *Children's Environments Quarterly* 82 (1991): 55–65; E. S. Paul, 'Love of pets and love of people', in A. L.

Podberscek, E. S. Paul, and J. A. Serpell (eds), *Companion animals and us* (Cambridge: Cambridge University Press, 2000); R. H. Poresky, 'The young children's empathy measure: Reliability, validity and effects of companion animal bonding', *Psychological Reports* 66 (1990): 931–936; R. H. Poresky, 'Companion animals and other factors affecting young children's development, *Anthrozoös*, 9, 4 (1996): 159–168; R. H. Poresky and C. Hendrix, 'Differential effects of pet presence and pet bonding on young children', *Psychological Reports* 67 (1990): 51–54.

8   A. M. Beetz and F. R. Ascione, *Empathy towards humans and animals and emotional intelligence*, Poster presented at the 10th International Conference on Human–Animal Interactions (Glasgow, October 6–10, 2004).

9   Ascione, 'Enhancing children's attitudes'.

10 Paul, 'Love of pets and love of people'.

11 J. D. Mayer and P. Salovey, 'What is emotional intelligence?', in P. Salovey and D. Sluyter (eds), *Emotional development and emotional intelligence: Implications for educators* (New York: Basic Books, 1997).

12 J. Bowlby, 'Grief and mourning in infancy and early childhood', *Psychoanalytic Study of the Child*, 15 (1960): 19–52.

13 H. F. Harlow and R. R. Zimmermann, 'Affectional responses in the infant monkey', *Science* 130 (1995): 421–431.

14 J. Bowlby, *A secure base: Parent–child attachment and healthy human development* (New York: Basic Books, 1988).

15 See J. Cassidy and P. R. Shaver (eds), *Handbook of attachment: Theory, research, and clinical applications* (New York: The Guilford Press, 1999).

16 Bowlby, 'Grief and mourning in infancy'.

17 G. Spangler, 'Die Rolle kindlicher Verhaltensdispositionen für die Bindungsentwicklung', in G. Spangler und P. Zimmermann (eds), *Die Bindungstheorie. Grundlagen, Forschung und Anwendung* (Stuttgart: Klett-Cotta, 1995).

18 M. D. S. Ainsworth, M. C. Blehar, E. Waters, and S. Wall, *Patterns of attachment: A psychological study of the strange situation* (Hillsdale, NJ: Lawrence Erlbaum, 1978).

19 Spangler, 'Die Rolle kindlicher Verhaltensdispositionen'.

20 E. Fremmer-Bombik, 'Innere Arbeitsmodelle von Bindung', in G. Spangler und P. Zimmermann (eds), *Die Bindungstheorie. Grundlagen, Forschung und Anwendung* (Stuttgart: Klett-Cotta, 1995).

21 I. Bretherton, 'Open communication and internal working models: The role in the development of attachment relationships', in R. Thompson (ed.), *Socioemotional development: The Nebraska symposium on motivation* (Lincoln: University of Nebraska Press, 1990), pp. 57–113.

22 M. Main, 'Metacognitive knowledge, metacognitive monitoring and singular (coherent) versus multiple (incoherent) model of attachment: Findings and directions for future research', in C. M. Parkes, J. Stevenson-Hinde, and P. Marris (eds), *Attachment across the life cycle* (London: Tavistock; New York: Routledge, 1991).

23 C. E. Scheidt und E. Waller, 'Bindungsforschung und Psychosomatik', in B. Strauß, A. Buchheim und H. Kächele (eds), *Klinische Bindungsforschung* (Stuttgart & New York: Schattauer, 2002).

24 J. Bowlby, *Attachment and loss*, vol. 1: *Attachment* (London: Pimlico, 1969); *Attachment and loss*, vol. 2: *Separation: Anxiety and anger* (New York: Basic Books, 1973).

25 V. Carlson, D. Cicchetti, D. Barnett, and K. G. Braunwald, 'Finding order in disorganization: Lessons from research on maltreated infants' attachment to their caregivers', in D. Cicchetti, and V. Carlson (eds), *Child maltreatment* (Cambridge: Cambridge University Press, 1989), pp. 494–528.

26 J. Solomon and C. George, 'The place of disorganization in attachment theory: Linking classic observations with contemporary findings', in J. Solomon and C. George (eds), *Attachment disorganization* (New York: Guilford Press, 1999).

27 Bowlby, *Attachment and Loss*, vol. 2; Solomon and George, 'The place of disorganization'.

28 M. Main and E. Hesse, 'Parents' unresolved traumatic experiences are related to infant disorganized attachment status: Is frightened and /or frightening parental behavior the linking mechanism?', in M. T. Greenberg, D. Cicchetti, and E. M. Cummings (eds), *Attachment in the preschool years: Theory, research, and intervention* (Chicago: The University of Chicago Press, 1990), pp. 161–182.

29 B. Janke, 'Naive Psychologie und die Entwicklung des Emotionswissens' in W. Friedlmeier und M. Holodynski (eds), *Emotionale Entwicklung* (Heidelberg: Spektrum Akademischer Verlag, 1999), pp. 70–98.

30 A. Beetz und P. Zimmermann, *Bindung und emotionale Intelligenz*, Poster am 44. Kongress der Deutschen Gesellschaft für Psychologie, Georg-August-Universität Göttingen, 26–30 September 2004; A. Beetz, *Bindung, emotionale Intelligenz und Emotionsregulation*, Poster am 45. Kongress der Deutschen Gesellschaft für Psychologie, 17–21 September 2006, Nürnberg; A. Beetz, C. Mayer, and A. Reiter, *Relationship quality and emotion regulation in adolescence*, Poster accepted at the European Conference of Developmental Psychology, Jena, August 2007; K. Kafetsios, 'Attachment and emotional intelligence abilities across the life course', *Personality and Individual Differences* 37 (2004): 129–145.

31 H. Steele, M. Steele, C. Croft, and P. Fonagy, 'Attachment as an organizational construct', *Child Development* 49 (1999): 1184–1199; G. J. Suess, K. E. Grossmann, and L. A. Sroufe, 'Effects of infant attachment to mother and father on quality of adaptation in preschool: From dyadic to individual organization of self', *International Journal of Behavioral Development* 15 (1992): 43–65.

32 Beetz and Ascione, *Empathy towards humans and animals and emotional intelligence*.

33 G. Rizzolatti, L. Fadiga, L. Fogassi, and V. Gallese, 'From mirror neurons to imitation: facts and speculations', in A. Mektzoff and W. Prings (eds), *The imitative mind* (Cambridge: Cambridge University Press, 2002).

34 J. Bauer, *Warum ich fühle was du fühlst: Intuitive Kommunikation und das Geheimnis der Spiegelneurone* (Hamburg: Hoffmann und Campe, 2005). This book provides an introduction into mirroring processes; if not otherwise indicated, the information in this sub-section is cited from this overview.

35 U. Dimberg, M. Thunberg, and K. Elmehed, 'Unconscious facial reactions to emotional facial expressions', *Psychological Science* 11 (2000): 86–89.

36 M. Jabbi, M. Swart, and C. Keysers, 'Empathy for positive and negative emotions in the gustatory cortex', *NeuroImage* 34, 4 (2007): 1744–1753; T. Singer, B. Seymour, J. O'Doherty, H. Kaube, R. J. Dolan, and C. D. Frith, 'Empathy for pain involves the affective but not sensory components of pain', *Science* 303, 5661 (2004): 1157–1162; B. Wicker, C. Keysers, J. Plailly, J.-P. Royet, V. Gallese, and G. Rizzolatti, 'Both of us disgusted in my insula: the common neural basis of seeing and feeling disgust', *Neuron* 40 (2003): 656–664.

37 Respectively, V. Gazzola, L. Aziz-Zadeh, and C. Keysers, 'Empathy and the soma-

totopic auditory mirror system in humans', *Current Biology* 16 (2006): 1824–1829; and Jabbi *et al.*, 'Empathy for positive and negative emotions'.

38 H. Theoret, E. Halligan, M. Kobayashi, F. Fregni, H. Tager-Flusberg, and A. Pascual-Leone, 'Impaired motor facilitation during action observation in individuals with autism spectrum disorder', *Biology* 15 (2005): 84–85.

39 T. Falck-Ytter, G. Gredebäck, and C. von Hofsten, 'Infants predict other people's action goals', *Nature Neuroscience* 9 (2006): 878–879.

40 J. Bauer, *Warum ich fühle was du fühlst*.

41 J. Bauer, *Warum ich fühle was du fühlst*.

Emotional Abuse of Children and Animals

FRANKLIN D. McMILLAN

Neglect and abuse of animals and children provokes a deep-seated sense of outrage among a large proportion of the public. A good portion of this reaction likely stems from the widely-held view of children and animals as innocent and defenceless and hence especially unworthy of any form of cruelty.[1] However, a major problem has been identified in both animal and child maltreatment: a disproportionate focus on physical neglect and abuse, with scant attention devoted to emotional maltreatment.

In children, this disparity in reaction and response (legal and otherwise) has been attributed to the fact that childhood emotional abuse does not generate the public interest or call to action that physical and sexual abuse do, in part because emotional maltreatment is harder to recognize, as it does not leave visible scars or overtly recognizable injury, like that found in physical neglect and abuse.[2]

As evidence of this lopsided focus in animals, of the cruelty statutes of the fifty United States and the District of Columbia, none include language specifically acknowledging or addressing emotional neglect, abuse, or suffering in their definitions of cruelty. Furthermore, nine states expressly prohibit consideration of emotional suffering by specifying that any injury or suffering be physical in nature.[3]

The emotions relevant to the issue of emotional maltreatment are those associated with unpleasant affects (feelings). Unpleasant emotions for which substantial evidence exists in animals include fear (and phobias), anxiety, separation anxiety (or separation distress), loneliness (and isolation-related emotions), boredom, frustration, anger, grief, helplessness, hopelessness, and depression.[4] This argues for assigning a high priority on addressing emotional maltreatment in animals.

Problems of Definition

A consensus on definitions and terminology in the study of emotional maltreatment in children – and its component parts, emotional neglect and emotional abuse – has not yet been achieved.[5] In contrast to physical abuse, childhood emotional abuse is exceedingly hard to recognize clearly, because there is no consensus as to what constitutes emotional abuse, its harm is in the form of emotional rather than physical scars, there are no pathognomonic findings on examination, and the harm characteristically varies, often dramatically, from one child to another.[6]

The problems inherent in the seemingly straightforward task of describing the signs of physical neglect and abuse pale in comparison to the challenges of describing the signs of emotional maltreatment. It is the ambiguity about what constitutes maltreatment that is one of the main obstacles to crafting enforceable animal cruelty legislation.[7]

Actual or potential harm is the central factor for any definition of maltreatment. This victim-oriented view has led many researchers to propose that intent should not be considered when defining maltreatment in children[8] and animals,[9] and current definitions of child abuse and neglect are not predicated on the intention to harm the child. Intent is, however, a factor in categorizing the acts of maltreatment as neglect or abuse.

Incorporating criteria for quantity in definitions of maltreatment has been a serious challenge. At what point, or quantity, does an act that is aversive to the animal become maltreatment? In units of time, where is the point at which keeping a horse isolated from other horses turns from an acceptable action into emotional neglect or abuse? One hour? Three days? Six months? Twelve years? Quantification in the form of number of aversive events necessary to meet the definition of maltreatment is no longer an issue: in children, because single acts may cause harm, proposed definitions include single events as well as patterns of behaviour.[10]

Maltreatment, Neglect, and Abuse

The forms of maltreatment to which animals may be subjected have extensive parallels with the forms seen in children.[11] Animals may be neglected or abused, physically, sexually, and emotionally. The similarities of animal and child maltreatment makes it useful to draw from the terminology used for children when developing definitions for use in animals.

Maltreatment may be defined as actions or inactions that are neglectful, abusive, or otherwise threatening to an individual's life or well-being. It is commonly used as a collective term for its two constituent parts: neglect and abuse.[12]

Neglect is widely considered to be a passive process, or an act of omission, in which the basic needs – physical or emotional – of a dependent individual are not adequately met by the caregivers.[13] Because basic needs may be physical or emotional in nature, the neglect arising from the failure to meet needs may also be broken down into two types corresponding to the same categories. In animals, physical needs include clean water, appropriate quantity and type of food, breathable air, shelter from the elements, hygienic living space, and veterinary care. Proposed emotional needs are presented below.

It is widely believed that in both children and animals, the most commonly seen form of maltreatment is neglect. Data has shown that neglect comprises 60 per cent of reported cases of child maltreatment and is the most common cause of death in maltreated children.[14] Neglect in animal maltreatment has been estimated to comprise most,[15] the overwhelming majority of,[16] 80 per cent or more of,[17] and almost all[18] cases of animal maltreatment.

Abuse, in contrast to the passive nature of neglect, is an active form of maltreatment consisting of acts of aggression with intent to harm the victim. Like neglect, harm may be physical or emotional; abuse correspondingly exists in both forms.

Emotional Maltreatment

The most widely-accepted classification of maltreatment in children identifies four major types: physical abuse, sexual abuse, neglect, and emotional abuse.[19] Similar categories have been proposed for use in animals.[20] In categorizing maltreatment in animals, due to the fact that both neglect and abuse may be subdivided into physical and emotional components,[21] the clearest approach would be to subdivide animal maltreatment into four categories: physical abuse, physical neglect, emotional abuse, and emotional neglect. As for the classification schemes in children, considerable overlap may occur within and between the classes.

Emotional Neglect

Serpell has suggested that emotional needs, such as the need for social companionship, have acquired many of the properties of a physical need such as hunger, and that satisfying these needs is required for a state of happiness and fulfilment.[22] Knowledge of the emotional needs of the individual is necessary in order to recognize and prevent emotional neglect. This is a substantial challenge in infants and toddlers, as it certainly is in animals. Deprivation of any of the emotional needs by a parent or caregiver's inactions, when sufficient to cause or risk harm to the child, constitutes emotional neglect.

Emotional needs in animals vary widely according to such factors as species, sex, age, and individual traits. However, a number of emotional needs have been widely accepted as being shared by most sentient animals, and include:

- control (ability to exert meaningful change to situations, especially those of an unpleasant nature, in one's life)[23]
- sufficient living space[24]
- mental stimulation[25]
- safety, security, and protection from danger, such as access to hiding places[26]
- social companionship (for social animals)[27]
- adequate predictability and stability to life events[28]

Of particular relevance in animal care is the fact that confinement of animals in man-made environments – such as zoological parks, farms, research laboratories, and even private homes – frequently create (and prolong) emotional needs, such as social companionship and stimulating activities. In a natural setting these can be easily fulfilled, but man-made environments typically prevent, or otherwise lack the resources necessary for, the animal to fulfil these needs.

Emotional Abuse

Emotional abuse has been described in children to differ from emotional neglect in that it is an active process in which there is some deliberate action on the part of the parent against the child that has the potential to cause serious behavioural, cognitive, emotional, or mental disorders.[29] Emotional abuse may be defined similarly in all sentient species (including human): the deliberate infliction of emotional distress on another individual.

Several categories of emotional abuse identified in children have direct application to animal care.[30] Those appearing to have the greatest usefulness include *rejecting, terrorizing, taunting, isolating, abandonment,* and *over-pressuring.* Whereas *ignoring* is a passive inattention to the individual's emotional needs and involves no intent of harm, *rejecting* is an active, purposeful denial of the emotional needs of a child or an animal, causing emotional deprivation. *Terrorizing* refers to the creating of a 'climate of fear' or unpredictable threat or hostility, preventing the victim from ever enjoying feelings of safety and security. Included in this category is the use of discipline and punishment that is inconsistent and capricious, extreme, or bizarre. *Taunting* includes any teasing, provoking, or harassing which causes frustration, anger, or mental anguish. *Isolating* involves the active preventing of social interactions and companionship. *Abandonment* is the desertion and termination of care of a dependent individual by the caregiver. This category of abuse overlaps with neglect by failing to meet the victim's needs; however, it is an active rather than passive behaviour on the part of the caregiver.

Proposed Definition of Emotional Maltreatment

The following is a proposed definition of emotional maltreatment: actions (or inactions) of the animal caregiver or other person(s) which, intentionally or unintentionally, cause, perpetuate, permit, or intensify emotional distress. Emotional distress is here defined as unpleasant emotional affect at a level that exceeds coping capacity. Such actions (or inactions), when intentional, are not maltreatment when there is a reasonable expectation that the ultimate outcome will be a meaningful net increase in that animal's overall well-being. Emotional maltreatment consists of two major types – passive neglect and active abuse – with some additional less distinctly classifiable forms.

Emotional Maltreatment as the Core of All Maltreatment

In children it has been recognized by many researchers that all physical abuse and neglect has a psychological component.[31] No form of childhood maltreatment is believed to occur without co-existing fear, terror, anxiety, loneliness, hopelessness, helplessness, or other negative emotional states. Emotional maltreatment is assumed to be part of or an inevitable consequence of all other kinds of abuse and neglect, and all maltreated children are regarded to be victims of emotional harm, the impact of which may persist long after the physical injuries have healed;[32] for this reason emotional maltreatment is now regarded as the core issue and major destructive force in the broader topic of child maltreatment.[33]

The Harms of Emotional Maltreatment

Contrary to the common perception that physical harm is more damaging to the individual, substantial evidence now exists to support the notion that in both animals[34] and children[35] the harm caused by emotional maltreatment is frequently worse than that from physical neglect and abuse. There is a growing consensus among childcare professionals that emotional maltreatment has the potential to harm the child in ways over and beyond the effects of physical injuries and is more damaging in the long-term than other forms.[36] In animals, some unpleasant emotional states appear to have a greater impact on animal well-being than physical pain.[37]

The harms of emotional maltreatment in animals appear to bear considerable similarities with those in children;[38] a large proportion of the research on human maltreatment, in fact, utilizes animal models.[39] It is important, however, to exercise prudent caution when drawing analogies between children and animals, as much of the harm in children involves harm to one's self-concept and self-esteem.[40] Nevertheless, many other relatively complex effects identified in children appear possible and even likely in animals, such as impaired ability to learn, inability to build or maintain satisfactory social relationships, inappropriate behaviour and feelings under normal circumstances (e.g., separation anxiety), a pervasive mood of unhappiness or depression, and a tendency to develop physical symptoms.[41]

Immediate Harm

The most obvious immediate harm of emotional maltreatment in any sentient species is the emotional pain and distress of the unpleasant emotional states elicited by the maltreatment. Unpleasant emotions, such as fear, anxiety, isolation and social deprivation, boredom, frustration, anger, helplessness, grief, and depression appear to be capable of causing distress and suffering of great intensity in animals.[42]

Long-term Harm

The harm that persists after experiencing emotional maltreatment is highly age-dependent. The effects of maltreatment on the young developing brain differ substantially from the effects on the mature brain-mind. Emotional maltreatment occurring in adulthood is studied primarily as post-traumatic stress disorder (PTSD); however, harm from early life maltreatment may also manifest as PTSD.

Maltreatment in Early Life

Convincing evidence from a large body of animal and human research in neurobiology and epidemiology has demonstrated that stressors in early life cause long term changes in multiple brain circuits and systems which lead to enduring brain dysfunction that adversely affects health and quality of life throughout the lifespan.[43] A particularly vulnerable point for stressful events during infancy is the mother-infant attachment.[44] For example, Agrawal *et al.* found that when puppies are socially isolated from three days to twenty weeks of age, regardless of having their physiological needs met, they are emotionally disturbed for life.[45] Serpell and Jagoe noted that long periods of daily social isolation or abandonment by the pet owner appear to intensify some dogs' attachments for their owners and may lead to separation-related emotional distress problems in adulthood.[46] Decades of research have provided unequivocal evidence that survivors of childhood maltreatment experience an increased prevalence of psychiatric disorders in adulthood, including major depressive disorder (MDD), PTSD, substance abuse disorders, borderline personality disorder, and eating disorders.[47]

Post-traumatic Stress Disorder in Maltreated Animals and People

Post-traumatic stress disorder is a potentially devastating condition with the ability to cause immense – and ongoing – psychological suffering. The disorder may result from emotional trauma experienced at any age[48] and specific traumas that have been determined to be highly associated with PTSD are rape, physical attack, combat exposure in war, accident, natural disaster, neglect, childhood physical abuse, and childhood sexual abuse.[49]

The harm of PTSD is particularly insidious and compounded by its persistent and repetitive nature. Patients may act or feel as if they are actually reliving the traumatic experience, often evoking an emotional response very similar to the one experienced at the time of the original traumatic events.[50]

The similarities of PTSD in human and animal studies have been noted by numerous researchers and, in fact, much of the research on PTSD has utilized animal models.[51] A study in which rats that were separated from their mothers as infants and then subjected to inescapable foot shocks as adults revealed that early life stress may aggravate some effects of exposure to a stressor during adult age, which the researchers interpreted as behavioural and physiological effects paralleling the effects observed in human PTSD patients.[52] A review by Siegmund and Wotjak noted that basic research in rats and mice has demonstrated that a single exposure to a severe stressor may cause long-lasting increases in anxiety-like behaviour, changes in neurochemistry, neuroendocrinology, startle responses, and electrical excitability of the fear circuitry.[53]

Little is known about PTSD in animals in their natural environment. A recent report on wild elephants by Bradshaw *et al.* described the events following elephant calves witnessing the culling and poaching deaths of relatives and bonded companions.[54] The investigators determined that these calves are high-risk candidates for later disorders, including an inability to regulate stress-reactive aggressive states. They suggested that elephants have demonstrated symptoms associated with human PTSD, such as an abnormal startle response, depression, unpredictable social behaviour, and hyperaggression.

Resilience

It has long been known that individuals differ markedly in the frequency with which they experience stressful life events and in their vulnerability – or its converse, resilience – in response to stressful challenges.[55] A recent description by Hoge *et al.* states that 'the notion of resilience encompasses psychological and biological characteristics, intrinsic to an individual, that . . . confer protection against the development of psychopathology in the face of stress'.[56]

Much research on resiliency has been conducted with animals. Because the laboratory evidence argues very strongly for not only the presence of long-term effects in non-human animals but also for clear patterns of resilience that vary among individuals, it would be reasonable to assume that similar psychological processes also exist in animals outside the laboratory.

Hoge *et al.* have noted that most of the research on PTSD has focused on variables that confer risk factors for developing this disorder after a trauma and that far fewer studies have focused on variables that buffer risk or serve as factors contributing to resilience. They point out growing research interest in determining and understanding factors that promote resilience to psychopathology in individuals after they experience a traumatic event. For example, Collishaw *et al.* investigated the development of resilience to psychopathology in adulthood years after childhood maltreatment.[57] This group found that a substantial minority (10 per cent) of individuals who reported repeated or severe physical or sexual abuse in childhood reported no mental health problems in adult life. The researchers were able to identify factors that were associated with the resilience exhibited by these individuals, which included parental care, adolescent peer relationships, the quality of adult love relationships, and personality style. They concluded that, 'Good quality relationships across childhood, adolescence, and adulthood appear especially important for adult psychological well-being in the context of childhood abuse'. These results are consistent with a literature that contains numerous reports demonstrating that social support is a strong protective factor against the harmful effects of a wide variety of traumatic stressors that may occur in adulthood as well as that occurring in early life.[58]

A second major protective factor is one discussed extensively in the stress literature: a perception of control. Considerable research involving a wide variety of animal species, including humans, has demonstrated the importance of a sense of control for emotional well-being.[59] The sense that one has control, even if it is not exerted, is highly effective in reducing the intensity and harmful effects of physiologic and emotional stress.[60]

Animal studies have demonstrated that genetic factors play a substantial role in the development of resilience.[61] In one study it was determined that rat strains were found to differ in their stress response and their vulnerability to certain stress-related illness.[62] Another study showed that infant rhesus monkeys who carry two copies of the long serotonin transporter (SERT) allele exhibit smaller HPA (maternal separation alters hypothalamic-pituitary-adrenal) responses to separation in response to repeated, unpredictable separations.[63]

Compounding the Distress of Maltreatment

The victim of emotional maltreatment is often dealing with numerous negative affects at once, all having complex interactions and all the object of the maltreated individual's best efforts to alleviate. Unfortunately, at times two or more unpleasant affects are active at the same time and in conflict, forcing the individual to choose one over the other as their priority – to choose the lesser of two evils and bring about the least suffering. A much too common example of this dynamic is the battered woman who stays in the abusive relationship because she fears the loneliness and isolation if she leaves.[64] To this woman the pain of loneliness will hurt more than the beatings she receives from her abuser.

Child psychologists have observed that in some, but not all, instances where an infant or toddler is being maltreated by his or her primary caregiver the child is at risk of a disorganized/disoriented attachment status, that is, a pattern of behaviour toward the caregiver in which the child shows conflicting patterns of avoidance and approach.[65] Some attachment theorists and psychologists believe that for disorganized infants, the parent – who should be a dependable source of safety and protection – is simultaneously a threat and a biologically-based, expected source of comfort.[66] When the child's attachment behavioural system is activated, these infants are caught in an irresolvable emotional conflict.[67]

Scientist as well as non-scientist observers of canine behaviour have known for hundreds of years that a physically-abused dog will often continue to seek affection from, and even show affection to, his or her abuser.[68] The emotional need for social companionship in highly social animals, sadly, often elicits such severe emotional pain that it keeps the abused animal – or person – coming back only to receive more abusive treatment from the person they simply want to share comfort and affection with.

Recognizing Emotionally Maltreated and Resilient Individuals

A problem that research in animal maltreatment faces to a far higher degree than does the field of childhood maltreatment is being able to recognize clinical victims of emotional maltreatment. The primary barriers are that the emotional maltreatment itself is not readily visible to outside onlookers, a vast number of the animals for which we most suspect emotional maltreatment have unknowable histories due to placement in shelters and foster homes and re-homing (often multiple times), and, of course, the inability of animals to communicate information of current or past maltreatment to us the way a human being can. Recognition of victims is important in instituting interventions, assessing success of such interventions, and for assisting the legal process in animal cruelty cases.

In children, McDonald has described patterns of behaviour that should raise concern about the possibility of emotional abuse, which include social withdrawal, excessive anger or aggression, eating disorders, failure to thrive, developmental delay, and emotional disturbances (e.g., depression, anxiety, fearfulness, and a history of running away from home).[69] Veterinarians have nothing of this nature to work with. In contrast to the advancements in recognition of signs of physical abuse and neglect, behavioural studies have thus far rarely been used as part of the assessment of animals who are the victims of abuse or neglect.[70] Marder and Engle looked at a small sample of dogs seized by the ASPCA for reasons of physical abuse, neglect, or abandonment.[71] These seventeen dogs were compared with eighteen owner-relinquished dogs on ninety different scores. The researchers found few consistent differences between the groups. Both groups were likely to show signs of fear in some situations, but with no consistent or distinguishing pattern.

In this near-complete void, the clinical picture of the maltreated animal, particularly the abused animal, has emerged through a fog of conjecture, assumption, logical reasoning, imagination, and misapplied anthropomorphism. The result – and the current state of affairs – is that animals (usually dogs) that show fear or anxiety, especially when cowering at the approach of a person or just a hand, are frequently assumed to have been, at some time in their unknown earlier life, 'probably abused'.[72] Unfortunately, there is currently no way to know in which cases the assumption is true.

Treating Victims of Emotional Maltreatment

Promising research has begun to show some of the ways that the adverse effects of emotional trauma may be alleviated and potentially reversed. Multiple studies have demonstrated that the effects of early life adversity can be modified by the subsequent caregiving environment. Francis *et al.*, studying infant rats, first determined that postnatal maternal separation increased HPA and behavioural responses to stress. They then modified the animals' living conditions and found that environmental enrichment during the peripubertal period completely reversed the effects of maternal separation on both HPA and behavioural responses to stress. The researchers concluded that 'environmental enrichment leads to a functional reversal of the effects of maternal separation through compensation for, rather than reversal of, the neural effects of early life adversity'.[73]

In a more recent study using a rat model of PTSD, Imanaka *et al.* examined the effects of early adversity (neonatal isolation) on the severity of PTSD symptoms later in life (elicited by a single prolonged stress) with and without intervention with environmental enrichment.[74] The results of the study demonstrated that early adversity strengthened PTSD-like symptoms, but environmental enrichment alleviated some of the enhanced behaviours. The researchers concluded that these findings suggested that early adversity may worsen dysfunction of the amygdala and hippocampus in PTSD, and early positive intervention may alleviate the early adversity-mediated enhancement of hippocampal dysfunction in PTSD.

A study of maltreated preschool children by Fisher *et al.* showed similar potential benefits.[75] Children who had been removed from their parents due to maltreatment were placed in foster care. The intervention was to incorporate positive parenting strategies by training foster parents to be more sensitive and responsive caregivers. During the first three months in foster care children in the intervention group demonstrated a more normative regulation of the HPA axis (restoration of typical physiological cortisol levels) and a decline in behaviour problems. In contrast, children whose foster families did not receive the intervention did not show improvements either in HPA function or behaviour.

Preventing Emotional Maltreatment

Education of the public is a critical step in the prevention of emotional maltreatment. Aware that most of the emotional neglect in children is a result not of malice but of an inadequate understanding of the child's emotional needs, child protection workers have focused on educating the well-meaning parents to make the home more nurturing and emotionally fulfilling for the child. Recently, authors on animal maltreatment have adopted a similar view. Butler *et al.* reported that animal control officers have reported that while some harmful actions are done intentionally, most maltreatment stems from high levels of frustration, a lack of resources, and insufficient knowledge about the animals' needs and about responsible ways to care for animals.[76] Sinclair *et al.* recently wrote that in their view, the majority of animal neglect situations are best resolved by education and monitoring of the caretaker.[77]

An effective prevention programme must include enactment and strong enforcement of humane laws which recognize and clearly define emotional maltreatment. Current state animal cruelty statutes need to be amended to include *emotional* injury, pain, suffering, and trauma. In addition, progress in child protective services demonstrates the benefits of mandated reporting of all forms of maltreatment. Ascione and Barnard have pointed out that the advent of definitions and mandated reporting statutes for child neglect and abuse resulted in substantial strengthening of the response to cases of child maltreatment.[78] They proposed that taking the same steps in the recognition and reporting of animal maltreatment would similarly strengthen the response to animal maltreatment.

Future Considerations

From an ethical and scientific standpoint, the rationale and principles for managing pain are essentially the same for physical and emotional pain. Unpleasant emotions harm the child or animal by way of the distress and suffering they cause, by the adverse health effects with which they are associated, and often result in a pattern of ongoing emotional suffering that can persist for one's entire lifetime. When neglect and abuse inflict emotional pain upon an animal or young child it is reasonable to believe that the victim experiencing the unpleasant feelings does not care about the source of the discomfort – whether it has an emotional or physical origin – but that he or she be rid of the unpleasantness. This applies to all forms of adversity throughout a child's or animal's life, but particularly to the distress and suffering caused by neglect and abuse.

Certainly one of the largest impediments to moving forward in our efforts to tend to emotional maltreatment in animals is the difficulty inherent in recognizing it when it occurs and discerning the signs of emotional harm. However, the same problem plagued the early efforts in the field of childhood emotional maltreatment. Johnson, in a summary view of the state child maltreatment in 2002, remarked that if early recognition is to occur there must be clearly-defined and uniform criteria that define abuse and the significant consequences.[79] Yet the challenging nature should not be a deterrent, Ludwig noted when he commented that the difficulties in defining maltreatment are not a reason to shrink from the duty to protect children.[80]

With his colleagues, Cornell University's James Garbarino,[81] perhaps the most widely recognized researcher on childhood emotional maltreatment, aptly stated, 'rather than casting psychological maltreatment as an ancillary issue, subordinate to other forms of abuse and neglect, we should place it as the centrepiece of efforts to understand family functioning and to protect children'. This is wise and compassionate advice in caring for any sentient species.

Notes

1   A. Arluke, *Just a dog: Understanding animal cruelty and ourselves* (Philadelphia, PA: Temple University Press, 2006).

2   D. Iwaniec, *The emotionally abused and neglected child: Identification, assessment and intervention* (Chichester: John Wiley & Sons, 1995); L. W. Kowal, 'Recognizing animal abuse: What veterinarians can learn from the field of child abuse and neglect', in *Recognizing and reporting animal abuse: A veterinarian's guide* (Denver, CO: American Humane Association, 1998).

3   Animal Protection Institute, 'State animal cruelty laws' (2001): http://www.api4animals.org.

4   J. Panksepp, *Affective neuroscience: The foundations of human and animal emotions* (New York: Oxford University Press, 1998).

5   A. Kent and G. Waller, 'Childhood emotional abuse and eating psychopathology', *Clinical Psychology Review* 20 (2000): 887–903; D. A. Wolfe, *Child abuse: Implications for child development and psychopathology* (Thousand Oaks, CA: SAGE Publications, 1999).

6   L. K. Jellen, J. E. McCarroll, L. E. Thayer, 'Child emotional maltreatment: A 2-year study of US Army cases', *Child Abuse and Neglect* 25 (2001): 623–639; M. Owen and P. Coant, 'Other forms of neglect', in S. Ludwig and A. E. Kornberg (eds), *Child abuse: A medical reference*, 2nd edn (New York: Churchill Livingstone, 1992).

7   J. Lofflin, 'Animal abuse: What practitioners need to know', *Veterinary Medicine* 101 (2006): 506–518.

8   D. Glaser, 'Child abuse and neglect and the brain: A review', *Journal of Child Psychology and Psychiatry* 41 (2000): 97–116. S. Ludwig, 'Defining child abuse:

Clinical mandate – evolving concepts', in S. Ludwig and A. E. Kornberg (eds), *Child abuse: A medical reference*, 2nd edn (New York: Churchill Livingstone, 1992).

9   H. Vermeulen and J. S. J. Odendaal, 'Proposed typology of companion animal abuse', *Anthrozoös* 6 (1993): 248–257.

10 Glaser, 'Child abuse and neglect'.

11 F. R. Ascione, 'Animal abuse and youth violence', *Juvenile Justice Bulletin* (Office of Juvenile Justice and Delinquency Prevention) (September 2001): 1–15; H. Cheever, 'Recognizing and investigating equine abuse', in L. Miller and S. Zawistowski (eds), *Shelter medicine for veterinarians and staff* (Ames, IA: Blackwell Publishing, 2004); G. J. Patronek, 'Animal cruelty, abuse and neglect: issues for veterinarians', Proceedings, American Animal Hospital Association Annual Meeting 1997, San Diego, pp. 375–379; Vermeulen and Odendaal, 'Proposed typology'.

12 US Department of Health, Education, and Welfare, 'Interdisciplinary glossary on child and neglect', in S. Ludwig and A. E. Kornberg (eds), *Child abuse: A medical reference*, 2nd edn (New York: Churchill Livingstone, 1992).

13 R. K. Oates, *The spectrum of child abuse: Assessment, treatment, and prevention* (New York: Brunner/Mazel, 1996); Owen and Coant, 'Other forms of neglect'; H. M. C. Munro, 'The battered pet syndrome', in *Recognizing and reporting animal abuse: A veterinarian's guide* (Denver, CO: American Humane Association, 1998).

14 M. D. DeBellis, 'The psychobiology of neglect', *Child Maltreatment* 10 (2005): 150–172; K. C. McDonald, 'Child abuse: approach and management', *American Family Physician* 75 (2007): 221–228.

15 A. J. German, 'Obesity in companion animals: Causes and consequences', Proceedings: American College of Veterinary Internal Medicine 2007 Forum, Seattle, Washington, 8 June 2007; Lofflin, 'Animal abuse'.

16 Cheever, 'Recognizing and investigating'.

17 R. Hubrecht, 'The welfare of dogs in human care', in J. Serpell (ed.), *The domestic dog: Its evolution, behaviour and interactions with people* (Cambridge: Cambridge University Press, 1995); Patronek, 'Animal cruelty'; G. J. Patronek, 'Issues and guidelines for veterinarians in recognizing, reporting, and assessing animal neglect and abuse', in *Recognizing and reporting animal abuse: A veterinarian's guide* (Denver, CO: American Humane Association, 1998).

18 L. Donley, G. J. Patronek, C. Luke, 'Animal abuse in Massachusetts: A summary of case reports at the MSPCA and attitudes of Massachusetts veterinarians' *Journal of Applied Animal Welfare Science* 2 (1999): 59–73.

19 D. A. Wolfe, *Child abuse: Implications for child development and psychopathology* (Thousand Oaks, CA: SAGE Publications, 1999).

20 F. R. Ascione and S. Barnard, 'The link between animal abuse and violence to humans: Why veterinarians should care', in *Recognizing and reporting animal abuse: A veterinarian's guide* (Denver, CO: American Humane Association, 1998); Vermeulen and Odendaal, 'Proposed typology'.

21 Oates, *The spectrum of child abuse*; Wolfe, *Child abuse*.

22 J. Serpell, *In the company of animals* (Cambridge: Cambridge University Press, 1996).

23 M. E. Seligman, *Helplessness: On depression, development, and death* (San Francisco, CA: W. H. Freeman and Company, 1975).

24 M. W. Fox, *Farm animals: Husbandry, behavior, and veterinary practice* (Baltimore, MD: University Park Press, 1984).

25 F. Wemelsfelder, 'Boredom and laboratory animal welfare', in B. E. Rollin and M. L. Kesel (eds), *The experimental animal in biomedical research* (Boca Raton, FL: CRC Press, 1990); F. Wemelsfelder, 'Animal boredom: Understanding the tedium of confined lives', in F. D. McMillan (ed.), *Mental health and well-being in animals* (Ames, IA: Blackwell Publishing, 2005).

26 Hubrecht, 'The welfare of dogs'.

27 J. Panksepp, 'Affective-social neuroscience approaches to understanding core emotional feelings in animals', in F. D. McMillan (ed.), *Mental health and well-being in animals* (Ames, IA: Blackwell Publishing, 2005); Serpell, *In the company of animals*.

28 M. B. M. Bracke, B. M. Spruijt, J. H. M. Metz, 'Overall animal welfare reviewed, Part 3: Welfare assessment based on needs and supported by expert opinion', *Netherlands Journal of Agricultural Science* 47 (1999): 307–322; Seligman, *Helplessness*.

29 Oates, *The spectrum of child abuse*; Wolfe, *Child abuse*.

30 J. A. Monteleone, *Recognition of child abuse for the mandated reporter*, 2nd edn (St. Louis, MO: G.W. Medical Publishing, Inc, 1996).

31 S. Hamarman and W. Bernet, 'Evaluating and reporting emotional abuse in children: parent-based, action-based focus aids in clinical decision-making', *Journal of the American Academy of Child and Adolescent Psychology* 39 (2000): 928–930; C. J. Hobbs, H. G. I. Hanks, J. M. Wynne, *Child abuse and neglect: A clinician's handbook* (Edinburgh: Churchill Livingstone, 1993); Jellen *et al.*, 'Child emotional maltreatment'; E. C. Jorgensen, *Child abuse: A practical guide for those who help others* (New York: Continuum, 1990); Kent and Waller, 'Childhood emotional abuse'; Monteleone, *Recognition of child abuse*; Oates, *The spectrum of child abuse*; Wolfe, *Child abuse*.

32 Hamarman and Bernet, 'Evaluating and reporting'; Hobbs *et al.*, 'Child abuse'; Jorgensen, *Child abuse*.

33 S. N. Hart and M. R. Brassard, 'A major threat to children's mental health: Psychological maltreatment', *American Psychologist* 42 (1987): 160–165; Jellen *et al.*, 'Child emotional maltreatment'; Monteleone, *Recognition of child abuse*; Oates, *The spectrum of child abuse*; I. L. Spertus, R. Yehuda, C. M. Wong *et al.*, 'Childhood emotional abuse and neglect as predictors of psychological and physical symptoms in women presenting to a primary care practice', *Child Abuse and Neglect* 27 (2003): 1247–1258

34 H. C. Agrawal, M. W. Fox, and W. A. Himwich, 'Neurochemical and behavioral effects of isolation-rearing in the dog', *Life Science* 6 (1967): 71–78; T. L. Wolfle, 'Control of stress using non-drug approaches' *Journal of the American Veterinary Medical Association* 191 (1987): 1219–1221; T. L. Wolfle, 'Policy, program, and people: The three P's to well-being', in J. A. Mench and L. Krulisch (eds), *Canine research environment* (Bethesda, MD: Scientists' Center for Animal Welfare, 1990).

35 J. Garbarino, E. Guttman, J. W. Seeley, *The psychologically battered child: Strategies for identification, assessment, and intervention* (San Francisco, CA: Jossey-Bass, 1986); Iwaniec, *The emotionally abused*; Jellen *et al.*, 'Child emotional maltreatment'; Monteleone, *Recognition of child abuse*; Oates, *The spectrum of child abuse*; K. P. O'Hagan, *Emotional and psychological abuse of children* (Buckingham: Open University Press, 1993); Wolfe, 'Child abuse'.

36 D. P. Chapman, C. L. Whitfield, V. J. Felitti *et al.*, 'Adverse childhood experiences and the risk of depressive disorders in adulthood', *Journal of Affective Disorders* 82

(2004): 217–225; Iwaniec, *The emotionally abused*; O'Hagan, *Emotional and psychological abuse*.

37 F. D. McMillan, 'Emotional pain management', *Veterinary Medicine* 97 (2002): 822–834; Wolfe, 'Control of stress'; Wolfe, 'Policy, program, and people'.

38 R. F. Anda, V. J. Felitti, J. D. Bremner *et al.*, 'The enduring effects of abuse and related adverse experiences in childhood: A convergence of evidence from neurobiology and epidemiology', *European Archives of Psychiatry and Clinical Neuroscience* 256 (2006): 174–186; M. Gunnar and K. Quevedo, 'The neurobiology of stress and development', *Annual Review of Psychology* 58 (2007): 145–173; M. Reite, 'Infant abuse and neglect: Lessons from the primate laboratory', *Child Abuse and Negligence* 11 (1987): 347–355; M. M. Sanchez, C. K. Lyon, P. L. Noble *et al.*, 'Maternal separation alters hypothalamic-pituitary-adrenal (HPA) axis function in rhesus macaques: Effects of sex and serotonin transporter gene variation', Proceedings, 60th Annual Meeting of the Society of Biological Psychiatry, 19–21 May 2005, Atlanta, Georgia, USA.

39 H. Cohen, M. A. Matar, G. Richter-Levin *et al.*, 'The contribution of an animal model toward uncovering biological risk factors for PTSD', *Annals of the New York Academy of Sciences* 1071 (2006): 335–350; A. Siegmund and C. T. Wotjak, 'Toward an animal model of posttraumatic stress disorder', *Annals of the New York Academy of Sciences* 1071 (2006): 324–334; M. H. Teicher, A. Tomoda, and S. L. Andersen, 'Neurobiological consequences of early stress and child hood maltreatment: Are results from human and animal studies comparable?' *Annals of the New York Academy of Sciences* 1071 (2006): 313–323.

40 Jellen, 'Child emotional maltreatment'; Monteleone, *Recognition of child abuse*.

41 Jellen, 'Child emotional maltreatment'.

42 Panskepp, *Affective neuroscience*.

43 Anda *et al.*, 'The enduring effects of abuse'.

44 De Bellis, 'The psychobiology of neglect'.

45 H.C. Agrawal, M. W. Fox, and W. A. Himwich, 'Neurochemical and behavioral effects of isolation-rearing in the dog', *Life Sciences* 6 (1967): 71–78.

46 J. Serpell and J. A. Jagoe, 'Early experience and the development of behaviour', in J. Serpell (ed.), *The domestic dog: Its evolution, behaviour and interactions with people* (Cambridge, UK: Cambridge University Press, 1995).

47 L. M. Bierer, R. Yehuda, J. Schmeidler *et al.*, 'Abuse and neglect in childhood: Relationship to personality disorder diagnoses', *CNS Spectrums* 8 (2003): 737–754; J. D. Bremner, 'Long-term effects of childhood abuse on the brain and neurobiology', *Child and Adolescent Psychiatric Clinics of North America* 12 (2003): 271–292; L. L. Carpenter, J. P. Carvalho, A. R. Tyrka *et al.*, 'Decreased adrenocorticotropic hormone and cortisol responses to stress in healthy adults reporting significant childhood maltreatment', *Biological Psychiatry* 25 Jul 2007 [electronic publication]; D. Cicchetti, 'Child maltreatment: Implications for developmental theory and research', *Human Development* 39 (1996): 18–39; Cohen *et al.*, 'The contribution of an animal model'; D. Cukor and L. K. McGinn, 'History of child abuse and severity of adult depression: The mediating role of cognitive schema', *Journal of Childhood Sexual Abuse* 15 (2006): 19–34; M. R. Gunnar and P. A. Fisher, 'Early experience, stress, and prevention network: Bringing basic research on early experience and stress neurobiology to bear on preventive interventions for neglected and maltreated children', *Development and Psychopathology* 18 (2006): 651–677; C. Heim, N. J. Newport, R. Bonsall *et al.*, 'Altered pituitary-adrenal axis responses to

provocative challenge tests in adult survivors of childhood abuse', *American Journal of Psychiatry* 158 (2001): 575–581; J. Kaufman and D. Charney, 'Effects of early stress on brain structure and function: Implications for understanding the relationship between child maltreatment and depression', *Development and Psychopathology* 13 (2001): 451–471; C. Moreau and S. Zisook, 'Rationale for a posttraumatic stress spectrum disorder', *Psychiatric Clinics of North America* 25 (2002): 775–790; K. M. Penza, C. Heim, and C. B. Nemeroff, 'Neurobiological effects of childhood abuse: Implications for the pathophysiology of depression and anxiety', *Archive of Women's Mental Health* 6 (2003): 15–22; B. A. van der Kolk and C. A. Courtois, 'Editorial comments: Complex developmental trauma', *Journal of Traumatic Stress* 18 (2005): 385–388.

48   Glaser, 'Child abuse'; L. A. King, D. W. King, J. A. Fairbank *et al.*, 'Resilience-recovery factors in post-traumatic stress disorder among female and male Vietnam veterans: Hardiness, postwar social support, and additional stressful life events', *Journal of Personality and Social Psychology* 74 (1998): 420–434; K. C. Koenen, J. M. Stellman, S. D. Stellman *et al.*, 'Risk factors for course of posttraumatic stress disorder among Vietnam veterans: A 14-year follow-up of American Legionnaires', *Journal of Consulting and Clinical Psychology* 71 (2003): 980–986; K. L. Overall, *Clinical behavioral medicine for small animals* (St. Louis, MO: Mosby, 1997); S. Perry, J. Difede, G. Musngi *et al.*, 'Predictors of posttraumatic stress disorder after burn injury', *American Journal of Psychiatry* 149 (1992): 931–935; Serpell and Jagoe, 'Early experience'; S. B. Thompson, 'Pharmacologic treatment of phobias', in N. H. Dodman and L. Shuste (eds), *Psychopharmacology of animal behavior disorders* (Malden, MA: Blackwell Publishing, 1998).

49   R. C. Kessler, A. Sonnega, E. Bromet *et al.*, 'Posttraumatic stress disorder in the National Comorbidity Survey', *Archives of General Psychiatry* 52 (1995): 1048–1060.

50   O. Bonne, C. Grillon, M. Vythilingam *et al.*, 'Adaptive and maladaptive psychobiological responses to severe psychological stress: implications for the discovery of novel pharmacotherapy', *Neuroscience and Biobehavioural Review* 28 (2004): 65–94.

51   Anda *et al.*, 'The enduring effects'.

52   L. A. Diehl, P. F. Silveira, M. C. Leite *et al.*, 'Long lasting sex-specific effects upon behavior and S100b levels after maternal separation and exposure to a model of post-traumatic stress disorder in rats', *Brain Research* 1144 (2007): 107–16.

53   Siegmund and Wotjak, 'Toward an animal model'.

54   G. A. Bradshaw, A. N. Schore, J. L. Brown *et al.*, 'Elephant breakdown', *Nature* 433 (2005): 807.

55   H. Akil and M. Morano, 'Stress', in F. Bloom and D. Kupfer (eds), *Psychopharmacology: The fourth generation of progress* (New York: Raven, 1995).

56   E. A. Hoge, E. D. Austin, and M. H. Pollack, 'Resilience: research evidence for conceptual considerations for posttraumatic stress disorder', *Depression and Anxiety* 24 (2007): 139–152.

57   S. Collishaw, A. Pickles, J. Messer *et al.*, 'Resilience to adult psychopathology following childhood maltreatment: Evidence from a community sample', *Child Abuse and Neglect* 31 March 2007: 211–229 [electronic publication].

58   King *et al.*, 'Resilience-recovery factors'; Koenen *et al.*, 'Risk factors'; Perry *et al.*, 'Predictors'.

59   J. R. Averill and T. A. More, 'Happiness', in M. Lewis and J. M. Haviland (eds), *Handbook of emotions* (New York: The Guilford Press, 1993); H. Markowitz and K.

Eckert, 'Giving power to animals', in F. D. McMillan (ed.), *Mental health and well-being in animals* (Ames, IA: Blackwell Publishing, 2005); J. A. Mench, 'Thirty years after Brambell: Whither animal welfare science?' *Journal of Applied Animal Welfare Science* 1 (1998): 91–102; Seligman, *Helplessness*; M. A. Visintainer, J. E. Volpicelli, and M. E. P. Seligman, 'Tumor rejection in rats after inescapable or escapable shock', *Science* 216 (1982): 437–439.

60 Mench, 'Thirty years after'; R. M. Sapolsky, *Why zebras don't get ulcers: A guide to stress, stress-related diseases, and coping* (New York: W.H. Freeman and Company, 1994).

61 C. S. Barr, T. K. Newman, M. Schwandt *et al.*, 'Sexual dichotomy of an interaction between early adversity and the serotonin transporter gene promoter variant in rhesus macaques', *Proceedings of the National Academy of Sciences* 101 (2004): 12358–12363; H. Cohen, A. B. Geva, M. A. Matar *et al.*, 'Post-traumatic stress behavioural responses in inbred mouse strains: Can genetic predisposition explain phenotypic vulnerability?', *International Journal of Neuropsychopharmacology* 27 (2007): 1–19 [electronic publication]; S. R. Jaffee, A. Caspi, T. E. Moffitt *et al.*, 'Nature X nurture: genetic vulnerabilities interact with physical maltreatment to promote conduct problems' *Development and Psychopathology* 17 (2005): 67–84; A. M. Milde, H. Sundberg, A. G. Roseth *et al.*, 'Proactive sensitizing effects of acute stress on acoustic startle responses and experimentally induced colitis in rats: Relationship to corticosterone', *Stress* 6 (2003): 49–57; D. A. Morilak, G. Barrera, D. J. Echevarria *et al.*, 'Role of brain norepinephrine in the behavioral response to stress', *Progress in Neuropsychopharmacology and Biological Psychology* 29 (2005): 1214–1224.

62 E. Redei, W. P. Pare, F. Aird *et al.*, 'Strain differences in hypothalamic-pituitary-adrenal activity in stress ulcer', *American Journal of Physiology* 266 (1994): R353–R360.

63 Sanchez, 'Maternal separation'.

64 A. D. LaViolette and O. W. Barnett, *It could happen to anyone: Why battered women stay*, 2nd edn (Thousand Oaks, CA: Sage Publications, Inc, 2000).

65 M. Main and J. Solomon, 'Procedures for identifying infants as disorganized/disoriented during the Ainsworth strange situation', in M. T. Greenberg, D. Cicchetti, and M. E. Cummings (eds), *Attachment in the preschool years: Theory, research, and intervention* (Chicago: University of Chicago Press, 1990).

66 E. Hesse and M. Main, 'Disorganized infant, child, and adult attachment: collapse in behavioral and attentional strategies', *Journal of the American Psychoanalytic Association* 48 (2000): 1097–1127; K. L. Hildyard and D. A. Wolfe, 'Child neglect: developmental issues and outcomes', *Child Abuse and Neglect* 26 (2002): 679–695; A. R. Tarullo and M. R. Gunnar, 'Child maltreatment and the developing HPA axis', *Hormones and Behaviour* 50 (2006): 632–639.

67 C. George, 'A representational perspective on child abuse and prevention: Internal working models and attachment and caregiving', *Child Abuse and Neglect* 20 (1996): 411–424.

68 J. M. Masson, *Dogs never lie about love* (New York: Crown Publishers, 1997).

69 McDonald, 'Child abuse'.

70 Patronek, 'Animal cruelty'; Patronek, 'Issues and guidelines'; L. Sinclair, M. Merck, and R. Lockwood, *Forensic investigation of animal cruelty: A guide for veterinary and law enforcement professionals* (Washington, DC: Humane Society Press, 2006).

71 A. Marder and J. Engle, 'Are there behavioral indicators of animal abuse?'

Proceedings, Veterinary Society of Animal Behavior Meeting, Baltimore, MD, 25 July 1998.

72 Katz 2007; Sinclair *et al.*, *Forensic investigation*.

73 D. Francis, J. Diorio, P. M. Plotsky *et al.*, 'Environmental enrichment reverses the effects of maternal separation on stress reactivity', *Journal of Neuroscience* 22 (2002): 7840–7843.

74 A. Imanaka, S. Morinobu, S. Toki *et al.*, 'Importance of early environment in the development of post-traumatic stress disorder-like behaviors', *Behavioural Brain Research* 173 (2006): 129–137.

75 P. A. Fisher, R. Gunnar, P. Chamberlain *et al.*, 'Preventive intervention for maltreated preschool children: Impact on children's behavior, neuroendocrine activity, and foster parent functioning', *Journal of the American Academy for Child and Adolescent Psychology* 39 (2000): 1356–1364.

76 C. Butler, L. Lagoni, and P. Olson, 'Reporting animal cruelty', in *Recognizing and reporting animal abuse: A veterinarian's guide* (Denver, CO: American Humane Association, 1998).

77 L. Sinclair, M. Merck, and R. Lockwood, *Forensic investigation of animal cruelty: A guide for veterinary and law enforcement professionals* (Washington, DC: Humane Society Press, 2006).

78 Ascione and Barnard, 'The link between animal abuse'.

79 C. F. Johnson, 'Child maltreatment 2002: Recognition, reporting and risk', *Pediatrics International* 44 (2002): 554–560.

80 Ludwig, 'Defining child abuse'.

81 Garabino *et al.*, *The psychologically battered child*.

PART

III

Children, Family Violence, and Animals

Part III focuses on a major issue that figures prominently in research about the link: the relationship between animal abuse, child abuse, and family violence.

Sabrina Tonutti (*Cruelty, Children and Animals: Historically One, Not Two, Causes*) begins by explaining why cruelty to animals and cruelty to children are, historically speaking, one and the same cause. We know that is the case, she argues, because the early pioneers of a cruelty-free world for animals were themselves frequently active in anti-child-cruelty campaigns. In both cases the same philanthropic appeal was evident, and it was commonly accepted that those who were cruel to animals would be cruel to children, and vice versa. 'Cruelty towards animals hardens a man's heart, even towards his equals', expostulated Giuseppe Consolo in 1856, '[while] compassion towards animals necessarily makes men meeker and more gentle towards each other'. As Tonutti makes clear, 'The two causes stemmed from the same ideological roots, shared common moral visions, and even resulted in similar forms of social intervention'.

Frank R. Ascione (*Examining Children's Exposure to Violence in the Context of Animal Abuse*) reviews the empirical evidence for that claim in relation to children. Specifically, he examines the work detailing children's exposure to violence in the context of animal abuse. Ascione maintains that the studies cited 'clearly illustrate the maturation of our understanding about how animal abuse may be implicated in interpersonal violence and how exposure to and perpetration of IPV and animal abuse may be intricately related'. Clifton P. Flynn (*Women-Battering, Pet Abuse, and Human–Animal Relationships*) amplifies that conclusion in relation to women-battering and companion animal abuse. Traditional approaches, he says, have tended to regard companion animals as secondary players in domestic violence, but sociological research reveals that they are 'minded social actors, who participate fully in relationships with their human caretakers'. It is precisely, he argues, 'because of their close relationship that women and animals are victimized'.

Given this recognition, it is odd that child welfare work has so overlooked the place of animals within the home. That is a deficiency that Christina Risley-Curtiss seeks to address (*The Role of Animals in Public Child Welfare Work*). Her starting point is the almost universal fact that households in the US have companion animals – no less than sixty-nine million – and yet their presence is seldom regarded as significant by child welfare professionals despite the clear links that have emerged between child and animal abuse. She holds that 'a serious consequence of disregarding human–animal relationships is that it short-changes one's ability to help child welfare clients by failing, *inter alia*, to recognize serious problem behaviours and hence to facilitate early intervention'. Her recommendations to professionals include a thorough investigation of the place of animals in the home, 'specifically asking questions about the presence, meaning, and treatment of animals, including non-household animals'. Only by taking these, and other steps, can child care agencies 'maximize their potential' to their clients.

Cruelty, Children, and Animals: Historically One, Not Two, Causes

SABRINA TONUTTI

Psychological and socio-statistical research enables us to place the issues of human (child) abuse and animal maltreatment within a frame of reference that indicates the extent to which they represent different aspects of the same attitude. However, it would seem that the most prevailing interpretation is one that views human abuse and animal abuse as two distinct categories, and accordingly considers the anti-cruelty measures adopted by child protection or human rights organizations generally, and those adopted by animal protection associations, as having different frames of reference.

There are many factors that lead to the tendency towards a separate view of human and animal issues,[1] and while it is not possible to address them all here, it is worth emphasizing that the separation is a contingent one and the result of historical-cultural processes. It is also important to stress that the very concept of 'childhood' has a history, as does 'animality' (with its sub-categories, 'pets', 'farm-animals', 'laboratory-animals', etc.), as do the concepts of 'personhood', 'rights', 'use' or 'abuse', private property, etc. Similarly, ideas concerning the limits of parental authority or the intervention of state or public institutions in matters concerning private property have also changed over time, and are equally the result of a stratification of meanings and connotations.

In this chapter, I will reflect on the original solidarity that existed between the human and animal anti-cruelty causes in the nineteenth century, with specific reference to the subsequent burgeoning of the international animal advocacy movement.

Philanthropy, Animals, and the Battle Against Cruelty

If we were to ask a nineteenth-century philanthropist for a comment on the existence of a relationship between animal abuse and human violence, he or she would probably remark it was a matter of fact – and perhaps cite, in explanation, the shared origins and the close links which exist between the two forms of violence. This view, which was common among British philanthropists of the time, was shared on the Continent and in the USA, as can be attested from documents and archives of publications from the period. Consider, for example, this passage written by Giuseppe Consolo, barrister, correspondent of the University of Venice, and member of the Society for the Prevention of Cruelty to Animals in Trieste: 'cruelty towards animals hardens a man's heart, even towards his equals, [while] compassion towards animals necessarily makes men meeker and gentler towards each other'.[2]

Like Consolo, nineteenth-century philanthropists not only believed that cruelty to humans and cruelty to animals shared a common root, but also that both required the same policy measures and sanctions to address the problem. From their point of view, concern for humans and animals was inseparable, as evidenced by the many joint campaigns organized at that time. Both had a common aim: to oppose cruelty in all its forms, be it against humans or animals.

The Mobilization for the Plight of Animals

The development and spread of this new concern for animals occurred at the beginning of the nineteenth century and constitutes a social, cultural, and philosophical phenomenon that is extremely important for understanding the historical roots of the animal advocacy movement and the links that connected the human and animal causes promoted at the time.

The rise of this sensibility resulted in the foundation of a number of associations in Britain,[3] on the Continent,[4] and across the ocean.[5] The most influential of the European societies was the Society for the Prevention of Cruelty to Animals (SPCA), which in 1840 became the Royal Society for the Prevention of Cruelty to Animals (RSPCA). The organization catalyzed the support and mobilization of animal advocates, to the extent that it became a model for the entire international movement. In addition, the Societies of Munich and Paris became a point of reference for the animal protection movement generally, and greatly contributed to its international growth and development. They provided a model for the foundation of similar initiatives in other countries (as far as structure, statutes, relations with governments, appeal to the public, etc., were concerned) and for the specific content of their campaigns – the translation of educational novels for children, posters, scientific treatises, and so forth.[6]

Indeed, European and American associations, which followed the pioneering experience of those SPCAs (London, Munich and Paris), are referred to as 'sister' or 'daughter' societies in many publications of the latter half of nineteenth century. Going through the literature of the history of animal advocacy – and also the documents collected in the archives and publications of that time – it is possible to notice the existence of a close net of relations which linked members and representatives of animal protection associations from different countries: societies from European nations (such as France, Austria, Germany, Belgium, the Netherlands, Switzerland, Scandinavia, Portugal, Italy) were in contact with the RSPCA and other British associations. The purpose of these links was not only to gain moral support for the cause, but also to acquire information and useful suggestions for the organization of the movement in the countries mentioned above. Parallel to this, members of the British Society themselves decided to launch similar initiatives abroad, as in France (Paris) or in Italy (Naples and Turin),[7] where some of these animal advocates were living as diplomats, working as businessmen, or were engaged in their Grand Tour of southern Europe. Another representative of the RSPCA, John Colam, was in contact with Henry Bergh of New York, and this collaboration was the basis for the creation of the American Society for the Prevention of Cruelty to Animals in 1866, the New York Society for the Prevention of Cruelty to Animals having already been founded the previous year.

The Cultural Background of Animal Advocacy in the Nineteenth Century

This new attitude towards animals began to take root in Britain in conjunction with the so-called 'Age of Sensibility' (the late eighteenth century).[8] This was corroborated by the ideals of Romanticism, Evangelicalism, and other religious reform movements both in Britain and abroad. As Brian Harrison wrote, in the UK 'during the late eighteenth century, a powerful combination of evangelical piety, romantic poetry and rational humanitarianism gradually alerted the public to the plight of animals'.[9]

Starting from this period, emphasis was placed on pain and suffering. An all-embracing compassion was espoused towards beings who were suffering individually or collectively from various calamities and 'misfortunes' (such as poverty, oppression, war, illness, etc.) and towards animals. The moral concern that informed the humanitarian reforms of the time also informed animal protection campaigns. The two causes stemmed from the same ideological roots, shared common moral visions, and even resulted in similar forms of social intervention. It is also important to stress that rather than developing separately, they developed side by side – as declinations of the same moral trend which advocated kindness, mercy, and protection and opposed cruelty, violence, and abuse in all its forms. Moreover, mutual connections between the two movements helped to sustain the organization and spread of both.[10]

Another important cultural trend which influenced the development of animal advocacy – as well as humanitarian reformism – was Christianity, and in particular Evangelicalism. As a reform movement, Evangelicalism was active throughout the century, instigating many charitable projects in favour of the lower classes and inspiring reform campaigns regarding moral causes (such as the abolition of the slave trade, temperance, and criminal reform).[11] It was against this cultural and religious background that a new concern for animals, and the animal advocacy movement which sprung from it, arose.

For much of the eighteenth century, the activities and campaigns of the European animal advocacy movement were imbued with religious values, as their rhetoric testifies. Reference to the notions of charity, compassion, humanity, faithfulness, and God's will were common, as an extract from the fifth annual report of the SPCA of Trieste, published in 1857, demonstrates. From this we learn that the Society's aim was humanitarian, since it worked 'to develop and fortify the principle of charity in the hearts of men by awakening a sense of compassion towards animals'.[12] These animal advocates and philanthropists saw the development of compassion towards animals as linked to the civilization of society:

> Thus to love animals is the most efficient means to understand, educate, direct them, since charity is the best way of educating men and making them feel united . . . . To protect the defenceless, to respect one's inferiors, whatever their nature, is a sign of the moral status and social progress of populations. [. . .] Through a concern to restore harmony between animals and humans, man will become accustomed to living in peace with his equals, since natural order is linked to social order, and the latter to religion. Public welfare and social progress, as well as individual well-being, depend greatly upon man fulfilling his foremost duty – correct conduct towards animals as indicated by God and the end of creation. . . .[13]

These philanthropists and animal advocacy pioneers aimed to educate the public and to instil a sense of compassion and proper moral values within society so as to eliminate, or at least reduce, cruel behaviour. Within this framework, care of animals constituted a natural extension of these philanthropists' commitment to humans – a widening of their sphere of compassion.[14] It is worth mentioning here the similarity between this 'widening' of the 'circle of compassion' and the recent articulation of the same pattern of inclusion in Peter Singer's theory of animal liberation, in which he urged 'the expansion of the circle' of moral consideration from human beings to other animals.[15]

The striking differences between the two movements tend to make the similarities appear almost insignificant. While there are marked differences due to historical contexts, language, and discourse about human–animal relations, it is important to notice that in both cases, even if for different aims and reasons, animal advocates often appeal to the existence of links between the protection of humans and animals.[16] In the past, the protection of animals often represented – and was promoted as a means of – protecting human beings from cruelty and violence, and was articulated within a religious framework (a characteristic that was later heavily criticized by opponents of the moral and religious orthodoxy of the time). As a consequence of the secularization of culture which began in the second half of the nineteenth century, animal advocacy not only gradually eliminated this rhetoric, but also changed its ideological and moral set of references. The plight of animals *per se* – as beings with an inherent value and not merely as means to achieve a reduction in cruelty in society – was stressed more and more. However, direct and indirect references to the living conditions of and discrimination against certain categories of humans were not eliminated in twentieth-century animal advocacy (reference continued to be made to slaves, for example, and later to women, homosexuals, disabled people, minorities, etc.). The keywords of this new rhetoric became justice instead of kindness, respect instead of compassion, rights instead of protection, while pain and various forms of suffering remained a central focus of this concern.[17]

Human and Animal Concern and Voluntary Organizations

Going back to the nineteenth century, human and animal causes were interconnected and the campaigns promoted by organizations against human (child) and animal abuse often overlapped. The case of the Humane Societies in the USA constitutes a clear example of this tendency, since they were engaged in raising public consciousness towards both animals and children (and occasionally towards women and elderly people).[18]

The ASPCA – the first organization of its kind in the USA – was founded by Henry Bergh in 1866,[19] and its example was followed by many other organizations across the USA. The ASPCA's main aim was to protect animals from cruelty and abuse; however, it also included child protection within the scope of its mission. ASPCA volunteers were often called to intervene in child abuse cases, as in 1874, when the baby Mary Ellen was rescued from abuse inflicted by her adoptive parents. At that time, the intervention of the ASPCA was in opposition to the policy of the police, who were reluctant to intervene in private family matters as this was perceived as infringing upon parents' rights and individual liberties.

It was the absence of child protection laws and policies and a heightened sensitivity towards defending the weak generally that led Bergh and other philanthropists to set up the SPCC in 1874.[20] Across the country, many societies for the protection of animals gradually included child protection among their aims: these dual-focused organizations were – and still are – called Humane Societies, and to this day the scope of their mission continues to include both animal welfare and humanitarian issues.[21]

For many nineteenth-century philanthropists, there was no contrast between taking care of children and protecting animals, since both were God's creatures, defenceless, dependent, and unable to protect their own interests. Like other European societies of their kind, the Humane Societies considered cruelty towards animals as a slippery slope that could lead to the abuse of other humans. John Shortall of the Humane Society of Illinois maintained that 'he who is cruel to his beast will abuse even his own child'.[22] These words sound quite similar to those written in the mid-nineteenth century by G. M. Malvezzi, an Italian barrister and animal protection supporter, who held that 'the shift from animal maltreatment to human abuse is often very quick; . . . those among the common people who have a tendency to maltreat their own beasts will end up abusing their own wives, their own children'.[23]

The same moral vision emerges from what J. J. Zagler – one of the most influential animal protection advocates in Europe at the time and connected with the SPCA of Munich – asserted in his pamphlet on the maltreatment of animals and human duties towards them:

> it has been proved again and again by experience that those men who act inhumanely and insensibly towards animals, behave in quite the same way towards other men. Thus, by reducing the abuse of animals, we not only ensure that the animals themselves benefit, but also contribute to the welfare of the entire human race: roughness and barbarousness, these terrible enemies of all living beings, will be progressively limited; this is an important step towards better conditions for all of living creation.[24]

The strong association between the concern for humans (mainly children) and the concern for animals is demonstrated by other examples. At the time of the development of the SPCC and Humane Societies in the United States and the SPCC and RSPCA in Britain, other associations were created with the aim of easing the plight of both children and animals. Societies in Palermo and in Gorizia devoted their effort and commitment to animals and children at the same time. The following paragraphs will provide a brief overview of these two societies.

The Society of Palermo

As we mentioned earlier, there was a flourishing of voluntary associations across Europe in the second half of the nineteenth century, which developed in parallel with the increase in industrial development, urbanization, and in the levels of literacy. Many of these associations were dedicated to the protection of children and to the weaker members of society.[25]

Across Europe, animal protection societies were united by common values, language, and aims, were in contact with each other, and created a shared cultural outlook that motivated and sustained their activities. In Sicily, the presence of the aristocracy and the industrial middle classes made Palermo a central meeting place for members of European high society, and in 1896 the Società Siciliana Umanitaria-Educativa e per la protezione degli animali (The Sicilian Humanitarian-Educational Society and Society for the Protection of Animals) was founded by Joseph Isaac (Pip) Whitaker and his wife Tina Scalia, along with other important figures of the time. The Society's principal activities were educational or aid-related and were aimed at educating the public in order to reduce the incidence of 'maltreatments, insults, abuses against children, the elderly, the disabled, and animals'.[26] The Society divided its activities into three branches: education in schools, animal protection, and abandoned children. Humans and animals were both put at the centre of the Society's moral concern. Again, as in the examples of societies mentioned above, there was no distinction for these philanthropists between these two categories of beings as far as their rights to be defended from cruelty were concerned. They had been neglected by society, lacked protection, and were equally in need of help. It was imperative, the Society stated, to educate the public to be compassionate towards the disadvantaged, the poor, the disabled, and the animals suffering from human cruelty. Respecting animals was therefore the first step towards the civilization of men's hearts and the general improvement of society as a whole. These issues were promoted in schools where the Society provided educational programmes aimed at 'educating hearts to be respectful towards the elderly, to children, to be compassionate towards and assist the poor, and defenceless or suffering beings generally, and to protect animals'.[27]

Also in this Society's discourses on humans, animals, cruelty and suffering, the key words and expressions were based on notions of charity, compassion, moral duty and humanitarianism, and the idea that humans and animals were both God's creatures.

The Society continued to work through its three branches until 1927, when, due to financial reorganization and following the introduction of laws regarding children and motherhood, two different societies – one for orphans and the other for animals – were created. However, it seems that the latter ceased its activities during the Second World War.

The Society of Gorizia

The historical and social context which led to the foundation of the SPCA in Gorizia, in 1845, was quite different from that of Palermo. Even so, the principles and motivations outlined above are the same in this case.

The man responsible for promoting this initiative was a clergyman, Valentin Stanig, referred to by Alojz Rebula as 'God's ecologist',[28] for his respect towards nature and the earth's inhabitants. Stanig was a humanist, a poet, and alpinist. He was ordained a priest in 1802 and was in service for many years on the Adriatic coast. His biographers all confirm his commitment to the betterment of his parishioners' living conditions and to the beasts of burden. He was particularly concerned with those who were most neglected – such as the disabled and the poor – and had always been upset by animal abuse. In 1840 he was among the founders of the Institute for deaf-mutes in Gorizia and was also one of its first teachers. His love for nature and his firm belief in the educational and health benefits that derived from a good relationship with the natural environment influenced his decision to take disabled people on trips to the mountains: once there, these people would not only find fresh air and an occasion to improve their health through exercise, but would also be given a lesson by Stanig on how God had infused nature with harmony and love.

While a chaplain in Bajnšice, he promoted more sensible and compassionate treatment of animals, and even reproached his parishioners when they whipped animals or burdened their beasts with excessive weight. When he happened to witness a situation like this, he helped the beasts and their conductors pushing the cart.[29] At the same time, he provided the farmers among his parishioners with instruction in carpentry and handwork, gave medical assistance, treated the sick and taught members of his parish how to recognize healing herbs.[30]

In 1845, the Reports of the Munich SPCA[31] regarding their activities in 1843 and 1844 were distributed across the regions of the Empire thanks to the interest of the Society's patron, Ludwig I of Bavaria (reigned 1825–1848), and to the commitment of Austrian Chancellor Metternich. One of these copies – including the treatise written by J. J. Zagler – reached the Archdiocese of Gorizia, and subsequently Stanig, who was impressed by the contents and the ideals which had inspired the initiative. He immediately joined the Society of Munich, managed to enrol a hundred members and eventually founded an autonomous Society in Gorizia. The year was 1845, and this Society was the first animal protection association to be founded in Slovenian territory in the Habsburg period, and given the current borders, the first in Italy.

All the initiatives of the Society revolved around this fundamental principle: compassion towards animals constituted a Christian duty towards God, since such behaviour reflected the inherent good nature of humans. Educating people was one of the main activities of the Society, which carried out initiatives in schools and provided teachers with a number of books on the subject, which were translated into three languages (Slovenian, German, and Italian) by Stanig himself.

Stanig died in 1847, leaving the Society anchorless, so much so to that it gradually ceased its activities and subsequently joined the Viennese Society in 1864.

Conclusion

The firm belief that a link existed between cruelty to animals and to humans was a characteristic feature of the nineteenth-century associations that opposed cruelty, promoted humanitarian reforms, and were motivated by educational purposes.

As seen from the specific perspective of the animal protection movement, no distinction was made between the efforts of humanitarian philanthropists concerned with the living conditions of human beings and the efforts of those committed to the protection of animals. Cruelty was their enemy, whatever its declinations and victims. The betterment of society, in the name of God's teachings and Christian values, was their aim. Societies that campaigned against human abuse and for animal protection shared this moral vision and often worked under the same name and organization.

At the end of the nineteenth century – and later in the twentieth century, following the secularization and historical transformation of society – not only did the language of these Societies change, but so too did the discourse about the relationship between humans and animals, and the ideologies on which these views were grounded. The thought of protecting animals from abuse merely as a way of curbing violence between humans might seem strange and even reprehensible to an animal advocate of our day. But the very concept of 'protection' has changed. Within the animal advocacy movement a 'revolution' took place in the 1960s and 1970s which led to the idea that animals have rights based on their inherent value, and that unjust discrimination between living beings solely on the basis of their species should not be tolerated.

Notwithstanding the enormous changes which have occurred in animal advocacy from its origin to the present day, the link between the conditions of and discrimination against certain human beings – for example, on the basis of gender, race, ethnic minority, or age – and the exploitation of animals still has a firm place on the movement's agenda and is part of the movement's ideological perspective, as is also attested by the participation of many animal rights activists and volunteers in campaigns for human rights.[32] Again, pain, suffering, cruelty, discrimination, and exploitation are the enemy, no matter who their victims are.

Notes

1   B. Noske, *Beyond boundaries: Humans and animals* (Montreal, New York, London: Black Rose Books, 1997); R. Marchesini, *Post human:Verso nuovi modelli di esistenza* (Torino: Bollati Boringhieri, 2002); R. Marchesini and S. Tonutti, *Manuale di zooantropologia* (Rome: Meltemi, 2007).

2   G. Consolo, *Sulla convenienza ed utilità d'istituire nelle Province Venete una Società contro il maltrattamento degli animali,* Memoria letta nell'Ateneo di Venezia il dì 10 Aprile 1856 (Padova: Pietro Prosperini, 1856), p. 7.

3   1809 Liverpool, 1824 London.

4   1837 Stuttgart, 1842 Munich, 1845 Paris, Gorizia and Budapest, 1846 Linz, 1847 Vienna, 1852 Trieste, and so on.

5   1865 New York.

6   The Society of Munich, for example, inspired many animal lovers and philanthropists all over the Austro-Hungarian Empire, and similar Societies were founded as a consequence. The SPCA in Trieste followed the example of Vienna. When founding the Italian Society - promoted by Giuseppe Garibaldi - Italian animal advocates appealed to the Society of Paris for support and sympathy.

7   R. D. Ryder, *Animal welfare and the environment* (London: Duckworth, 1992); R. Preece and L. Chamberlain, *Animal welfare and human values* (Ontario: Wilfrid Laurier University Press, 1993).

8   D. Harwood claims that 'between 1700 and 1800, the point of view on man's rela-

tion to other living creatures changed more completely than in all the centuries since the death of Christ' (*Love for animals and how it developed in Great Britain*, ed. R. Preece and D. Fraser [Lampeter: The Edwin Mellen Press, 2002], p. 144). At the end of the eighteenth century, in literature and poetry, but also in philosophy, a 'revolution of the heart' took place, which gave rise to a new 'sensibility' that encompassed the plight of animals within its sphere of moral concern, compassion, and empathy. In 1711, *The Characteristics* by Shaftesbury was published, subsequently becoming one of the key texts of the time and one which exerted great influence over the culture and moral vision of nineteenth-century society. It helped give compassion for animals the dignity of philosophical argument; Shaftesbury claimed that since humanity is naturally orientated towards goodness, cruelty is completely wrong, and must be renounced even when it concerns lower creatures.

9 B. Harrison, 'Animals and the state in nineteenth-century England', *The English Historical Review* 88, 349 (1973), p. 788.

10 C. Li, 'The animal cause and its greater traditions', *History and Policy* (2004), http://www.historyandpolicy.org/archived.html.

11 Cruel behaviour was commonly associated with ignorance and the lower classes specifically, and reforms were thus targeted at 'civilizing' and educating this section of society. It was only later that philanthropists extended their criticism to the cruel activities and traditions of the upper classes.

12 Società triestina contro il maltrattamento degli animali, *Pensieri zoologici, apologhi e racconti pei fanciulli, ed atti della Società*, 5th year (Trieste: Lloyd Austriaco, 1857), p. 81.

13 *Ibid.*, pp. 7–8.

14 As an example of this attitude, we should mention the work of William Wilberforce and Thomas Fowell Buxton. Social reformers and leading opponents of the slave trade in the UK, they were also supporters of the animal protection movement and took part in the foundation of the SPCA in London in 1824.

15 P. Singer, *The expanding circle: Ethics and sociobiology* (Oxford: Clarendon Press, 1981).

16 In this context our aim is to understand animal advocates' self-perception as members of a movement, their interpretation of history, their construction of their own identity with reference to ideologies, traditions and social movements from the past; we will not focus on the pertinence of these associations and processes from an historical point of view.

17 S. Tonutti, *Diritti animali: Storia e antropologia di un movimento* (Udine: Forum, 2007).

18 Preece and Chamberlain, *Animal welfare*, p. 35; C. D. Niven, *History of the humane movement* (London: Johnson, 1967); W. J. Shultz, *The humane movement in the United States, 1910–1922* (New York: Columbia University Press, 1924); S. Pearson, '*The arm of the law*': *Protecting animals and children in Gilded Age America*, draft, Northwestern University Department of History (see http://www.abf-sociolegal.org/armofthelawseminar.pdf).

19 Again, the existence of international personal relations between animal advocates and representatives is also shown in this case: while in London, Bergh came to know John Colam, Secretary of the RSPCA, who gave him suggestions for the organization of a Society in the USA.

20 This initiative inspired Colam of the RSPCA in London to become involved in the

promotion of a similar organization, the NSPCC, which was initially hosted by the RSPCA at its own headquarters.

21 Preece and Chamberlain, *Animal welfare.*

22 Cited in Pearson, *The arm of the law*, p. 5.

23 G. M. Malvezzi, *Sui maltrattamenti delle bestie* (Venice: Cecchini, 1851), pp. 13–14.

24 J. J. Zagler, *Sui maltrattamenti delle bestie e sui doveri che abbiamo verso di loro*, trans. and ed. Giacinto Silvestri (Milan: Silvestri, 1845), pp. 38–39. Very often cruelty was described as a relic of barbarism, an enemy of civilization and religious conduct by philanthropists who opposed cruelty in its various forms.

25 D. L. Caglioti, *Associazionismo e sociabilità d'élite a Napoli nel XIX secolo* (Naples: Liguori, 1996), p. 5. There were even striking differences between associations from different European countries, mostly due to the political, economic, and social context in which they were grounded. In many Italian states, for example, before 1848 the freedom of speech, association, and publishing was under direct government control, and following the riots of 1848, this control was exerted by the police. The situation changed with the unification of Italy. The number of associations progressively increased, the 'spirit' of voluntary association spread, creating a mass phenomenon. A number of these associations were aimed at the prevention of cruelty to animals (Caglioti, *Associazionismo*, p. 70).

26 L. Bonafede Muscolino, 'La Società per la protezione e l'assistenza dell'infanzia abbandonata di Palermo e l'opera di Joseph Isaac Whitaker', in C. D'Aleo and S. Girgenti (eds), *I Whitaker e il capitale inglese tra l'Ottocento e il Novecento in Sicilia* (Trapani, Libera Università del Mediterraneo, 1992), p. 59.

27 Società Siciliana Umanitaria-Educativa e per la Protezione degli Animali 1898, *Resoconto 1897* (Palermo: Stabilimento Tipografico Virzì, 1898). I would like to thank Mr Mirmina of the Whitaker Foundation in Palermo for sending me the First Report of the Society, dated 1898, and Mr Urso from the SPCA of Trieste for the documents regarding the early history of the local society.

28 Quoted in L. Bratuž, 'Valentin Stanig (Stani): Cultura e impegno sociale di un sacerdote nel Goriziano', in S. Cavazza and M. Gaddi (eds), *Figure e problemi dell'Ottocento Goriziano* (Gorizia: Istituto di storia sociale e religiosa, 1998), p. 38.

29 T. Peterlin-Neumaier, 'Valentin Stanig e la Società Goriziana contro il maltrattamento degli animali (1845–1847)', in J. Vetrih (ed.), *L'arcidiocesi di Gorizia dall'istituzione alla fine dell'Impero Asburgico (1751–1918)* (Udine: Forum, 2001), p. 496.

30 Bratuž, 'Valentin Stanig'.

31 The Munich Society was founded by the jurist and Court Counsellor Perner, who carried out a correspondence, in four languages, with other animal advocates from different regions of the Empire and other nations, such as England, France, Italy, and Russia (Peterlin-Neumaier, 'Valentin Stanig', p. 495).

32 Tonutti, *Diritti animali.*

CHAPTER 7

Examining Children's Exposure to Violence in the Context of Animal Abuse

FRANK R. ASCIONE

A substantial research literature now exists examining the potentially delete-rious mental health correlates of children's exposure to intimate partner violence.[1] As noted by Moffitt and Caspi, 'demographic statistics suggest that young children and partner violence are concentrated together in the same segment of the population, with the result that many children witness adults' partner violence'.[2] It is now also evident that in homes with companion animals or pets, animal abuse may occur in the context of intimate partner violence (IPV).[3] This paper explores recent research addressing the following risk factors related to mental health variables: exposure to IPV, exposure to animal abuse, perpetrating animal abuse, and children's emotional responses to expo-sure to animal abuse.

The framework for this review reflects the diverse samples of children and adults involved in such research: normative samples of young people, college-attending adults, incarcerated adults, victims of child maltreatment, victims of and those exposed to IPV, and young people with psychiatric disorders (specif-ically, Conduct Disorder[4]). Although animal abuse that occurs outside of the home may be considered a form of community violence, I am not aware of any research on exposure to community violence that has included measures of animal abuse.

Setting the context for what follows, I note a recent report on a large Northeast American city examining 1,517 substantiated domestic violence incidents, with police involvement, over a one-year period.[5] In 43 per cent of these incidents, children were present. Of these children, 81 per cent experi-enced 'sensory exposure' to IPV: they heard the IPV incident, saw it, or were injured in some way during the incident. Most of these children (60 per cent) were less than six years of age. Another study examined children's behav-ioural responses to IPV exposure.[6] Even one-year-old infants may display symptoms of trauma associated with exposure to severe IPV.[7] Reflecting the concerns raised by such findings, some physicians, social workers, and psychologists have recommended screening for IPV in paediatric settings,[8] screening that includes questions about pet abuse. The links among child maltreatment, IPV, and exposure to animal abuse have also been noted.[9] What research tells us about these links is the focus of the remainder of this paper.

Definition and Assessment

As a starting point, I define animal abuse as non-accidental, socially unacceptable behaviour that results in harm to and/or the death of a non-human animal.[10] The age of onset, frequency, and severity of such abuse may vary – as may the species of animal abused. Harm may involve physical, sexual, and emotional components. In my first review of the topic of animal abuse, I could only guess about the potential effects of witnessing animal abuse: 'One may speculate that witnessing marital aggression may be a form of observational learning through which children may learn violent problem-'solving' behaviours. If companion animals are present in such situations and are also targets of parental aggression, children may imitate parents' behaviour'.[11] When colleagues and I developed the first comprehensive assessment of animal abuse issues in childhood and adolescence,[12] we included items related to both perpetrating and witnessing animal abuse. However, just as measures of exposure to IPV vary from study to study, there currently is no standard assessment for measuring young people's exposure to or perpetration of animal abuse. Addressing these measurement issues is beyond the scope of this paper. At the conclusion of this paper, I will offer methodological and conceptual recommendations related to future research on this topic.

Normative Samples

Exposure to animal abuse appears to be a common childhood experience. Baldry[13] surveyed 1,356 nine- to seventeen-year-olds in Rome, Italy about their animal-related experiences and home environments. Exposure to animal abuse perpetrated by peers was reported by 63.7 per cent of respondents and exposure to non-parental adult animal abuse by 60.9 per cent. Exposure to mothers (5.1 per cent) and fathers (9.0 per cent) harming animals was also reported. Children's perpetration of animal abuse was related to their exposure to IPV and exposure to animal abuse. In a similar study of five hundred and thirty-two nine- to twelve-year-old Roman school children,[14] 70.1 per cent of boys and 60.3 per cent of girls reported exposure to animal abuse perpetrated by others. Children who had witnessed parental IPV (broadly defined to include verbal and emotional, as well as physical abuse) or who had witnessed animal abuse were approximately three times more likely to have abused animals themselves than non-exposed children.

Pagani, Robustelli, and Ascione[15] studied eight hundred Roman children who were between nine and eighteen years of age. Witnessing some form of animal abuse was reported by 65 per cent of the respondents. More girls (seventy-eight per cent) than boys (51 per cent) reported feeling 'very sorry' at the time animal abuse had been witnessed. This emotional reaction to witnessing animal abuse persisted for many children to the time of the study's assessment: continuing to feel 'very sorry' was reported by 65 per cent of girls and 36 per cent of boys.

Studying an Australian sample of two hundred and eighty-one adolescents between twelve and eighteen years of age, Thompson and Gullone measured animal abuse the adolescents perpetrated and/or witnessed.[16] Witnessing animal abuse at least once was reported by 77.5 per cent of the sample. Perpetrators included strangers (58.7 per cent), friends (33.8 per cent), parents (10 per cent), siblings (17.1 per cent), and other relatives (14.6 per cent). Animal abuse perpetration scores were higher for adolescents who had witnessed animal abuse and were higher if animal abuse had been witnessed 'frequently' as distinct from witnessed 'a few times'. Witnessing a parent, sibling, friend, or relative perpetrate animal abuse was associated with higher perpetration scores (witnessing a stranger as perpetrator was associated with lower animal abuse perpetration scores).

Henry asked one hundred and sixty-nine college students about exposure to and perpetration of animal abuse as well as self-reported delinquency (more common for men) and general attitudes toward the treatment of animals (more humane for women).[17] Animal abuse was witnessed at least once by 50.9 per cent of the participants (64.9 per cent of men and 39.1 per cent of women) and more than once by 37.3 per cent of the sample (54.5 per cent of men and 22.8 per cent of women). Perpetration of animal abuse at least once was reported by 35.1 per cent of men and 3.3 per cent of women; more frequent perpetration was reported by 24.7 per cent of men and 2.2 per cent of women. Perpetration of animal abuse was significantly higher (25.6 per cent) for participants who had witnessed animal abuse than for those who had not (9.6 per cent). Witnessing animal abuse before thirteen years of age was associated with higher perpetration rates (32 per cent) than witnessing occurring at thirteen years of age or later (11.5 per cent). Past year self-reported delinquency was higher for those who witnessed animal abuse. Attitudes toward animals were less humane for men who witnessed animal abuse but more humane for women who had witnessed animal abuse; this finding may be related to the sex difference in children's emotional response to animal abuse reported by Pagani, Robustelli, and Ascione.

In a similar study with a sample of two hundred and six college students, Henry found that 62.1 per cent of men and 37.9 per cent of women reported witnessing animal abuse.[18] Perpetrating animal abuse was again associated with exposure to animal abuse (and age of exposure), specifically for men.

Perpetration of animal abuse was reported by 39 per cent of men exposed to animal abuse before thirteen years of age and 15 per cent of men exposed at thirteen years of age or later. These sex differences as well as the apparent significance of the developmental timing of exposure to animal abuse warrant further study. Despite the differing assessments and methodologies in these studies, it is clear that exposure to animal abuse is a significant and relatively common developmental phenomenon.

Incarcerated Men

Early research on the animal abuse issue often focused on samples of male and female prison inmates. More recently, Merz-Perez and Heide[19] interviewed fifty violent and fifty non-violent male criminals at a maximum-security prison in Florida about their animal-related experiences. Although no difference was found between the two groups in exposure to animal abuse (seventy-five acts were reported by the violent men and sixty-seven by the non-violent men), non-violent criminals were more likely to express remorse about the animal abuse they had observed.

Hensley and Tallichet surveyed two hundred and sixty-one men incarcerated in two medium-security and one maximum-security prison in the southern part of the United States.[20] Although the authors did not report frequencies or percentages for responses to questions about abusing or witnessing the abuse of animals, they noted that witnessing animal abuse was associated ($r = .30$) with the frequency of perpetrating animal abuse. The younger the age at which witnessing occurred, the younger the age at which the first perpetration of animal abuse occurred ($r = .49$). The significance of the age at which animal abuse was first witnessed reported with this sample of incarcerated men and its relation to perpetrating animal abuse reinforces the findings of Henry, noted earlier.

Exposure to IPV and Other Stressors

A recent case-control study of four hundred and twenty-seven women who were victims of IPV and four hundred and eighteen who were not victims found that partners' threats to and/or actual abuse of pets yielded an adjusted odds ratio of 7.59 in predicting victim/non-victim status.[21] Despite a failure to control for the presence of pets in homes, this study found that victims of IPV were nearly eight times more likely to report that their partner had threatened and/or abused pets than women who were not victims of IPV. Similar results have been reported in a number of studies reviewed by Ascione.[22]

Becker, Stuewig, Herrera, and McCloskey studied, over a ten-year period, children (six to twelve years of age) of one hundred and ninety-one women who were victims of IPV and a comparison group of one hundred and seventy-two women who were not IPV victims.[23] Children from violent homes were more than twice as likely to be reported as cruel to animals (assessed via maternal reports or child self reports) than children from non-violent homes (11.4 per cent vs. 5.3 per cent). Children's fire setting was also higher if women's partners had abused pets (16.3 per cent) than if they had not abused pets (7.7 per cent).

Boys in residential treatment (eight to seventeen years of age at admission) for Conduct Disorder were divided into two groups in a study by Duncan, Thomas, and Miller.[24] One group of fifty boys had documented animal abuse perpetration in their histories and the other group of fifty did not. The group with documented animal abuse had higher rates of physical and/or sexual abuse victimization as well as exposure to domestic violence. In a recent report from Japan with a small sample of abused children residing in an institution, approximately 40 per cent reported exposure to animal abuse and 18.2 per cent admitted to perpetrating animal abuse.[25]

Ascione, Friedrich, Heath, and Hayashi reported on a sample of five hundred and forty children with no known history of abuse (normative), four hundred and eighty-one children who were victims of sexual abuse, and four hundred and twelve children who were in outpatient psychiatric care but did not have a history of sexual abuse victimization.[26] The children were between six and twelve years of age. The authors also noted the presence of parental physical fighting (a proxy for exposure to IPV) and whether children had been victims of physical abuse. Parental physical fighting was reported for 5.9 per cent of the normative group, 35.7 per cent of the sexually abused group, and 18.5 per cent of the psychiatric group. Reports of cruelty to animals for these three groups were 3.1 per cent, 17.9 per cent, and 15.6 per cent, respectively. Even higher rates of perpetrating animal abuse were reported for other subgroups: cruelty to animals was reported for 36.8 per cent of boys and 29.4 per cent of girls who were sexually abused, physically abused, *and* from homes with parental physical fighting. These results suggest than an accumulation of adverse childhood experiences may be related to children's perpetration of animal abuse.

Currie studied women who had children between five and seventeen years of age.[27] Forty-seven women were victims of IPV and forty-five were not. More children from homes with IPV were reported to be cruel to animals than children from homes without IPV (seventeen vs. seven per cent; odds ratio = 2.95). It should be noted that there was no assessment, in this study, of the presence of pets in the homes of participants. Thus, the reported percentages may be underestimates.

Ascione *et al.* reported on one hundred and one women residing at five different Utah shelters for IPV victims.[28] Thirty-nine of these women granted permission for their accompanying children to be interviewed. Actual harm or killing of pets by partners was reported by 54 per cent of these women (pet abuse was reported by 5 per cent of a comparison group of one hundred and nineteen women who were not victims of IPV). For IPV victims' children, 66.7

per cent reported that they had seen or heard one of their pets hurt. In most cases, the perpetrator was either a parent figure (46.4 per cent) or a male sibling (7.1 per cent). Being 'very upset' or 'sort of upset' was reported by 92.6 per cent of children who had been exposed to pet abuse. Fifty-one per cent of children reported that they had tried to protect their pet from being hurt. Clearly, these children were concerned about the welfare of their pets. However, if concern turns into active intervention, children's welfare may be endangered. Programmes designed to shelter the pets of IPV victims,[29] and the inclusion of pets in orders of protection,[30] might reduce such dangers.

In Ascione's review, five other studies assessed children's exposure to animal abuse.[31] The percentage so exposed ranged from 29 per cent to 75.5 per cent. Allen, Gallagher, and Jones reported on a small sample of women who were IPV victims in Ireland.[32] 52.4 per cent reported their partners had abused pets. According to maternal reports, 50 per cent of children had witnessed threats to family pets and 41.2 per cent witnessed actual abuse of pets.

The issue of pet abuse in the context of IPV has now moved beyond being the concern primarily of animal welfare professionals and is emerging as a mainstream issue in research on domestic violence. Strauchler *et al.* examined items from sixteen assessment instruments used to measure IPV and found that while 21.2 per cent of items addressed physical violence, 0.06 per cent of items tapped animal abuse experiences.[33] These authors noted that physical violence is, of course, a critical element of IPV but that insufficient attention has been given to abusive partners' humiliation, manipulation, and control tactics. They recommend use of the Artemis Intake Questionnaire, an assessment instrument that includes two items on animal abuse: my partner 'threatened to abuse my pets'; my partner 'abused my pets'. In a factor analysis of the responses of four hundred and eighty-five IPV victims to this questionnaire, the pet abuse factor accounted for 3.94 per cent of the variance (a child abuse factor accounted for 3.90 per cent of the variance).

In a similar study, Simmons and Lehmann interviewed 1,283 pet-owning women seeking shelter at domestic violence refuges in Texas.[34] Twenty-five per cent of women reported that their partner had engaged in verbal or physical abuse of their pets. For the entire sample, 9 per cent of women reported that their children had watched animals abused in their homes (since the percentage of women who had children was not reported, the 9 per cent figure is likely an underestimate of the prevalence of children's exposure to pet abuse). In cases where any pet abuse had occurred, women were more likely to report that their partner engaged in sexual violence, marital rape, emotional violence, and stalking than in cases where pet abuse was absent. The authors' own assessment measure of IPV and controlling behaviours includes ten sub-scales (e.g., isolation, blaming, and economic abuse). Women who reported any pet abuse (as distinct from no pet abuse) or who reported that one of their pets had been killed by their partner (as distinct from cases where pets had not been killed) had significantly higher victimization scores on each of the ten sub-scales.

The studies cited in this paper clearly illustrate the maturation of our understanding about how animal abuse may be implicated in interpersonal violence and how exposure to and perpetration of IPV and animal abuse may be intricately related. What follows are recommendations that, I hope, will further enhance our understanding of these phenomena.

- Perpetration of animal abuse has most often been assessed via single items that may appear on checklists of children's problem behaviours[35] or single items peculiar to a specific research study ('were you ever mean or cruel to animals . . . ?'[36]). A number of newly developed assessments with multiple items can now be recommended. These include the Dadds *et al.* (2004) assessment of animal abuse perpetration that has both parent-report and child self-report forms,[37] Henry and Sanders' animal-related assessment for adults,[38] and Ascione *et al.'s* measures of animal abuse in the context of IPV that can be used with adult victims and with their children.[39]
- Just as measures of children's exposure to IPV are becoming more detailed (see, for example, Fantuzzo and Fusco's measure of 'sensory exposure'[40]), so too must we be more specific about measuring the dimensions of children's exposure to animal abuse (e.g., type of animal abused, quality of the child's relations with and attachment to the animal abused, age at first exposure, type of exposure, frequency and chronicity of exposure, identity of the perpetrator, children's affective responses to exposure). This will require careful consideration of ethical issues in directly querying children about their experiences of violence.[41]
- Studies of animal abuse and IPV have most often relied on samples of victims at shelters. Comparative research is needed that includes IPV victims who remain in the community as well as women who experience marital distress but who are not victims of IPV. I am also unaware of any research that has examined animal abuse in the context of dating or courtship violence.
- A recent study examined batterers' views of the effects of their children's exposure to IPV.[42] Similar research is warranted in cases where batterers have threatened or abused family pets. Pet abuse may also be related to emerging batterer typologies.
- A survey of psychologists who practice as therapists indicated that the overwhelming majority (87 per cent) considered animal abuse to be a mental health issue.[43] Animals may also facilitate the healing process.[44] It is time for critical and methodologically-rigorous exploration of the therapeutic value of animals in addressing the needs of children who are exposed to violence, children who are themselves victims of violence, and children who perpetrate violence.[45]

Notes

1 L. Pawelko and C. Koverola, 'Children in the crossfire: Impact of exposure to intimate partner violence', in K. Kendall-Tackett and Sarah Giacomoni (eds), *Intimate Partner Violence* (Kingston, NY: Civic Research Institute, 2006).

2 T. E. Moffitt and A. Caspi, 'Preventing the inter-generational continuity of antisocial behavior: Implications of partner violence' in D. P. Farrington and J. W. Coid (eds), *Early prevention of adult antisocial behavior* (Cambridge: Cambridge University Press, 2003), p. 111.

3 F. R. Ascione, 'Emerging research on animal abuse as a risk factor for intimate partner violence', in K. Kendall-Tackett and S. M. Giacomoni (eds), *Intimate partner violence* (Kingston, NY: Civic Research Institute, Inc., 2007), pp. 3–17.

4 American Psychiatric Association, *Diagnostic and statistical manual of mental disorders: DSM-IV-TR*. 4th edn (Washington, DC: American Psychiatric Association, 2000).

5 J. Fantuzzo and R. Fusco, 'Children's direct sensory exposure to substantiated domestic violence crimes', *Violence and Victims* 22 (2007): 158–171.

6 J. L. Edleson, L. F. Mbilinyi, S. K. Beeman, and A. K. Hagemeister, 'How children are involved in adult domestic violence: Results from a four-city telephone survey', *Journal of Interpersonal Violence* 18 (2003): 18–32.

7 G. A. Bogat, E. DeJonghe, A. A. Levendosky, W. S. Davidson, and A. von Eye, 'Trauma symptoms among infants exposed to intimate partner violence', *Child Abuse and Neglect* 30 (2006): 109–125.

8 R. M. Siegel, T. D. Hill, V. A. Henderson, H. M. Ernst, and B. W. Boat, 'Screening for domestic violence in the community pediatric setting', *Pediatrics* 104 (1999): 874–877; R. M. Siegel, E. C. Joseph, S. A. Routh, S. G. Mendel, E. Jones, R. B. Ramesh, and T. D. Hill, 'Screening for domestic violence in the pediatric office: A multipractice experience', *Clinical Pediatrics* 42 (2003): 599–602.

9 F. Finlay and S. Lenton, 'Cross-reporting of animal abuse', *Veterinary Record* 161 (2007): 34–35; M. Greenfields, 'Letters to the editors', *Child Abuse Review* 16 (2007): 74–76.

10 F. R. Ascione, *Research on the LINK® between animal abuse and family violence*, Keynote address at the meeting of the American Humane Association, Alexandria, VA, 28 September 2007.

11 F. R. Ascione, 'Children who are cruel to animals: A review of research and implications for developmental psychopathology', *Anthrozoös* 6, 4 (1993), p. 237.

12 F. R. Ascione, T. M. Thompson, and T. Black, 'Childhood cruelty to animals: Assessing cruelty dimensions and motivations', *Anthrozoös* 10, 4 (1997): 170–177.

13 A. C. Baldry, 'Animal abuse and exposure to interparental violence in Italian Youth', *Journal of Interpersonal Violence* 18 (2003): 258–281.

14 A. C. Baldry, 'Animal abuse among preadolescents directly and indirectly victimized at school and at home', *Criminal Behaviour and Mental Health* 15 (2005): 97–110.

15 C. Pagani, F. Robustelli, and F. R. Ascione, 'Italian youths' attitudes toward and concern for animals', *Anthrozoös* 20, 3 (2007), 275–293.

16 K. L. Thompson and E. Gullone, 'An investigation into the association between the witnessing of animal abuse and adolescents' behavior toward animals', *Society & Animals* 14 (2006): 221–243.

17 B. C. Henry, 'Exposure to animal abuse and group context: Two factors affecting participation in animal abuse', *Anthrozoös* 17 (2004): 290–305.

18 B. C. Henry, 'The relationship between animal cruelty, delinquency, and attitudes toward the treatment of animals', *Society & Animals* 12 (2004): 185–207.

19 L. Merz-Perez and K. M. Heide, *Animal cruelty: Pathway to violence against people* (Walnut Creek, CA: AltaMira Press, 2004).

20 C. Hensley and S. E. Tallichet, 'Learning to be cruel?: Exploring the onset and frequency of animal cruelty', *International Journal of Offender Therapy and Comparative Criminology* 49 (2005): 37–47.

21 B. J. Walton-Moss, J. Manganello, V. Frye, and J. C. Campbell, 'Risk factors for intimate partner violence and associated injury among urban women', *Journal of Community Health* 30 (2005): 377–389.

22 Ascione, 'Emerging research'.

23 K. D. Becker, J. Stuewig, V. M. Herrera, and L. A. McCloskey, 'A study of firesetting and animal cruelty in children: Family influences and adolescent outcomes', *Journal of the American Academy of Child and Adolescent Psychiatry* 43 (2004): 905–912.

24 A. Duncan, J. C. Thomas, and C. Miller, 'Significance of family risk factors in development of childhood animal cruelty in adolescent boys with conduct problems', *Journal of Family Violence* 20 (2005): 235–239.

25 S. Yamazaki, 'A pilot study on the relationship between child abuse and animal abuse', Presentation at the triennial meeting of the International Association of Human–Animal Interaction Organizations, Tokyo, Japan, 8 October 2007.

26 F. R. Ascione, W. N. Friedrich, J. Heath, and K. Hayashi, 'Cruelty to animals in normative, sexually abused, and outpatient psychiatric samples of 6- to 12-year-old children: Relations to maltreatment and exposure to domestic violence', *Anthrozoös* 16, 3 (2003), 194–212.

27 C. L. Currie, 'Animal cruelty by children exposed to domestic violence', *Child Abuse and Neglect* 30 (2006): 425–435.

28 Ascione *et al.*, 'Battered pets'.

29 Ascione, F. R., *Safe havens for pets: Guidelines for programs sheltering pets for women who are battered* (Logan, UT: http://www.vachss.com/guest_dispatches/safe_havens.html).

30 J. Zorza, 'Maine's encouraging law protecting animals in domestic violence situations', *Domestic Violence Report* 11 (2006): pp. 65, 78.

31 Ascione, 'Emerging research'.

32 M. Allen, B. Gallagher, and B. Jones, 'Domestic violence and the abuse of pets: Researching the link and its implications in Ireland', *Practice* 18 (2006): 167–181.

33 O. Strauchler, K. McCloskey, K. Malloy, M. Sitaker, N. Grigsby, and P. Gillig, 'Humiliation, manipulation, and control: Evidence of centrality in domestic violence against an adult partner', *Journal of Family Violence* 19 (2004): 339–354.

34 C. A. Simmons and P. Lehmann, 'Exploring the link between pet abuse and controlling behaviors in violent relationships', *Journal of Interpersonal Violence* 22 (2007): 1211–1222.

35 See Ascione *et al.*, 'Cruelty to animals'; Currie, 'Animal cruelty'.

36 Suzanne R. Goodney Lea, *Delinquency and animal cruelty* (New York: LFB Scholarly Publishing, 2007).

37 M. R. Dadds, C. Whiting, P. Bunn, J. A. Fraser, J. H. Charlson, and A. Pirola-Merlo, 'Measurement of cruelty in children: The Cruelty to Animals Inventory', *Journal of Abnormal Child Psychology* 32 (2004), 321–334.

38 B. C. Henry and C. E. Sanders, 'Bullying and animal abuse: Is there a connection?' *Society & Animals* 15 (2007): 107–126.

39 Ascione *et al.*, 'Cruelty to animals'.

40 Fantuzzo and Fusco, 'Children's direct sensory exposure'.

41 J. Carroll-Lind, J. W. Chapman, J. Gregory, and G. Maxwell, 'The key to gate-keepers: Passive consent and other ethical issues surrounding the rights of children to speak on issues that concern them', *Child Abuse and Neglect* 30 (2006): 979–989; J. Cashmore, 'Ethical issues concerning consent in obtaining children's reports on their experiences of violence', *Child Abuse and Neglect* 30 (2006): 969–977.

42 E. F. Rothman, D. G. Mandel, and J. G. Silverman, 'Abusers' perceptions of the effect of their intimate partner violence on children', *Violence against Women* 13 (2007): 1179–1191.

43 K. D. Schaefer, K. A. Hays, and R. L. Steiner, 'Animal abuse issues in therapy: A survey of therapists' attitudes', *Professional Psychology: Research and Practice* 38 (2007): 530–537.

44 N. Thomas, T. Thomas, and B. Thomas, *Dandelion on my pillow, butcher knife beneath* (Glenwood Springs, CO: Families by Design, 2002).

45 F. R. Ascione, *Children and animals: Exploring the roots of kindness and cruelty* (West Lafayette, IN: Purdue University Press, 2005).

Women–Battering, Pet Abuse, and Human–Animal Relationships

CLIFTON P. FLYNN

In his now classic analysis written three decades ago, sociologist Clifton Bryant took his fellow sociologists to task for failing to acknowledge and investigate what he called the 'zoological connection'. He concluded that article by saying that 'Our behavior, our lives, and our destiny are directed in part by the shadow of the beast'.[1] For many battered women and their children, this is doubly true; that is, there are at least two beasts. Without meaning to disparage non-human animals, the shadow of the first, the human beasts whose violence terrorizes women and other family members (both human and non-human), looms large over their lives, both present and future.

Yet there is often another beast whose shadow is neither dark nor terrifying. It is the non-human beast whose shadow manages somehow to shed light on the lives of battered women and their children. For it is women's close relationships with their animal companions that can shape their reactions to their battering, their pet's abuse, and their views of themselves – in short, 'their behaviour, their lives, and their destiny'. It is to the complex relationships between battered women and these two beasts that I now turn.

Not surprisingly, studies of animal abuse have almost always been anthropocentric; that is, animal abuse was conceptualized either as a sign of psychopathology or studied because of its relation to other forms of violence towards humans.[2] So the abuse of animals was seen as evidence of mental illness, as a predictor of subsequent violence against humans, as a marker of family violence, or as another form of wife (or child) abuse.

Such an approach, in my view, is anthropocentric for two reasons. First, it includes animals only at the periphery of the social interaction, not as central participants. Second, it conceptualizes animals as tools of violence, as objects used in expressing psychiatric illness, as important only because of their connection with us, rather than seeing other animals as individuals whose lives and victimization are worthy of scholarly attention and moral consideration in their own right, and who are legitimate partners in relationships with battered women. This perspective is harmful to the women as well as the animals, as it tends to devalue their non-human relationships, which may be the most meaningful and valuable ones in their lives.

The goal of this chapter is to bring the companion animals of battered women to the centre of the analysis, examining the connections between women's and animals' victimization, and seeing non-human animals as individuals (as 'persons'), and as relationship partners. Theoretically, this requires what I am calling a feminist-interactionist perspective – a combination of symbolic interactionism with feminist theory.[3] Practically, this necessitates policies, laws, and training that value animals as individuals and recognize the importance of their relationships with battered women.

Pet Abuse and Battered Women

There have literally been only a handful of studies examining the relationship between animal abuse and woman-battering.[4] The first, published in 1998, and the most recent, which came out in 2007, were both conducted by Frank Ascione. Ascione has been a leader in research on animal abuse, its causes and its connections with other forms of human violence. What have we learned from these studies?

First, a connection between pet abuse and woman-battering has been empirically established. This should not be surprising, given a long-standing empirical base in the family violence literature demonstrating the co-existence of multiple forms of violence in families. Among battered women with pets, between approximately one-half and three-fourths report that their companion animals have been threatened or actually harmed by their intimate partners. Thus a significant number of violent relationships also include violence against a non-human member of the household. Most studies have focused only on samples of battered women from shelters with no comparison group. However, Ascione *et al.* also included a comparison group of non-shelter women from the community. They found that battered women were eleven times more likely than the community sample to report that their pets had also been abused – 54 per cent versus 5 per cent.

Pets were important sources of emotional support for the women in dealing with their abuse. This was particularly true for women whose pets had been abused, as well as for women without children. One could reasonably argue that male batterers may be targeting pets precisely because their partners are strongly attached to them. And for women without children, companion animals may take on an even greater meaning as surrogate children, as family members, which implies that the abuse they suffer is all the more hurtful to the woman. Battered women's relationships with their companion animals may be especially important, given the isolation and low-self-esteem that is known frequently to accompany abuse. Pets may be the only individuals (besides their children) who cannot only be valuable relationship partners, but also make the women feel worthy.

These two factors – pet abuse and the absence of human children – could help explain why women are slow to leave abusive relationships. Studies show that approximately 20 per cent of the women delayed leaving due to their concern about the safety of their companion animals. Putting off leaving her batterer was even more likely if he had also abused her pet.[5] And women with no children were more likely than women with children to delay seeking shelter.[6]

But coming to the shelter meant leaving the companion animal behind, because few shelters allow women to bring their pets. Depending on the study, in anywhere from 4 to 50 per cent of the cases, the animal was still with the abusive partner or ex-partner. This created much anxiety and concern among the women, who were not only worried about their animals' well-being, but who were now also vulnerable to batterers' attempts to control them by threatening to harm their companion animals. And even if the animal is in better or more trusted care, the women (and their children) are separated from and concerned about their non-human companion.

All of these features – a pet with whom women share a close relationship, who is abused (and sometimes killed), who often cannot be protected and must be left behind – combine to create a powerful form of emotional abuse that includes fear, guilt, and grief.[7] Many battered women have reported that their children had witnessed their companion animals' victimization and, like the women, the children were both angered and terrified. In many ways, the impact of children witnessing the violence toward their animal companions parallels the effects of wife abuse on children. Not only was a loved one, a valued member of the family being harmed, but they were powerless to do anything about it at the time, and often prevented from comforting the animal immediately following the abuse. In general, the abuse contributed to a climate of control, intimidation, and terror for the children, women, and animals.

Animal abuse has clearly been established as another method of wife (and child) abuse. But it is also important to remember that the women and children strongly consider their companion animals as members of the family. Thus, animal abuse should be conceptualized not just as a type of wife or child abuse, but also as a separate form of family violence in itself. Consequently, pets were also victimized when women were abused. When companion animals witnessed the woman being assaulted, they typically played either one of two roles: comforter, providing emotional support to women after a violent episode; or protector, sometimes risking their own physical safety. Either way, witnessing a woman's abuse was often very emotionally upsetting for her animal companion. Women reported several physical manifestations of stress in their pets when the animals witnessed her abuse that were similar to symptoms in humans, including shivering or shaking, cowering, hiding, and urinating.

These examples reveal the multi-dimensional nature of domestic violence involving companion animals. It is important to see that both women and animals are victimized by abuse of the other. A man's violence toward an animal also hurts his partner (and children), just as his violence toward her also hurts the animal.

Feminist Theory

Feminist perspectives, which have been extremely valuable in explaining domestic violence,[8] and violence toward women in general, have also been successfully applied to the analysis of animal abuse and its relation to violence against humans. Adams argues that the abuse of animals is part of a larger dominance and exploitation by males of less powerful others – women, children, and animals.[9] From this perspective, patriarchy has led dominant males to use violence as a means to control other less powerful individuals, including other animals. 'A hierarchy in which men have power over women and humans have power over animals, is actually more appropriately understood as a hierarchy in which men have power over women, (feminized) men and (feminized) animals'.[10]

Studies on pet abuse and woman-battering, both quantitative and qualitative, reveal the central role of gender, power, and control in male violence toward both women and animals.[11] Batterers control, intimidate, and silence their partners by threatening or actually harming and killing their companion animals. Some female victims are unwilling participants in their pets' abuse, coerced by their batterers to witness, or actually engage in, sexual acts with animals. One recent study found that batterers have even threatened pet abuse in order to coerce their female victims into committing illegal behaviour.[12]

Clearly, feminist theoretical perspectives have been invaluable in helping to explain interpersonal violence, including woman-battering and pet abuse. Yet, the argument here is that the picture would be more complete if it included a view of animals that sees them as competent, legitimate partners in intimate relationships with humans – i.e., if feminist theory were combined with symbolic interactionism.

Symbolic Interactionism

Another theory that has been employed in the analysis of animal abuse is symbolic interactionism.[13] From this perspective, through interactions with others, individuals give meaning to their experiences and actively construct reality. To interact symbolically, and to develop a sense of self, actors must be able to role-take – to imagine how others define the situation, including how the actors themselves are perceived by others.

Animals as Individuals and Relationship Partners

Because symbolic interaction, according to Mead, requires the ability to speak, sociologists in general and interactionists in particular have limited their study of close relationships to those existing only between humans. Yet Sanders has recently taken issue with this view,[14] arguing that it excludes an extremely common and important type of close relationship that has all of the central qualities that characterize other human close relationships – i.e., interactions that are frequent, diverse, intense (emotional), and that endure over time.[15] These close relationships are the ones between humans and their companion animals. According to Sanders,

> I maintain that this characterization of close relationships [existing only between human beings] is overly restrictive. It excludes from consideration a class of affiliations that are commonplace, imbued with emotion, and central to the shaping of the identities and selves of those involved. Traditionally, conventional sociologists have ignored or denigrated relationships between people and their companion animals. However, the intense, involving, and routine interactions forming these relations are worthy of serious attention and have the potential of adding significantly to the sociology of intimate exchanges.[16]

Why are humans and companion animals able to establish routine and patterned interactions? That is, how are they able to form close relationships? Increasingly, sociologists such as Sanders, Alger and Alger, and Irvine, have challenged traditional sociological thought that since only humans have language, only humans are capable of symbolic interaction.[17] In opposition to Mead, this new perspective argues that animals are minded, social actors who have selves, can role-take, can create shared meanings with humans (and sometimes other animals) with whom they interact, and thus are also capable of interacting symbolically.[18]

In their work with caretakers of severely disabled family members, Bogdan and Taylor argued that caretakers, in the absence of spoken language, construct a social identity that enables them to see the disabled as minded and as still capable of engaging in interaction.[19] According to Bogdan and Taylor, the four features of this process of attributing 'personhood' to nonverbal, disabled others involve seeing them as: (1) minded, social actors; (2) individuals with unique personalities; (3) reciprocating partners in the relationship; and (4) legitimate relationship partners who are afforded a social place in the family.

Both Sanders, in his study of dog caretakers, and the Algers, in their study of feline caretakers, found that both groups attributed personhood to their companion animals.[20] Both dog and cat owners considered their animals to be thinking individuals who contributed to the relationship, and who were seen as members of the family.

Studies of battered women with pets offer evidence that these women similarly regard their companion animals as 'persons'. Most women think of their pets as family members, as their children. In Flynn's study, two respondents even brought photo albums to the interview that were filled with pictures of their companion animals – much like a parent memorializing the experiences of their human child.[21] They described their animals as intelligent individuals with their own personalities. Many battered women saw their companion animals as being very upset upon witnessing the woman's battering, often trying to protect her during the attack or comfort her afterward. Their pets were capable of expressing emotion and were attuned to the women's emotional states. The women saw these actions as evidence of their pets' mindedness – intentional, reciprocal, and thoughtful behaviour.

Yet it is precisely because the women view their pets as persons – as individuals, as valued relationship partners, as family members – that the abuse of the animal is so terrifying and so effective. As noted earlier, given their social isolation, battered women are likely to have limited opportunities for meaningful human interaction. Similarly, their low self-esteem may also prevent them from maintaining strong relationships with others. So their relationship with their companion animals may be particularly important and valued. When animals are threatened or harmed, it is not merely a prized possession or a sentimental object that may be lost. As Carol Adams recognized, 'What is so anguishing to the human victim about the injury of an animal is that it is a threat or actual destruction of a cherished relationship in which the animal has been seen as an individual'.[22]

Yet batterers, perhaps as well as anyone, understand the power of this relationship, and unfortunately are able to use it to create a climate of terror in the home. 'The degree to which she or the children have an intense respectful relationship with an animal is the extent to which he can harm her by harming the animal'.[23]

Implications

Implications for Theory and Research

If other animals are capable of symbolic interaction, then empirical investigation of their abusive treatment by humans needs to expand to new and challenging levels. What does animal abuse mean to animals? How do animals and their human companions respond to victimization of the other? Animal abuse is no longer relevant merely as an indicator of human psychopathology or an instrument of male power and control over women, but as another form of violence against individuals who can experience terror and pain, and should receive attention for that reason alone. In general, researchers need to expand their notion of personhood, and to broaden their conception of close relationships, following the lead of researchers like Sanders and Leslie Irvine, who makes a compelling argument for companion animal 'selfhood'.[24] As Sanders notes, 'Serious attention to human–animal relationships requires that the anthropocentric "commonsense of science" be replaced with the "ordinary commonsense" of everyday social actors derived from their routine experiences with their animal companions'.[25]

When companion animals are viewed as minded, social actors, as individuals with unique personalities, who are reciprocating and intentional – and not as objects or tools or commodities – then they are more likely to become full participants in close relationships with humans, and less likely to be harmed. And it is important for researchers of domestic violence as well to acknowledge and examine the relationship that battered women have with their companion animals.

Implications for Professionals and Policy

Those who work with battered women must take women's (and their children's) relationships with their companion animals seriously. Shelter workers, for example, need not only to ask women about whether they have pets, but also respect those relationships. Women who have left their batterer to come to a shelter, particularly those without children and whose pets have been abused, do not need the added burden of having their emotional responses (worry, guilt, fear, concern, or even grief) to their companion animals dismissed or taken lightly. Understanding the importance of women's relationships with their pets, particularly since a significant minority delay leaving out of concern for their animals, should lead all shelters to provide services for companion animals. Although few battered women's shelters allow on-site housing of pets, increasing numbers are establishing foster programmes for their clients' pets.[26]

In discussing the implications of battered women's close relationships with their pets for social workers, Strand and Faver stress the importance of assessing the level of attachment that women, and even their children, have with a pet.[27] Higher levels of attachment may affect women's decisions to come to the shelter, and their emotional response to being separated from their companion animals. According to Strand and Faver,

> If battered women indicate that (a) their pets are like children, (b) their pets are family members, (c) their pets got them through a difficult time or a major life transition in the past, (d) they 'rescued' or 'were rescued' by their pet, or (e) they had a significantly difficult time grieving at the loss of a former pet, then it is likely that these women have a strong attachment to their pets.[28]

With regard to legal policy, animals must be seen as legitimate victims of criminal behaviour. This requires more than just taking animal abuse more seriously – although this undoubtedly needs to be done. Beyond this, however, the status of animals in the law must be elevated above that of property. Until companion animals are recognized as 'persons' and not property, as family rather than furniture, their abuse will likely continue with minimal consequences.

Family courts need to value pets and women's relationships with them as they consider issues of divorce, custody, and restraining orders. For example, the abuse of companion animals should be seen as powerful evidence of parental unfitness, and could be used as a valuable tool to help battered women retain the family home and obtain orders of protection for themselves, their children, and their pets. With the limited success that battered women have experienced in the criminal justice system, stricter enforcement of male batterers' abuse of the family pet could be a secret weapon that enables prosecutors more successfully to convict perpetrators who have previously managed to escape responsibility for their violence.

Conclusion

Understanding, responding to, and ultimately ending interconnected forms of violence requires that we understand those interconnections, and the role of patriarchy in perpetuating the use of violence as a means of power and control against less powerful human and non-human others. But it also requires that companion animals be seen by all those involved as individuals, as persons, with whom battered women (and often their children) have established genuine and meaningful relationships. So a feminist-interactionist approach would heed the words of Arluke and Sanders, who argue that, 'Rather than a world separated into subjects (scientists, men, the powerful) and objects (women, animals, "savages"), the image of the world ultimately offered is one composed of subjects-in-interaction, human and non-human actors cooperating and struggling with the historical, political, and cultural forces in which their activities are embedded'.[29] It would also incorporate the wisdom of Carol Adams, who says that, 'Recognizing harm to animals as interconnected to controlling behaviour by violent men is one aspect of recognizing the interrelatedness of all violence in a gender hierarchical world. The challenge now, as it has been for quite some time, is to stop it'.[30]

Let's get to work.

Notes

1   C. D. Bryant, 'The zoological connection: Animal-related human behavior', *Social Forces* 58 (1979), p. 417.
2   A. Arluke, 'Animal abuse as dirty play', *Symbolic Interaction* 25, 4 (2002): 405–430; P. Beirne, 'Rethinking bestiality: Towards a concept of interspecies sexual assault', *Theoretical Criminology* 1, 3 (1997): 317–340; P. Beirne, 'For a nonspeciesist criminology: Animal abuse as an object of study', *Criminology* 37 (1999): 117–147; G. Cazaux, 'Legitimating the entry of "the animals issue" into (critical) Criminology', *Humanity and Society* 22 (1998); D. Solot, 'Untangling the animal abuse web', *Society & Animals* 5 (1997): 257–265.
3   See S. Brennan, 'Animals as disregarded pawns in family violence: Exclusionary practices of feminist based refuge policies', *Electronic Journal of Sociology* (2007).
4   F. R. Ascione, 'Battered women's reports of their partners' and their children's cruelty to animals', *Journal of Emotional Abuse* 1 (1998): 119–133; F. R. Ascione,

C. V. Weber, T. M. Thompson, J. Heath, M. Maruyama, and K. Hayashi, 'Battered women and domestic violence: Animal abuse reported by women experiencing intimate violence and by non-abused women', *Violence Against Women* 13, 4 (2007): 354–373; C. P. Flynn, 'Woman's best friend: Pet abuse and the role of companion animals in the lives of battered women', *Violence Against Women* 6, 2 (2000): 162–177; C. P. Flynn, 'Battered women and their animal companions: Symbolic interaction between human and non-human animals', *Society & Animals* 8, 2 (2000): 99–127; C. A. Faver and E. B. Strand, 'To leave or to stay? Battered women's concern for vulnerable pets', *Journal of Interpersonal Violence* 18, 12 (2003): 1367–1377; M. T. Loring and T. A. Bolden-Hines, 'Pet abuse by batterers as a means of coercing battered women into committing illegal behavior', *Journal of Emotional Abuse* 4 (2004): 27–37.

5 Ascione *et al.*, 'Battered women'; Flynn, 'Woman's best friend'.
6 Ascione *et al.*, 'Battered women'; Faver and Strand, 'To leave or to stay?'
7 Faver and Strand, 'Fear, guilt, and grief'.
8 K. Yllo, 'Through a feminist lens: Gender, power, and violence', in R. Gelles and D. Loseke (eds), *Current controversies on family violence* (Newbury Park, CA: Sage, 1993).
9 C. J. Adams, 'Bringing peace home: A feminist philosophical perspective on the abuse of women, children, and pet animals', *Hypatia* 9 (1994): 62–84; C. J. Adams, 'Woman-battering and harm to animals', in C. J. Adams and J. Donovan (eds), *Animals and women: Feminist theoretical explorations* (Durham, NC: Duke University Press, 1995), pp. 55–84.
10 Adams, 'Woman-battering', p. 80.
11 Ascione, 'Battered woman's reports'; Faver and Strand, 'To leave or to stay?'; Flynn, 'Woman's best friend'; Flynn, 'Battered women'; Loring and Bolden-Hines, 'Pet abuse by batterers'.
12 Loring and Bolden-Hines, 'Pet abuse by batterers'.
13 H. Blumer, *Symbolic interactionism: Perspective and method* (Englewood Cliffs, NJ: Prentice-Hall, 1969); G. H. Mead, *Mind, self, and society* (Chicago: The University of Chicago Press, 1962).
14 C. R. Sanders, 'Actions speak louder than words: Close relationships between human and nonhuman animals', *Symbolic Interaction*, 26, 3 (2003).
15 H. Kelley, E. Berscheid, A. Christensen, J. Harvey, T. Huston, G. Levinger, E. McClintock, L. A. Peplau, and D. Peterson, *Close relationships* (New York: W. H. Freeman, 1983).
16. Sanders, 'Actions speak louder than words', p. 406.
17 C. R. Sanders, 'Understanding dogs: Caretakers' attributions of mindedness in canine–human relationships', *Journal of Contemporary Ethnography* 22 (1993); C. R. Sanders, *Understanding dogs: Living and working with canine companions* (Philadelphia, PA: Temple University Press, 1999); Sanders, 'Actions speak louder than words'; J. M. Alger and S. F. Alger, 'Beyond Mead: Symbolic interaction between humans and felines', *Society & Animals* 5 (1997); J. M. Alger and S. F. Alger, 'Cat culture, human culture: An ethnographic study of a cat shelter', *Society & Animals* 7 (1999); L. Irvine, *If you tame them* (Philadelphia, PA: Temple University Press, 2004).
18 G. H. Mead, *Mind, self, and society*.
19 R. Bogdon, and S. Taylor, 'Relationships with severely disabled people: The social construction of humanness', *Social Problems* 36 (1989).

20 Sanders, 'Understanding dogs'; Alger and Alger, 'Beyond Mead'.
21 Flynn, 'Battered women'.
22 C. J. Adams, 'Woman-battering and harm to animals', p. 59.
23 *Ibid.*, p. 77.
24 Sanders, 'Understanding dogs'; Sanders, *Understanding dogs*; Sanders, 'Actions speak louder than words'; Irvine, *If you tame them.*
25 Sanders, 'Actions speak louder than words', p. 420.
26 Ascione *et al.*, 'Battered women'; L. R. Kogan, S. McConnell, R. Schoenfeld-Tacher, and P. Jansen-Lock, 'Crosstrails: A unique foster program to provide safety for pets of women in safehouses', *Violence Against Women*, 10, 4 (2004): 418–434.
27 E. B. Strand and C. A, Faver, 'Battered women's concern for their pets: A closer look', *Journal of Family Social Work* 9, 4 (2005): 39–58.
28 *Ibid.*, p. 54.
29 A. Arluke and C. R. Sanders, *Regarding animals* (Philadelphia, PA: Temple University Press, 1996), p. 57.
30 C. J. Adams, 'Woman-battering', p. 80.

The Role of Animals in Public Child Welfare Work[1]

CHRISTINA RISLEY-CURTISS

More than 70 per cent of US households with minor children have companion animals (i.e., pets).[1] Thus many of the families that child welfare agencies serve have companion animals. Furthermore, close to one hundred per cent of these human families may consider their animal companions to be family members.[2] Thus, other animals are part of families' ecologies and as family members belong in family-centred practice.

A considerable body of research supports the existence of relationships between humans and other animals that are beneficial as well as harmful to both. These relationships are especially common for children[3] and manifest themselves in both animal abuse as well as the protective effects of bonding with an animal companion or responding to animal-assisted activities (AAA) and therapy (AAT). Nonetheless, while, for instance, many experts now acknowledge the co-occurrence of child maltreatment and animal abuse, child welfare agencies continue to be reluctant to include animals in policy, assessment, and intervention. The purpose of this article is to describe the interrelatedness of humans and other animals in three areas that are critical to child welfare work. Suggestions for integrating animals into child welfare research, policy, training, and practice are made.

Inclusion of Animals in Child Welfare Practice

Ample research on human–animal relationships indicates an interrelatedness between humans and other animals that is critically relevant to good child welfare practice. Recent related research, unfortunately, suggests that integration of the human–animal bond into human service work, such as child welfare, may not necessarily be happening. A study of two hundred and three psychologists found while 94 per cent believed animal abuse to be connected to other human behavioural disturbances, only 14 per cent assessed for such abuse.[4] A study of cross-reporting between child welfare workers and humane society workers in Canada found that a number of child welfare workers thought cross-reporting was unimportant and were resistant to including animal welfare in their assessments. These child welfare workers also under-reported concern for animal well-being.[5] In an unpublished study by Risley-Curtiss,[6] only seven out of two hundred and thirty schools of social work in the US that responded to a survey included much content on the human–animal bond in their courses, and what was offered was most often about AAT. Ascione, a developmental psychologist and one of the foremost experts on the link between animal abuse and other forms of family abuse, asserts that 'developmental psychology and related disciplines have virtually ignored the positive role that companion animals and other animals may play in the lives of children'.[7]

Finally, in a recent US national study of 1,649 social work practitioners, Risley-Curtiss found that 66.2 per cent of the participants do not include questions about other animals in their intake assessments.[8] Even fewer include other animals as part of their interventions in social work practice (23.2 per cent). Approximately 31 per cent do ask if their clients have companion animals, but only 12 per cent ask if anyone in the family has hurt other animals. In regard to training about the human–other animal bond, 95.7 per cent of the 1,621 who responded to the survey question had not had any special training in including other animals in their social work practice. Furthermore, 82.2 per cent of those who did include other animals in assessment and/or treatment said they had received no special training to do so. Almost 63 per cent of respondents said they had no social work course content regarding other animals or did not remember having such content. For those who did have such content, 22.4 per cent said they had information on animal abuse, 25.7 per cent had information on the positive effects of other animals on people, and 12.6 per cent had information on animal-assisted activities/therapy.

Animals in Child Welfare

The interrelatedness between humans and animals plays out in many ways but three are of essential importance for child welfare: (1) if kept as pets, companion animals are usually considered to be family members and are thus an integral part of family systems; (2) animal abuse by children or adults is a very deviant behaviour indicating a need for mental health services as well as potentially being an indicator of victimization, and a marker for other antisocial behaviour; and (3) the protective impact animals can have on the functioning of children and adults means including other animals in child welfare interventions. While each of these areas is discussed in more detail below, note that they are not discrete categories but very much intertwined. For example, in relation to other animal abuse (2), research suggests that it is linked to family violence (1) and also that abused children may be likely to see their companion animals as a source of support (1 and 3).

Other Animals as Family

Leaving consideration of other animals and the roles they play in families out of safety, risk, and ongoing assessment and treatment means potentially leaving out a significant member of the family system. This can compromise the accuracy of those assessments.

Keeping companion animals is a common phenomenon. In the US approximately sixty-nine million households have a companion animal, including 90.5 million cats and 73.9 million dogs.[9] The majority of those with companion animals consider them family members. Risley-Curtiss *et al.*, in two different studies on ethnicity and companion animals, found that 97 per cent[10] and 87 per cent[11] of participants agreed that their pets are members of their families. For example, Patty, one of the participants in the qualitative study on women of colour and companion animals said, 'I like to spoil my dog and I don't treat my dog [like] he's just an animal. I treat him like part of our family. He's my baby, you know . . . I treat him as a part of me'. Another participant, Roz, explained the family nature of the relationship in terms of her pet's devotion to people: 'She was . . . very much so a member of the family, and it was so wonderful. Like when you come home from being tired and so stressed out from work and there would be Sparkles greeting you at the door, smiling and so happy to see you'.[12]

The Pew Research Center found that 85 per cent of those with dogs and 78 per cent of those with cats felt the same way.[13] When asked how close participants felt to their dog, cat, mother, and father, they ranked themselves as being closest to their dogs first, followed by mom, cats, and then dad. Participants with dogs, in an earlier study by Barker and Barker, also reported feeling closer to their dogs than to any human family member.[14] Johnson and Meadows examined twenty-four community-dwelling Latina/os over age fifty with regard to their relationships with their companion animals (dogs).[15] The majority of participants viewed their dogs as equals (54 per cent) and as members of their family (79 per cent). Sixty-seven per cent stated their dog was the reason they got up in the morning and 62 per cent stated their dog comforts them. The authors concluded that dog companions are considered, among these elderly Latina/os, to be valued members of their families.

Human family members may talk to, and confide in, their animal family members, seeing them as a source of comfort and constancy: 'When I was by myself, he (her cat) always knew when to come and sit on my lap – just sit there while I was watching TV . . . When I was [feeling sad], he was always there too'.[16] Another survey found that 52 per cent of those with companion animals felt their pets listened to them better than their spouse or significant other.[17] 'We often overlook the fact that pets are important not only for children but for every member of the family'.[18]

The consideration of other animals as family members has also been evidenced in dangerous environments such as during natural disasters or family violence. As previously documented by Lockwood,[19] and more recently witnessed through Hurricane Katrina, many humans will risk their lives (some died) and refuse to evacuate unless they can be assured of their other animals' safety. In a different yet similar vein, battered women have delayed entering domestic violence shelters due to concern for their other animals.[20] Allen, Gallagher and Jones, in their study of battered women, found in the women's own words that, 'Fear for my pets caused me to stay for years', and 'I delayed leaving for months, until I found a safe home for my dog'.[21] They also found that consideration of their children's attachment to their pets influenced their staying or returning: 'The children wouldn't leave, one child would always insist on staying behind. I felt pressure to stay to keep my son happy'.[22]

Considering other animals as family members means that companion animals are one of the sub-systems within the complex family system and as such both influence, and are influenced by, every other family system.[23] As seen, the presence of companion animals can influence staying or not staying in dangerous situations. In addition, companion animals can become tools that abusers use to gain power and control over their other family members. As a protective factor, Allen, Blascovich, and Mendes found that the presence of companion animals often lowered reactivity to stressful situations more than the presence of spouses.[24] They concluded that animals clearly act as social supports and that social support can cross species. In addition, Albert and Anderson found that women talked about how their companion animals raised family morale.[25] Cain found in her study of the characteristics of companion animals relationships in sixty families that 81 per cent felt their companion animals were sensitive to the moods of other family members and some related that when their family was stressed or in conflict that their companion animal manifested physical symptoms such as loss of appetite and diarrhoea.[26] Thus companion animals may mirror family tensions and critical situations.[27]

In a study of eight hundred and ninety-six military families, Catanzaro found companion animals to be of great importance during the temporary absence of a spouse or child, childhood and adolescence, lonely or depressed times, crises such as the illness or death of other family members, or relocation and unemployment.[28] Companion animals can act as stabilizers in these situations because of their offer of love, affection, and unconditional acceptance. For example, Lilly related that for her, '[Animals are] so loyal, and they like you regardless, and they see you as gods even though you're not at your best. You know, you could be a murderer, and your dog still loves you'.[29] The presence of companion animals can help children and adults navigate the mourning process with less pain,[30] and help families learn about certain life experiences such as responsibility (who takes care of the animal), care giving (the actual act of nurturing and caring for), and loss and death (the death of the animal itself). Companion animals may also sacrifice their own health or give their lives for family members by 'functioning as sentinels of unsafe environmental conditions'.[31]

Being a member of the family means that not only do humans and other animals benefit from that association – they can also be victims of it. So while family human–animal interactions can result in such behaviours as companion animals sleeping with family members, sharing meals and snacks, travelling with family members, playing with and celebrating their companion animals' birthdays, they can also result in interactions where the other animals are, among other things, kicked, punched, burned, stomped, starved, hung, drowned, tortured, and killed. Moreover children and other family members are terrorized by such behaviour.

Including questions about the past and current presence of other animals in child welfare households, the meaning those animals have for each family member, their care, and whether any of them have been hurt or killed is essential to family centred practice given that in many families companion animals are a meaningful and relevant part of the family system. Information collected can help caseworkers make a more accurate assessment of child and family; detect and support findings of child abuse and neglect as well as identify other victims (i.e., humans and animals) and problems (i.e., domestic violence, animal abuse); establish key supports in a child's eco-system which may help if the child remains at home or be lost if removed from his or her family (also cause for grief and bereavement); and suggest the inclusion of specific types of animal-assisted interventions.

Animal Abuse

Animal abuse is illegal in all fifty United States and the District of Columbia, and is often an indicator of a seriously troubled child and/or family. Using Ascione's definition of cruelty to animals – socially unacceptable behaviour that intentionally causes unnecessary pain, suffering or distress to and/or death of an animal – questions regarding the treatment of animals in child welfare households can enhance the accuracy of safety and risk assessments as well as help support decisions with regard to the occurrence or non-occurrence of child maltreatment and domestic violence. In addition, given the serious nature of animal abuse and the potential for prevention, identifying such aberrant behaviour in children by caseworkers is critical for referral to treatment, thereby helping them to carry out their mission of protecting children.

Not every child or parent engaged in the child welfare system will abuse other animals. Nonetheless, despite its limitations, research from a diversity of data sources is persistently finding of the co-occurrence of animal abuse and other antisocial behaviours. For example Quinlisk, in two studies of domestic violence clients, found that of those reporting having companion animals, 79 per cent and 72 per cent said there was animal abuse, including kicking, hitting, punching, mutilation, and killing.[32] Arkow reported that of one hundred and twenty-two battered women seeking entry to safe houses, 23.8 per cent reported abuse of their other animals.[33] In a study of one hundred battered lesbian women, 38 per cent reported their partners had abused their companion animals,[34] while over two-thirds of one hundred battered women seeking safety in domestic violence shelters studied by Ascione reported their companion animals being threatened or killed by their partners.[35] Walton-Moss *et al.*, in a study of four hundred and twenty-seven abused women across eleven geographically dispersed US cities, found threat or actual abuse of a companion animal to be one of five partner characteristics that was statistically significant when compared to a control group of non-abused women.[36] Quinlisk also surveyed a small group of perpetrators and while all reported they had not abused animals as adults, one third did report threatening to give companion animals away.[37]

Another link that is increasingly being supported is the abuse of animals by children who have been abused themselves or witnessed abuse of others (i.e., animals, domestic violence). Merz-Perez and Heide suggest that abuse to other animals by individuals can be an indicator of those who are at risk themselves of having violence committed against them.[38] For example, children who have been physically or sexually abused are more likely than non-abused children to abuse other animals.[39] DeViney, Dickert and Lockwood, in a study of fifty-three child abusing families, found that animal abuse/neglect had occurred in 60 per cent of the families; in 26 per cent of the families children had abused their companion animals.[40] In 88 per cent of the families in which physical abuse was substantiated, animal abuse was also found. This was in comparison to animal abuse in 34 per cent of those families where no physical abuse was found. Robin, ten Bensel, Quigley, and Anderson found in a study of abused children and their companion animals that, in comparison to non-abused children, the companion animals of abused children were almost three times more often killed, accidentally or intentionally.[41] Friedrich (as reported in Ascione) compared two hundred and seventy-one cases of substantiated sexual abuse in two- to twelve-year-olds to eight hundred and seventy-nine non-abused children, and found that parents reported one in three sexually abused boys and one in four abused girls were cruel to animals.[42] In comparison to non-abused children the rates were seven times higher for abused boys and eight times higher for abused girls. In a retrospective study of sexual offenders, Ressler, Burgess, Hartman, Douglas, and McCormack found that during childhood or adolescence a significantly greater proportion of offenders who had been sexually abused had abused other animals compared to non-sexually abused offenders.[43]

Quinlisk found in one study that 76 per cent of the battered women who reported abuse towards their companion animals also reported their children witnessing the abuse, and 54 per cent reported their children also committing animal abuse.[44] In a smaller study, Quinlisk found that 43 per cent of thirty-two battered women reported their children had witnessed animal abuse and 39 per cent reported their children had been cruel to other animals.[45] Ascione found, out of twenty-two women with children and animals who sought safe shelter, 32 per cent reported their children had hurt their companion animals.[46] Ascione, Weber, and Wood also found in their study of companion animal abuse experiences of abused and non-abused women, that 61.5 per cent of the abused women reported their children witnessing companion animal abuse.[47] This was in contrast to 3.3 per cent of the non-abused women. More than 13 per cent of the children who had witnessed such abuse reported they themselves had hurt a companion animal by doing such things as throwing, hitting, or stepping on the animal.[48]

A sometimes unrecognized connection between domestic violence, animal abuse, and child maltreatment is the emotional abuse of women and/or children that occurs when animal abuse is committed in the presence of the child, or as a threat to family members, or as a means to coerce women into committing illegal acts.[49] Merz-Perez and Heide identify this form of abuse for a number of participants in a study of non-violent and violent offenders who reported having observed their cherished companion animals being abused by their parents.[50] In the case of battered women, Adams describes companion animal abuse as one unique form of battering.[51] Women whose companion animals are threatened, harmed, or killed experience fear for themselves and their other animals. They may decide they have to give up their companion animals to a shelter (where they may be euthanized) or to others in order to avoid harm. In these cases women can experience tremendous grief over the loss of their companion animal and the relationship with that other animal. When they have children who also experience this loss, they also suffer this loss with them. Ascione et al. interviewed thirty-nine children of battered mothers: 66.7 per cent had witnessed companion animals being hurt by, among other things, strangulation, poisoning, and being shot.[52] More than half (51.4 per cent) said they had protected a companion animal from a perpetrator. 'In front of the children he would talk about giving the dog away, or worse still about killing him. This made the children very frightened as they loved the dog'.[53]

Finally animal abuse by children is itself a very serious behaviour that should not be dismissed. It is one of the early manifestations of conduct problems associated with 'low empathy and callous disregard',[54] and requires some form of intervention whether simply correction and education, or something more intensive. A substantial body of research also suggests that animal abuse is one of what is often a cluster of dysfunctional behaviours that can be an early indicator of an inclination for later violence against humans as well as property (see Merz-Perez and Heide for an extensive review of this research).[55] Felthous, in a study of aggressive psychiatric patients (APP) compared to non-aggressive psychiatric patients as well as non-psychiatric patients, found that APPs gave a history of killing cats or dogs over 2.5 times that of the two control groups.[56] In a study of childhood and adolescent characteristics of forty-three paedophiles and twenty-one rapists, Tingle et al. reported childhood other animal abuse by 47.6 per cent of rapists and 27.9 per cent of child molesters.[57] Ascione found in data from the Utah Division of Youth Corrections that 21 per cent of youth undergoing evaluation and 15 per cent of youth currently incarcerated reported torturing or intentionally hurting other animals within the past twelve months.[58]

Including assessment for other animal abuse as part of a child abuse investigation, as well as on-going case management, has many critical benefits for child welfare practice. Identification of other animal abuse by children or adults is useful since its frequent co-occurrence with child maltreatment and/or domestic violence signifies a need to assess for other forms of family problems. Identification of other animal abuse by children is also useful for identifying those who are possibly disturbed and engaging in a variety of deviant behaviours; identifying children as victims; in signaling the need for prevention treatment efforts for said children; in notifying substitute caregivers with companion animals who may care for such children; and in referring to relevant animal-assisted interventions.

Positive Impact of Animals on Humans

The literature, both professional and popular, is replete with evidence of a variety of positive effects that animals can have on humans – more than can be adequately reviewed here. However, examples include both long- and short-term health and wellness effects, as well as psychosocial benefits. Research on cardiovascular health has demonstrated that companion animals may assist people in buffering against the development, or slowing the progression, of coronary heart disease.[59] Examples of other findings include lower heart rate and reduced blood pressure for both children,[60] and adults,[61] decreased depression among the elderly,[62] as well as those with AIDS,[63] and the positive influence of service dogs on well-being, self-esteem, and integration into the community for those with disabilities.[64] Risley-Curtiss *et al.* found the women in their study identified receiving friendship, fun, love, comfort, constancy, and/or protection either for themselves, their children, or both, from their relationships with their animal companions.[65]

These women also talked about their own childhood experiences with companion animals, relating that their animal companions provided them with, among other things, support, friendship, protection, fun, play, and love. Felicia, for example, described a childhood dog as 'always at our side; [he] went everywhere with us. He was real protective over us'.[66] It is important to note that these relationships do not have to be long-term but can develop almost immediately. Marie shared her experience with a stray cat when she was five years old: 'It was kind of like my only friend that I could talk to . . . . I didn't have good communication in the family . . . so it was kind of like my friend – my cat, my buddy that I talked to and stuff'.[67] In fact, children often report confiding their secrets, fears, and angers to their companion animals,[68] and abused children may be more likely to do so than non-abused children.[69] Robin *et al.* also found abused children were three times more likely than non-abused children to report their companion animals as support for overcoming loneliness and boredom.[70] Companion animals also provided someone to love, and be loved by, for 47 per cent of the abused children, compared to 29 per cent of non-abused children. As stated by a child in the study 'A pet is important as it gives the child something to hold and love when his parents or one parent doesn't love him'.[71] Fortunately for such children, holding and confiding in other animals does not have to be developmentally outgrown as they age. This is in contrast to, for example, the developmental pattern of children gradually individuating from their parents and siblings.[72]

Garrity and Stallones, in a review of the research on effects of companion animal contact on human well-being, cautiously concluded that benefits from companion animal association occur on the psychological, physical, social, and behavioural levels, and are probably both a direct benefit to humans as well as a protective or buffering factor when humans face life crises.[73] Strand's review of the research also supports the buffering impact of the child-animal bond in families with interparental conflict, and she recommends inclusion of that bond to enhance child coping in such families.[74] Melson, professor of child development and family studies, writes 'the study of children has been largely "humancentric", assuming that only human relationships . . . are consequential of development',[75] yet 'the ties that children forge with their pets are often among the most significant bonds of childhood, as deeply affecting as those with parents, sibling, and friends'.[76] Becker, a veterinarian, writes of the healing power of companion animals and their 'amazing ability to make and keep people happy and healthy'.[77]

Because of the powerful connections that humans can have with other animals, other animals can also be positive adjuncts in treatment of clients such as children and their caretakers.[78] This positive impact has been recognized as far back as the mid-eighteenth century with the planned introduction of companion animals into the care of the mentally ill at 'The York Retreat' in England.[79] In the US, 'Boris Levinson was the first professionally trained clinician to formally introduce and document the way that companion animals could hasten the development of rapport between therapist and patient thereby increasing the likelihood of patient motivation'.[80] Levinson published his seminal book *Pet-oriented child psychotherapy* in 1969. In it he described how the inclusion of other animals could be helpful in psychological assessment, in psychotherapy, in pet-oriented therapy in residential settings, in working to motivate the exceptional child for learning, and in family therapy. In 1984 Anderson, Hart, and Hart published *The pet connection: Its influence on our health and quality of life*, which includes reports of the positive impact of other animals on children who are emotionally disturbed, or who have language disorders or autism. Little more than a decade later, Cusack reviewed research on the positive connection between mental health and companion animals specifically related to depression, stress and anxiety, and psychiatric patients, as well as children, adolescents, family, the elderly, the physically challenged, and those in prison.[81] About the same time the National Institutes of Health (NIH) convened a workshop on the human health benefits of companion animals. Beck and Glickman concluded the workshop by proposing that for all future studies of human health to be comprehensive they would have to include the presence or absence of other animals with which the humans may share their lives, and where present, the nature of this relationship as a significant variable.[82]

The evidence supports inclusion of the human–animal bond in treatment of children, and perhaps adults, in abusive families. The form this treatment takes can vary in multiple ways including: placing troubled children and youth in residential centres that include AAA/AAT programmes such as Green Chimneys in Brewster, NY, USA; requesting AAA/AAT programmes in crisis or transitional settings for maltreated children who are going into foster care (e.g., Gabriel's Angels, Mesa, AZ, USA); encouraging foster caretakers to get companion animals so that foster children may have an immediate non-threatening ally, advocating for children going into foster care to be able to take a treasured companion animal with them, and referring individual children and adults to therapists who use AAT programmes designed specifically for treatment of maltreatment (e.g., garden therapy programme in Sonoma, CA, USA; equine psychotherapeutic programmes). Treatment can also include educational, concrete, and referral services, such as helping a family keep a child's treasured companion animal by linking them to low-cost veterinary services, as well as food banks that provide other animal food. Through budgeting and casework, caseworkers can even assist individuals (e.g., the foster child aging out of the system) and families (e.g., getting a child a companion animal as a supportive ally) in deciding whether a companion animal would be appropriate and, if so, what kind of companion animal would be appropriate, what their care entails, and if they can afford such an animal. Anecdotal evidence suggests that many children aging out of the substitute care system are getting companion animals. Unfortunately they are usually unprepared for this responsibility and the companion animals may end up being harmed. For example, one young woman who got herself a ferret did not realize that ferrets can smell quite bad. She told her caseworker she didn't want the ferret any longer and was going to turn it loose in a park. She erroneously believed ferrets come from the wild. Caseworkers can also validate the importance of non-human family members to their client families and maximize their work with those families by drawing on the positive impact such other animals can have for family members.

Implications for Practice in Child Welfare

There is more than enough documentation of the above-described connections between humans and animals to recognize that animals can have significant roles in child welfare work. In fact, Andrew Vachss writes, in the foreword to Ascione's recent book on children and animals: 'As a lawyer, I am confident I now have the evidence to argue successfully that any report of animal abuse is sufficient probable cause to trigger a child protection investigation of the home in which it occurred'.[83] Nonetheless evidence suggests reluctance by child welfare professionals and agencies to address human–animal relationships, indicating a preference for a 'humancentric' focus rather than one that embraces a true ecological perspective inclusive of non-human species.

Unfortunately, a serious consequence of disregarding human–animal relation-ships is that it short-changes one's ability to help child welfare clients by failing to recognize serious problem behaviours and hence to facilitate early inter-vention; to recognize the potential for supporting resiliency through the powerful healing potential of human–animals interactions; to include an accu-rate family-centred assessment; and to validate important members of many families. These failures can challenge the efficacy of child welfare practice.

The evidence available supports the premise that child welfare professionals and agencies can significantly improve client service with a more thorough understanding of the impact of other animals on individuals and families. This implies the need for even more research; for example, to explore further the relationships between child abuse and animal abuse, especially prospectively and longitudinally. Tremendous amounts of significant information are lost when, for example, such research projects as the National Survey of Child and Adolescent Well-Being Study undertaken by the US Administration for Children and Families do not include questions about companion animals and animal abuse. Both can be indicators of and/or contributors to a child's well-being. Current and future research can be used to educate and train child welfare professionals at all levels. Administrators and managers, for example, must understand the importance of human–animal interactions in order to support and develop policies and procedures for cross-reporting other animal and child abuse, advocate for the addition of other animal related questions or categories in safety and risk assessments, and mandate inclusion of such infor-mation into worker training and case management records. They can support attendance at outside training that is available on such topics as children and other animals, and treatment of animal abuse, as well as contracting with agen-cies that provide other animal-assisted interventions. They can also encourage policies that support children taking their companion animals into foster, rela-tive or adoptive care, and of foster homes acquiring companion animals.

All child welfare case practitioners should be asking their clients about the presence, meaning, and treatment of other animals including non-household animals (farm, wild). Identifying other animal abuse may well be a means of identifying parallel dynamics within the larger family group,[84] and thereby enhance detection of child abuse and domestic violence (a form of maltreat-ment). The indicators of physical, emotional, and neglectful child maltreatment are similar to those of non-human animal abuse, including: conflicting or inad-equate explanations for injuries; self destructive, withdrawn, or aggressive behaviour; consistent and/or extreme fear, cowering, and anxiety, especially in presence of caretaker; running away; avoidance of physical contact; toilet acci-dents; depression; failure to thrive; apathy; being dirty, too cold, too hot, thirsty and/or hungry, as well as having untreated medical issues.[85]

Home-based services are the core of child welfare service provision, including during investigation. This affords child welfare practitioners the opportunity repeatedly to interact with humans and their other animals in a non-threatening manner. In DeViney *et al.'s* investigation of animal abuse and maltreating families, caseworkers actually observed animal abuse/neglect first-hand in 38 per cent of the families.[86] In all of the cases that Zilney and Zilney examined in depth, the type of child abuse/neglect mirrored the type of animal abuse/neglect, or vice versa.[87] Thus, observation of these interactions can well be a window into underlying dynamics in a family, both protective and harmful. Moreover, child welfare workers should be identifying clients with animal abuse histories and referring them for treatment. Identifying and treating animal abuse early may help clients avoid related troubles in the present and/or future. It is also important to educate foster parents, and residential facilities with other animals, about the need for careful supervision of abusing children, especially if other animals and children reside in the same home.

Child welfare workers also need to assess for loss and trauma when children lose their companion animals through animal abuse or when moved to substitute care or adoption. Not doing so fails to recognize additional significant losses experienced by children who already have lost so much. Additionally, while child welfare practitioners do not need to do animal-assisted work, they should understand the potential benefits, the differences between AAA and AAT, and consider referrals to programmes that do include animals (e.g., hippotherapy, equine-assisted psychotherapy, and humane education).

Finally, many child welfare professionals come from the ranks of social work students and a lot of child welfare research comes from social work researchers. It is incumbent upon social work education to integrate the human–animal bond into their BSW, MSW, and PhD curricula, and so join other professions and disciplines in efforts to delve into, and build on, the human–other animal bond.

The global mission of child welfare practice is to protect children and enhance families. By taking full advantage of current and growing knowledge regarding humans and other animals, child welfare agencies can maximize their potential to do so.

Notes

1   American Pet Products Manufacturers Association, 'Statistics and Trends: Pet Ownership' (2005/2006): www.appma.org/press/press_industrytrends.asp.

2   C. Risley-Curtiss, L. C. Holley, and S. Wolf, 'The animal–human bond and ethnic diversity', *Social Work* 51 (2006).

3   F. R. Ascione, *Children and animals: Exploring the roots of kindness and cruelty* (West Lafayette, IN: Purdue University Press, 2005); G. F. Melson, 'Companion animals and the development of children', in A. Fine (ed.), *Handbook on animal assisted therapy: Theoretical foundations and guidelines for practice* (CA: Academic Press, 2000).

4   P. Nelson, *The survey of psychologists' attitudes, opinions, and clinical experiences with animal abuse,* unpublished doctoral dissertation, The Wright Institute Graduate School of Clinical Psychology, 2002.

5   L. A. Zilney and M. Zilney, 'Reunification of child and animal welfare agencies: Cross-reporting of abuse in Wellington County, Ontario', *Child Welfare* 84 (2005).

6 C. Risley-Curtiss, *Human–other animal bond related content and programs in schools of social work*, unpublished study, Arizona State University, 2004.

7 Ascione, *Children and animals*, p. 5.

8 C. Risley-Curtiss, 'Social work practitioners and the human–other animal bond: A national study', *Social Work*, in press.

9 American Pet Products Manufacturers Association, 'Statistics and Trends'.

10 Risley-Curtiss *et al.*, 'The animal–human bond'.

11 C. Risley-Curtiss and L. C. Holley, T. Cruickshank, J. Porcelli, C. Rhoads, D. Bacchus, S. Nyakoe and S. B. Murphy, '"She was family": Women of colour and their animal–human connections', *AFFILIA* 21 (2006).

12 Risley-Curtiss *et al.*, '"She was family"', p. 441.

13 Pew Research Center, *Gauging family intimacy: Dogs edge cats (dads trail both): A social trends report* (Washington, DC: Author, 2006).

14 S. B. Barker, and R. T. Barker, 'The animal–canine bond: Closer than family ties?' *Journal of Mental Health Counseling* 10 (1988).

15 R. A. Johnson and R. L. Meadows, 'Older Latinos, pets and health', *Western Journal of Nursing Research* 24 (2002).

16 Risley-Curtiss *et al.*, '"She was family"', p. 438.

17 American Pet Products Manufacturers Association, 'Leading trade organization releases study finding pets owned by more than half of all U.S. households', 14 April 2003, www.appma.org/press/press_releases/2003/nr_04–14–03.asp.

18 B. M. Levinson, *Pet-oriented child psychotherapy*, 2nd edn (Springfield, IL: Charles C. Thomas, 1997), p. 122.

19 R. Lockwood, *Through hell and high water: Disasters and the human–animal bond* (Washington, DC: The Humane Society of the United States, 1997).

20 For example: C. P. Flynn, 'Woman's best friend: Pet abuse and the role of companion animals in the lives of battered women', *Violence Against Women* 6, 2 (2000): 162–177.

21 M. Allen, B. Gallagher, and B. Jones, 'Domestic violence and the abuse of pets: Researching the link and its implications in Ireland' *Practice*, 18, 3 (September 2006), p. 174.

22 *Ibid.*

23 G. F. Melson, *Why the wild things are: Animals in the lives of children* (Cambridge, MA: Harvard University Press, 2001).

24 K. Allen, J. Blascovich, and W. B. Mendes, 'Cardiovascular reactivity and the presence of pets, friends, and spouses: The truth about cats and dogs', *Psychosomatic Medicine* 64 (2002).

25 A. Albert and M. Anderson, 'Dogs, cats and morale maintenance: Some preliminary data', *Anthrozoös* 10 (1997).

26 A. O. Cain, 'A study of pets in the family system', in A. H. Katcher and A. M. Beck (eds), *New perspectives in our lives with companion animals* (NY: The Haworth Press, 1983).

27 Levinson, *Pet-oriented child psychotherapy*.

28 T. E. Catanzaro, 'The human–animal bond in military communities', in R. K. Anderson, B. L. Hart and L. A. Hart (eds), *The pet connection* (Philadelphia, PA: University of Pennsylvania Press, 1984).

29 Risley-Curtiss *et al.*, '"She was family"', p. 438.

30 K. R. Kaufman, and N. D. Kaufman, 'And then the dog died', *Death Studies* 30 (2006); P. Sable, 'Pets, attachment, and well-being across the life cycle', *Social Work* 40 (1995).

31 M. R. Jalongo, M. L. Stanek, and B. S. Fennimore, 'Companion animals at home: What children learn from families', in M. R. Jalongo (ed.), *The world's children and their companion animals: Developmental and educational significance of the child/pet bond* (Olney, MD: Association for Childhood Education International, 2004), p. 54.

32 J. A. Quinlisk, 'Animal abuse and family violence', in F. R. Ascione and P. Arkow (eds), *Child abuse, domestic violence, and animal abuse: Linking the circles of compassion for prevention and intervention* (West Lafayette, IN: Purdue University Press, 1999), pp. 168–175.

33 P. Arkow, 'Animal abuse and domestic violence: Intake statistics tell a sad story', *The Latham Letter* 15, 2 (Spring 1994): 17.

34 C. M. Renzetti, *Violent betrayal: Partner abuse in lesbian relationships* (Thousand Oaks, CA: Sage Publications, Inc., 1992).

35 Ascione, *Children and animals*.

36 B. J. Walton-Moss, J. Manganello, V. Frye, and J. C. Campbell, 'Risk factors for intimate partner violence and associated injury among urban women', *Journal of Community Health* 30 (2005).

37 Quinlisk, 'Animal abuse and family violence'.

38 L. Merz-Perez, and K. M. Heide, *Animal cruelty: Pathway to violence against people* (New York: Altamira Press, 2004).

39 Ascione, *Children and animals*.

40 E. DeViney, J. Dickert, and R. Lockwood, 'The care of pets within child abusing families', *International Journal for the Study of Animal Problems* 4 (1983): 321–329.

41 M. Robin, R. W. ten Bensel, J. Quigley, and R. K. Anderson, 'Abused children and their pets', in R. K. Anderson, B.L. Hart and L.A. Hart (eds), *The pet connection* (Minneapolis, MN: University of Minnesota, 1984).

42 Ascione, *Children and animals*.

43 R. K. Ressler, A. W. Burgess, C. R. Hartman, J. E. Douglas, and A. McCormack, 'Murderers who rape and mutilate', in R. Lockwood and F. R. Ascione (eds), *Cruelty to animals and interpersonal violence* (West Lafayette, IN: Purdue University Press, 1998).

44 Quinlisk, 'Animal abuse and family violence'.

45 *Ibid.*

46 F. R. Ascione, 'Battered women's report of their partner's and their children's cruelty to animals', *Journal of Emotional Abuse* 1 (1998): 119–133.

47 F. R. Ascione, C. V. Weber, and D. S. Wood, *Final report on the project entitled: Animal welfare and domestic violence* (submitted to the Geraldine R. Doge Foundation, Logan, UT: Authors, 1997).

48 See also: C. A. Faver and A. M. Cavazos Jr., 'Animal abuse and domestic violence: A view from the border' (under review, 2006); Flynn, 'Woman's best friend'; Melson, 'Why the wild things are'; K. L. Thompson, and E. Gullone, 'An investigation into the association between the witnessing of animal abuse and adolescents' behaviour toward animals', *Society & Animals Forum* 14, 3 (2006).

49 M. T. Loring, and T. A. Bolden-Hines, 'Pet abuse by batterers as a means of coercing battered women into committing illegal behaviour', *Journal of Emotional Abuse* 4 (2004): 27–37.

50 Merz-Perez and Heide, *Animal cruelty*.

51 C. J. Adams, 'Woman-battering and harm to animals', in C. J. Adams and J. Donovan (eds), *Animals and women: Feminist theoretical explorations* (Durham, NC: Duke University Press, 1995), pp. 55–84.

52   Ascione *et al.*, *Final report*.
53   Allen *et al.*, 'Domestic violence and the abuse of pets', p. 172; see Faver and Strand (in press) for an excellent review of the current research support for psychological costs of companion animal abuse for battered women and their children.
54   M. R. Dadds, C. Whiting, and D. J. Hawes, 'Associations among cruelty to animals, family conflict, and psychopathic traits in childhood', *Journal of Interpersonal Violence* 21 (2006): 411–429.
55   Merz-Perez and Heide, *Animal cruelty*.
56   A. R. Felthous, 'Childhood antecedents of aggressive behaviours in male psychiatric patients', in R. Lockwood and F. R. Ascione (eds), *Cruelty to animals and interpersonal violence* (West Lafayette, IN: Purdue University Press, 1998).
57   D. Tingle, G. W. Barnard, G. Robbins, G. Newman, and D. Hutchinson, 'Childhood and adolescent characteristics of pedophiles and rapists', *International Journal of Law and Psychiatry*, 9 (1986), 103–116.
58   F. R. Ascione, 'Children who are cruel to animals: A review of research and implications for developmental pathology', in R. Lockwood and F. R. Ascione (eds), *Cruelty to animals and interpersonal violence* (West Lafayette, IN: Purdue University Press, 1998).
59   A. Fine (ed.), *Handbook of animal-assisted therapy* (San Diego, CA: Academic Press, 2000).
60   E. Friedman, A. H. Katcher, S. A. Thomas, J. J. Lynch, and P. R. Messent, 'Social interaction and blood pressure: Influence of animal companions', *Journal of Nervous and Mental Disease* 171, 8 (1983): 461–464.
61   Allen *et al.*, 'Cardiovascular reactivity'; A. Katcher, E. Freidmann, A. Beck, and J. Lynch, 'Looking, talking, and blood pressure: Physiological consequences of interaction with the living environment', in A. H. Katcher and A. M. Beck (eds), *New perspectives on our lives with companion animals* (Philadelphia, PA: University of Pennsylvania Press, 1983).
62   T. F. Garrity, L. Stallones, M. B. Marx, and T. P. Johnson, 'Pet ownership and attachment as supportive factors in the health of the elderly', *Anthrozoös* 3, 1 (1989).
63   J. M. Siegle, F. J. Angulo, R. Detels, J. Wesch, and A. Mullen, 'AIDS diagnosis and depression in the multicenter AIDS cohort study: The ameliorating impact of pet ownership', *AIDS Care* 11 (1999).
64   K. Allen and J. Blascovich, 'The value of service dogs for people with severe ambulatory disabilities: A randomized controlled trial', *JAMA* 275 (1996).
65   Risley-Curtiss *et al.*, '"She was family"'.
66   Risley-Curtiss *et al.*, '"She was family"', p. 438.
67   *Ibid.*
68   Melson, 'Companion animals'.
69   Robin *et al.*, 'Abused children and their pets'.
70   *Ibid.*
71   *Ibid.*, p. 114.
72   Melson, 'Companion animals'.
73   T. F. Garrity, and L. Stallones, 'Effects of pet contact on human well-being', in C. C. Wilson and D. C. Turner (eds), *Companion animals in human health* (Thousand Oaks, CA: Sage Publications Inc., 1998).
74   E. B. Strand, 'Interparental conflict and youth maladjustment: The buffering effects of pets', *Stress, Trauma and Crisis* 7 (2004), p. 3.
75   Melson, 'Companion animals', p. 5.

76   *Ibid.*, p. 16.
77   M. Becker, *The healing power of pets: Harnessing the amazing ability of pets to make and keep people happy and healthy* (New York: Hyperion, 2002).
78   Levinson, *Pet-oriented child psychotherapy*; A. H. Fine (ed.), *Handbook of animal-assisted therapy*.
79   Levinson, *Pet-oriented child psychotherapy*.
80   *Ibid.*, p. vii.
81   O. Cusack, *Pets and mental health* (New York: The Haworth Press, 1988).
82   A. M. Beck and L. T. Glickman, *Future research on pet facilitated therapy: A plea for comprehension before intervention*, paper presented at the NIH Technology Assessment Workshop: Health Benefits of Pets, Washington, DC, 10–11 September 1987.
83   Ascione, *Children and animals*, p. xiv.
84   J. S. Hutton, 'Animal abuse as a diagnostic approach in social work: A pilot study', in A. H. Katcher and A. Beck (eds), *New perspectives on our lives with companion animals* (Philadelphia, PA: University of Pennsylvania Press), pp. 444–447; L. Loar, '"I'll only help you if you have two legs" or, why human service professionals should pay attention to cases involving cruelty to animals', in F. R. Ascione and P. Arkow (eds), *Child abuse, domestic violence, and animal abuse*, pp. 120–136; B. Rosen, 'Watch for pet abuse – It might save your client's life', in R. Lockwood and F. R. Ascione (eds), *Cruelty to animals and interpersonal violence*.
85   Loar, '"I'll only help"'.
86   DeViney *et al.*, 'The care of pets'.
87   Zilney and Zilney, 'Reunification'.

PART
IV

Animal Abuse and Serial Murder

Part IV comprises two pioneering studies on the link between animal abuse and serial murder, but both have different methodologies and reach differing conclusions.

Can acts of animal abuse at an early age predict later violence towards humans, specifically serial murder? Does it follow that early animal abusers automatically graduate to human victims – the so-called 'graduation hypothesis'? Or is the 'deviance generalization hypothesis' correct, which views animal abuse as but 'one expression of a wider delinquent repertoire'?

An Australian research team comprising Llian Alys, J. Clare Wilson, John Clarke, and Peter Toman (*Developmental Animal Cruelty and its Correlates in Sexual Homicide Offenders and Sex Offenders*) found that 'sexual homicide offenders reported greater developmental animal cruelty than the sex offenders who did not kill and the controls, thus supporting the violence graduation hypothesis', but their study also found support for both hypotheses. They conclude that animal cruelty in childhood and adolescence is associated with many antisocial behaviours, but a history of animal cruelty is not exclusive to serial killers, and cannot therefore be regarded as a sole predictor of serial killing.

American researchers Jack Levin and Arnold Arluke (*Reducing the Link's False Positive Problem*), on the other hand, found that 73 per cent of forty-four sadistic repeat killers had also killed or harmed animals. But what Levin and Arluke call the 'link's false positive problem' emerges in that 'so many ordinary non-violent individuals engage in animal abuse in childhood, but never go on to commit violence against humans'. However, they indicate that their 'results suggest that the false positive problem can be substantially reduced – if not almost eliminated – by limiting predictive acts of animal abuse to those in which dogs and cats are tortured in a hands-on manner'. In other words, according to Levin and Arluke, cruelty to animals, specifically dogs and cats, can be seen as predictive of later sadistic serial killing of humans.

Whether animal abuse is only a partial indicator or a predictor when only some species of animal are involved, it seems clear that it is a significant factor in assessing future dangerousness, including the possibility of serial killing.

Developmental Animal Cruelty and its Correlates in Sexual Homicide Offenders and Sex Offenders

LLIAN ALYS, J. CLARE WILSON, JOHN CLARKE, AND PETER TOMAN

The possible link between developmental animal cruelty and violence towards humans is a topic of great importance to practitioners working to diminish violence. Indeed, animal cruelty has been linked to the extremely violent behaviour of sexual homicide.[1] The violence graduation hypothesis suggests that animal cruelty predicts later interpersonal violence while the deviance generalization hypothesis sees it as but one expression of a wider delinquent repertoire.[2] This study examined the aetiology of animal cruelty and its hypothesized association with later delinquency and violent behaviour. Twenty male incarcerated sexual homicide offenders, twenty male sex offenders in a Sex Offender Treatment and Assessment Programme and twenty male mature students (from an adult education course) matched for age completed a questionnaire on childhood (zero to twelve years) and adolescent (thirteen to seventeen years) animal cruelty, antisocial behaviour, child abuse, and paternal alcoholism. Sexual homicide offenders reported greater developmental animal cruelty than the sex offenders who did not kill and the controls, thus supporting the violence graduation hypothesis. However, developmental animal cruelty was associated with developmental antisocial behaviour such as stealing, destroying property, and cruelty to children, thus endorsing the deviance generalization hypothesis. Paternal alcoholism was found to predict physical and psychological abuse, which in turn predicted animal cruelty, factors which are also associated with adult violent behaviour.

'When Animals are Abused, People are at Risk – And Vice Versa'[3]

Studies of delinquents and aggressive criminals have proposed an association between childhood animal abuse and interpersonal violence both in childhood[4] and in adulthood.[5] Indeed, animal cruelty may be considered a pathological symptom. Physical cruelty to animals was added to the list of criteria for a DSM-III diagnosis of conduct disorder in 1987.[6] Research has suggested that a history of childhood animal cruelty was associated with antisocial personality disorder, antisocial personality traits, and polysubstance abuse in a sample of criminal defendants.[7]

It is proposed that cruelty to animals may lead to desensitization to violence or to enjoyment of inflicting pain.[8] This may facilitate or fuel graduation to interpersonal violence,[9] in particular as perpetrating animal abuse may result in the potential inhibition or distortion of empathy.[10] The violence graduation hypothesis suggests that individuals advance from cruelty towards animals in childhood and adolescence to violence towards human beings in adulthood.[11] Alternatively, the deviance generalization hypothesis suggests that animal cruelty is just one of the antisocial behaviours which can be expected to occur from childhood onwards,[12] due to common underlying factors[13] – thus, animal cruelty will not automatically precede other antisocial behaviours.[14]

The present study aimed to examine the onset of violence to both humans and animals in violent sexual offenders and controls. It further explored the relationship between the presence of familial violence and animal abuse, as the two may be indicative of one another.[15] Understanding why individuals are cruel to animals is an important part of any policy to eliminate violence,[16] and greater understanding of the association between interpersonal violence and animal cruelty will result in more successful prevention and intervention strategies.[17]

Prevention targeted at children appears to be the most promising, as children who are especially cruel to animals may be more likely to be aggressive or violent toward others.[18] In case histories of delinquent children, bullying, fighting, destructiveness, fire-setting, and stealing were common, as well as animal cruelty.[19] Indeed, more aggressive criminals may report more childhood animal cruelty than non-aggressive criminals and non-criminals.[20] Further, a significant association has been found between childhood cruelty to animals and later violence against humans and, further, violent offenders had perpetrated more childhood abuse of pets than non-violent offenders.[21] Research appears to emphasize the significance of cruelty to *pet* animals in particular as a precursor to later violence against humans.[22] However, the problem with predicting extreme violence based on animal cruelty is an issue of base rates; that is, animal cruelty is substantially more common than sexual homicide.[23] Further, animal cruelty may also be associated with antisocial behaviour in general, not exclusively with violence.[24] For example, animal abusers were also more likely to commit non-violent offences (e.g., property, drug, and public disorder).[25] Further, experiences of animal cruelty may not differentiate between types of offender (e.g., homicide, violent, sex, other offences).[26] Given these findings, it was expected that developmentally animal cruelty may be associated with developmental antisocial behaviour such as stealing, destroying property, and cruelty to children.

Animal Cruelty, the Ego Triad and Sexual Homicide

Cruelty to animals is often cited as a precursor to the violent crimes of serial killers.[27] Nonetheless, the reported numbers of serial killers with histories of animal cruelty are not high. One study examined twenty-eight sexual murderers (mostly serial), 36 per cent reported childhood animal cruelty, 46 per cent were cruel to animals as adolescents, and 36 per cent continued their abusive nature toward animals as adults.[28] Similarly, of the three hundred and fifty-four cases of serial murder that Wright and Hensley examined, only seventy-five (21 per cent) were known to have committed cruelty toward animals.[29] Despite the modest numbers, the arguments made for the significance of developmental animal cruelty in serial murder are compelling. Wright and Hensley suggested that the murderers displaced the anger they felt at their (sometimes abusive) parents towards animals, and then graduated to humans to increase their gratification.[30] Further, the killers appeared to use the same method of killing on their human and animal victims.[31]

MacDonald proposed that three factors were common in the childhood histories of serial killers, the ego triad or homicidal triad (enuresis, fire-setting, and cruelty to animals),[32] with each factor being predictive of one another.[33] MacDonald maintained that the ego triad behaviours were indicative of a lack of affective bonds between the child and other people and suggested that they were precursors to similar behaviours directed towards others,[34] or a manifestation of the child's revengeful and sadistic developing fantasies.[35] However, the predictive validity of the ego triad has been limited. Wax and Haddox suggested that the triad was useful for predicting violent behaviour,[36] but Prentky and Carter found a low frequency of triad factors in their sample of sex offenders, and found no evidence for the triad as a predictor of adult criminal behaviour.[37] Nonetheless, there was an association between one or more of the factors and an abusive home life, and thus the triad may be a reaction to abuse before and during adolescence.[38] The present study expected that sexual homicide offenders would report more developmental animal cruelty than sexual offenders and control subjects. It was also anticipated that the self-report nature of this study may capture more reliable information than investigations which examine written case studies.

Animal Cruelty and Familial Violence

Research has also shown a relationship between cruelty to animals and familial violence[39] and family dysfunction.[40] Animal cruelty may be a symptom of a disturbed family life,[41] and childhood cruelty to animals may also indicate child abuse or other forms of domestic violence.[42] For example, 32 per cent of the battered women who had children said that one or more of their offspring had hurt or killed pets, and in 71 per cent of these cases the partner had threatened or committed animal cruelty.[43] Abusive parents and partners have sometimes been reported to threaten to harm – or actually to have harmed – animals as a way to control and intimidate victims.[44] Abuse of pets and other animals has been found to co-occur with familial physical and sexual violence in situations of violence against female partners in heterosexual[45] and homosexual relationships,[46] violence against children,[47] and violence against siblings.[48]

The relationship between animal (particularly pet) abuse and child abuse appears to show a significant association.[49] For example, a participant (convicted of sexual battery) described how he would throw stones and bricks at stray animals 'to beat and hurt them like my parents hurt me'.[50] DeViney, Dickert, and Lockwood found that pet abuse was present in 88 per cent of the investigated families in which there was physical child abuse and thus proposed that cruelty towards pets may be an indicator of familial violence towards humans.[51] Fathers constituted two-thirds of the pet abusers, while the remaining third of abusers were children.[52] Paternal abuse and alcoholism in particular appear to be common in the backgrounds of children who are cruel to animals.[53] Further, Wax and Haddox's male adolescent delinquents also demonstrated disordered home backgrounds and erratic childrearing.[54] Indeed, Becker, Stuewig, Herrera, and McCloskey proposed that family variables (marital violence, paternal and maternal harsh parenting) increase the likelihood of animal cruelty, which in turn is associated with self-reported violent crime in adolescence.[55] Thus, an abusive family background may be a better predictor of adult violence than childhood animal cruelty per se.[56] Indeed, as childhood abuse is associated with both childhood animal cruelty and adult violence, it may explain the apparent link between the factors.[57]

Learning theory would use modelling to predict that the child models the animal–human abuse perpetrated by the parent.[58] Animal cruelty on the part of the parent thus provides a model of inappropriate behaviours with animals.[59] Further, within an abusive family environment, controlling or punitive parenting styles are employed.[60] Children in such contexts may model these controlling or punitive styles on their pets.[61] Identification with the aggressor and imitation, curiosity and peer reinforcement, modification of mood state, and using animals to self-injure were the reported motivations for animal cruelty from a sample of children who abused animals.[62] Alternatively, psychoanalytic theories would conceptualize the child abuse/dysfunctional home lives as interfering with the ego development of the child,[63] and causing projection (where the child acts like the adult abuser towards the animal) or displacement (where the child displaced the anger and hostility they cannot cope with onto the animal) by the abused child onto the abused animal.[64] Thus, this study hypothesized that animal cruelty would be associated with child abuse, particularly physical abuse and that paternal alcoholism may predict child abuse, which would in turn predict animal cruelty.

The Present Study

The present study aimed to investigate the associations between childhood animal cruelty and delinquency, adult offending and violence, and a dysfunctional background. It was hoped that it would find evidence for the violence graduation or, at least, the deviance generalization hypothesis, due to the importance of establishing (or disproving) that childhood animal cruelty predicts later interpersonal violence. Establishing this link would provide practitioners with valuable information for identifying and assessing future violent offenders and putting preventative strategies into action.

Further evidence is required before animal cruelty can be considered a significant target for early intervention to stop adult violent offending. This study thus examined developmental animal cruelty, developmental antisocial behaviour (destroying property, stealing, cruelty to children), a dysfunctional background (paternal alcoholism, child abuse) in samples of sexual homicide offenders, sex offenders who do not kill, and matched non-criminal subjects. Tallichet and Hensley maintained that research has failed to investigate repeated acts of animal cruelty, and that repeated acts of animal cruelty may be significant in predicting later violence.[65] Thus, this study examined the presence and absence of animal cruelty and its frequency. The method was a retrospective self-report with participants responding to a Developmental Experiences questionnaire. Sexual homicide offenders are investigated due to the hypothesized link between serial sexual murder and animal cruelty and due to the extreme violence of their offences. Sex offenders on the other hand, are included as a sample of non-violent offenders, to see whether animal cruelty is in fact associated with violence (violence graduation) or offending in general (deviance generalization).

Method

Participants

The Sexual Homicide Offender group consisted of twenty Australian incarcerated male sexual homicide offenders with a mean age of 34.9 years ($SD = 12.5$). The Sex Offender group consisted of twenty Australian sex offender outpatients at a Sexual Offender Treatment and Assessment Programme. The mean age for the Sex Offender group was 44.6 years ($SD = 14.9$). The Control group consisted of Australian male students enrolled in an introductory Psychology course for Adult Continuing Education students at the University of Sydney. The mean age for the Control group was 34.7 years ($SD = 12.4$).

The three groups were matched for gender and ethnicity. Participation was voluntary and participants received no incentive or reward. Participants were also assured that their contribution was anonymous and confidential and that their responses would only be reported as group data.

Materials

The questionnaire firstly asked for demographic information such as age, ethnicity, education, and employment. These were included for matching purposes. These questions were a mixture of open, forced, and multiple-choice answers.

Secondly, questions addressed paternal history of alcohol abuse, and experiencing physical abuse, psychological abuse, or sexual abuse. These were forced yes or no questions.

Thirdly, eight questions addressed the frequency of destroying property, stealing, cruelty to children and cruelty to animals in childhood and adolescence. Childhood was defined as between zero and twelve years of age, and adolescence was classified as between the ages of thirteen and seventeen. These were likert-scale type answer questions, ranging from Always, Often, Sometimes and Rarely, to Never.

Procedure

The data for the Sexual Homicide Offenders and Controls was collected by Clarke and Wilson (in preparation) as part of a larger study. The data on the Sex Offender group was collected for the purpose of this study. Information sheets, consent forms, questionnaires, and debriefing sheets were sent to a Sex Offender Treatment and Assessment Programme to be distributed to willing participants. Questionnaire completion took approximately twenty minutes.

For the Sexual Homicide Offender group, the response rate was one hundred per cent. The response rate for the Sex Offender group was 77 per cent. For the Control group, the response rate was one hundred per cent.

Data Coding

Cruelty to animals and children in childhood (zero to twelve years) and adolescence (thirteen to seventeen years) were coded as Always (3), Often (2), Sometimes (1), A little (0), Never (0). Categories of Antisocial Behaviour in Childhood and Antisocial Behaviour in Adolescence were created by summing the scores of three likert-scale type questions regarding frequency of property destruction, stealing and cruelty to animals (in childhood and in adolescence, respectively). Questions concerning property destruction and stealing in childhood (zero to twelve years) and adolescence (thirteen to seventeen years) were coded as Always (2), Often (1), Sometimes (0), A little (0), Never (0). Questions concerning cruelty to children in childhood (zero to twelve years) and adolescence (thirteen to seventeen years) were coded as Always (3), Often (2), Sometimes (1), A little (0), Never (0). The maximum score for these categories was seven.

Results

Animal Cruelty

The numbers of Sexual Homicide Offenders, Sex Offenders who don't kill and Control subjects to have committed acts of Animal Cruelty (in Childhood and in Adolescence) were examined (see Table 10.1).

Table 10.1 Number of Sexual Homicide Offenders, Sex Offenders who don't kill and Control subjects to report committing Animal Cruelty in Childhood and Adolescence

	Animal Cruelty in Childhood		Animal Cruelty in Adolescence	
	Yes	No	Yes	No
Sexual Homicide Offenders	19	1	18	2
Sex Offenders who don't kill	0	20	0	20
Control subjects	14	6	9	11

Nineteen of the Sexual Homicide Offenders reported being cruel to animals in childhood and eighteen reported doing so in adolescence. None of the Sex Offenders who do not kill reported significant Animal Cruelty in Childhood or in Adolescence (note: significant refers to at least 'Sometimes'); whereas fourteen of the Controls reported Animal Cruelty in Childhood and nine reported it in Adolescence.

A Pearson's Chi-square revealed a relationship between group (Sexual Homicide Offenders, Sex Offenders who do not kill and Control subjects) and committing Animal Cruelty in Childhood, x^2 (2) = 39.19, $p < .01$. The relationship between the variables was strong, Cramér's $V = .81$, $p < .01$. Another Pearson's Chi-square revealed a relationship between group and committing Animal Cruelty in Adolescence, x^2 (2) = 32.73, $p < .01$ and again, the relationship was strong, Cramér's $V = .74$, $p < .01$.

The frequency of animal cruelty committed by the perpetrators in the Sexual Homicide Offenders and Control group was then examined (see Table 10.2). (None of the Sex Offenders reported animal cruelty, thus they were omitted from the following analyses, unless otherwise stated.)

Table 10.2 Frequency of Animal Cruelty in Childhood and Adolescence for the Sexual Homicide Offenders and Control subjects

	Frequency of Animal Cruelty in Childhood			Frequency of Animal Cruelty in Adolescence		
	Mean	Standard deviation	n	Mean	Standard deviation	n
Sexual Homicide Offenders	2.74	.56	19	2.67	.59	18
Control subjects	1.43	.65	14	1.78	.83	9

As shown in Table 10.2, Sexual Homicide Offenders were frequently crueller to animals than the Control group, in childhood, $F(1, 31) = 38.49, p < .01, n^2 = .55, 1- = 1.00$; and adolescence $F(1, 25) = 10.26, p < .01, n^2 = .29, 1- = .87$.

Table 10.3 Correlations between Animal Cruelty in Childhood and Adolescence and Antisocial Behaviour in Childhood and Adolescence (Stealing, Destroying Property and Cruelty to Children)

	Sexual Homicide Offenders (n = 20)		Control subjects (n = 20)	
	Animal Cruelty in Childhood	Animal Cruelty in Adolescence	Animal Cruelty in Childhood	Animal Cruelty in Adolescence
Animal Cruelty in Adolescence	.85**		.76**	
Antisocial Behaviour in Childhood	.35	.32	.73**	.55*
Antisocial Behaviour in Adolescence	.45*	.40	.72**	.58**
Cruelty to Children in Childhood	.29	.27	.53*	.52*
Cruelty to Children in Adolescence	.36	.34	.54**	.45*
Stealing in Childhood	.02	-.02	.60**	.28
Stealing in Adolescence	.30	.24	.60**	.42
Destroy Property in Childhood	.43	.41	.53*	.52*
Destroy Property in Adolescence	.38	.35	.54*	.45*

Logistic regressions tested the violence graduation hypothesis. Animal Cruelty in Childhood and Adolescence were examined as possible predictors of group membership (Sexual Homicide Offender or Control). Animal Cruelty in Childhood approached significance as a predictor of group membership (OR = 8.14, B = 2.10, SE = 1.14, p = .07). In comparison, Animal Cruelty in Adolescence was a significant predictor of group membership (OR = 11.00, B = 2.40, SE = .87, p = .01) and it explained 29 per cent of the variance (Nagelkerke R^2 = .29). Further, to assess whether the frequency of animal cruelty is a more significant factor than the simple presence or absence of animal cruelty, the frequency of animal cruelty was also examined as a predictor. Frequency of Animal Cruelty in Childhood was a significant predictor of group membership (OR = 6.12, B = 1.81, SE = .51, p < .01) and it explained 59 per cent of the variance (Nagelkerke R^2 = .59). Frequency of Animal Cruelty in Adolescence was also a significant predictor of group membership (OR = 3.42, B = 1.23, SE = .36, p < .01) and it explained 47 per cent of the variance (Nagelkerke R^2 = .47).

SEXUAL HOMICIDE OFFENDERS   As shown in Table 10.3, Cruelty to Animals in Childhood was significantly associated with Cruelty to Animals in Adolescence and Antisocial Behaviour in Adolescence. Many of the other variables' associations with animal cruelty approached significance. The associations between Cruelty to Animals in Adolescence and Antisocial Behaviour in Adolescence also approached significance (p = .08). The correlations between Animal Cruelty in Childhood and Destroying Property in Childhood and in Adolescence approached significance (p = .06, p = .10, respectively) as did the relationship between Cruelty to Animals in Adolescence and Destroying Property in Childhood (p = .08).

Unsurprisingly, Cruelty to Animals in Childhood predicted Cruelty to Animals in Adolescence (= .85, p < .01). The variable explained approximately 72 per cent of the variance (r^2 = .72), which was significant, $F(1, 18)$ = 47.23, p < .01. Cruelty to Animals in Childhood also predicted Antisocial Behaviour in Adolescence (= .45, p = .05). The variable explained approximately 20 per cent of the variance (r^2 = .20), which was significant, $F(1, 18)$ = 4.48, p = .05.

CONTROLS   Cruelty to Animals in Childhood was associated with Cruelty to Animals in Adolescence. Cruelty to Animals (in Childhood and Adolescence) was also associated with Antisocial Behaviour (in Childhood and Adolescence). Specifically, Cruelty to Animals in Childhood and Adolescence was correlated with Cruelty to Children in Childhood and Adolescence, with Stealing in Childhood and Adolescence and with Destroying Property in Childhood and Adolescence. The association between Cruelty to Animals in Adolescence and Stealing in Adolescence also approached significance (p = .07).

Cruelty to Animals in Childhood predicted square root of Cruelty to Animals in Adolescence (= .77, p < .01). The variable explained approximately 59 per cent of the variance (r^2 = .59), which was significant, $F(1, 18)$ = 26.11, p < .01. Cruelty to Animals in Childhood was a significant predictor of square root of Antisocial Behaviour in Adolescence (= .75, p < .01). The variable explained approximately 55 per cent of the variance (r^2 = .55), which was significant, $F(1, 18)$ = 22.40, p < .01.

Cruelty to Animals in Childhood also predicted square root of Cruelty to Children in Adolescence (= .46, p = .04). The variable explained approximately 21 per cent of the variance ($r^2 = .21$), which was significant, $F(1, 18) = 4.76, p = .04$.

Cruelty to Animals in Childhood was a significant predictor of Stealing in Adolescence ($= .60, p = .01$). The variable explained approximately 36 per cent of the variance ($r^2 = .36$), which was significant, $F(1, 18) = 10.08, p = .01$.

Cruelty to Animals in Childhood predicted square root of Destroying Property in Adolescence ($= .59, p = .01$). The variable explained approximately 35 per cent of the variance ($r^2 = .35$), which was significant, $F(1, 18) = 9.54, p = .01$.

Logistic regressions also assessed whether childhood animal cruelty predicted later delinquent behaviour or whether animal cruelty is predicted by general antisocial behaviour as suggested by the deviance generalization hypothesis. Animal Cruelty in Childhood was a significant predictor of Antisocial Behaviour in Adolescence (OR = 25.38, B = 3.23, $SE = .71$, $p < .01$) and it explained 51 per cent of the variance (Nagelkerke $R^2 = .51$). Frequency of Animal Cruelty in Childhood was also a significant predictor of Antisocial Behaviour in Adolescence (OR = 4.45, B = 1.49, $SE = .39$, $p < .01$) and it explained 49 per cent of the variance (Nagelkerke $R^2 = .49$).

Antisocial Behaviour in Childhood was a significant predictor of Animal Cruelty in Childhood (OR = 112.00, B = 4.72, $SE = 1.12$, $p < .01$) and it explained 67 per cent of the variance (Nagelkerke $R^2 = .67$). Antisocial Behaviour in Adolescence was a significant predictor of Animal Cruelty in Adolescence (OR = 10.06, B = 2.31, $SE = .65$, $p < .01$). The variable explained 31 per cent of the variance of Animal Cruelty in Adolescence (Nagelkerke $R^2 = .31$).

Paternal Alcoholism and Child Abuse

Next, to examine whether Paternal Alcoholism is associated with child abuse, chi-square analyses were conducted (see Table 10.4). The data included Sexual Homicide Offenders, Sex Offenders who do not kill and Control subjects.

Table 10.4 Rates of Sexual, Physical and Psychological Abuse among participants with and without alcoholic fathers

		Sexually Abused		Physically Abused		Psychologically Abused	
		Yes	No	Yes	No	Yes	No
Paternal	Yes	12	8	15	5	16	4
Alcoholism	No	10	30	9	31	12	28

There was a significant relationship between Sexual Abuse and Paternal Alcoholism, $x^2 (1) = 7.03, p < .01$, but the strength of the association was low, $= .34, p < .01$. There was a significant relationship between Physical Abuse and Parental Alcoholism also, $x^2 (1) = 15.31, p < .01$ and the strength of the association was moderate, $= .51, p < .01$. There was also a significant relationship between Psychological Abuse and Parental Alcoholism, x^2 (1) = 13.39, $p < .01$, and again, the strength of the association was moderate, = .47, $p < .01$.

Logistic regressions were computed to see whether Paternal Alcoholism (presence or absence) predicted child abuse (sexual, physical, and psychological). Paternal Alcoholism was a significant predictor of Sexual Abuse (OR = 4.50, B = 1.50, SE = .59, p = .01) but the variable only explained 15 per cent of the variance of Sexual Abuse (Nagelkerke R^2 = .15). Paternal Alcoholism was also a significant predictor of Physical Abuse (OR = 10.33, B = 2.34, SE = .64, $p < .01$) and it explained 31 per cent of the variance of Physical Abuse (Nagelkerke R^2 = .31). Paternal Alcoholism was also a significant predictor of Psychological Abuse (OR = 9.33, B = 2.23, SE = .66, $p < .01$) and it explained 28 per cent of the variance (Nagelkerke R^2 = .28).

To examine whether child abuse is associated with Animal Cruelty in Childhood and Adolescence, chi-square analyses were conducted (see Table 10.5). The data included Sexual Homicide Offenders, Sex Offenders who do not kill, and Control subjects.

Table 10.5 Rates of Sexual, Physical and Psychological Abuse among participants who committed Animal Cruelty in Childhood and Adolescence and those who did not

		Sexually Abused		Physically Abused		Psychologically Abused	
		Yes	No	Yes	No	Yes	No
Animal Cruelty in Childhood	Yes	12	21	17	16	19	14
	No	10	17	7	20	9	18
Animal Cruelty in Adolescence	Yes	12	15	17	10	18	9
	No	10	23	7	26	10	23

There was no significant relationship between Sexual Abuse and Animal Cruelty in Childhood, x^2 (1) = .00, p = .96; or Animal Cruelty in Adolescence, x^2 (1) = 1.28, p = .26 The association between Physical Abuse and Animal Cruelty in Childhood was significant however, x^2 (1) = 4.05, p = .04, but the strength of the association was low, = .26, p = .04. There was also a significant relationship between Physical Abuse and Animal Cruelty in Adolescence, x^2 (1) = 10.79, $p < .01$, and again the strength of the association was moderate, = .42, $p < .01$. The relationship between Psychological Abuse and Animal Cruelty in Childhood approached significance, x^2 (1) = 3.51, p = .06. However, the relationship between Psychological Abuse and Animal Cruelty in Adolescence was significant, x^2 (1) = 7.89, p = .01, and the strength of the association was low, = .36, p = .01.

Logistic regressions were also computed to see whether Physical and Psychological child abuse predicted Animal Cruelty (in Childhood and

Adolescence). Physical Abuse was a significant predictor of Animal Cruelty in Childhood (OR = 3.04, B = 1.11, SE = .56, p = .05) but the variable only explained 9 per cent of the variance (Nagelkerke R^2 = .09). Physical Abuse was also a significant predictor of Animal Cruelty in Adolescence (OR = 6.31, B = 1.84, SE = .58, p < .01) but the variable only explained 23 per cent of the variance (Nagelkerke R^2 = .23).

Psychological Abuse only approached significance as a predictor of Animal Cruelty in Childhood (OR = 2.71, B = 1.00, SE = .54, p = .06). However, Psychological Abuse was a significant predictor of Animal Cruelty in Adolescence (OR = 4.60, B = 1.53, SE = .56, p = .01) and the variable explained 17 per cent of the variance of Animal Cruelty in Adolescence (Nagelkerke R^2 = .17).

Discussion

This study examined developmental animal cruelty in three samples, Sexual Homicide Offenders, Sex Offenders, and Control subjects. As expected, the Sexual Homicide Offenders reported more developmental animal cruelty than the Sex Offenders who did not kill and the Control group. However many of the Control group had abused animals in childhood too. This suggests that animal cruelty may be widespread and not a causal factor predictive of sexual homicide. Further, the rates of animal abuse in this study were much higher than those of Flynn (one in five),[66] and Miller and Knutson (one in ten).[67] This may be because the questionnaire did not define what was meant by animal cruelty (the item was 'I hurt animals . . . '). As such, it is subjective, and participants may have been referring to innocuous behaviours (or 'legal' behaviours such as hunting). Further, participants may have denied animal cruelty because they did not view their actions as causing pain (whether they did or not).

None of the Sex Offenders admitted significant cruelty to animals in childhood or adolescence. However, they were participants in outpatient treatment, and perhaps they may have been less than honest for fear it may jeopardize their parole conditions. Alternatively, as participation was voluntary, one cannot ensure that a representative sample is obtained. The type of offender who would agree to participate may have certain characteristics, e.g., being less violent, meeker or more likely to lie for social desirability's sake. Also, the Sex Offenders may have interpreted their actions and their consequences in different ways to the Sexual Homicide Offenders and Control subjects. Researchers propose that sex offenders are likely to distort cognitively in order to minimize or deny the harm they cause their victims.[68] Perhaps they acquired or developed this way of thinking to relieve the guilt and allow them to continue abusing their animal victims.

To answer Tallichet and Hensley's concern that repeated animal cruelty has not been examined in childhood animal cruelty/adult violence research, frequency of offending was investigated.[69] In line with the original hypothesis, the Sexual Homicide Offenders had a higher mean frequency of developmental animal cruelty than the Control group. Presence of childhood animal cruelty approached significance as a predictor of whether an individual was a Sexual Homicide Offender or Control subject, while Animal Cruelty in Adolescence was a significant predictor. It only explained 29 per cent of the variance, but participants with a history of animal cruelty were eleven times more likely to be Sexual Homicide Offenders than Controls. Frequency of Animal Cruelty in Childhood and Adolescence were much stronger predictors and explained 59 per cent and 47 per cent of the variance of group membership, respectively. However, individuals with a greater frequency of childhood (adolescent) animal cruelty were only six times (three times) more likely to be Sexual Homicide Offenders than Controls. These findings provide some support for the violence graduation hypothesis but the association between developmental animal cruelty and sexual homicide does not appear strong. This is somewhat in keeping with the serial killer literature however, as the numbers of offenders who are known to have abused animals in childhood are not as robust as one might expect (for example, 21 per cent of the three hundred and fifty-four cases examined by Wright and Hensley[70]).

It was expected that developmental animal cruelty would be associated with developmental antisocial behaviour such as Stealing, Destroying Property and Cruelty to Children. The present study found that individuals reporting childhood animal cruelty were more likely to be antisocial in adolescence. Group comparisons were then made. For the Sexual Homicide Offenders, childhood animal cruelty explained 72 per cent of the variance in adolescent animal cruelty and 20 per cent of the variance in Antisocial Behaviour in Adolescence. For the Control group, childhood animal cruelty explained 59 per cent of the variance in adolescent animal cruelty and 55 per cent of the variance in Antisocial Behaviour in Adolescence. This suggests the influence of additional factors in the development of Sexual Homicide Offenders. Further, for the Controls, childhood animal cruelty predicted the three types of adolescent antisocial behaviour examined in this study. It explained 21 per cent of the variance in Cruelty to Children, 36 per cent of the variance in Stealing, and 20 per cent of the variance in Destroying Property. These findings suggest that childhood animal cruelty may be associated with antisocial behaviour and delinquency in normal populations (although the total variances explained by animal cruelty demonstrate that other influences are also at work) and is not exclusively related to violent offending but to more general offending (e.g., property offences).

This study has some evidence in support of the violence graduation hypothesis but what about its alternative, the deviance generalization hypothesis? It proposes that animal cruelty is but one behaviour in a repertoire of delinquency, i.e., it is not a predictor but a correlate of other delinquent behaviours. There was some evidence to support this hypothesis too. Childhood and adolescent antisocial behaviour were significant predictors of childhood and adolescent animal cruelty, respectively (explaining 67 per cent and 31 per cent of the variances). Thus, over half the variance of childhood animal cruelty was predicted by childhood antisocial behaviour. It appears therefore that the association between animal cruelty and general delinquency is stronger for children than for adolescents.

This study also examined the aetiology of animal cruelty. It was hypothesized that Paternal Alcoholism may predict child abuse which will in turn predict developmental animal cruelty. As expected, Paternal Alcoholism predicted all types of abuse. Paternal Alcoholism explained 15 per cent of the variance of Sexual Abuse, 31 per cent of the variance of Physical Abuse, and 28 per cent of the variance of Psychological Abuse. This would appear consistent with anecdotal and research evidence showing links between alcoholism and physical and psychological abuse of spouses and offspring.[71]

Contrary to expectation, Sexual Abuse was not associated with animal cruelty. Animal cruelty was associated with Physical and Psychological Abuse, however. Participants who were physically abused were three times more likely to abuse animals in childhood and six times more likely to abuse animals in adolescence. Participants who were psychologically abused were two to three times more likely to abuse animals in adolescence, but Psychological Abuse only explained 17 per cent of the variance of adolescent animal cruelty. The findings provide some evidence for the hypothesis that Paternal Alcoholism predicts child abuse and that child abuse in turn (physical and psychological) predicts animal cruelty. However, the predictors do not explain much of the variance of the dependent variables, thus suggesting that other factors are involved.

Finding those other factors can be difficult, as serial killers (our sample of sexual homicide offenders) are one of the rarest groups of offenders and may be very idiosyncratic individuals. Thus, one of the main limitations of the present study was the sample size. However, that significant findings were found at all with such small groups may be evidence that the associations are strong and require further investigation. Another issue with asking developmental information about sexual homicide offenders is that there may be a strong need in the offender (and in their families) to justify or deny certain behaviours (for example, it may be more acceptable to report animal cruelty as a possible 'explanation' of their behaviour than other behaviours, such as fantasies) and this may limit the validity of some of the information obtained. Another limitation was that the control subjects were not asked whether they had ever committed a crime, particularly a violent one. Further evidence would have been provided for or against the violence graduation and deviance generalization hypotheses if such information was available. Different types of offender will also help to define the relationships between antisocial behaviour, violence, aggression, and animal cruelty. This study highlights the need for clarity when defining animal cruelty and ensuring that participants understand and concur on what is abuse. Interviews may be particularly useful for future studies as they allow the researcher to gain specific information on incidences of animal cruelty and the participant's thoughts and feelings at the time. There are many specific details to animal cruelty which may or may not, individually or collectively, be predictive of later interpersonal violence.[72] This study suggests that frequency of animal cruelty may be a better predictor of antisocial behaviour than its presence or absence alone.

To summarize, this study found support for both the violence graduation hypothesis and the deviance generalization hypothesis. Therefore, neither can be discarded as yet. While they may ascribe different weightings of significance to animal cruelty, both hypotheses are congruent with the fact that animal cruelty is antisocial and unacceptable. This study also found support for animal cruelty in childhood being strongly related to later antisocial behaviour. However, there may be better predictors of sexual homicide offending than relying exclusively on animal cruelty. Finally, whether a predictor of future violence or part of a wider delinquent repertoire, animal cruelty signifies that something is wrong and that intervention is needed. Its associations with a dysfunctional family background and abuse is further evidence that it is a warning, an indicator to social workers and other professionals that they need to intervene, especially given the possible ramifications for both the individual and society.

Notes

1 R. Ressler, A. Burgess, and J. Douglas, *Sexual homicide: Patterns and motives* (Lexington, MA: Lexington, 1988).

2 A. Arluke, J. Levin, C. Luke, and F. R. Ascione, 'The relationship of animal abuse to violence and other forms of antisocial behavior', *Journal of Interpersonal Violence* 14 (1999).

3 P. Arkow, 'The relationships between animal abuse and other forms of family violence', *Family Violence and Sexual Assault Bulletin* 12 (1996).

4 J. D. Rigdon and F. Tapia, 'Children who are cruel to animals: A follow-up study', *Journal of Operational Psychiatry* 8 (1977).

5 A. R. Felthous and S. R. Kellert, 'Violence against animals and people: Is aggression against living creatures generalized?' *Bulletin of the American Academy of Psychiatry and the Law* 14 (1986).

6 F. R. Ascione, 'Children who are cruel to animals: A review of research and implications for developmental psychology', *Anthrozoös* 6 (1993); Arkow, 'Relationships between animal abuse'.

7 R. Gleyzer, A. R. Felthous, and C. E. Holzer III, 'Animal cruelty and psychiatric disorders', *Journal of the American Academy of Psychiatry and the Law* 30 (2002).

8 National Association for Humane and Environmental Education, *Understanding animal cruelty* (Washington, DC: Author, 2001).

9 J. Wright and C. Hensley, 'From animal cruelty to serial murder: Applying the graduation hypothesis', *International Journal of Offender Therapy and Comparative Criminology* 47 (1) (2003).

10 Ascione, 'Children who are cruel to animals'; M. J. P. Zruesi, 'Cruelty to animals and CSF 5–HIAA [Letter]' *Psychiatry Research* 28 (1989); L. Merz-Perez, K. M. Heide, and I. J. Silverman, 'Childhood cruelty to animals and subsequent violence

against humans', *International Journal of Offender Therapy and Comparative Criminology* 45 (2001).

11 Arluke *et al.*, 'The relationship of animal abuse to violence'.

12 *Ibid.*

13 D. W. Osgood, L. Johnston, P. O'Malley, and J. Bachman, 'The generality of deviance in late adolescence and early adulthood', *American Sociological Review* 53 (1988).

14 Arluke *et al.*, 'The relationship of animal abuse to violence'.

15 B. W. Boat, 'The relationship between violence to children and violence to animals: An ignored link?' *Journal of Interpersonal Violence* 10 (1995).

16 A. Arluke, and C. Luke, 'Physical cruelty toward animals in Massachusetts, 1975–1990', *Society & Animals* 5 (1997).

17 Ascione, 'Children who are cruel to animals'.

18 Felthous and Kellert, 'Violence against animals and people'.

19 F. Tapia, 'Children who are cruel to animals', *Clinical Psychiatry and Human Development* 2 (1971).

20 S. R. Kellert and A. R. Felthous, 'Childhood cruelty toward animals among criminals and noncriminals', *Human Relations* 38 (1985).

21 Merz-Perez *et al.*, 'Childhood cruelty to animals'.

22 *Ibid.*

23 A. Duncan and C. Miller, 'The impact of an abusive family context on childhood animal cruelty and adult violence', *Aggression and Violent Behavior* 7 (2002); K. S. Miller and J. F. Knutson, 'Reports of severe physical punishment and exposure to animal cruelty by inmates convicted of felonies and by university students', *Child Abuse and Neglect* 21 (1997); C. P. Flynn, 'Why family professionals can no longer ignore violence toward animals', *Family Relations* 49 (2000).

24 Arluke *et al.*, 'The relationship of animal abuse to violence'.

25 *Ibid.*

26 Miller and Knutson, 'Reports of severe physical punishment'; Arluke *et al.*, 'The relationship of animal abuse to violence'.

27 R. Lockwood and A. Church, 'Deadly serious: An FBI perspective on animal cruelty', in R. Lockwood and F. A. Ascione (eds), *Cruelty to animals and interpersonal violence* (West Lafayette, IN: Purdue University Press, 1998).

28 Ressler *et al.*, *Sexual homicide*.

29 Wright and Hensley, 'From animal cruelty to serial murder'.

30 *Ibid.*

31 *Ibid.*

32 J. M. MacDonald, 'The threat to kill', *American Journal of Psychiatry* 120 (1963).

33 H. Yarnell, 'Firesetting in children', *American Journal of Orthopsychiatry* 10 (1940).

34 MacDonald, 'The threat to kill'.

35 A. W. Burgess, C. R. Hartman, R. K. Ressler, J. E. Douglas, and A. McCormack, 'Sexual homicide: A motivational model', *Journal of Interpersonal Violence* 1 (1986).

36 D. E. Wax and V. G. Haddox, 'Enuresis, firesetting, and animal cruelty: A useful danger signal in predicting vulnerability of adolescent males to assaultive behavior', *Child Psychiatry and Human Development* 4, 3 (1974).

37 R. A. Prentky and D. L. Carter, 'The predictive value of the triad for sex offenders', *Behavioral Sciences and the Law* 2 (1984).

38 *Ibid.*; B. Justice, R. Justice, and I. A. Kraft, 'Early-warning signs of violence: Is a triad enough?' *American Journal of Psychiatry* 131 (1974).

39 R. Lockwood and F. R. Ascione, *Cruelty to animals and interpersonal violence: Readings in research and application* (West Lafayette, IN: Purdue University Press, 1998).

40 E. S. L. Luk, P. K. Staiger, L. Wong, and J. Mathai, 'Children who are cruel to animals: A revisit', *Australian and New Zealand Journal of Psychiatry* 33 (1999).

41 R. Lockwood and G. R. Hodge, 'The tangled web of animal abuse: The links between cruelty to animals and human violence', *The Humane Society News* (Summer 1986).

42 Arkow, 'Relationships between animal abuse'; F. R. Ascione, 'Battered women's report of their partner's and their children's cruelty to animals', *Journal of Emotional Abuse* 1 (1998).

43 Ascione, 'Battered women's report'.

44 R. J. Gelles and M. A. Straus, *Intimate violence* (New York: Simon and Schuster, 1988).

45 M. A. Dutton, *Empowering and healing the battered woman* (New York: Springer, 1992).

46 C. M. Renzetti, *Violent betrayal: Partner abuse in lesbian relationships* (Newbury Park, CA: Sage, 1992).

47 E. Deviney, J. Dickert, and R. Lockwood, 'The care of pets within child abusing families', *International Journal of the Study of Animal Problems* 4 (1983).

48 Vernon R. Wiehe, *Sibling abuse* (New York: Lexington, 1990).

49 Boat, 'The relationship between violence to children'.

50 Merz-Perez *et al.*, 'Childhood cruelty to animals'.

51 Deviney *et al.*, 'The care of pets'.

52 *Ibid.*

53 Flynn, 'Family professionals'; Tapia, 'Children who are cruel to animals'; F. R. Ascione and P. Arkow, *Child abuse, domestic violence, and animal abuse: Linking the circles of compassion for prevention and intervention* (West Lafayette, IN: Purdue University Press, 1999); Kellert and Felthous, 'Childhood cruelty'.

54 Wax and Haddox, 'Enuresis, firesetting, and animal cruelty'.

55 Duncan and Miller, 'The impact of an abusive family context'; K. D. Becker, J. Stuewig, V. M. Herrera, and L. A. McCloskey, 'A study of fire setting and animal cruelty in children: Family influences and adolescent outcomes', *Journal of the American Academy of Child and Adolescent Psychiatry* 43 (2004).

56 Duncan and Miller, 'The impact of an abusive family context'.

57 *Ibid.*

58 *Ibid.*

59 Boat, 'The relationship between violence to children'.

60 G. R. Patterson, B. D. DeBaryshe, and E. Ramsey, 'A developmental perspective on antisocial behavior', *American Psychologist* 44, 3 (1989).

61 Ascione, 'Children who are cruel to animals'; Duncan and Miller, 'The impact of an abusive family context'.

62 F. R. Ascione, T. M. Thompson, and T. Black, 'Childhood cruelty to animals: Assessing cruelty dimensions and motivations', *Anthrozoös* 10 (1997).

63 A. R. Felthous, 'Aggression against cats, dogs, and people', *Child Psychiatry and Human Development* 10, 3 (1980).

64 Boat, 'The relationship between violence to children'.

65 S. E. Tallichet and C. Hensley, 'Exploring the link between recurrent acts of childhood and adolescent animal cruelty and subsequent violent crime', *Criminal Justice Review* 29 (2004).

66 Flynn, 'Family professionals'.
67 Miller and Knutson, 'Reports of severe physical punishment'.
68 T. Ward, S. M. Hudson, L. Johnston, and W. L. Marshall, 'Cognitive distortions in sex offenders: An integrative review', *Clinical Psychology Review* 17, 5 (1997).
69 Tallichet and Hensley, 'Exploring the link'.
70 Wright and Hensley, 'From animal cruelty to serial murder'.
71 K. E. Leonard and T. Jacob, 'Alcohol, alcoholism and family violence', in V. D. Van Hasselt, R. L. Morrison, A. S. Bellach, and M. D. Herson (eds), *Handbook of family violence* (New York: Plenum Press, 1988).
72 Merz-Perez *et al.*, 'Childhood cruelty to animals'.

11

Reducing the Link's False Positive Problem[1]

JACK LEVIN AND ARNOLD ARLUKE

Introduction

Serial murder involves a string of four or more homicides committed over a period of days, weeks, months, or even years.[2] Most murders are solved within forty-eight hours, but serial killers can stay on the loose for long periods of time amassing very large body counts. For example, Seattle's Gary Ridgway, a.k.a. the Green River Killer, took the lives of at least forty-eight prostitutes over a span of twenty years; Dennis Rader, a.k.a. B.T.K., of Wichita, Kansas, avoided apprehension for some three decades, while he was killing ten innocent people.

Using a variety of sources – newspaper articles, books, and internet profiles, Fox and Levin gathered together a list of five hundred and fifty-eight known serial killers operating in the United States since 1900.[3] The trend is relatively flat during the first half of the twentieth century, represented by approximately ten serial killers per decade. The pattern differs sharply during the second half of the century. In the 1960s, there were some forty serial killers on the loose. Then, during the next two decades, the number of killers increased dramatically. During the 1980s, there were more than one hundred and fifty serial killers operating in the United States. This number declined somewhat during the closing decade of the century, perhaps because of technological advances in crime-fighting (e.g., DNA testing). But it is just as possible that 'linkage blindness' – that is, the inability of law enforcement to recognize that a single killer is responsible for a number of murders in separate police jurisdictions – prevented authorities from recognizing many serial murders until the opening years of this century.[4]

It is difficult to estimate the number of individuals victimized by these five hundred and fifty-eight serial killers. Almost certainly, the total falls somewhere between 4,000 and 5,000 individuals. Very few offenders stay on the streets long enough to become serial killers, but those who do are responsible for a very large number of deaths.

Since the 1960s, criminologists and psychiatrists have sought to generate a set of warning signs in childhood to predict who would grow up to become a prolific serial killer. From the beginning, investigators focused on animal cruelty as symptomatic of later violence-proneness in general and serial murder in particular.[5]

It makes sense that so much attention would be focused on animal abuse as a predictor of extreme forms of violence including serial murder. Most criminologists accept the notion that violence begets violence and that the best predictor of violence directed against humans or animals is previous violence directed against humans or animals.

Yet not all research investigating the predictive value of animal abuse has confirmed its connection with human violence let alone serial murder.[6] In 1963, John Macdonald proposed that assaulting small animals was one of three precursors – along with fire setting and enuresis – of extreme cruelty toward humans. In a controlled study of personal histories, however, Macdonald himself failed to confirm the hypothesis that violent psychiatric patients would be significantly more likely than non-violent psychiatric patients to have abused animals.

By contrast, the overall thrust of more recent research is fairly supportive of the link between animal abuse and human violence. In 1985, Kellert and Felthous uncovered significantly more animal cruelty in the childhoods of 'aggressive criminals' than in the childhoods of 'non-aggressive criminals' or 'non-criminals'. Estimates of the percentage of extremely violent individuals who have engaged in animal cruelty tend to be substantially higher than in the general population. In their study of serial killers, Wright and Hensley found that seventy-five or 21 per cent had a known history of childhood animal cruelty – although the authors failed to report either the nature or the extent of that animal cruelty.[7] Ressler et al. similarly determined that a large number of their thirty-six convicted sexual murderers – many of them serial killers – admitted having engaged in animal cruelty.[8] More than half of these sexual killers had perpetrated animal abuse as either children or adolescents.

Arluke, Levin, Luke, and Ascione,[9] using official reports of animal cruelty and criminal records, determined in a comparative study of one hundred and fifty-three animal abusers and one hundred and fifty-three of their non-abusive neighbours that the abusers were much more likely to be engaged in antisocial behaviour generally – in perpetrating interpersonal violence, but also in committing property offences, drug offences, and public disorder offences. The finding that animal cruelty may be related to antisocial behaviour generally rather than just human violence may help to explain the failure of previous studies consistently to uncover significant differences between violent and non-violent criminals. Given the presence of animal cruelty among property and drug offenders, it would seem important to employ a non-criminal comparison group. Moreover, as far as animal abuse as a precursor to human violence is concerned, animal abuse episodes in the Arluke et al. study did not always precede human violence. In some cases, children started by abusing people and then later graduated to animals. The authors suggested that their findings support the generalization of deviance model which argues that animal cruelty may or may not precede or follow any antisocial behaviour – rather than the graduation or escalation hypothesis which argues that animal cruelty precedes subsequent acts of human violence.

Study 1

In Study 1, we examined true-crime books supplemented by crime websites depicting the offences and backgrounds of fifty-two serial killers. From the original sample, we then focused only on the forty-four (85 per cent) who had reportedly tortured their victims. That is, beyond causing the death of a human being, they had intentionally inflicted pain and suffering.

This large proportion is not surprising. It is the sadism in serial murder – especially the sexual sadism – that makes for the most popular true crime books. Thus, our sample represented high-profile, visible serial killers whose identities are known. The relatively few non-sadistic killers about whom true-crime books were written either perpetrated grotesque crimes on the corpses of their dead victims (for example, Jeffrey Dahmer who sedated his victims before he strangled them and practiced necrophilia) or amassed a large body count (for example, one of the DC snipers – Lee Malvo – shot his victims from a distance), but they did not seek to inflict pain and suffering on their victims.

By contrast, the sadistic killers were up close and personal – they tortured their victims by strangling, suffocating, stabbing, raping, sodomizing, electrocuting, burning, eating alive, hanging, or holding them under water. Some videotaped the tortures; others audio-taped their victims as they screamed and begged for mercy. Many collected trophies from their victims – their jewellery, underwear, photos, or body parts – to help them later reminisce about their most cherished moments when victims were kept in the throes of unspeakable misery before their lives ended.

Among the forty-four sadistic repeat killers in our sample, thirty-two (or 73 per cent) had reportedly also injured or killed animals. Almost all had engaged in animal cruelty during childhood or adolescence before they began committing serial murder. Twenty-four of the forty-four sadistic killers – 55 per cent – also tortured the animals they abused, by strangling, engaging in bestiality, decapitating while alive, beating, suffocating, stabbing, burning, skinning alive, hanging, or holding them under water.

It may not be a coincidence that these methods of perpetrating animal abuse are so similar to the methods the killers employed to end the lives of their human victims. At least eighteen of the twenty-four (75 per cent) used the same modus operandi in both cases. For example, as a child, Kansas City's Robert Berdella decapitated a duck; he later beheaded one of his male victims; Richard Chase drank both animal and human blood; Carroll Edward Cole strangled puppies and people; John Norman Collins strangled a cat and later on strangled six women; Adolfo de Jesus Constanzo first ritually sacrificed animals as a child and then ritually sacrificed humans as an adult; and Arthur Shawcross practiced bestiality growing up and later raped two of his female victims.

Even the relatively few – four out of eight – serial killers who had not tortured their human victims but abused animals seemed to employ the same modus operandi for both animal and human victims. For example, Jeffrey Dahmer, at the age of ten, collected and dissected road kill. He later dismembered his human victims, keeping their body parts in his refrigerator. As a child, Lee Malvo used a slingshot and marbles to kill stray cats. As one of the DC Snipers, he shot his human victims with a long-distance rifle.

Finally, twenty-one (or 88 per cent) of the twenty-four killers who tortured animals targeted dogs and cats, but not usually in their own home or neighbourhood. Seventeen of the twenty-four sadistic killers who tortured animals (71 per cent) victimized those they did not know. It should be noted that the overwhelming majority of sadistic serial killers similarly targeted humans who were absolute strangers, typically having a small circle of family and friends who were off limits when it came to being victimized and concentrating their attacks on people with whom they had no relationship.

The close resemblance between human and animal victims in the modus operandi of serial killers has been observed in some previous research.[10] In our study, not only did the methods used by serial killers to injure and kill their human victims closely resemble their methods for torturing animals, so did the selection of strangers in the case of both animal and human victims. The graduation hypothesis received some support: many serial killers apparently learn the malicious behaviour as a child with animals and then apply what they have learned in subsequently attacking their human victims. At the same time, serial killers may graduate in a number of different ways, not only from animal cruelty. They might, for example, escalate their violence from sexual assault to murder. Or, they might begin by targeting playmates or younger children. Animal abuse may turn out to be an important, but hardly exclusive, pivotal point for certain children who later become repeat killers.

Study 2

Even if each and every killer had abused animals during childhood, the false positive factor would still prevent making predictive statements from earlier acts of animal cruelty. This is because so many ordinary non-violent individuals engage in animal abuse during childhood, but never go on to commit violence against humans. According to a study by Offord et al.,[11] almost 10 per cent of all children reported to investigators that they had engaged in animal abuse. Kellert and Felthous' study of offenders found that 16 per cent of their comparison group of non-offenders reported committing three to four incidents of abuse.[12] In a study of five hundred and seventy residents of Bloomington, Indiana, Lea[13] reported that 13 per cent answered in the affirmative to the following measure of animal abuse: 'When you were a child or a teenager, were you ever mean or cruel to animals or did you intentionally hurt animals (mammals, not insects, etc.)?' Similarly, Miller and Knutson found that almost 21 per cent of three hundred and eight undergraduate students they studied reportedly perpetrated one or more acts of animal cruelty.[14] In a study of undergraduates majoring in psychology or sociology, Flynn found 34.5 per cent of male students and 9.3 per cent of female students had abused animals.[15] Baldry determined that 51 per cent of Italian youngsters, aged nine to seventeen, engaged in animal cruelty.[16]

Baldry and Agnew have warned that the identification of an abuse episode largely depends on how 'animal cruelty' is defined.[17] Large differences between estimates of the prevalence of animal abuse can be explained, at least in part, by variations in the manner in which the investigators have operationalized animal cruelty. Studies that employ a broad definition of animal abuse – for example, by including insects and reptiles – would be expected to find larger numbers of abusers in the general population. Studies that limit animal abuse to, say, dogs and cats, or to intentional acts of sadism (i.e., torture), would be expected to uncover substantially less abuse. Thus, Miller and Knutson and Flynn derived their relatively low estimate of animal cruelty by investigating extreme forms of abuse;[18] Baldry's operationalization was much broader and therefore more inclusive.[19]

In Study 2, we administered a questionnaire to two hundred and sixty undergraduate students – one hundred and forty-five females and one hundred and fifteen males – at a large Northeastern university who were enrolled in a sociology course. During a regularly scheduled class period, students volunteered to answer a series of questions concerning whether or not they had committed an act of animal abuse during childhood or adolescence. More specifically, they were asked (a) to indicate any and all of the animals they had intentionally injured or killed, (b) the methods they had used in order to inflict injury or death, (c) their degree of familiarity (from pet to stray or wild animal) with the animals they had abused, and (d) whether they had intended to cause pain and suffering to their victims.

Results obtained in Study 2 support the finding of previous investigations that many ordinary people – those who presumably would never commit a serious act of human aggression – perpetrate acts of animal cruelty. We found that 28 per cent admitted having been abusive toward animals. However, the proportion of students who reported abusing dogs and cats was substantially smaller – specifically, only 5 per cent overall. Moreover, 13 per cent of all respondents admitted employing an up close and personal method such as strangulation, bludgeoning, or beating to death. Finally, only 5 per cent admitted that they had intended to inflict pain and suffering on (i.e., to torture) a dog, cat, or other warm-blooded animal. Combining all three criteria – abusing dogs and cats and using a hands-on method and reporting a need to inflict pain and suffering, only three of the two hundred and sixty students (about one per cent) fell into the abusive group.

In sum, then, by limiting incidents of animal cruelty in a normal population to those resembling the modus operandi of many sadistic serial killers – that is, targeting dogs and cats, using a hands-on method, and inflicting pain and suffering – it is possible to make a vast reduction in the false positive problem. Using a narrow standard will undoubtedly cause some cases of future violence to slip between the cracks, but it will also reduce the tendency to identify as potential Hillside Stranglers and Green River Killers those children for whom animal abuse is part of a temporary phase.

Discussion and Conclusion

Our results suggest that a common denominator underlying extreme violence against both humans and animals may be the desire to inflict pain and suffering for pleasure. For some serial killers, the injury and death they cause are means to an end – to silence possible eyewitnesses to their crimes, to retaliate for perceived injustices they have suffered, and so on. But for many other serial killers, the pain and suffering they cause are meant to give them great personal pleasure. Goldberg has suggested that this kind of sadistic violence results from the humiliation and internalized shame certain individuals experience during childhood.[20] In order to compensate, they develop a generalized malevolence whereby they inflict pain and suffering onto others.

According to Kellert and Felthous, some animal cruelty has the same objective.[21] Inflicting injury, suffering, or death on an animal, absent of provocation or hostility, gives an individual tremendous psychological pleasure. In this regard, Dadds *et al.* distinguishes between developmental immaturity and malice in the motivation for abusing animals.[22] The immature child may never progress to the commission of human violence. But the malicious youngster rehearses his sadistic attacks – perhaps on animals, perhaps on other people, perhaps on both – and continues into his adult years to perpetrate the same sorts of sadistic acts on human beings. His attacks on animals are serious and personal. He chooses 'socially valued' or culturally humanized animals – for example, dogs and cats – against which to carry out his sadistic aims, but he is likely to repeat his abusive behaviour on a variety of animals.[23] If he later finds a socially acceptable means of compensating for his sense of powerlessness, then he might very well escape the grip of violence perpetrated against humans. If not, his early experiences with animal cruelty may become a training ground for later committing assaults, rape, and even murder.

Sadistic gratification often involves a desire to exercise power and control over the lives of others. The sadistic serial killer decides who lives and who dies. With his own hands, he regulates the degree of pain and suffering experienced by his victims. Certain cases of both animal cruelty and human destructiveness are similarly motivated: they serve to compensate for a person's feelings of powerlessness and vulnerability; they give such an individual a sense of strength and superiority.[24]

Torture may be the variable that links animal cruelty with serious acts of human violence. Animal abuse may, in certain cases, provide a child or adolescent with a way of reducing his feelings of inferiority, at least temporarily, by displacing the aggression that he feels toward a vulnerable animal. In the short term, some psychologists have even argued that there may actually be some sort of therapeutic advantage for a child who is desperately in need of feeling a sense of personal power.[25] In the long run, however, animal abuse seems also to teach young people that violence is a satisfactory method for gaining a sense of superiority.[26] Moreover, as shown in the repeat violence of serial killers, a single violent episode may not be sufficient. The serial killer continues, over and over again, to target his victims, rarely satisfying his sadistic need for dominance and control in a permanent sense.

The weak or inconsistent evidence connecting animal abuse with human violence may reflect the use of a very broad operationalization of animal cruelty. Shooting birds from a distance may be a result of boredom, fear of rejection from friends, or the need for a challenge – as in hunting. Killing rodents or snakes may be widely regarded as culturally acceptable, not necessarily indicating severe psychopathology in the perpetrator. But our results in Study 1 indicate that torturing animals in an up close and personal way, especially animals like dogs and cats that have been heavily anthropomorphized in our culture, is much more likely to be a red flag. The majority of serial killers who tortured their human victims had also tortured their animal victims, often using the same modus operandi in both cases.

It appears then that the torture of animals early on may have served as a rehearsal for the human violence that came later. Inflicting pain and suffering may be indicative of a strong sadistic impulse – a need to feel powerful and strong at the expense of victims. The hands-on approach suggests that the killer seeks to control his victim. He may gain pleasure from his victims' pain; he may feel superior to the extent that he degrades and belittles his victim.

It could still be argued that any attempt to predict human violence from animal abuse is bound to fail, even if each and every killer can be shown to have tortured animals. The false positive problem is not reduced by showing a strong relationship between animal abuse and human violence, because there are apparently millions of normal people who have committed animal cruelty. However, our results suggest that the false positive problem can be substantially reduced – if not almost eliminated – by limiting predictive acts of animal abuse to those in which dogs and cats are tortured in a hands-on manner. Animal abuse, as broadly defined, may be pervasive; but not necessarily predictive of subsequent violence against humans.

Finally, it should be noted that the false positive issue is problematic only if it serves as a basis for stigmatizing and punishing children. If instead we reach out to youngsters who abuse animals to help them, in order to give them an improved sense of self-esteem and confidence, the false positive problem is minimized. At worst, we might give a few children our assistance when it is not needed. In the process, we will also be reducing animal cruelty.

Notes

1 We are grateful to Sarah Bakanosky and Eric Madfis who competently assisted us with the data collection and analysis phases of our two studies, and the Kenneth A. Scott Charitable Trust, a KeyBack Trust, for supporting this research.

2 Jack Levin, *Serial killers and sadistic murderers: Up close and personal* (Amherst, NY: Prometheus Books, 2008).

3 James A. Fox and Jack Levin, *Extreme killing* (Thousand Oaks, CA: Sage Publications Inc., 2005).

4 Steven Egger, 'Linkage blindness: A systemic myopia', in S. Egger (ed.), *Serial murder: An elusive phenomenon* (New York: Praeger, 1990).

5 Jack Levin and James Alan Fox, *Mass murder: America's growing menace* (New York: Berkley True Crime, 1991).

6 See Suzanne R. Goodney Lea, *Delinquency and animal cruelty* (New York: LFB Scholarly Publishing, 2007).

7 Jeremy Wright and Christopher Hensley, 'From animal cruelty to serial murder: Applying the graduation hypothesis', *International Journal of Offender Therapy and Comparative Criminology* 47 (2003), 71–88.

8 Robert K. Ressler, Ann W. Burgess, and John E. Douglas, *Sexual homicide: Patterns and motives* (New York: The Free Press, 1988).

9 Arnold Arluke, Jack Levin, Carter Luke, and Frank Ascione, 'The relationship of animal abuse to violence and other forms of antisocial behavior', *Journal of Interpersonal Violence* 14 (1999): 963–975.

10 Wright and Hensley, 'From animal cruelty'; Linda Merz-Perez, Kathleen M. Heide, and Ira J. Silverman, 'Childhood cruelty to animals and subsequent violence against humans', *International Journal of Therapy and Comparative Criminology* 45 (2001): 556–573.

11 D. R. Offord, M. H. Boyle, and Y. A. Racine, 'The epidemiology of antisocial behavior in childhood and adolescence', in D. J. Pepler and K. H. Rubin (eds), *The development and treatment of childhood aggression* (Hillsdale, NJ: Lawrence Erlbaum Associates, 1991).

12 Stephen R. Kellert and Alan R. Felthous, 'Childhood cruelty toward animals among criminals and noncriminals', *Human Relations* 38 (1985): 1113–1129.

13 Lea, *Delinquency*.

14 K. S. Miller and J. F. Knutson, 'Reports of severe physical punishment and exposure to animal cruelty by inmates convicted of felonies and by university students', *Child Abuse and Neglect* 21 (1997): 59–82.

15 C. P. Flynn, 'Animal abuse in childhood and later support for interpersonal violence in families', *Society & Animals* 7 (1999): 161–172.

16 A. C. Baldry, 'Animal abuse and exposure to interpersonal violence in Italian youth', *Journal of Interpersonal Violence* 18 (2003): 258–281.

17 *Ibid.*; Robert Agnew, 'The causes of animal abuse: A social psychological analysis', *Theoretical Criminology* 2 (1998): 177–209.

18 Miller and Knutson, 'Reports'; Flynn, 'Animal abuse'.

19 Baldry, 'Animal abuse'.

20 Carl Goldberg, *Speaking with the devil: A dialogue with evil* (New York: Viking, 1996).

21 Kellert and Felthous, 'Childhood cruelty'.

22 Mark R. Dadds, Cynthia M. Turner, and John McAloon, 'Developmental links between cruelty to animals and human violence', *The Australian and New Zealand Journal of Criminology* 35 (2002): 363–382.

23 *Ibid.*

24 Kellert and Felthous, 'Childhood cruelty'.

25 J. Bossard and E. Boll, *The sociology of child development*, 4th edn (New York: Harper and Row, 1966).

26 Arnold Arluke, *Just a dog: Understanding animal cruelty and ourselves* (Philadelphia, PA: Temple University Press, 2006).

PART

V

Ethical Perspectives on Human–Animal Relations

Part V focuses on the underlying ethical perspectives that should inform our judgment about the link. No matter how much empirical evidence can be adduced in favour, the evidence still needs to be evaluated, and that, crucially, depends upon our ethical perspective.

Conor Gearty (*Is Human Rights Speciesist?*) begins by questioning whether humans alone can have rights. 'Speciesism' may be defined as the *arbitrary* favouring of one species over another. After surveying the history of rights language, he concludes that the 'collapse of intellectual confidence in the specialness of the human, the decline in arguments for human uniqueness *vis-à-vis* the rest of living things on the planet, now offers a window of opportunity for other animals, or rather to be accurate for their human protagonists'. This is an opportunity to say that 'certain animals too deserve to fit within the world of right behaviour and of entitlement to proper treatment that hitherto has been the preserve of humans alone'.

Mark H. Bernstein (*Responding Ethically to Animal Abuse*) takes issue with philosophers who argue that animal abuse is wrong only by virtue of such a practice having negative effects on intra-human behaviour. Animal abuse, he argues, is intrinsically wrong in the same way that human abuse is morally wrong. It is wrong because 'it harms or mistreats innocent creatures who, because of the kind of beings they are, have a right not to have their welfare denigrated without exceptionally good reasons'. Elizabeth Clawson (*The New Canaries in the Mine: The Priority of Human Welfare in Animal Abuse Prosecution*) largely concurs. After reviewing the evidence of animal abuse prosecutions in one US State, she detects philosophical and moral anomalies in the way in which heavy emphasis is placed on human welfare to the detriment of animals. Animals, she claims, have become the 'new canaries' in the mine: 'animal abuse deserves attention not only as an indicator of a danger to humans'. Rather, 'Animals merit respectful treatment as inherently valuable beings', she concludes.

Mark Rowlands (*The Structure of Evil*) challenges the notion that evil consists only in intentional acts. 'Stupidity of belief and derogation of duty can do their work only when the victim is powerless – helplessness is the canvas on which the portrait of human evil is painted', he argues. But if that is correct 'then there are more evil acts, and more evil people than we would care to imagine or admit'. After reviewing two cases of animal and child abuse, Rowlands concludes that:

> Humans don't merely treat the weak badly. Humans make things weak so that they may treat them badly. If we wanted a one-sentence definition of humans, this one would do: humans are the animals that engineer the possibility of their own evil.

In a similarly reflective mode, Daniel B. Williams (*'Vile attentions': On the Limits of Sympathetic Imagination*) ponders the limits of human imagination. Using the novels of J. M. Coetzee, he suggests ways in which 'failures to treat animals with kindness and ethical sense are constitutive of, and share structural features with, similar incapacities to treat human beings in ways that take seriously their own relation to suffering'. Our incapacity to perceive animal suffering – specifically to *see* their gaze and *hear* their voices – is part and parcel of a general structure of ethical insensitivity from which we all suffer. Williams concludes that instead of 'disvaluing these voices, we should take courage and pursue their ethical suggestion, namely the calling into question of any expression or action that predicates violence on a morally considerable human/animal distinction'. Moreover, all 'gestures of linguistic diminution and degradation' should be challenged '"even" and especially with respect to animals'.

12

Is Human Rights Speciesist?[1]

CONOR GEARTY

This question seems absurd until one thinks of it as a deliberately contrived way of putting a deeper point, one that I will argue in what follows is difficult easily to dismiss: what makes human beings so special that they – and they alone among the animals – warrant the protection that flows from being entitled to rights? The usual stock responses to this are not as satisfactory as once they were. In this essay I shall review these orthodox explanations for the species-specificity of human rights, and in doing so will develop an argument for the justification of rights which is not necessarily limited to humans alone. This then takes us into a new field, the terrain of animal (including human) rights. The paper will end with some brief reflections on what might be entailed in such a (revolutionary?) approach to our subject.

It is clear that the development of the idea of human rights has indeed been tied up with the story of the human. On the standard account, it starts with the Greeks (Plato; Aristotle; Epictetus), picks up some Roman pedigree on its way (Cicero) via the Catholic Church (from St Paul through Plotinus to St Thomas Aquinas) to northern Europe, where it settles down in England (Hobbes; Locke) and France (Rousseau), before setting up further outposts in the United States.[2] The hit list of early human rights documents referenced in the textbooks is a hymn to the civilizing progress of what we now think of as western statehood: Magna Carta in 1215, the American Declaration of Independence in 1776, the French Declaration of the Rights of Man and of the Citizen in 1789, and so on. The emphasis is on the rights of humans, of course, but what I want to note here is that it is about the control of power as well – each of these documents reflects a trend in the culture from which it emerged which is assertive of a right to resist abusive authority: Magna Carta was concerned with limiting the power of King John; the 1776 Declaration with establishing the freedom from external coercion of the American colonies; and the French Declaration with overthrowing an entire system of magisterial rule. These examples could be expanded to include other documents, such as the English Bill of Rights of 1688. The important point for the present purpose is that while to a greater or lesser extent the drafters of these fundamental texts were alighting upon the language of rights to make their point, they were doing so as rhetoricians of revolt, as liberation philosophers whose focus was more on the first than second of these two words. To put this another way, they were activist opponents of the abuse of power first and 'human rights' campaigners second. The language of human rights was either deployed at the time (as with the French and the Americans) or imposed later (as with Magna Carta and the English Bill of Rights) as a way of capturing in words the essence of what the drafters were about, and what they were doing was opposing the abuse of power in a series of acts of revolutionary solidarity; what they were *not* engaged in was pondering the essential features of the human species. On this analysis, 'human rights' stops being a description of some essential truth about a species and becomes a subset of a larger idea – resistance to abusive power.

The same underlying theme can be detected in later developments in the philosophy of human rights.[3] The concept of objective right – the idea of a natural law determining right behaviour which stood above the people of the world and ordered their conduct – is an old one, having found expression through the intellectual work done in the first centuries of the Christian era and then in the early medieval period; the writings of St Paul, St Augustine and St Thomas Aquinas remain embedded within Western culture to this day (and indeed more widely than that through the reach of the universal Catholic Church). Gradually, even in the period prior to what is routinely called the 'Enlightenment' (a term to which I shall return), there emerged the notion of a subjective human right, a right that individuals could have in view of their humanity and which required of others that they behave in a certain way towards them. This idea has paved the way for our modern version of rights as entitlements each of us has, as a person, and which are inherent in us on account of our humanity. Where does this notion of subjective rights come from? What purpose did it serve? Is the species restriction necessary to its coherence? Let me take each of these questions in turn.

First, the origins of subjective right. In the sixteenth century, at the high-point of Spanish imperial expansion, regal power required – and secured – various theoretical and theological justifications as to why it was right to wage war against the Indians, or, as we would call them today, the indigenous people of the Americas. One such apologist was Ginés de Sepúlveda, whose great contribution to progress has not been his own reactionary writings but rather the response he provoked from Bartolomé de las Casas. An early pioneer who had known Columbus, de las Casas was so repelled by Spanish excesses that he became a Dominican priest and dedicated his life to what we would now call anti-imperialist and anti-racist work. Searching for a way to express his opposition to the attitudes of his fellow nationals towards the natives, he found it in the language of human rights, rooted in the religion which he shared with the oppressors. His *In Defence of the Indians* published in 1584 stands as an early human rights classic in which the emphasis is on the shared, God-ordained humanity of the colonialist and the local, and how this should make ethically impossible the barbarism of the wars against the latter.[4] Taking such a line was certainly a good tactic at the time, but it came at a high price for the rest of the animal kingdom. De las Casas contrasted the native Americans with animals to the advantage of the former (and naturally, therefore, to the disadvantage of the latter). The natives were 'not ignorant, inhuman or bestial'.[5] Rather, it was the 'merciless man acting against human reason' who was the barbarian, plunging 'blindly into crimes that only the wildest beasts of the forests would commit'.[6] Quoting Aristotle, de las Casas noted that 'just as the man who obeys right reason and excellent laws is superior to all the animals, so too, if he leaves the path of right reason and law, he is the wickedest, worst, and most inhuman of animals'.[7]

The intention here is not to abandon the animals, just as it was not to jettison the Jews and Saracens whose informed unbelief was for de las Casas 'much more serious and damnable than the unbelief of [the] idolaters [i.e., Indians]'[8] who had not had the chance to hear the word of God. Rather, the argument was opportunistic, drawing on religious texts and on rights arguments as instruments to achieve the desired outcome, which was that the natives be treated better by the imperialists. All theology and philosophy was subjugated to this goal. So in identifying this reason for this idea of subjective right, we can see also that the species boundary is not a necessary one. Just as had been the case with the drafters of Magna Carta and the various other revolutionaries that were to follow this Dominican radical, de las Casas was concerned primarily with the abuse of power and how both to stop and then prevent it. His focus was on marginalized and exploited humans, but this species restriction was not necessitated by his governing position, which was about the prevention of cruelty that followed from the abuse of power.

Let me now return to the 'Enlightenment', the most prominent thinker of which, for human rights purposes, is Immanuel Kant (1724–1804). The achievement here was once again at a price to other animals: Kant reconfigured our understanding of the human so as to maintain the specialness of the species, but now without the need for any kind of immaterial soul which was what had hitherto been believed to have rendered these human creatures different from the many other animals on the planet. Following the theme of the present discussion, we can characterize this as primarily an act of revolt against the power of the Church, and in particular the control Rome had hitherto exercised over the individual mind, telling it what to think, what to believe and (especially) what not to say.[9] While this rebellion manifested itself in a rejection of Church authority, however, it did not go so far as to deny an underlying premise of Christian thinking, namely the uniqueness of man (and woman) in the world. Rather it merely shifted the basis for this belief away from the heavens and into the human person itself. Our species was no longer special because we had a soul, but on account of our capacity for autonomous decision-making about the world around us. Our consciousness enabled us to reason and to reflect, to make life plans and sort out the kind of projects upon which we wished to embark. Our rights flowed out of this interest in freedom and liberty, which in turn hinged upon our remarkable autonomy, the mind replacing the soul as the fount of our uniqueness.

But how species-specific are these Enlightenment ideas? My colleague at the London School of Economics, Dr Alasdair Cochrane, has analyzed this question from the perspective of animal rights, asking the important question of the extent to which the 'intrinsic interest in liberty that humans possess . . . founded upon their status as autonomous agents' can be translated across the species.[10] To start with, Cochrane 'rules out as possessors of autonomous agency those animals that lack any conscious experience at all'. To be able to have goals and pursue them, 'some conscious experience will undoubtedly be necessary'. The relevant distinction in the non-human animal world is probably between 'vertebrates who possess complex nervous systems, and invertebrates who do not'.[11] It would seem to be the case that 'the physiological structure of animals such as mammals, birds, reptiles, amphibians and fish strongly suggests that they have the capacity for conscious experience, whereas that of insects, molluscs, crustaceans, arachnids and so on suggests that they do not'.[12] If these animals have a capacity for conscious experience then they – like humans – will have a capacity to feel pleasure and pain. Furthermore a number of them will feel desire and then a sub-category of these may well be able to act on their desire, to reflect on the feeling of desire and make choices accordingly – in other words, to display autonomy. Now it may well be the case that only very few animals can do this, great apes for example (chimpanzees and gorillas) and cetaceans (whales and dolphins): Cochrane is agnostic on this and he is right when he says that further research is required, both with regard to these animals and generally. But the goal here is not to build a case for animal rights as such; it is to challenge the species-specificity of autonomy. So if we can establish even a single analogous capacity for autonomy outside the human species, in which direction the literature (at least as regards the higher mammals) does tilt, then we will have shown that this state of consciousness is not unique to humans, and by doing this we will have demonstrated that the emergence of a philosophy of subjective rights in the eighteenth century is not *necessarily* restricted to the human species and that species alone. Armed with this insight, we can more confidently return to our starting point for human rights talk in this period of world history, namely the role of the idea as an emancipatory force against the abuse of power. Clearly, at this level of generality there is no inhibiting species barrier in play at all.

The contention that the true basis for human rights in the Enlightenment is concern about the abuse of power rather than a foundational commitment to a uniquely human autonomy draws further strength from the difficulty that non-autonomous humans have always posed for this theory of rights. Plenty of (particularly powerless) humans fail the test of engagement with the world that Kant and his followers have determined to be the key to personhood. The most obvious and by far the largest categories are babies and very young persons, but here the sensible answer is to point to their potential for autonomy, and then to say that by protecting them now we are investing in their future success as 'real' (i.e., autonomous) people. While this is the case, what about an anencephalic baby which, though a live human organism, is simply lacking in the bits of matter (in particular the brain) which would ever allow it to pass Kant's test? Or other 'ex-persons' whose capacity to reason and engage in autonomous decision-making has been irretrievably destroyed by injury – the patient in a permanent vegetative state, for example? There is debate about these marginal persons, with some theorists following the logic of their commitment to autonomy and recognizing that the implication of their restricted approach to personhood is that such human creatures have either never lived as true persons (the anencephalic baby) or have died as persons in advance of the body to which they have been tethered. But other proponents of human rights strongly deny this, claiming the need to protect such humans remains, indeed is stronger than ever, while the law (in the United Kingdom at least) muddies the water by allowing death to follow from the (mere) withdrawal of treatment but insisting at the same time that nothing should be done deliberately to bring about such an end-result.[13] This dispute over the reach of autonomy as the organizing principle of rights, even in relation to human creatures, further demonstrates that it cannot be an exclusive foundation for rights, that there are other values jostling for attention, the (religious) sanctity of human life certainly, but also some strong sense of the need to protect the weak from the abuse of power, in other words the meta-idea behind rights for which this essay is contending.

So far we have said little about non-human animals as such. The move towards compassion for animals which was reflected in the enactment of animal welfare legislation in the UK and elsewhere in the nineteenth century flowed from a different ethical stream from that which had produced the human rights language of earlier generations, but it was not very different in sentiment from the feelings which produced the anti-slavery and humanitarian movements of the same period. As far as the first of these is concerned, the unfinished business of de las Casas focused on convincing opinion that mattered that those unlucky men and women who were in law the mere property of others were in fact – and despite this proprietorial complication – truly members of the human species. Bizarre though it seems to modern opinion, in many ways this leap of understanding in the nature of the slave, from mere chattel into full member of the species (and therefore no longer property, being necessarily free), required a larger job of persuasion than any equivalent effort today to convince the public of the entitlement of at least certain animals to a limited range of rights. As late as 1857, the United States Supreme Court could confidently assert the property status of the slave,[14] and as is well known in that jurisdiction it took more than the verbal persuasive powers of the anti-slave-holding North to win the day. As far as the humanitarian advances of the nineteenth century were concerned, the effort to develop a more humane attitude to one's opponents in the battlefield, which began in the 1850s, received a major impetus with the formation of the Lieber Code during the civil war of 1860–65 that followed the 1857 US Supreme Court decision on slaves. The persuasive challenge facing the proponents of the Code, one that to this day remains controversial, was to get military forces to see that their opponents in the field had not forfeited their right to be treated with respect as humans merely on account of the hostile activity in which they were engaged. Whereas the slaves had to be argued into membership of the human species, the soldiers in conflict had to be protected from de facto expulsion from humanity, with all the cruelty and unnecessary killing that would result. The underlying idea behind each of these progressive movements was a strong commitment to the protection of the vulnerable (slaves/captured soldiers) from abuse of power (by their owners/captors). The analogy with the animal welfare movement, which was building a strong momentum at the same time, is clear.[15]

Let me sum up where the argument has taken us so far. Our historical survey reveals a fundamental idea which lies behind the various elaborations of human rights down the ages, elaborations which encompass specific rights-talk but also go beyond such discourse to include events and documents which have long been claimed by human rights protagonists – and rightly so – as belonging to their story. This idea is the familiar one that power should not be abused, that those who are victims of abuse of this nature should have an entitlement to resist, and that such resistance can be (perhaps even – depending on the particular culture and moment – prudently ought to be) phrased in the language of human rights. The various religious and philosophical explanations of human rights are, on this analysis, not complete in themselves, but are rather reflections of this underlying sensitivity to the abuse of power. And where in turn does this attitude to power come from? Here once again the nineteenth century provides a critical contribution, albeit this time of a destabilizing sort. The pioneering work of Darwin and Nietzsche (and the twentieth-century followers of each) has shown us that the difference between man and the other animals is no more than one of kind (Darwin), and furthermore may even be merely the result of how we use words and phrases to organize our world into created rather than objective categories (Nietzsche). If these nineteenth-century thinkers did indeed teach us that we are now merely clever animals who are 'beyond good and evil', how can we form an adverse opinion of any sort on the abuse of power, much less call resistance to such abuse a matter of asserting our human rights? And if 'abuse of power' is neither good nor bad for inter-relationships within the human species, how can it be different for the human in his or her interaction with other animals?

It is certainly the case that some post-modern philosophers draw from these Nietzschean observations the conclusion that while the abuse of power remains a bad thing, there can nevertheless be no such thing as 'human rights' through which to articulate our disapproval of such conduct, since there are no foundations outside language capable of underpinning the kind of universal ethical judgement inherent in use of the term.[16] Not surprisingly this is usually not good enough for people who think of themselves as human rights scholars. Among this group are those who acknowledge the force but desire to avoid the implications of such anti-foundationalism, and who therefore seek to locate their objections to the abuse of power in something more grounded than neutral observation or unspoken assumption.[17] From such a perspective, it is tempting to draw out of the human inclination to do 'good' – in other words, to avoid abuses of power but rather to act with hospitality towards the stranger – a new kind of (highly generalized) natural law based on compassion and empathy which can then sensibly and without difficulty be said to find contemporary expression in the language of human rights, as a kind of 'Esperanto of the virtuous'.[18] This approach allows the activist/scholar who adopts it to ground his or her commitment to human rights as opposition to the abuse of power in a set of (very) basic (and therefore universal) observations about the nature of that animal that he or she is happy to classify as human for the purpose of organizing the living world into (among other categories) species.

It should be said immediately that the implication of this is not to separate the human from other animals who might show similar characteristics, or to rule out natural reactions to animals that might similarly be given linguistic expression in terms of rights. The approach set out above does not insist that because humans can be observed to act altruistically/ compassionately/empathetically towards their fellows, it therefore follows that as a matter of moral obligation (deploying this term in the traditional sense of a form of reasoned duty) they ought to act only or ever in this way: there is no incoherent deduction of an 'ought' from an 'is' in this reading of the foundations of human rights, and therefore no insistence upon a moral attitude that only humans can understand and act upon.[19] Rather, the language of human rights is being used to describe a thread of behaviour that is natural and, from the point of view of the flourishing of the species, valuable. It is because we intuit the latter that we bolster our tendency to do this kind of good with the language of moral obligation, to persuade ourselves of its general rightness and to bolster us against irresolution – against the tendency to go for short-term selfishness at the expense of medium- to long-term species-gain. The moral obligation apparently inherent in the term 'human rights' is therefore not a moral truth as such in the traditional sense described above; rather, on this account, it is a kind of linguistic moral mask we assume to foster our sense of hospitality, and thereby to help keep us on the right long-term path for our species. (It is worth noting that 'human rights' is only one of many varieties of language engaged in this kind of word-game, today's 'natural/homeland security' or, in past ages, 'racial purity', fulfil similar linguistic functions, albeit deducing very different conclusions from observations of other, darker elements of human nature.)

Where does all this leave animal rights? The collapse of intellectual confidence in the specialness of the human, the decline in arguments for human uniqueness *vis-à-vis* the rest of the living things on the planet, now offers a window of opportunity for other animals – or rather, to be accurate, for their human protagonists – to be able to say much more convincingly than in the past that certain animals also deserve to fit within the world of right behaviour and of entitlement to proper treatment, which hitherto has been the preserve of the human alone. The usual stock responses as to why this should not be so (the human soul; the autonomy of the human person) are not as readily available as they once were, while the contemporary answers that tend to convince on the foundations of human rights (the need to protect the vulnerable from the abuse of power; the importance of compassion) are not necessarily limited to the human species at all – indeed can have a special relevance to the non-human animal whose life chances are so entirely in the hands of its human master (or mistress). The strength of human rights language has always lain in its power to expand its net of solicitude outwards towards categories of humans (women, slaves, prisoners-of-war; and also children, prisoners, those with mental and physical disabilities, and many others) previously invisible to the powerful. There is no reason in principle why this outward momentum should be permanently blocked at a species barrier that is, after all, only a human construct. The kind of reflections about nature that produce observable conduct classifiable as reflecting a 'human rights approach' might be replicated by similar observations producing a more general language of animal rights. What this entails in terms of exact rights would need to be worked through; which rights are available to each kind of animal (including the human) would naturally depend on the nature of the species under discussion, its capacity to feel pain, its ability to engage with the world around it, its conscious involvement with the world outside itself, and many other factors. But in this the sixtieth anniversary year of the Universal Declaration of Human Rights, those who are truly dedicated to human rights should not be afraid of characterizing their subject as a subset of a wider topic, that of animal rights, albeit a subset without which the larger category would never have been effectively articulated as such. This does not diminish the importance of *human* rights, which would inevitably remain more sophisticated and complete than their animal counterparts, but it might well do long-term good to the subject by putting its intellectual foundations on a firmer basis than they presently enjoy.

Notes

1   I am indebted to the Reverend Professor Andrew Linzey, through whose writings I first became aware of the value of the idea of speciesism. See A. Linzey and D. Yamamoto (eds), *Animals on the agenda: Questions about animals for theology and ethics* (Chicago, IL: University of Illinois Press, 1998). For an excellent overview of the contributions to this subject of various thinkers, see A. Linzey and P. B. Clarke (eds), *Animal rights: A historical anthology* (New York: Columbia University Press, 2004).

2   J. Mahoney, *The challenge of human rights* (Oxford: Blackwell, 2007); M. R. Ishay, *The human rights reader*, 2nd edn (London: Routledge, 2007).

3   For a good recent study, see M. J. Perry, *Towards a theory of human rights: Religion, law, courts* (New York: Cambridge University Press, 2007), chapter 2.

4   See M. R. Ishay, *The human rights reader*, pp. 165–68.

5   *Ibid.*, p. 166.

6   *Ibid.*, p. 165.

7   *Ibid.*; the reference to Aristotle is from the *Politics*, book 1, chapter 2.

8   *Ibid.*, p. 168.

9 See generally A. C. Grayling, *Towards the light: The story of the struggles for liberty and rights that made the modern west* (London: Bloomsbury, 2007). Also of interest is L. Hunt, *Inventing human rights: A history* (New York: W. W. Norton, 2007).

10 'Do animals have an interest in liberty?', *Political Studies* (forthcoming), mss with author, p. 8.

11 *Ibid.*, citing D. DeGrazia, *Taking animals seriously: Mental life and moral status* (Cambridge: Cambridge University Press, 1996); M. Rowlands, *Animals like us* (London: Verso, 2002); and R. Garner, *Animal ethics* (Cambridge: Polity, 2005).

12 *Ibid.*

13 *Airedale National Health Trust v. Bland* [1993] AC 789. See also Mental Capacity Act 2005, s 4(5).

14 *Dred Scott v. Sandford* 60 US 393 (1857).

15 H. Kean, *Animal rights: Political and social change in Britain since 1800* (Chicago, IL: Reaktion, 1998).

16 See especially R. Rorty, 'Human rights, rationality and sentimentality', in S. Shute and S. Hurley (eds), *On human rights* (New York: Basic Books, 1993), and for a more general perspective the same author's *Contingency, irony and solidarity* (Cambridge: Cambridge University Press, 1989).

17 A fascinating writer in this regard is Costas Douzinas. See his *The end of human rights* (Oxford: Hart Publishing, 2000) and *Human rights and empire: The political philosophy of cosmopolitanism* (Abingdon: Routledge-Cavendish, 2007).

18 These points are explored further in C. A. Gearty, *Can human rights survive?* (Cambridge: Cambridge University Press, 2006), chapter 2.

19 For a stimulating discussion of the complex relationship between 'ought' and 'is' in this field, see J. Griffin, *On human rights* (Oxford: Oxford University Press, 2008).

Responding Ethically to Animal Abuse

MARK H. BERNSTEIN

I am confident that all of us reading this chapter, along with an overwhelming majority of the population, concur that animal abuse is morally wrong. Although such a thesis garners nearly unanimous support, it is not trivial. Rather it is a substantive moral thesis that transcends the meanings of the terms involved; the thesis, to put it in philosophical jargon, is not analytic. We abuse our automobiles (by not getting the proper periodic tune-ups for the car), abuse the rules of etiquette (by using the large fork for eating our salad), and abuse our health (by eating a diet bloated with saturated fats) without – obviously, at least – doing anything morally untoward. Thus, it may be objected that, despite broad support, I cannot justifiably begin with the commonsensical idea that animal abuse, even *prima facie*, is immoral. This objection does not deny that animals are abused or even that there is something wrong about abusing animals, but does question the supposition that this behaviour should be discussed in moral terms.

This is a sophisticated complaint. At root, it raises the difficult and murky area of delineating moral assessments from other kinds of normative evaluations. I do not pretend to have anything approaching a satisfactory answer even when we leave the arena of non-human animals and move to the domain consisting of purely human practices. That is, a committed sceptic, on similar grounds, may insist on some justification for viewing human abuse as an ethical matter. Still, the fact that most people think of animal abuse as a moral issue should count for something, and to assume it to be such should prove offensive to only a few professional philosophers. This virtual unanimity of opinion makes me confident of the assumption, although not dogmatically so.

Of course, to concede that animal abuse is a practice that legitimately calls for moral assessment, and is presumably morally wrong, does not gesture toward the reason for its wrongness. It is this question – 'what constitutes the moral wrongness of animal abuse?'; or, equivalently, 'what is it about animal abuse that makes it morally wrong?' – that does elicit disparate answers. My own answer, in short, is that animal abuse is wrong because it harms or mistreats innocent creatures who, because of the kind of beings they are, have a right not to have their welfare denigrated without exceptionally good reasons. But my aim here is not to defend this specific answer. Instead I want to focus my discussion on a very different kind of answer, one that situates, at least in large measure, the wrongness of animal abuse in the causal relationship such abuse has with human abuse.

I

I want first, to distinguish two kinds of answers to the question of what makes abusing animals immoral. One type of answer, of which my own is an example, makes the immorality primarily a function of the negative effects that the abuse has on the animal herself. This kind of reply thinks of various non-relational or intrinsic properties of the animal as valuable to the animal. It conceives abuse as an unjustified means of reducing or eliminating these valuable qualities and frequently producing negative attributes in their stead. So, for example, physical abuse causes animals to suffer. Suffering is a non-relational state (animals can suffer in isolation) that is harmful to its subject. Unless there are overriding reasons to produce this suffering, the abuse is morally wrong. Abuse can take many forms, from frustrating animals to mitigating their autonomy and free will. For our purposes, the central point is that all of these suggestions share the idea that the wrongness of animal abuse is primarily located in the diminution of the animal itself and not in virtue of any functional or relational role the animal plays.

Compare this to a second kind of view that primarily, if not exclusively, situates the moral wrongness of animal abuse not in the harm done to the animal *per se*, but instead in harm done to other beings that are related to the abused animal in particular ways. A prime example of this second type of view is purveyed by those who claim, roughly, that animal abuse is wrong because it leads to, or makes more probable, human abuse. Animal abuse, therefore, is instrumentally wrong and not intrinsically wrong, and so differs from human abuse in this significant way.

Immanuel Kant, the great eighteenth-century Prussian philosopher, is paradigmatic of the instrumentalist view of the wrongness of animal abuse. For Kant, the immorality of harming non-human animals resided exclusively in the fact that such behaviour would likely 'harden our hearts' against our fellow human beings. A bit more carefully, Kant believed, what has been subsequently confirmed, that animal abuse makes it more likely that human abuse will occur. At bottom, Kant is making a point about human psychology. He believed that we are the sort of creatures who are disposed to act cruelly toward our own species in virtue of acting in similar ways toward at least some non-human animals.

II

Thus we have two views regarding the constitution of the badness of animal abuse. The non-instrumentalist believes that the badness primarily consists of the harm the abused animal suffers, while for the instrumentalist, exemplified in its starkest terms by Kant, the badness is exclusively a matter of making human abuse more likely than it would otherwise be. It is interesting to note that there is nothing in this distinction that should lead one to conclusions about the comparative badness either of the abuse committed or the seriousness of the punishment that should be meted out. As a purely autobiographical comment, people seem to think that non-instrumentalists consider animal abuse to be worse than instrumentalists do, and that they also treat animal abuse as a more serious offence that deserves a harsher response than do instrumentalists. But there is no reason for someone not to believe that animal abuse is just as immoral, and perhaps even more so in virtue of it causing an increased propensity in human abuse than because of the harm it causes the abused animal herself. There is no logical impediment, that is, for a Kantian to think of animal abuse as equally wrong – if not more wrong – and deserving of repercussions at least as serious as the non-instrumentalist who believes that the wrongness of animal abuse lies primarily in the harm the animal suffers directly. Yet the Kantian position that attributes only instrumental disvalue to animal abuse is deeply troubling, offending basic moral intuitions. Let us consider, briefly, three scenarios.

(1) (**PC**) Consider a case involving pre-emptive causation. John, a young man, is about to abuse some animals. Were he to abuse these animals, he would, in fact, 'harden his heart' and subsequently abuse human beings. Just as he is about to begin his animal abuse, he unwittingly takes a pill that has the same causal effect that the animal abuse would have had. That is, as a result of swallowing the pill the same amount and quality of human abuse is brought about. Since the Kantian ascribes no intrinsic moral significance to animal abuse, he would need to judge both possibilities ('worlds') as morally equivalent. This surely seems wrong; the world with animal abuse and human abuse seems morally worse than the world with equal human abuse absent the animal abuse.

(2) (**Both**) Consider, simply, a John who both abuses animals and as a result abuses humans. Compare this to Jack who simply abuses humans to exactly the same degree as John. *Pace* Kant, John seems to be morally worse than Jack.

(3) (**Death**) While (PC) and (Both) traded on the scarcely radical idea that abusing animals is not necessary for human abuse, (Death) relies on the idea that abusing animals cannot be sufficient for human abuse. Suppose John abuses animals and dies shortly afterward. Even if the animal abuse raised the likelihood of his abusing humans, since death prevented the abuse from taking place, it would seem the Kantian would need to say, counter-intuitively, that nothing John actually did was morally untoward.

Kant attributed no intrinsic or direct moral significance to non-human animals because he believed that animals lack the requisite kind of rationality necessary for the self-legislation of moral principles and are thereby excluded from our moral domain. In simpler language, animals are unable, by their very nature, to act from moral principles, and since such motivation is necessary for their pain, suffering, and frustrations to count morally and non-instrumentally, the only wrong that can accrue to animal abuse is indirect.

Kant's response is an instance on a type of common response for those who wish to attribute non-relational value to humans while attributing only relational or instrumental value to non-human animals. The general form of argument is as follows. There is a particular property that an individual must have, or have to a certain degree, that confers intrinsic moral significance upon the individual. Animals either completely lack this property or have this property to a limited extent, and so their pain, suffering, and frustration are eliminated as candidates for our direct moral concern; these animals have no intrinsic moral significance.

The most popular response to this reasoning has come in the form of the so-called marginal case argument. There are 'marginal human beings' that also either lack the given property or have it to a degree no greater than that of animals. Thus, if intrinsic significance requires this property (or having this property to a certain degree) then there are some human beings who lack intrinsic significance and so, at best, their pain, suffering, and frustration are only of instrumental import. So, for example, there are severely brain-damaged and senile humans who clearly lack the type of rationality that Kant suggests as necessary for intrinsic significance. Thus, on Kant's own grounds, these humans lack intrinsic import. Unless one wants to bite the bullet in cases like these and accept the fact that some humans lack intrinsic significance, such a conclusion is intolerable and thus serves as a *reductio* of the Kantian strategy. Other properties that have been proffered and serve as grist for the marginal case argument are autonomy, free will, and language use.

Although it is difficult to deny the empirical premise that some humans fall below the threshold for having the morally significant quality in question, there are a host of responses available to the Kantian instrumentalist. First, he might not think that biting the bullet comes at too expensive a cost. He may suggest that it is a mistake to think that all human lives have equal value or even that all human lives have intrinsic moral significance. Those unfortunate humans who suffer from very advanced Alzheimer's disease or who are extremely retarded ought to have their moral import considered on a par with non-human animals with similar mental ability. The Kantian may suggest that in very extreme cases – for example anencephalics, who are born with no brain except for a stem – nothing other than pure sentimentalism keeps us from considering their moral significance as anything other than instrumental.

A second strategy concedes that not all humans meet a minimum threshold for having intrinsic moral significance, and so to this extent are similar to non-human animals; but, unlike animals, these marginal human beings have, or at least had, the *capacity* to obtain the morally significant property that confers intrinsic significance. So, for example, the person who is brain-damaged and can no longer hope to reach the Kantian threshold for rationality required for her obtaining intrinsic moral importance, had the capacity for this kind of rationality prior, say, to her tragic car accident. In this way, she is fundamentally different from animals who at no time have the capacity to manifest this morally significant property.

A third strategy also concedes that not all humans meet the requisite minimum for intrinsic moral significance, but highlights the fact that the normal condition for human beings is to have the morally significant property in question, while this is not true regarding any particular non-human animal. Humans gain intrinsic significance, regardless of their individual deficiencies, by virtue of the fact that, typically, humans have the intrinsically significant bestowing property. The fact that deficiently rational humans are members of a species that is normally rational in the way that confers intrinsic significance suffices for the marginalized human to be intrinsically valuable.

Undoubtedly other responses can be suggested. But rather than address each individually, I wish to suggest a general problem with all the attempts to confer intrinsic moral significance only upon humans by positing a special empirical property: why should we accept the assumption that any of the empirical properties have the moral significance that its proponents attribute to it?

Let us consider two commonly offered examples to exemplify my general concern. Kant says that rationality of a certain sort bestows intrinsic moral significance upon its possessors. It is worth noting, at first, that when we limit our discussion to human beings, all of whom are alleged to have intrinsic moral value, that rationality seems to play no role. All else being equal, priority of care at a doctor's office is not influenced whatsoever by the difference of rationality possessed by two suffering people. If two people enter a physician's office at the same time, with equally severe and painful injuries, one's pain and frustrations are not given preferential concern by virtue of having greater rationality. Very roughly put, being more intelligent than another seems not to have any general moral implications. One might respond that the case involving only humans differs from the case involving a human and an animal since the former always involves a matter of degree while the latter is a matter of kind. But this is not true. There simply are some humans without rationality and, furthermore, without the capacity for developing such rationality, especially of the somewhat sophisticated form that Kant envisages. We need not allude even to marginal human beings. Consider a one-year-old infant who, because of a deadly genetic illness, will not live more than another few months. Although this baby lacks rationality, and even the capacity to obtain it, it seems counterintuitive that her interests in having her pain and suffering relieved should, in virtue of this fact alone, be given a diminished priority.

A second example, popularized by the seventeenth-century French philosopher René Descartes, granted critical moral consequence to language use. But, just as is the case with rationality, we do not bestow this moral significance on language use in cases involving only humans. All else being equal, attending to the suffering of an English professor does not have priority over treating an equal amount of suffering in an illiterate. And once again, any attempt to try to distinguish the case of intra-human suffering from the case where one member is an animal and one is a human, by reference to the latter's capacity to use language, can be nullified by the example of the tragic infant.

These objections to the typical empirical candidates for intrinsic moral significance do not rely on some broader meta-ethical thesis such as there being an unbridgeable gap between 'is' and 'ought'. Indeed, I believe that in a sense there is an empirical characteristic, the possession of which does have enormous moral implications. I believe that sentience – roughly the ability to suffer and enjoy – is both necessary and sufficient for intrinsic moral significance. Such a capacity cuts across species lines. There are human beings who lack the capacity and there are animals that have it. One might say that sentience is a condition of attributing direct moral significance to an individual. My mantra, developed in other venues, is not merely that we can traverse from an 'is' to an 'ought' but that we can travel from a 'can' to an 'ought'; whatever can be intelligibly treated as having intrinsic moral significance should be considered as having intrinsic moral significance.

I would be remiss if I did not mention a final tactic for uniquely bestowing intrinsic significance on humans that seems to escape the talons of the marginal case argument. The suggestion here is the demotic religious one where only humans are created in God's image and are given souls. In this case the strategy of the marginal case appears inapplicable, for we can no longer say, as we did for candidates such as rationality, linguistic ability, and autonomy, that there are some humans who either lack them completely or have them to a lesser degree than possessed by some animals. Presumably, souls do not come in degrees. All humans have them regardless of their mental and physical deficiencies and no non-humans have them regardless of their mental and physical prowess. Only humans have intrinsic moral significance because this is the way that God set up the world.

There have been luminaries – John Wesley, the founder of Methodism among them – who disagree with the orthodox view that God graced only humans with souls. There is also the popular parlour game of selectively highlighting passages in both the Hebrew Bible and New Testament that can support either the instrumentalist or intrinsicist position; I have participated myself in such an exercise. Transcending the issue of situating the value of non-human animals, an omni-benevolent creator would surely not condone that a segment of his innocent creation be routinely abused. For their own sakes, as well as those of animals, believers ought to act accordingly.

CHAPTER 1

14

The New Canaries in the Mine: The Priority of Human Welfare in Animal Abuse Prosecution

ELIZABETH CLAWSON

Law review articles on animal cruelty seem to favour a specific pattern. The first paragraph details a true story of gruesome torture and murder. The innocent and trusting victim only realizes its fate when it is too late to escape. The killer, once caught, gets away with a slap on the wrist. Finally, the Big Reveal: the victim was an animal, and a heinous crime has gone unpunished because its victim was the wrong species. The point is clear, but the shock value of these introductions wears off after a number of them. More shocking, perhaps, are the cases no one mentions: countless instances in which animal cruelty was *not* reported. Plenty has been written about adults who abuse animals and pay only minimal penalties. When children abuse animals, on the other hand, the act may be overlooked.

In the Seattle metropolitan area, the criminal justice system has responded to growing evidence that violence against animals is a gateway to violence against human beings. This has not raised the profile of animal abuse as a crime. Instead, it has raised the profile of rehabilitation for juvenile offenders – the priority is on the needs of the child. There is nothing wrong with addressing the emotional needs of troubled children and young adults. But in these situations, is the animal little more than a warning sign?

The link between cruelty to animals and violence against humans both informs the rehabilitation of young animal abusers in King County (which includes the city of Seattle) and reveals the tension[1] between animal interests and human interests. In order to reduce the exploitation, however inadvertent, of abused animals, this tension must be resolved by objective, non-speciesist mechanisms.

In general, speciesism is 'a prejudice or attitude of bias in favour of the interests of one's own species and against those of members of other species'.[2] In the context of animal cruelty laws, it refers to the privilege of human welfare over the welfare of other species. The concept is both straightforward and firmly entrenched. When abused animals are taken less seriously than abused humans, in general, the most likely reason is speciesism, and it is this bias that must be overcome in order fully to address these animals' pain and suffering.

Statutes and Their Application

Currently, anti-cruelty statutes exist in all fifty US states. These statutes 'generally recognize that animals ought to be protected from cruelty, abandonment, and poisoning, and that they must be provided with necessary sustenance, including food, water, and shelter'.[3] They vary, however, in definitions of key terms such as 'animal' and 'cruelty'. The penalties for animal cruelty also vary widely by state: the maximum fine in Wisconsin is $10,000; in Pennsylvania and Arkansas it is $5,000; in Missouri, it is only $50. Prison sentences likewise vary, from a maximum of five years in Oklahoma to zero prison time in Ohio and Virginia.[4] This variation makes animal protection a regional consideration, with no national consensus on how severely to punish or condemn it.

Laws in the state of Washington appear to firmly condemn animal cruelty. The first definition of first-degree anti-cruelty, a class-C felony,[5] reads as follows:

> A person is guilty of animal cruelty in the first degree when, except as authorized by law, he or she intentionally a) inflicts substantial pain on, b) causes physical injury to, or c) kills an animal by a means causing undue suffering, or forces a minor to inflict unnecessary pain, injury or death on an animal.[6]

This definition of cruelty focuses on the results of action – pain,[7] suffering, and death – rather than on the type of action. Almost any imaginable action that results in the pain and suffering of an animal can be punished under this statute. But almost any action can also be *exempted* from the statute by the slew of modifiers: 'except as authorized by law', 'intentionally', 'substantial', 'undue', and 'unnecessary'.

The above statute applies not only to adults, but also to children and youths under twenty-one years of age. However, the legal treatment of children and youths recognizes that they are not simply small adults. In King County, juvenile offenders may undergo 'capacity hearings' to assess their ability to judge right from wrong.[8] Juvenile offenders' moral judgment is generally determined by age. Children under age eight are deemed for legal purposes not to be culpable for otherwise criminal actions, simply because they cannot judge right from wrong. As a result, they are not subject to prosecution for these actions.[9] Between the ages of eight and twelve the law invokes a 'rebuttable presumption': the child still is not presumed capable of determining right from wrong, but the state has the opportunity to rebut this by proving, through school records or similar history, that the child is in fact capable of moral distinction.[10] After age twelve, the presumption reverses: juveniles are understood as being capable of judging right from wrong, and are therefore culpable for criminal actions.[11]

Furthermore, juvenile offenders benefit from an array of sentencing options tailored to their backgrounds, ages, and crimes. Even one single option, confinement, has many variations. Washington is unique in its use of a 'determinate sentencing' structure for the confinement of juvenile offenders, in which 'sentencing length is determined using a point system that takes offence seriousness and criminal history into account'.[12] This structure highlights the goal of preventing the escalation of crime severity or frequency. Along the same lines, first-time juvenile offenders may be referred to the community to carry out restitution or service projects.[13] The goal is rehabilitation, not punishment. The belief at work here is that effective treatment can prevent juvenile offenders from becoming adult offenders. Judges in King County recognize that effective rehabilitation of these young offenders demands a 'holistic' approach 'geared to the child's needs'.[14] Risk factors such as family instability or mental health issues are also taken into account. In some situations, court intervention may not even be appropriate; when the offender is a child, 'not everything needs to be criminalized'.[15]

According to juvenile court judges, animal cruelty is under-represented in King County courts.[16] Because of rebuttable presumption, any instances of animal cruelty that a child commits before age eight are not criminal offences, and tend to appear only as background notes written by probation counsellors if the child is charged with a crime later in life. In addition, animal cruelty cases may 'get overlooked; maybe they get handled through diversion, maybe parents are able to bring some counselling or control so they don't come into court . . . or maybe other charges are brought because that's what finally draws attention'.[17]

When animal cruelty appears in an offender's case history, its reception is ambivalent. On one hand, it adds weight to other crimes. For a child with a history of animal cruelty, 'the length of time in probation tends to be longer than a child who is simply involved with theft . . . [or] those kind of things'.[18] On the other hand, it is a low priority. A judge in King County Juvenile Court attests that it 'isn't high on the array of crimes . . . even though . . . we know it can be a predictor for other, very serious problems'.[19] This statement tells us two things about how animal cruelty is perceived: first, it is a relatively unimportant crime; second, the reason that judges may attach any level of importance to it is that it indicates future 'problems', possibly including criminal behaviour. A mention of the *wrongness* of animal cruelty is conspicuously absent. Between the under-representation of animal cruelty in court and its ambivalent reception in case history, it is clear that animal cruelty is not regarded as a serious crime, at least in juvenile justice.

One reason for this may be that animal abuse is something of a victimless crime. According to the Definitions section of the Washington State Constitution, a victim is 'any *person* who has sustained emotional, psychological, physical, or financial injury to person or property as a direct result of the crime charged'.[20] Unless we take the word 'person' liberally, the definition of 'victim' is restricted to human beings. An animal, then, can never be the victim of a crime. If it is abused, its owners, if it has them, may be victims, having sustained the loss of their property. But an animal that has been, say, severely beaten is denied the same victim status granted to a human beaten in the same manner. There are no victims in animal abuse, only objects.

The issue of victim status would be less crucial if it were merely a formality. But in Washington, victims are entitled to specific rights: the right to be informed of court proceedings, attend relevant trial and court proceedings, and make a statement at the plaintiff's sentencing and release proceedings.[21] The point is not to extend these specific rights to animals, since animals lack the capacities to exercise them. The point is that these rights recognize that society has certain duties to victims of crime, duties not extended to animals, though they may experience the same brutal acts as human victims. Animals, in contrast, remain objects of the law – property of humans or, in the case of juvenile justice, indicators of future human crime against human victims. With this in mind it is more understandable that animal cruelty is not considered a serious crime, since it is committed against an object. Just as animal cruelty is a symptom of potential delinquency, discounting animal cruelty is a symptom of a larger societal disorder.

The Inherent Value Model

The topic of animal interests – do they exist? What are they? How do they compare to human interests? – has been dissected at length by eminent theorists, so for now it is sufficient to build on their foundations. One such theorist, Tom Regan, sums up the topic handily: animals and humans alike have a condition of well-being or welfare, and therefore both can be said to have interests.[22] Thanks to the thorough work of Regan and others, it is reasonable to assume that animals have interests, many of which are similar to human interests. Granted, there is no firm consensus on the exact nature of animal interests; Regan, for example, distinguishes between *welfare-* and *preference*-interests, and other theorists use their own terminology. The nuances are less important here than the fact of their existence. Interests transform an object into a subject. They mean that certain acts have beneficial or detrimental effects to the subject, and that these benefits or detriments must be taken into account when justifying acts on the subject.

Crucially, many interests attributed to an animal may be *similar* to those attributed to a human – shelter, food and water, etc. – but they are *distinct from the interests of any human attached to the animal*, i.e., its owner or keeper. A pet is not merely a vessel for its owner's interests. But to assume that animals have interests does not mean that these interests will be respected by society. In addition to recognizing the existence of animal interests, it is vital to identify mechanisms to defend these interests from being dominated by the interests of humans.

One such threat of domination exists in the link between animal cruelty and violence against humans. That is, both animals and humans have an interest in avoiding pain and suffering, but an animal suffering today at the hands of a child can provide a specific benefit: it can indicate a youth who might cause human suffering in the future. What mechanisms might help ensure that this potential benefit does not come at the expense of the abused animal's interests?

One mechanism is hedonistic utilitarianism. This branch of ethics focuses on pleasure and pain, attempting to optimize the balance of both. This balance is the bottom line. If an action causes pain to some but increases overall pleasure, it is morally good. What matters, then, is not the type of 'receptacle' for the pleasure and pain – whether the body is human or animal – but the capacity for each being to contribute to the overall good.[23] Because it recognizes the pain of animals, it ensures that, all other things being equal, 'animals have a vote in the moral affairs of the world', equal to the overall human vote.[24] On the surface, hedonistic utilitarianism looks like an objective mechanism to decide conflicts between animal and human interests.

However, it falls prey to a major pitfall. Even counting animal pain alongside human pain, hedonistic utilitarianism would disadvantage animals if it held that good was optimized by privileging the interests of humans as a 'superior' species.[25] This possibility suggests a larger problem with utilitarianism: how do we quantify or qualify the pleasure and pain of different species? It may be possible with complex scientific research. But at the moment, we cannot even guess at this issue. There is no way to prove that using abused animals as indicators of future violence results in optimal overall good. We must, therefore, discard hedonistic utilitarianism as a method for arbitrating among interests – it is too easily dominated by human interests to be impartial.

Another alternative proposed by Regan is the concept of inherent value. Animals and humans alike, he says, are 'subjects-of-a-life'; they possess, among other things, 'beliefs and desires; perception, memory, and a sense of the future'; and 'an emotional life together with feelings of pleasure and pain'.[26] This is a compelling alternative to utilitarianism because it takes into account the complex interests of animals (and humans) beyond pleasure and pain. It also levels the playing field by asserting that '*all* who have inherent value . . . have it equally'.[27] Animals are therefore equal to humans as beings of inherent value. The interests of one species do not dominate the interests of others.

Having established the equal inherent value of animals and humans, Regan goes on to describe what it means in practice. According to his 'respect principle', '*we are to treat those individuals who have inherent value in ways that respect their inherent value*'. One example of failing to do this would be to treat them 'as if their value depended on their utility relative to the interests of others'.[28] This failure of the respect principle is visible in the abused animal instrumentality concept. If we take animal cruelty seriously only because it may indicate future violence, we reduce the animals involved to objects whose value extends only as far as their usefulness to human beings. Regarding abused animals as instruments does not respect their inherent value.

Competent adult humans are responsible for respecting inherent value because they have the capacity to deliberate among options. They are 'moral agents' because they 'can bring impartial reasons to bear on deciding how they ought to act'[29] with an active role in determining right actions. Impartial reasoning, Regan implies, confers moral accountability for decisions on those who make them. This category would include mentally competent adult humans. Animals, on the other hand, fall into the category of 'moral patients'. Like moral agents, they 'have desires and beliefs', they 'perceive, remember, and can act intentionally', and they 'have an emotional life' and 'a psychophysical identity over time', among other things.[30] But they lack the impartial reasoning ability of moral agents. Children too would be considered moral patients, particularly under Washington law, which absolves them of culpability until age eight. Only at age twelve does a child become a 'moral agent' in the eyes of the law.

As Regan notes, moral agents alone have duties to others.[31] Therefore, only moral agents can violate others' rights. A child who abuses an animal has not violated its rights, because it has no duties to that or any other animal. (Likewise, an animal of any age, though it may grievously injure another living being, cannot be said to violate its rights.) This is no double standard, since animals and children lack the 'abilities necessary for being held accountable for what they do or fail to do'.[32] Regan warns, however, against a double standard just for moral patients. Moral patients, as innocents, are to be protected from harm, but one type of moral patient (i.e., children) must not be protected more than another (i.e., animals).[33] All are due equal protection, regardless of species. It follows that one is not to be protected at the expense of the other. Even if harm to an animal would benefit a child, respect for the inherent value of the animal (and the child) would prohibit said harm.

It is difficult to criticize a justice system that aims to prevent violent children from becoming violent adults. What remains disturbing is the devaluation of animals in this system. Moral mechanisms that recognize the value of animals cannot stand without corresponding legal mechanisms. As long as animals lack legal mechanisms for redressing violence against them, their protection is subject to human discretion. How, then, to guarantee their protection from utilitarian legal practices?

Converging Interests

As it stands, the interests of animals are vulnerable to domination by the interests of humans as long as the two are perceived as being in competition. In the courts, animal interests are exchanged for human benefit in a practice dubbed 'legal welfarism'.[34] This is an accurate description of Washington animal cruelty law, in which many modifiers leave ample leeway to protect vital industries such as meatpacking and pharmaceuticals. But it reflects results, not intentions. It would be unreasonable to assume that these laws are drafted, interpreted, or enforced with the intention of exploiting animals. Instead, several factors contribute to the 'low priority' afforded to animal cruelty in the courts. The following have been offered as four of these factors:

1   Animals are considered less valuable than humans by society at large.
2   'Serious human issues' take precedence over non-human issues, making non-human issues appear less prevalent and serious.
3   A lack of media and court attention makes cruelty cases seem rare.
4   Animal abuse is not seen as relevant to human violence.[35]

The first and second factors reflect ideological challenges – values and perceptions that hold animals as unworthy of priority. The third and fourth factors reflect practical challenges – perceptions that might be receptive to reform based on changing facts. These two factors seem more easily reconciled with human interests because they do not require the overhaul of an entrenched worldview. If policy changes sent more animal cruelty cases to court, and these cases received a reasonable amount of media attention, animal cruelty might enjoy a higher priority. If studies could link animal cruelty to violence against humans – as is currently being done – animal cruelty might be taken more seriously as a legitimate problem.

Why should animal interests be given any higher priority than they currently enjoy? One answer, described above by Regan, is the equal inherent value of animals and humans that demands respectful treatment of both. Yet this alone is hardly compelling to the average citizen, or to her local legislators. Human societies have run roughshod over animal interests for millennia; something more enforceable than inherent value is necessary to guarantee respectful treatment of animals.

A practical stance is that, at least in animal abuse, animal and human interests often converge. However, the points at which they currently converge do not guarantee respect for the inherent value of animals. Take the assertion that 'the crux of requiring humane treatment of animals lies not in justice, but in the belief that cruelty to animals will beget cruelty to fellow human beings'.[36] If animal cruelty is seen to correlate with violence against humans, then reducing the one would reduce the other as well. Here the interests of both in avoiding pain and suffering are intertwined. However, animals in fact may not be treated as inherently valuable beings in this interpretation. Their respectful treatment would be a result not of their inherent value, but of their utility to humans.

Animal and human interests also appear to converge in the ownership of the former by the latter. The practice of keeping animals as private property can provide these animals a point of entry to the legal system. An owner or keeper can bring legal action for injury to her pet by another person, thus advocating for the injured animal. However, keeping animals as property results in subjective standards of treatment for animals. For example, an animal has no control over whether or not it even has an owner. Pets do not choose to be bred, sold, bought, adopted, or abandoned. The circumstances of an animal's property status are created by human beings, who then have complete control over the animal's existence. This control also varies person to person, and though standards may be dictated by law they have been enforced sporadically and often only after their violation draws attention to cruelty or neglect. Therefore, 'the quality of [animals'] care and the attitudes of their owners reveal much about the dynamics of power and the owner's capacity for *kindness*'.[37] It is kindness, optional goodwill, rather than justice that compels respectful treatment of animals. Animal well-being depends on the individual morals of owners and keepers, rather than on objectively enforced universal standards. Animals do not deserve this varied treatment, which has no basis in merit and is largely subjective.

For the reasons described above, the fields of animal welfare and animal rights are divided. 'Strict animal rights activists' advocate for the right of animals 'to be free from human cruelty and exploitation'.[38] The language of rights implies that humans would have a duty to treat animals fairly, and that animals would have access to forums such as courts of law to redress violations of this right.

Animal welfare proponents advocate 'more humane treatment of animals', rather than the elimination of 'all use and exploitation of them'.[39] 'The real goal', asserts an animal welfare enforcement officer in Florida, 'should always be elimination (or at least reduction) of victim pain and suffering'.[40] Whether or not the abused animal is legally considered a victim, its removal from an abusive situation is urgent. This immediate action recognizes the pain experienced by the animal as legitimate and in need of response.

The animal welfare ethic currently guides the treatment of animals in many countries; if a society believes that 'exploiting animals is significantly beneficial for humans', then 'the law permits it'.[41] This mindset is likewise visible in Washington anti-cruelty statutes. It establishes standards for the welfare of privately-owned animals, while leaving enough room for exploitative industries, such as slaughterhouses, to function for human benefit. The animal welfare movement recognizes that animals have moral worth but are still morally inferior to humans. Humans may 'use animals' as instruments to gain 'significant benefits'.[42] Utilitarian ethics are plainly visible in the animal welfare camp. The instrumental value of animals in juvenile justice would be justified as long as the benefits accrued by humans were sufficiently great.

Toward Ideological and Legal Reform

In light of these debates and balancing acts, what kinds of reforms would be most helpful here and now? Just as animal abuse may indicate a potentially violent youth, the oversight of juvenile animal abusers indicates the speciesism of legal mechanisms. These mechanisms therefore can effectively address speciesism in the law without directly addressing the problem of juvenile animal abusers.

Ideological changes would be ideal, since they tend to be more enduring than legal changes. In addition, laws tend to reflect social norms, so 'a change in society's perception of the moral worth of animals would lead to a change in their legal status'.[43] Yet legal changes, and the results they accomplish, can legitimize changing norms, creating a cycle of reform. The answer, then, is a two-pronged approach of legal and ideological reforms. These reforms would not specifically target juvenile animal abusers, who are often too young to be held culpable for their actions; likewise, older juveniles would probably not benefit from harsher penalties. Instead, the reforms would target public perceptions of the value of animals, perceptions that would trickle down to the treatment of animals by children.

An attractive route to guide this two-pronged approach is to promote animal rights. The legal rights of individuals 'arise as the result of the creative activity of human beings', making their creation appear a matter of a will and a pen stroke. Victims' rights, for example, would vastly improve the status of animals by making their abusers accountable in pre-existing ways already provided for humans. But there must be societal sanction for these rights, which requires changes in norms. Moreover, anti-cruelty statutes alone cannot ensure animals' rights; the statutes are 'prohibitory . . . in nature', not 'rights-granting'. 'They simply state what actions are prohibited without suggesting that any rights are being conveyed to the animals'.[44] Anti-cruelty legislation may be appropriate for responding to animal abuse on an individual basis, but as a tool of long-term status change it falls short.

One possibility for endowing animals with rights is to name them plaintiffs in their own cruelty cases, with a human advocate acting on their behalf. This idea is 'similar to that of a parent or guardian bringing suit on behalf of a minor or an incompetent individual'.[45] Just as the interests of children and mentally challenged persons are promoted by qualified advocates, the interests of animals could be represented in court. Moreover, having an owner or keeper would not be a requirement of this representation. And the pain of the animal would be recognized, rather than the property rights of its owner or keeper. In Washington, extending victim status to include animals would require this very advocacy: legally recognized victims can have their rights exercised by proxy in court if they are not competent to exercise these rights themselves. Advocacy for animal plaintiffs would restore attention to the target of the violence in animal cruelty cases.

Another possibility is to redraft existing violent crimes statutes, such as those covering assault and battery, to include animal victims.[46] These statutes already protect human beings, and while extending their reach to animals may not be the same thing as granting rights, it offers grounds for recognizing animal victims alongside human ones, given the same violent acts. The compelling thought behind this reform is that 'the law should punish violent criminals according to the acts that they perpetrate. Whether the victim is a human being or an animal, a violent crime is a crime against its intended victim, as well as a crime against society and its morals'.[47]

It may seem obvious that violence is violence even if its target is not human. Yet when committed against an animal, it may not legally be considered violence. The perpetuation of this double standard devalues animals and blurs the definition of violence itself. Redrafting existing statutes, like expanding victim status, aims for only what is already due: an equal recognition of victims, regardless of species, and the firm condemnation of violent acts themselves, which damage not only their target, but also the perpetrator and society.

Conclusion

The pain and suffering of animals deserves attention whether their abusers are children or adults. Much of the attention it currently draws is the result of studies linking animal abuse to violence against humans. Of course, any attention given to animal abuse is helpful, but animal abuse deserves attention not only as an indicator of danger to humans. Animals merit respectful treatment as inherently valuable beings. Respectful treatment demands not only that they are protected from violence, but that when they are subjects of violence, their experiences are taken seriously by society, and they are regarded as consistent with their value.

Notes

1   The phrase 'abused animal instrumentality' will be used throughout this discussion as shorthand for this tension: the link between cruelty to animals and violence against humans puts abused animals at risk of being perceived as indicators for future violence, potentially rendering them instruments for human interests.
2   Peter Singer, *Animal liberation*, 2nd edn (New York: Random House, 1990), p. 6.
3   Piers Beirne, 'For a nonspeciesist criminology: Animal abuse as an object of study', *Criminology* 37, 2 (1999), p. 126.
4   *Ibid.*, n. 6.
5   'RCW 16.52.205: Animal cruelty in the first degree', Revised Code of Washington, http://apps.leg.wa.gov/RCW/default.aspx?cite=16.52.205.
6   *Ibid.*
7   The statute does not explicitly recognize emotional pain and suffering, leaving open the interpretation that only physical pain and suffering constitutes animal cruelty.
8   The Honorable Carol Schapira, King County Juvenile Court Judge, personal interview, 20 July 2007.
9   The Honorable Patricia Clark, King County Juvenile Court Chief Justice, personal interview, 20 July 2007.
10 *Ibid.*
11 *Ibid.*
12 Department of Social and Health Services, 'Juvenile justice in Washington', Juvenile Rehabilitation Administration, www1.dshs.wa.gov/jra/JuvJustWA.html.

13 Gene DuPuis, Supervisor of King County Juvenile Court Probation Department, personal interview, 13 August 2007.

14 Clark interview.

15 Schapira interview.

16 Clark interview.

17 Schapira interview.

18 *Ibid.*

19 *Ibid.*

20 'Definitions', Revised Code of Washington; italics added.

21 Washington State Legislature, 'Victim bill of rights', Washington State Constitution, www.leg.wa.gov/LawsAndAgencyRules/constitution.htm.

22 Tom Regan, *The case for animal rights* (Berkeley: University of California Press, 1983), p. 88.

23 *Ibid.*, pp. 205–206.

24 *Ibid.*, p. 202.

25 *Ibid.*, p. 227.

26 *Ibid.*, p. 243.

27 *Ibid.*, p. 240.

28 *Ibid.*, pp. 248–249; italics in original.

29 *Ibid.*, p. 30.

30 *Ibid.*, p. 153.

31 *Ibid.*, p. 285; italics in original.

32 *Ibid.*

33 *Ibid.*, p. 297.

34 Beth Ann Madeline, 'Cruelty to animals: Recognizing violence against nonhuman victims', *University of Hawai'i Law Review* (Winter 2000), p. 328.

35 *Ibid.*, p. 327.

36 *Ibid.*, pp. 330–331.

37 Lynn Loar, 'I'll only help you if you have two legs', in F. R. Ascione and P. Arkow (eds), *Child abuse, domestic violence, and animal abuse: Linking the circles of compassion for prevention and intervention* (West Lafayette, IN: Purdue University Press, 1999), p. 121; italics added. Loar neglects to qualify the use of 'living creatures' to exclude, for example, plants. Nevertheless, her point remains clear.

38 Madeline, 'Cruelty to animals', p. 330.

39 *Ibid.*, pp. 329–330.

40 Sherry Schlueter, 'Animal abuse and law enforcement', in Ascione and Arkow (eds), *Child abuse*, p. 320.

41 Robert Garner, 'Animal welfare: A political defense', *University of Pennsylvania Law School Journal of Animal Law and Ethics* (May 2006), p. 163.

42 *Ibid.*, pp. 162, 171.

43 *Ibid.*, p. 169.

44 Madeline, 'Cruelty to animals', p. 332.

45 Shigehiko Ito, 'Beyond standing: A search for a new solution in animal welfare', *Santa Clara Law Review* (2006), p. 414.

46 Madeline, 'Cruelty to animals', p. 333.

47 *Ibid.*, p. 338.

The Structure of Evil

MARK ROWLANDS

I

Brenin was a wolf with whom I was fortunate to spend a decade or so of my life. I mention him because there are two episodes from his life that are peculiarly relevant to this chapter. The first occurred when he was a young wolf, and we were living in the United States. We used to go running together most days. But Brenin had been a little off-colour for the past couple of days, and I didn't want to risk him in the heat of an Alabama summer. So, today, I left him behind – a decision with which he vehemently disagreed and about which he made his displeasure known.

Brenin apparently managed to open the garden gate, and charged off after me. About ten minutes into my run, I heard a screeching of brakes following by a loud, sickening, thud. I turned to see Brenin lying in the road, having been hit by a Chevrolet Blazer. A Blazer, for those of you who are not American, is an SUV. It had passed seconds earlier, travelling at – I would estimate – somewhere in the region of forty to fifty miles per hour. Brenin lay in the road for a few heart-stopping seconds, howling, and then he picked himself up and ran off into the woods. It took me nearly an hour to find him. But when I did, he was largely okay. In a day or so he was back to normal. In fact, the Chevy came off distinctly worse.

The Blazer would have killed me. But Brenin's physical scars healed in just a few days. And, psychologically, there didn't seem to be any scarring at all. The very next day, he was pestering me to take him running, and never showed any subsequent fear of the cars that would fly past him on the road. Brenin was a very tough and together animal, both physically and psychologically. I want you to bear this in mind when I tell you the next story.

We are out running again, but this time it is a few years later. We have moved to Ireland and are running together along the banks of the River Lee in Cork. When we were on the return leg of the run, I grabbed hold of Brenin's collar, since I had seen, up ahead, Paco, a big St Bernard. Brenin was officially hostile to all large male dogs, and I didn't fancy having to step in to separate those two.

As I grabbed his collar, we ducked under one of the electric cattle fences. My elbow brushed the fence, and the shock passed through to Brenin. Brenin took off, scorching straight past a somewhat mystified Paco. And he didn't stop until he reached the car, a couple of miles away. He was there waiting for me when I eventually got back, anxious and breathless. We had gone on that same run most days, rain or shine, for the best part of a year. But he never went back again. He refused point blank, and his decision would remain unchanged no matter what the form of begging, bribery or coercion I employed. That, apparently, is how horrible electricity is for wolves.

Perhaps, you might think Brenin was just being a little histrionic. It was, after all, only a mild electric shock. If you are tempted to think this, just remember the Chevy Blazer. On balance, it seems that for a wolf a mild electric shock is a lot worse than being hit by an SUV!

II

With this in mind, consider some famous experiments conducted by experimental psychologists at a world-renowned university. The experiments involved a shuttlebox. This box consists in two compartments separated by a barrier. The floor of each compartment is an electrified grid. The psychologist and his collaborators would put a dog in one compartment, and then give an intense electric shock to its feet. Instinctively, the dog jumps over from one compartment to the other. They would then repeat this procedure over and over – several hundred times in a typical experiment. Each time, however, the jump is more and more difficult for the dog because the experimenters are gradually making the barrier higher and higher. Eventually the dog can't make the jump, and falls to the electrified grid beneath it. In a variation, the experimenters electrify the floor on both sides of the barrier. No matter where the dog jumps, it is going to be shocked. Nevertheless, the pain of the shock is intense, and the dog tries to escape, no matter how futile the attempt. And so the dog jumps from one electrified grid to the other. The researchers, when they wrote up the experiment, described the dog as giving a 'sharp anticipatory yip which turned into a yelp when he landed on the electrified grid.' The end result is the same. Exhausted, the dog lies on the floor urinating, defecating, yelping, shrieking, trembling. After ten to twelve days of these sorts of trials, the dog ceases to resist the shock. In these experiments, I think, we find an instructive distillation of the concept of human evil.

III

Evil has fallen on hard times lately – not in the sense that there isn't much of it around but, rather, in that most people are loathe to admit its existence. Evil, they will insist, is either a medical issue – the result of some form of mental illness – or it is a social issue – the result of some societal malaise or other. The guiding assumption is that evil deeds require evil people; and evil people must act from evil motives. And if you have no control over your motives – because you are medically ill or socially maladapted – then you have no control over the deeds. This connection between evil deeds and evil motives is no accident. It goes back to a distinction originally made in the middle ages – between moral and natural evil. Medieval philosophers noted that evil – which they thought of as pain, suffering, and associated ilk – could be caused by two different sorts of thing: natural events and human agency. Pain and suffering caused by earthquakes, floods, hurricanes, disease, and so on, they called natural evil. This they distinguished from the pain and suffering caused by human agency, which they called moral evil. But the idea of agency – of acting – involves the notion of a motive or intention. Therefore, people have inferred – though it doesn't strictly follow – morally evil acts require evil motives. And an evil person, therefore, is someone who acts from evil motives.

The result is a highly intellectualized concept of moral evil. A good example of this is provided by Colin McGinn, a friend and one of the best philosophers around, who understands moral evil as essentially a kind of *Schadenfreude* – taking delight in the pain, suffering or misfortune of someone else.[1] This may seem like a good way of understanding evil. Surely it is evil to delight in the pain, suffering, or misfortune of someone else? And surely the sort of person who does this is as good an example as any of an evil person? I want to undermine whatever confidence you have in this idea.

Here is a real case. A young girl is the victim of long-term abuse as a child, being regularly raped by her father from a very young age. Horrified, you might ask what her mother was doing in all of this. Didn't she realize what was happening? Her reply chilled me to the bone, and still does. When her father came back drunk, abusive, and spoiling for a fight her mother would tell her to, as she put it, go in there and keep him quiet! Whenever I need to keep an image of human evil firmly in my mind, I just think of this woman telling her daughter to go in there and keep him quiet.

There are two acts of evil involved here: the repeated episodes of rape by the father and the active complicity of the mother. And it is not easy to see which is worse. The mother was a victim – certainly – but was she any less evil? Her evil was, we must assume, fuelled by her terror – and not by any delight she took in the suffering of her daughter. But this doesn't change the fact that her actions were as evil as it is possible to imagine. Just think about that when you assume that victims can't be evil.

Who knows the motives of the man who called himself her father? Perhaps he understood that what he was doing was evil. But suppose he didn't. Suppose he thought it was a perfectly natural aspect of family life – maybe because he grew up in similar circumstances. All I can say is: who cares what he thought? There is no need to speculate about his motives. Even if he thought he was doing nothing wrong – even if he thought he was doing right – that diminishes his evil not one bit.

You can be evil – as was the mother – because you fail in your duties of protection, and whatever terror you feel here does not alter the evil of your acts or omissions. And you can be evil – as was the father in our wholly speculative reconstruction of his motives – because you are an irredeemably stupid man. But in neither case does your evil have anything to do in taking delight in the pain, suffering or misfortune of others. Deliberate malice has, I think, little to do with the essence of evil. Let's now flash forward a few years, at least in our imagination. Let's suppose the father and mother were eventually caught and punished. I'm not sure what, in these circumstances, the daughter's emotional reaction would be. Probably a little mixed, I would expect.

But suppose it wasn't mixed. Suppose she was absolutely delighted. Moreover, suppose she was delighted for one very simple reason: vengeance. She wanted her parents to suffer. Would this be an evil desire? I don't think so. I think her desire for vengeance may be regrettable. It may be evidence of permanent psychological scarring. Maybe. But it isn't evil. And is the woman evil for having this desire? This charge would be implausible. Delighting in the misfortune of evil people – especially when you have personally suffered at their hands – may not be a shining example of moral development. But it is a long way from being evil.

So, contrary to what McGinn – and the philosophical tradition – claims, I think *Schadenfreude* is neither a necessary nor a sufficient condition for being an evil person. It is not necessary because you can be evil even if you don't delight in the pain, suffering or misfortune of others. You can be evil, as was the mother, because you don't do your duty. And you can be evil, as was the father in our reconstruction of his motives, because you have fundamentally stupid beliefs. And *Schadenfreude* is not sufficient for being an evil person. Taking delight in the pain of evil others, when you have suffered at their hands, does not automatically make you evil.

IV

Many people would be appalled if I mentioned the animal experiments in the same breath as the abused child – as if that in some way diminishes her suffering. But, I've argued, the best way of understanding evil is not in terms of the motives of the person who acts, but in terms of the structure of the situation in which they act. So, with this in mind, let's look at the shared structure of the shuttlebox experiments and the abused child.

In both cases, of course, we might find fundamentally stupid beliefs on the part of the perpetrators: for example, the belief that torturing dogs with electricity is going to reveal anything at all about the nature of human depression – with its multifarious causes, etiologies, and syndromes. We often also find derogation of moral duty: for example, the duty to protect those who are defenceless against those who deem them inferior and therefore expendable. Stupidity and derogation are typically centrally involved in evil acts.

However, there is one further ingredient, and without this neither stupidity nor derogation is of any consequence: the helplessness of the victim. In this regard, I think Milan Kundera said something fundamentally important and correct about the nature of human goodness:

> True human goodness cannot show itself in all its purity and liberty except in regard to those who have no power. The true moral test of humanity (the most radical, situated on a level so profound that it escapes our notice) lies in its relations with those who are at its mercy: the animals. And it is here that exists the fundamental failing of man, so fundamental that all others follow from it.[2]

In effect, I am making the converse point about human evil. When the other – whether human or animal – is powerless, you have no self-interested motive for treating them with decency or respect. You do not fear them, nor do you covet their assistance. The only motive you can have for treating them with decency and respect is a moral one: you treat them in this way because that is the right thing to do. And you do this because that is the sort of person you are. And if you do not . . . that is when evil gains a foothold in the world. Stupidity of belief and derogation of duty can do their work only when the victim is powerless – helplessness is the canvas on which the portrait of human evil is painted.

If this is correct, then there are more evil acts, and more evil people, than we would care to imagine or admit. When we think of evil in terms of medical illness or social breakdown, then we assume that evil is exceptional: evil is something that resides at the margins of society. But, in fact, evil pervades society all the way in. It attaches to abusive fathers and complicit mothers. But it attaches no less to privileged and happy psychologists – supposed experts in the domain of mental health who acted, we can suppose, only out of the best intentions towards humanity.

Ultimately, there are more evil acts and more evil people than we would care to admit, because humans stand in a unique relationship to evil. Humans are not unique in that they treat the helpless badly. All animals do so – life is profoundly cruel. Humans are the animals that manufacture weakness. The abused child was naturally helpless. But the researchers' dogs were the product of 20,000 years of social and genetic engineering that led them, eventually but inexorably, to a shuttlebox. In this, we have taken the cruelty of life, refined it, and intensified it. Humans don't merely treat the weak badly. Humans make things weak precisely so that they may treat them badly. If we wanted a one-sentence definition of humans, this one would do: humans are the animals that engineer the possibility of their own evil.

Notes

1 Colin McGinn, *Ethics, evil and fiction* (Oxford: Oxford University Press, 1999).
2 Milan Kundera, *L'insoutenable légèreté de l'être* (Paris: Gallimard, 1984), p. 421. Translation mine.

'Vile Attentions': On the Limits of Sympathetic Imagination

DANIEL B. WILLIAMS

The possibility of pogroms is decided in the moment when the gaze of a fatally-wounded animal falls on a human being. The defiance with which he repels this gaze – 'after all, it's only an animal' – reappears irresistibly in cruelties done to human beings, the perpetrators having again and again to reassure themselves that it is 'only an animal', because they could never fully believe this even of animals.[1]

Theodor W. Adorno

Introduction

The disquietingly similar beings with which we share the world do not often return our gaze or fix their attention on our world in ways that we can for theirs. Yet when forced to comprehend animals, human attention is only too willing to accept ethical complacency. Although we evince sympathy and compassion as natural capabilities that radiate care and attention outwards, when faced with animals and a shared capacity for suffering, we tend to decouple such sentient capacities from our 'rational' selves. This tendency has defined centuries of willed distance from animals; what compassion issues from the Western tradition preserves this distance and has often led to our treating animals without kindness or moral reflection.[2]

The South-African-born novelist and critic J. M. Coetzee has consistently explored the cruelties that result from such failures of reflection. In the two fictional lectures that comprise *The lives of animals*, Coetzee's character Elizabeth Costello argues for a notion called 'sympathetic imagination', the illimitable capacity to 'think ourselves into the being of another', and finds it incomprehensible that 'kindness, human-kindness' can also be capable of, and complicit in, 'a crime of stupefying proportions' – the mass slaughter and maltreatment of animals.[3]

In this chapter, I suggest that failures to treat animals with kindness and ethical sense are constitutive of, and share structural features with, similar incapacities to treat human beings in ways that take seriously their own relation to suffering. More particularly, I shall be examining in Coetzee's novel *Waiting for the barbarians* the force and limits of 'sympathetic imagination' – what I shall call 'compassionate attention', extracting both rational and 'passionate' dimensions of ethical behaviour from Coetzee's deft pun, 'human-kindness'. 'Attention', in defining cognitive faculties as well as considerateness, forms a precondition for ethics and creates 'structures of value' around us in ways that mime the activity by which children learn – through 'close attention to objects'.[4] Yet when attention relates to the suffering of animals, the 'almost insuperable difficulty of looking properly at . . . human suffering' is intensified.[5] I shall be tracking the fates of this ethical imperative, focusing not only on what solicits sympathetic energy but also on the difficulties that threaten to blind attention and to turn its intimacies towards cruelty.

Freedom and 'Fullness of Being'

The central narrative voice of *Waiting for the barbarians*, the 'Magistrate' in an unnamed fort-town that is part of an unspecified 'Empire', seeks to live out his remaining days in uncomplicated languor – womanizing, hunting, and excavating a set of wooden ruins outside the town.[6] Although crime is rare, and the 'barbarians' that live in the desert give only occasional trouble by raiding livestock, the imperial powers have sent a military taskforce in response to rumours of an uprising. What follows is, in some respects, an 'allegory' of the political dynamics of dealing mercilessly with a perceived threat, and the attendant paranoia and social dissolution.[7] At its core, though, this novel is a consideration of the freedom of animal life when such life is constricted by spatial confinement, psychological degradation, and torture. The Empire rapidly shows itself not as a historical or political entity but as an 'empire of pain'.[8]

The infliction of extreme pain targets the unencumbered movement of the body, its capacity to act without being immobilized in a limited space. As such, pain curtails the freedom of movement that is a sure precondition of more developed liberties, rights to membership and association, and the determination of a life exempt from necessity. Without movement, and a space in which movement can take place, freedom is literally an 'aporia' – *a-poros*, without a means of passing, an opening, or a way. Humans share this biomechanical substrate with other animals, from whom we nonetheless undertake to deprive it, despite the fact that the mere animal 'aliveness' or 'bare life' that we presuppose in all 'higher' modes of existing underlies at once arguments about freedom and actions aiming at unfreedom.[9] Indeed, only by acknowledging the protection of such an animal freedom within the human might we salvage our broader notions of 'freedom', which such injurious behaviours as torture threaten by intimating that a body, any body, might be 'only an animal' – 'bloß ein Tier', 'merely' an animal.

In what follows I consider several angles of limitation by which freedom of movement and action, ethical or otherwise, is voided in situations of extreme pain. Further, I examine the radical 'unsharability' of pain, which compounds ethical paralysis, first by rendering compassion for a suffering body difficult without a spectator's sense of safe distance, second by interposing the felt vivacity of one's own concerns and thus extinguishing the reality of another's suffering from view.

'World Dissolution': Pain, Confinement, and Necessity

It is suggested in *The lives of animals* that a failure of imagination and sympathy with regard to other beings adumbrates confinement or violence, based on and justified by their assumed existential impoverishment. In a deceptively naïve misprision of Thomas Nagel's arguments concerning the subjective aspect of consciousness, Elizabeth Costello surmises that living organisms are all equally 'full of being' and opposes to philosophical reason the 'heavily affective sensation' of 'being a body with limbs that have extension in space, of being alive to the world'.[10] Crucially, this existential plenitude is 'hard to sustain in confinement', and so 'the freedom of the body to move in space is targeted as the point at which reason can most painfully and effectively harm the being of the other'.[11] The imaginative 'argument' of *The lives of animals* thus seeks to return an *affective* force to ethical attention and evaluation by moving beyond the accessibility of another's subjective experience, and instead concentrating on the key nodes – such as painful confinement – that link human and animal experience.

The sensation of pain, and especially *inflicted* pain, to which we accord an unarguable moral imperative, has exactly this foundational, substrate quality. Pain has a 'compelling vibrancy' and 'incontestable reality' for our own subjective experience, but is nevertheless structured in a way that ensures 'unsharability through its resistance to language'.[12] While other mental states that take a referential object attest to 'the human being's capacity to move out beyond the boundaries of his or her own body into the external, sharable world', pain has 'no referential content' and thus, 'more than any other phenomenon, resists objectification in language'.[13] Pain shrinks all 'vibrancy' and 'reality' to the space of bodily extension; it enervates our will to reciprocity and action in a shared world, not to mention an ethical world; and it curtails or obliterates this 'fullness of being', if only momentarily.

Pain contracts the space of possibility, erasing the world in a denuding, 'animalizing' gesture: extreme pain entails 'world contraction' and 'world dissolution'.[14] What remains within this shrunken and impoverished world is, paradoxically perhaps, a projection and magnification of the body's tangibility, since torture, with its 'specific acts of inflicting pain', 'bestows visibility on the structure and enormity of what is usually private and incommunicable, contained within the boundaries of the sufferer's body'.[15] However, if we cannot represent this implosion of language and agency, this 'overwhelming discrepancy' that arises 'between an increasingly palpable body and an increasingly substanceless world', then the 'subjective' accessibility of the experience is beside the point.[16] That there is palpable torment – in a human or animal body – should be enough to activate our attention.

Importantly, painful confinement entails not only suffering but also the character of *necessity*. Only the violence used in torture, writes Hannah Arendt, 'can match the natural force with which necessity itself compels', and this is why 'the Greeks derived their word for torture from *necessity*, calling it *anagkai*, and not from *bia*, used for violence as exerted by man over man'.[17] To torture, in the classical sense, is to apply an inherent necessity to a body which is barely distinguishable from an animal's in that its 'bare life', which the Greeks called *zoē*, is not the qualified living, *bios*, that Aristotle reserves for freemen.[18] Thus the contraction of space, the immobilization of sensation, and the effacement of vital force in confinement and torture involve the same reduction of beings to 'bare life', to being 'sacred' in the original sense of *sacer*, 'a life that may be killed by anyone – an object of a violence that exceeds the sphere both of law and of sacrifice'.[19] Elizabeth Costello formulates something similar in suggesting that we treat the animal as a prisoner of war: 'We can do what we want with him. . . . We can cut his throat, tear out his heart, throw him on the fire. There are no laws when it comes to prisoners of war'.[20]

Early scenes of hunting and the confinement and torture of prisoners in *Waiting for the barbarians* dramatize these linked notions of pain, necessity, and spatial contraction, tracking the limits of compassionate attention with respect to two themes around which the following sections will crystallize: first, the refusal to acknowledge the claim on ethical attention made by the *gaze* of another being; second, the willed refusal to respond to similar claims made by another's *voice*.

Although the Magistrate used to hold hunting in high regard, he is increasingly losing his nerve after the arrival of the ominous Colonel Joll. When he finds a waterbuck grazing on one expedition, there is a pause as he raises his gun: the animal 'turns his head and sees me. . . . [W]e gaze at each other.' He admits that, 'evidently it is not important to me that the ram die', but he is nevertheless immobilized: 'I find an obscure sentiment lurking at the edge of my consciousness. With the buck before me suspended in immobility, there seems to be time for all things, time even to turn my gaze inward and see what it is that has robbed the hunt of its savour'.[21] Later, there is a similar anxiety over the gaze of a horse put to death for not walking any further, 'even under the severest flogging': 'I can swear that the beast knows what is to happen. At the sight of the knife its eyes roll. With the blood spurting from its neck it scrambles free of the sand and totters a pace or two downwind before it falls'.[22] In neither of these situations, though, does the Magistrate attain the level of self-reflection that might yield an imaginative, compassionate reaction.

The Magistrate also remains impervious to various protesting voices, and despite his self-fashioned ethical awareness he does not acknowledge the link between the voices of animals – such as the birds 'crammed alive into wooden cages, screaming with outrage' – and the human cries that become undiscussably evident as the first interrogations of 'barbarians' take place in the town.[23] 'Of the screaming which people afterwards claim to have heard from the granary, I hear nothing. At every moment that evening as I go about my business I am aware of what might be happening, and my ear is even tuned to the pitch of human pain. But the granary is a massive building with heavy doors and tiny windows'.[24] Despite the characteristic simultaneity of tense here, what is alluded to in absentia is the ineluctable *presence* of a brutality whose victims know no present tense.[25] The Magistrate retains a prurient fascination for this 'pitch of human pain' that he claims not to hear. When he asks Colonel Joll about prisoners who tell the truth but are not believed, he is told that 'there is a certain tone [that] enters the voice of a man who is telling the truth'. Although he is incredulous, Colonel Joll specifies, 'I am speaking of a situation in which I am probing for the truth, in which I have to exert pressure to find it', such that the theme of spatial constriction, 'probing' the body, leads to the specious equation: 'Pain is truth; all else is subject to doubt'.[26]

Arendt states that the infliction of pain reduces the *logos* of human language to the *phonē* of animal sound, and that particularly in torture, animal communication becomes necessary on account of the impossibility of making up an untruth under extreme pain.[27] Yet, while pain actuates 'an immediate reversion to a state anterior to language, to the sounds and cries a human being makes before language is learned', the voice nevertheless operates as 'a final source of self extension; so long as one is speaking, the self extends out beyond the boundaries of the body, occupies a space much larger than the body'.[28] The voice of a damaged being might express nothing other than the inexpressibility of its state and the mute gaze of a dying animal might contain only a dull expression of sensations too palpable and overwhelming to find articulation. In both these cases – screaming and the mute gaze – something in the being of another addresses us, directs itself towards our ethical sensibility, and protests against being ignored merely on account of the inherent 'unsharability' of its experience.[29]

Pain as Incompletion and Blankness

The tendency of an injured body to become blank, 'incomplete', and effaced on account of its inability to objectify felt experience marks an important aspect of the incommunicability of pain. The 'unsharability' of pain can yield an opacity that elicits and frustrates responses of intimacy and compassionate understanding. In trying to approach such an unknowable entity, one which does *not* protest with its animal voice, there is a danger that one might seek to *obliterate* rather than sympathize with it.

'There has been something staring me in the face and still I do not see it'.[30] Thus culminates a set of fraught reflections concerning the 'barbarian' girl who was left behind in the town after her torture and taken in by the Magistrate. She has been blinded by heated metal placed close to her eyes and her feet have been broken. These sharp reminders of the restrictive targeting of the body in torture – the mobility of the feet; the capacity to look beyond a limited zone of agency – here give rise to a metaphoric constriction. The deep blankness and formlessness of the girl matches her broken body and resists the approaches of the Magistrate. From the first moment she gives only 'a strange regard, staring straight ahead', and from 'her empty eyes there always seemed to be a haze spreading, a blankness that overtook all of her'.[31] She stares as if in imitation of those animal gazes evoked in the poems of Rilke to which Coetzee refers in *The lives of animals*.[32] At the Magistrate's offer of work, she replies, '"You do not want someone like me." She gropes for her sticks. I know that she cannot see. "I am . . . " – she holds up her forefinger, grips it, twists it. I have no idea what the gesture means'.[33] Her inexpressible experience weighs heavy in the ellipsis, but her gesture at least intimates the general sign of what has been done to her: 'torture', from *torquere*, to twist, bend, or wring. Her 'swaddled, shapeless' feet and her 'twisted' body suggest a loss of the *forma humanis*, an incompleteness or deforming of the body.[34]

The girl's refusal to articulate her experience also finds physical expression in the tautness of her body: 'Her lips are clenched shut, her ears too no doubt'.[35] In attempting to uncoil her from this unresponsive and circumscribed space by the ritual of washing her injured feet, the Magistrate finds that at least 'her body yields' after 'moments when she stiffened at certain intimacies'.[36] Yet even though the body 'knits itself in sleep into ever sturdier health', the inarticulable character of her torture thwarts the Magistrate's obsession with recovering an 'image of her as she was before'.[37] He finds that trying to reach out to her actually and imaginatively yields 'no answering life' and it seems 'like caressing an urn or a ball, something which is all surface'.[38] The process of recollecting the 'still unmarked' body comes uncomfortably close to *creating* that body *ex nihilo*, and thus the Magistrate finds himself tracing, as if in negative form, the incisions and acts of damage that have left this body so obdurate: 'I try to recall her as she was before the doctors of pain began their ministrations'.[39] He cannot avoiding seeing her 'as a body maimed, scarred, harmed', and when finally the marks on her body – a burn under her eyelid, 'a phantom criss-cross of ridges under the skin' – are deciphered and the process of torture detailed, Coetzee carefully elides the moment when pain is actually effected.[40] By describing what precedes and follows the pain, or by concentrating on its instruments and visceral effects, the blank duration of suffering is accounted for in a matter-of-fact fashion.[41] Thus we learn how her blindness was induced by the heat of a 'kind of fork with only two teeth': 'The man brought it very close to my face and made me look at it. They held my eyelids open. . . . After that I could not see properly any more. There was a blur in the middle of everything I looked at; I could see only around the edges'.[42]

The marks on the girl's body are records of an intimacy forced upon the body with an extinguishing fullness unmatched by any other intimacy, perhaps the most devastating source of the injured body's inaccessibility to attention. The Magistrate thinks,

> it has not escaped me that in bed in the dark the marks her torturers have left upon her, the twisted feet, the half-blind eyes, are easily forgotten. Is it then the case that it is the whole woman I want, that my pleasure in her is spoiled until these marks on her are erased and she is restored to herself; or is it the case . . . that it is the marks on her which drew me to her but which, to my disappointment, I find, do not go deep enough?[43]

The tryst between the complex and corporal intimacies of sexual desire and the infliction of extreme pain begins at the resistant surface of the body, taunting erotic intimacy with the indices of a more total experience of possession. The girl seems deficient, 'as if there is no interior, only a surface across which I hunt back and forth seeking entry', the image suggesting that entering this body is part of an act of acquisition.[44] This perhaps explains but hardly excuses the Magistrate's startlingly offhand parallels made between lover and torturer, between caring and damaging: 'I behave in some ways like a lover – I undress her, I bathe her, I stroke her, I sleep beside her – but I might equally well tie her to a chair and beat her, it would be no less intimate'.[45] As attention is thwarted by an opaque, non-reciprocal being, the Magistrate thinks with terrible ambivalence of Colonel Joll and the 'intimate cruelties for which I abhor him'.[46]

That torture finds itself in the ambit of intimacy shows how even the most unthinkable acts can take on an aura of seductiveness, even necessity, with time.[47] Indeed, the passage of time plays a tacit role in our systems of justice, where 'the fact of even the most heinous of acts becomes familiar through repetition' such that 'the victim can no longer be remembered as undamaged'.[48] This novel gives shape to the gradual 'fading of anger' after a horrific act, an ebbing of moral sentiments through which 'our mind is forced to reimagine someone, and in so doing to convert the unthinkable into the contingent and, finally, into the necessary'.[49] How might we avoid this irreversible pull of necessity, and keep alive the unthinkable nature of what, certainly in the case of animals and perhaps even concerning the victims of torture, no longer seems unimaginable? Why do we convert the 'sad experience of standing at the rim of an unknowable mode of being', that of an animal or human victim, into a justification for brutality?[50] Perhaps an answer lies in acknowledging that the unedifying course of human communion with animals may issue from the natural temptation to press such silence and opacity into the register of fullness and speech, a temptation that all too often overtakes its object and turns into cruelty.

Pain as Intentional Voice

The dissevering effects of pain can make others appear inconceivable as beings with their own particular relation to suffering, since the body, 'thrown back upon itself, concentrates on nothing but its own being alive, and remains imprisoned in its metabolism with nature'.[51] The resulting impression of (animal) 'worldlessness' is only obliquely and with difficulty conveyed to the (human) world in which this reduction takes place. Thus, having concentrated intensely on deciphering a blank and broken body, the Magistrate finds himself confined and is forced to account for the violence that is meted out to him. His former juridical agency is tellingly surrendered at the level of narrative form, in the shift from the active to passive voice. The once law-making pronounce-ments – 'I gesture', 'I order', 'I sentence' – now express the frail passivity and pressing solitude of confinement: 'I am fed', 'I am led out', 'I am cast wholly upon myself'.[52] The Magistrate thinks initially that it 'seemed no great inflic-tion to move from the solitariness of everyday existence to the solitude of a cell when I could bring with me a world of thoughts and memories'. However, he quickly realizes how 'rudimentary' is the 'freedom to eat or go hungry; to keep my silence or gabble to myself or beat on the door or scream'. He finds himself banished from the human community, reduced to bare homeostatic functions, 'no more than a pile of blood, bone and meat that is unhappy'.[53] Indeed, 'the moral dimension of my plight, if that is what it is, a plight', has lost its force 'under the pressure of appetite and physical functions'.[54] When the 'intermit-tent vile attentions' of the torturers begin, the spatial restriction of 'pressure' is converted into the sharp flash of pain and the incessant demonstration of a body needing only 'to drink, to relieve itself, to find the posture in which it is least sore'.[55] His torturers

> were not interested in degrees of pain. They were interested only in demonstrating to me what it meant to live in a body, as a body, a body which can entertain notions of justice only as long as it is whole and well, which very soon forgets them when its head is gripped and a pipe is pushed down its gullet and pints of salt water are poured into it till it coughs and retches and flails and voids itself.[56]

Torture provides the paradigmatic experience of moral eclipse, shocking and voiding the body in order to demonstrate its capacity to be injured – 'to show [him] the meaning of humanity'.[57]

This reduction of the human to animal life begins to have the felt consis-tency of an animalizing experience, estranging human speech and privileging only increments of relief from pain and confinement. The Magistrate's time is structured according to when he is fed – 'A bestial life', he thinks, 'is turn-ing me into a beast' – and he is recognized by the people of the town only as 'the filthy creature who for a week licked food off the flagstones like a dog because he had lost the use of his hands', and by metaphoric implication, the loss of human content such as play and language.[58] He stares at the wall and realizes 'how tiny I have allowed them to make my world', and rushes around the cell 'with movements of vertiginous terror . . . jerking my arms about, pulling my beard, stamping my feet, doing anything to surprise myself, to remind myself of a world beyond that is various and rich'.[59] The culmination of these 'pettiest degradations' which leave him vacillating between two thoughts – 'I must live!' and 'When will I die?' – is a mock hanging.[60] The last sadistic section of this torture has him hanging from his arms, so that the tissue tears and he shouts – 'the noise comes out of a body that knows itself damaged perhaps beyond repair and roars its fright'.[61] The Magistrate, then, is finally reduced to the animal voice that is the obverse of the animal's opaque gaze, and just as the mute blankness of the 'barbarian' girl presented challenges to any kind of compassion, so his pained voice seems to offer its own resistance to being heard. Just like the two 'absurd prisoners' earlier in the novel – whom he would have preferred *not* to hear – the Magistrate finds himself in an 'absurd incarceration'[62] where he is in the deliberate and 'exceptional' position of a being that has assumed the true meaning of 'absurd': *insufferable to hear*.

The individual whose work has been predicated on a weighing of voices ultimately finds himself unable to respond to the animal substrate of the human voice. A brief incident, apparently unmotivated in the novel's plot, illustrates this ethical deficiency. The Magistrate buys a small fox-cub from a trapper, and keeps it in his rooms. Although it elicits no obvious response from the girl, other than 'Animals belong outdoors', she protests when he suggests releasing it by the lake: 'You can't do that, it is too young, it would starve to death or dogs would catch it'. So the animal remains, as a mere vocal presence, a 'noise in the night'.[63] The Magistrate fails to recognize the silently-made analogy between the vulnerability of the fox-cub and the broken body of the girl, instead quipping that it will be said that he keeps 'two wild animals in my rooms', later retracting: 'Of course it is not the same'.[64] Yet there is a basic level on which it *is* the same, where ignoring the pleas of terrified voices carries the same stain of ethical avoidance.

When he goes out of an evening to the ruins outside the fort, the Magistrate *does* attempt to hear the voices of 'history', but finally considers it misguided to 'find in the vacuousness of the desert a special historical poignancy'.[65] Similarly, in confinement, he stares blankly at the granary walls, trying unsuccessfully to search for indices of formerly occurring agonies: 'I stare all day at the empty walls, unable to believe that the imprint of all the pain and degradation they have enclosed will not materialize under an intent enough gaze; or shut my eyes, trying to attune my hearing to that infinitely faint level at which the cries of all who suffered here must still beat from wall to wall'.[66] The vocal register and the script of torture alluded to here emphasize the *signifying* character of these echoing silences, and attempting to recover the traces of those 'who after a visit here no longer felt that they wanted to eat and could not walk unaided' becomes the Magistrate's thwarted task.[67]

The important idea that unfamiliar sounds may have a signifying character is well illustrated in Augustine's example of someone who hears an archaic word of obscure provenance.[68] Augustine notes that this person would already know that the phonemes made up a word, as well as a sign that signified something. 'Hence', he writes,

> the more a thing is known, but not fully known, the more the mind desires to know the rest. . . . But because he already knew that it was not only a word, but also a sign, he wishes to know it perfectly. But no sign is known perfectly if it is not known of what thing it is a sign. If anyone, therefore, applies himself with ardent diligence to know, and inflamed with this zeal continues this search, can he be said to be without love?

What is loved, in the absence of meaning and understanding, is precisely the knowledge that these sounds 'signify something', that they have a possible meaning that might be disclosed. For Aristotle the form in which animals have a voice is as 'the indication [s meion] of pleasure or pain', since 'their nature attains to the perception [aisth sin] of pleasure and pain and the intimation [s mainein] of them to one another'.[69] The signifying function of animal sounds, the base level of phonē to which the human voice is reduced in situations of extreme pain – this is what calls forth from birds, horses, and cubs in apostrophic indignation, demanding to be attended to in default of concrete signification. In this strict sense, compassionate attention comes close to amor, both a will to knowledge, and a will to act even where knowledge is withheld behind mute and opaque eyes. Instead of devaluing these voices, we should take courage and pursue their ethical suggestion, namely the calling into question of any expression or action that predicates violence on a morally considerable human/animal distinction. And instead of reacting indignantly when abrupt comparisons are made between human and animal suffering, we should recognize that such gestures of linguistic diminution and degradation – 'es ist ja bloß ein Tier' – deserve to be challenged, 'even' and especially with respect to animals.

The voices and signs that are often mistaken in Waiting for the barbarians for allegorical indices of a historical register are fundamentally the voices of beings, human and animal, in extreme agony. Only an idea of history that takes into account this base substrate of pain, necessity, and restrictions on the freedom of all beings can remain ethically viable beyond its local context. Indeed, 'historical' criticism that attempts, not without reason, to find signs of 'historical poignancy' in Coetzee's work might do well to remember that 'poignancy' (from pungere, 'to pierce') initially means sharpness and keenness of pain, and that the necessary signs are already located in the screams of bodies locked in cages or enchained in squalid rooms, bodies that are subjected to burning, twisting, piercing, beating, and blinding, before they are disposed of as detritus.

Notes

1 Theodor W. Adorno, *Minima moralia: Reflections from damaged life*, trans. E. F. N. Jephcott (London: Verso, 1978), p. 105. The original contains both the phrases '"es ist ja bloß ein Tier"', 'it is merely an animal', and makes a substantive of 'das *"Nur ein Tier"*', 'only an animal'. See *Minima Moralia: Reflexionen aus dem beschädigten Leben*, vol. 4 of *Gesammelte Schriften*, ed. Rolf Tiedemann (Frankfurt am Main: Suhrkamp, 1997 [1951]), p. 118.

2 At once one of the staunchest and most striking examples of this tendency is Martin Heidegger's insistence on the ontological – as opposed to merely generic – difference between man and animal, formulated at length in the 1929–30 lecture course, *Die Grundbegriffe der Metaphysik: Welt, Endlichkeit, Einsamkeit* (Frankfurt am Main: Klostermann, 1983), and later upheld in the 'Brief über den Humanismus' (see 'Letter on Humanism', in *Basic writings*, ed. David Farrell Krell [San Francisco: HarperSanFrancisco, 1993], pp. 217–265). For commentary on the former, see Jacques Derrida, *De l'esprit: Heidegger et la question* (Paris: Galilée, 1987), chapter 6 and passim, and Giorgio Agamben, *The Open*, trans. Kevin Attell (Stanford: Stanford University Press, 2004), chapters 11–16; on the latter, see Peter Sloterdijk, *Regeln für den Menschenpark: Ein Antwortschreiben zu Heideggers Brief über den Humanismus* (Frankfurt am Main: Suhrkamp, 1999), pp. 24–25 and passim.

3 J. M. Coetzee *et al.*, *The lives of animals*, ed. Amy Gutmann (Princeton: Princeton University Press, 1999), pp. 35, 69.

4 Iris Murdoch, *The sovereignty of good* (London: Routledge, 1991), pp. 37, 31.

5 *Ibid.*, p. 73.

6 J. M. Coetzee, *Waiting for the barbarians* (New York: Penguin, 1982 [1980]). Further references will be indicated by *WB*.

7 Derek Attridge carefully examines the problems with considering this text an 'allegory' in *J. M. Coetzee and the ethics of reading: Literature in the event* (Chicago: University of Chicago Press, 2004), pp. 32–48.

8 Coetzee, *WB*, p. 23. In an interview Coetzee notes that the freedoms in this novel are 'elementary freedoms'. 'An interview with J. M. Coetzee', by Tony Morphet, *Social Dynamics* 10, 1 (1984), p. 63.

9 The figure of 'bare life' (*bloßes Leben*) occurs as a fulcrum joining law and violence in Walter Benjamin's 'Zur Kritik der Gewalt' (in *Zur Kritik der Gewalt und andere Aufsätze* [Frankfurt am Main: Suhrkamp, 1965], pp. 29–64). As Agamben suggests, this notion can aid us in investigating 'the sacred character of life, which our age assigns to human life and even to animal life', an investigation that Benjamin himself thought necessary. See *Homo Sacer: Sovereign power and bare life*, trans. Daniel Heller-Roazen (Stanford: Stanford University Press, 1998), pp. 65–66. A more general explication of 'sacred' or 'bare life' can be found in *Homo Sacer*, pp. 1–12, 63–67, 71–74 and 81–86, as well as in *The coming community*, trans. Michael Hardt (Minneapolis: University of Minnesota Press, 1993), pp. 86–87.

10 Coetzee, *Lives of animals*, p. 33. See also Thomas Nagel, 'What is it like to be a bat?' in *Mortal questions* (Cambridge: Cambridge University Press, 1979), pp. 165–180.

11 Coetzee, *Lives of animals*, pp. 33, 34. Confinement might also extinguish the faculty for empathy, as is suggested in Coetzee's later novel *Foe* (New York: Penguin, 1988 [1986]), p. 81: 'I wish to point out how unnatural a lot it is for a dog or any other creature to be kept from its kind; also how the impulse of love, which urges us toward our own kind, perishes during confinement, or loses its way'.

12 Elaine Scarry, *The body in pain: The making and unmaking of the world* (New York: Oxford University Press, 1985), pp. 13, 14.

13 *Ibid.*, p. 5.

14 *Ibid.*, pp. 29, 32. This existential emphasis on a 'world' that undergoes contraction or erasure should be set against Heidegger's exposition in *Die Grundbegriffe der Metaphysik* of three 'theses', namely that the stone is 'worldless' (*weltlos*), the animal 'poor-in-world' (*weltarm*), and the human 'world-forming' (*weltbildend*). Indeed, my entire discussion is premised on the assumption that there exist experiences or events that consign these categories to indistinction.

15 Scarry, *The body in pain*, p. 27.

16 *Ibid.*, p. 30.

17 Hannah Arendt, *The human condition* (Chicago: University of Chicago Press, 1958), p. 29. The word *anangk* , which means force, constraint, and necessity, can also cover the registers of torture, duress, and bodily pain. See Bernard Williams, *Shame and necessity* (Berkeley: University of California Press, 1993), pp. 109–117, for a discussion of the seemingly paradoxical arguments deployed by Aristotle to show that slavery was a 'necessary identity' – that it was both 'natural' and 'necessary', while at the same time admitting of elements contrary to nature in the sense that it was *biaion*, brought about by external force or constraint.

18 Aristotle's oft-cited discussion of property, slavery, and necessity, which includes a brief mention of the taming of animals, occurs in the *Politics*, 1253b24–1255a2, and it is hardly accidental that it is followed immediately by statements on hunting (see 1256b20–25). *The complete works of Aristotle: The revised Oxford translation*, vol. 2, ed. Jonathan Barnes (Princeton: Princeton University Press, 1984). Indeed, the raids to acquire slaves – notably 'barbarians', those who did not speak Greek – are figured in the *Politics* as a 'kind of hunting' (see Williams, *Shame and necessity*, p. 107).

19 Agamben, *Homo Sacer*, p. 86.

20 Coetzee, *Lives of animals*, p. 59.

21 Coetzee, *WB*, p. 39.

22 Coetzee, *WB*, p. 62. Such attention given to the moment of an animal's death is by no means rare in Coetzee. See, for example, the end of a significant chapter in the third-personal memoir, *Boyhood: Scenes from provincial life* (New York: Viking, 1997), pp. 101–2.

23 Coetzee, *WB*, p. 57.

24 Coetzee, *WB*, pp. 4–5.

25 The classic analysis of the present tense in this novel is Dorrit Cohn, '"I doze and wake": The deviance of simultaneous narration', in *The distinction of fiction* (Baltimore: Johns Hopkins University Press, 1999), pp. 96–108. Cohn shows that Coetzee's tensual style evades the usual narrative necessity of past tenses by being neither a 'historical present' nor a version of 'interior monologue'. Despite its acuity, I believe that this analysis avoids at least one experiential category that precludes the coincidence of 'telling' and 'experiencing', namely the situation of extreme pain. Indeed, Cohn does not mention the second occurrence of the paradigmatic phrase of 'simultaneous narration' – 'doze and wake' – where it describes the episodic life of a set of prisoners. It is crucial to recognize that moments of inflicted pain intervene between these states, briefly extinguishing one's world and language, as the Magistrate realizes in noting that during his confinement he 'disappeared, and then reappeared, and in between was not part of the world' (*WB*, p. 128).

26 Coetzee, *WB*, p. 5.

27 Arendt, *The human condition*, p. 129. The main difference between freemen and slaves, according to Demosthenes, 'was that the slave was answerable with his or her body. Evidence from slaves was acceptable in the courts solely on condition that it had been extracted under torture' (Williams, *Shame and necessity*, p. 108).

28 Scarry, *The body in pain*, pp. 4, 33.

29 The associations among pain, confinement, and necessity – and the linked notion that we refuse to acknowledge the (animal) voice in pain as capable of any articulation whatsoever – are neatly expressed in the first Discourse of Plutarch's 'On the eating of flesh': 'we go on to assume that when they utter cries and squeaks their speech is inarticulate [*phonas anarthrous*], that they do not, begging for mercy, entreating, seeking justice, each one of them say, "I do not ask to be spared in case of necessity [*anangken*]; only spare me your arrogance! Kill me to eat, but not to please your palate!"' (*Moralia*, vol. 12, trans. Harold Cherniss and William B. Helmbold [Cambridge, MA: Harvard University Press, 1957], 994E).

30 Coetzee, *WB*, p. 155.

31 Coetzee, *WB*, pp. 25, 86.

32 For instance, the eighth of the *Duiner Elegien* and 'Der Panther', in *Die Gedichte* (Frankfurt am Main: Insel, 1986), pp. 558–60, 451. For Coetzee's discussion, see particularly *Lives of animals*, p. 50; and *Stranger shores: Essays 1986–1999* (London: Secker & Warburg, 2001), pp. 60–73.

33 Coetzee, *WB*, p. 27.

34 Coetzee, *WB*, p. 28.

35 Coetzee, *WB*, p. 27.

36 Coetzee, *WB*, p. 30.

37 Coetzee, *WB*, p. 33.

38 Coetzee, *WB*, p. 49.

39 Coetzee, *WB*, pp. 33, 47.

40 Coetzee, *WB*, p. 31. Deciphering the blank body and decoding the wooden slips with barbarian language on them are linked undertakings, as has been noted by Attridge, *J. M. Coetzee and the ethics of reading*, p. 47.

41 Indeed, Coetzee's descriptions almost always typify the two metaphoric registers that Scarry associates with representing pain, namely the 'language of agency' inherent in the 'weapon', and the recognition of inflicted pain or 'damage' that is expressed by the 'wound'. The first identifies 'an external agent of the pain, a weapon that is pictured as producing the pain', and is accompanied by our 'mental habit of *recognizing* pain *in* the weapon' (Scarry, *The body in pain*, pp. 15, 16); the second, 'body damage that is pictured as accompanying the pain' (*Ibid.*, p. 15).

42 Coetzee, *WB*, p. 41.

43 Coetzee, *WB*, p. 64.

44 Coetzee, *WB*, p. 43.

45 Coetzee, *WB*, p. 43.

46 Coetzee, *WB*, p. 146.

47 The basic 'moral reflex' that directs us always against torturers begins to become confused when the interrogatory aspect is superadded to physical pain. In this, 'to have moved even a small amount in the direction of the torturer in this most clear-cut of moral situations is a remarkable and appalling sign of the seductiveness of even the most debased forms of power' (Scarry, *The body in pain*, pp. 35, 331 n. 21). In a short article, Coetzee himself discusses torture, and the justifying of 'a

concern with morally dubious people involved in a contemptible activity', as well as 'how to treat something that, in truth, because it is offered like the Gorgon's head to terrorize the populace and paralyze resistance, deserves to be ignored' ('Into the dark chamber: The novelist and South Africa', *New York Times Book Review* 12 January 1986, p. 35). He argues against the depiction of torture in order to avoid ideological complicity.

48 Philip Fisher, *The vehement passions* (Princeton: Princeton University Press, 2002), p. 107.

49 *Ibid.*, p. 108.

50 J. M. Coetzee, *Stranger shores*, p. 71.

51 Arendt, *The human condition*, p. 115.

52 Coetzee, *WB*, pp. 79–80.

53 Coetzee, *WB*, p. 85. Compare Gilles Deleuze on Francis Bacon: 'Bacon does not say, "Pity the beasts", but rather that every man who suffers is a piece of meat. Meat is the common zone of man and the beast, their zone of indiscernibility' (*Francis Bacon: The logic of sensation*, trans. Daniel W. Smith [Minneapolis: University of Minnesota Press, 2003], p. 21).

54 Coetzee, *WB*, p. 87.

55 Coetzee, *WB*, pp. 94, 115.

56 Coetzee, *WB*, p. 115.

57 Coetzee, *WB*, p. 115. There is an interesting parallel to this bodily reduction in Elizabeth Costello's example of an ape named Sultan, part of Wolfgang Köhler's experiments on apes in the early years of the twentieth century. She gives an account of how this ape is made to solve basic problems in order to get food, and is thus 'relentlessly propelled toward lower, practical, instrumental reason . . . and thus toward acceptance of himself as primarily an organism with an appetite that needs to be satisfied' (*Lives of animals*, p. 29).

58 Coetzee, *WB*, pp. 80, 124. Compare *Foe*: 'Yet it is not the heart but the members of play that elevate us above the beasts: the fingers with which we touch the clavichord or the flute, the tongue with which we jest and lie and seduce. Lacking members of play, what is there left for beasts to do when they are bored but sleep?' (p. 85). In *Was heisst Denken?*, ed. Paola-Ludovika Coriando (Frankfurt am Main: Klostermann, 2002), Heidegger articulates the idea that the hand embodies a uniquely human capacity, naturally deploying the German cognates that signify 'concept' (*Begriff*) and the actions of 'grasping' or 'gripping' (*greifen*). For commentary, see Derrida, '*Geschlecht* II: Heidegger's hand', trans. John P. Leavey Jr., in John Sallis (ed.) *Deconstruction and philosophy: The texts of Jacques Derrida* (Chicago: University of Chicago Press, 1987), p. 173.

59 Coetzee, *WB*, pp. 84, 85.

60 Coetzee, *WB*, p. 117.

61 Coetzee, *WB*, p. 121. Scarry calls pain and death 'the most intense forms of negation, the purest expressions of the anti-human, of annihilation, of total aversiveness, though one is an absence and the other a felt presence, one occurring in the cessation of sentience, the other expressing itself in grotesque overload'. Thus physical pain 'always mimes death and the infliction of physical pain is always a mock execution' (*The body in pain*, p. 31).

62 Coetzee, *WB*, p. 102.

63 Coetzee, *WB*, p. 34.

64 Coetzee, *WB*, pp. 34, 35.

65 Coetzee, *WB*, p. 17.
66 Coetzee, *WB*, pp. 79–80.
67 Coetzee, *WB*, p. 80.
68 Augustine, *The trinity* [*De Trinitate*], trans. Stephen McKenna (Washington: Catholic University of America Press, 1970), pp. 292–93. For this discussion of Augustine, I am indebted to Agamben, *Language and death: The place of negativity*, trans. Karen E. Pinkus and Michael Hardt (Minneapolis: University of Minnesota Press, 1991), pp. 33–34. Although I am articulating an idea of the voice that is in line with Agamben's interpretation, I should point out that he situates the problem of 'intention' and signification within his larger topics of potentiality, language, and death, whereas I am realigning this problem with what is common to animal and human voices when they express, or fail to express, pain.
69 Aristotle, *Metaphysics*, 1253a11–14.

PART
VI

Law Enforcement, Offenders, and Sentencing Policy

Part VI focuses on how law enforcement, criminal law, and sentencing policy should respond to the link between animal abuse and violence to people.

The section begins with an interview with former FBI Supervisory Agent Alan C. Brantley (*An FBI Perspective on Animal Cruelty*). Prior to his retirement from the FBI, Brantley was assigned to the National Center for the Analysis of Violent Crime and the Behavioral Analysis/Behavioral Science Units at the FBI Academy in Quantico, Virginia. He specialized in criminal investigative analysis and the assessment of dangerousness/threats, and was responsible for providing training in criminal psychology to law enforcement officers who attended the FBI's National Academy. He describes how the FBI first began to see a link – way back in the late 1970s – when they interviewed thirty-six multiple murderers in prison and found that, by self-report, 36 per cent 'described killing and torturing animals as children and 46 per cent said they did this as adolescents'. Animal cruelty is now one of the diagnostic tests employed by the FBI in assessing dangerousness. Brantley's comments are revealing: 'We try to tell people [police in training] that investigating animal cruelty and investigating homicides may not be mutually exclusive'. Again, 'People shouldn't discount animal abuse as a childish prank or childish experimentation'.

Joan Schaffner (*Laws and Policy to Address the Link of Family Violence*) considers the failure of US law to address the link: 'The laws criminalize behaviour that directly harms animals but in turn might lead to, or coincide with, violence against other humans'. Law 'independently addresses animal abuse, domestic violence, child abuse, and elder abuse, but does not directly target *the relationships among these abuses* and thus inadequately protects citizens from these crimes'. Schaffner considers a variety of remedies, both legal and practical, to deal with this lacuna, including humane education, stronger enforcement of animal cruelty statutes, cross-reporting, and earlier intervention.

Angus Nurse (*Dealing with Wildlife Offenders*) considers the causes of criminal behaviour in animal cruelty and wildlife crimes. He concentrates on the extent of animal cruelty offences and the causes of these crimes in the UK. A variety of animal welfare and wildlife protection legislation is on the statute books, but crimes such as bird of prey persecution, dog fighting, and the illegal killing, trapping, and use of animals such as badgers for sport continue. Criminological theory provides a basis for understanding why people commit crimes and what might be effective in dealing with offenders. Yet criminology has paid little attention to assessing animal cruelty, the link between these offences and human violence, and the motivations of those committing these crimes. Nurse assesses current criminal justice policy on animal abuse offences, as well as the rationale of offenders involved, to determine what criminal justice policies are needed to deal with animal offenders given what is known about crime, punishment, and justice in mainstream criminology. He concludes that there are distinct types of animal offender, and that criminal justice policy needs to consider each different type, rather than treating all offenders the same, and employing a purely punitive regime that relies heavily on custodial sentences.

Martin Wasik (*Implications for Criminal Law, Sentencing Policy and Practice*) takes a careful look at what might be the implications of a relationship between a person's history of offences committed against animals and a propensity on their part to go on to commit violence against human beings. Written from the perspective of a lawyer who is both an academic and a practitioner in the UK criminal courts, Wasik concludes that, *inter alia*, evidence of animal offences could be employed at the sentencing stage by being incorporated within the probation service's tool for risk assessment, and by being included in appropriate pre-sentencing reports by psychiatrists where there is a 'serious risk' to members of the public.

An FBI Perspective on Animal Cruelty

ALAN C. BRANTLEY INTERVIEWED BY RANDALL LOCKWOOD AND
ANN W. CHURCH

Q: What is the history of the Behavioral Science Unit/Investigative Support Unit?

Brantley: The Behavioral Science Unit originated in the 1970s and is located at the FBI Academy. Its purpose is to teach behavioural science to FBI trainees and National Academy students. The instructors were often asked questions about violent criminals, such as, 'What do you think causes a person to do something like this?' The instructors offered some ideas, and as the students went out and applied some of these ideas, it was seen that there might be some merit to using this knowledge in field operations. In the mid-1980s, the National Center for the Analysis of Violent Crime was founded with the primary mission of identifying and tracking serial killers, but it also was given the task of looking at any violent crime that was particularly vicious, unusual, or repetitive, including serial rape and child molestation. We now look at and provide operational assistance to law enforcement agencies and prosecutors worldwide, who are confronted with any type of violent crime.

Q: You have said that the FBI takes the connection between animal cruelty and violent crime very seriously. How is this awareness applied on a daily basis?

Brantley: A lot of what we do is called threat assessment. If we have a known subject, we want as much information as we can obtain from family members, co-workers, local police, and others, before we offer an opinion about this person's threat level and dangerousness. Something we believe is prominently displayed in the histories of people who are habitually violent is animal abuse. We look not only for a history of animal abuse, torment, or torture, but also for childhood or adolescent acts of violence toward other children and possibly adults, and for a history of destructiveness to property.

Sometimes this violence against animals is symbolic. We have had cases where individuals had an early history of taking stuffed animals or even pictures of animals and carving them up. That is a risk indicator.

You can look at cruelty to animals and cruelty to humans as a continuum. We first see people begin to fantasize about these violent actions. If there is escalation along this continuum, we may see acting out against inanimate objects. This may also be manifest in the writings or drawings of the individual affected. The next phase is usually acting out against animals.

Q: When did the FBI first begin to see this connection?

Brantley: We first quantified it when we did research in the late 1970s, interviewing thirty-six multiple murderers in prison. This kind of theme had already emerged in our work with violent criminals. We all believed this was an important factor, so we said, 'Let's go and ask the offenders themselves and see what they have to say about it.' By self report, 36 per cent described killing and torturing animals as children and 46 per cent said they did this as adolescents. We believe that the real figure was much higher, but that people might not have been willing to admit to it.

Q: You mean that people who commit multiple, brutal murders might be reluctant to admit to killing animals?

Brantley: I believe that to be true in some cases. In the inmate population, it's one thing to be a big-time criminal and kill people – many inmates have no empathy or concern for human victims – but they might identify with animals. I've worked with prisoners who kept pets even though they weren't supposed to. They would consider someone else hurting their pet as reason enough to commit homicide. Also, within prisons, criminals usually don't want to talk about what they have done to animals or children for fear that other inmates may retaliate against them or that they may lose status among their peers.

Q: Where is violence against animals coming from? Are criminals witnessing it in others? Convicted serial killer Ted Bundy recounted being forced to watch his grandfather's animal abuse.

Brantley: For the most part, in my experience, offenders who harm animals as children pretty much come up with this on their own. Quite often they will do this in the presence of others and teach it to others, but the ones with a rich history of violence are usually the instigators. Some children might follow along to be accepted, but the ones we need to worry about are the one or two dominant, influential children who initiate the cruelty.

Q: What components need to be present for you to think a child or adolescent is really in trouble?

Brantley: You have to look at the quality of the act and at the frequency and severity. If a child kicks the dog when somebody's been aggressive toward him, that's one issue, but if it's a daily thing or if he has a pattern of tormenting and physically torturing the family dog or cat, that's another. I would look to see if the pattern is escalating. I look at any type of abuse of an animal as serious to begin with, unless I have other information that might explain it. It should not be dismissed. I've seen it too often develop into something more severe.

Some types of abuse – for example, against insects – seem to be fundamentally different. Our society doesn't consider insects attractive or worthy of affection. But our pets are friendly and affectionate and they often symbolically represent the qualities and characteristics of human beings. Violence against them more likely indicates violence that may well escalate into violence against humans.

You also need to look at the bigger picture. What's going on at home? What other supports, if any, are in place? How is the child doing at school? Is he drinking or doing drugs?

Q: We are familiar with the 'classic' cases of serial killers, like Jeffrey Dahmer, who had early histories of animal abuse (see the Summer 1986 *HSUS News*). Are there any recent cases you have worked on?

Brantley: The Jason Massey case jumps out as being a prominent one. This was a case from 1993 in Texas. This individual, from an early age, started his career killing many dogs and cats. He finally graduated, at the age of twenty, to beheading a thirteen-year-old girl and shooting her fourteen-year-old step-brother to death.

He was convicted of murder. I was brought in for the sentencing phase to testify as to his dangerousness and future threat to the community. The prosecutors knew that he was a prolific killer of animals, and that he was saving the body parts of these animals. The prosecutor discovered a cooler full of animal remains that belonged to Massey and brought it to the courtroom for the sentencing hearing. It caused the jurors to react strongly, and ultimately the sentence was death.

Q: Mr Massey had been institutionalized at his mother's request two years before the murders since she was aware of his diaries, which recorded his violent fantasies, and his animal killings, yet he was released. Do you think that mental health officials have been slower than law enforcement agencies in taking animal abuse seriously?

Brantley: We've made this a part of a lot of our training for local police, and I think most police recognize that when they see animal mutilation or torture that they need to check it out; but police have to triage and prioritize their cases. We try to tell people that investigating animal cruelty and investigating homicides may not be mutually exclusive.

We are trying to do the same for mental health professionals. We offer training to forensic psychiatrists through a fellowship programme and provide other training to the mental health community. I think psychiatrists are receptive to our message when we can give them examples and case studies demonstrating this connection. The word is getting out.

Q: Do you think more aggressive prosecution of animal-cruelty cases can help get some people into the legal system who might otherwise slip through?

Brantley: I think that it is a legitimate way to deal with someone who poses a threat. Remember, Al Capone was finally imprisoned for income-tax evasion rather than for murder or racketeering – charges which could never be proven.

Q: Have you ever encountered a situation where extreme or repeated animal cruelty is the only warning sign you see in an individual, where there is no other violent behaviour? Or does such abuse not occur in a vacuum?

Brantley: I would agree with that last concept. But let's say that you do have a case of an individual who seems not to have had any other adjustment problems but is harming animals. What that says is that while, up to that point, there is no documented history of adjustment problems, there are adjustment problems now and there could be greater problems down the road. We have some kids who start early and move toward greater and greater levels of violence, some who get into it starting in adolescence, and some who are adults before they start to blossom into violent offenders.

Q: Do you find animal cruelty developing in those who have already begun killing people?

Brantley: We know that certain types of offenders who have escalated to human victims will, at times, regress back to earlier offences such as making obscene phone calls, stalking people, or killing animals. Rarely, if ever, do we see humans being killed as a precursor to the killing of animals.

Q: How would you respond to the argument that animal cruelty provides an outlet that prevents violent individuals from acting against people?

Brantley: I would disagree with that. Animal cruelty is not as serious as killing human beings, we have to agree to that, but certainly it's moving in a very ominous direction. This is not a harmless venting of emotion in a healthy individual; this is a warning sign that this individual is not mentally healthy and needs some sort of intervention. Abusing animals does not dissipate those violent emotions; instead, it may fuel them.

Q: What problems do you have in trying to assess the dangerousness of a suspect or a known offender?

Brantley: Getting background information is the main problem. People know this person has done these things, but there may be no record or we haven't found the right people to interview.

Q: That's one of the reasons why we have put an emphasis on stronger anti-cruelty laws and more aggressive enforcement – to get such information in the record.

Brantley: A lot of the time people who encounter this kind of behaviour are looking for the best in people. We also see cases where people are quite frankly afraid to get involved, because if they are dealing with a child or adult who seems to be bizarre or threatening, they are afraid that he or she may no longer kill animals but instead come after them. I've seen a lot of mental health professionals, law enforcement officers, and private citizens who don't want to get involved because they are afraid – and for good reason. There are very scary people out there doing scary things. That's largely why they are doing it and talking about it: they want to intimidate and shock and offend, sometimes regardless of the consequences.

Q: Is there hope for such an individual?

Brantley: The earlier you can intervene, the better off you'll be. I like to be optimistic. I think in the vast majority of cases, especially if you get to them as children, you can intervene. People shouldn't discount animal abuse as a childish prank or childish experimentation.

Q: Have you ever seen any serial killers who have been rehabilitated?

Brantley: I've seen no examples of it and no real efforts to even attempt it! Even if you had a programme that might work, the potential consequences of being wrong and releasing someone like that greatly outweigh the benefits of attempting it, in my opinion.

Q: There is also a problem in trying to understand which acts against animals and others are associated with the escalation of violence, since police records, if they exist, are often unavailable or juvenile offences are expunged. Sometimes only local humane societies or animal-control agencies have any record. The Humane Society of the United States (HSUS) hopes to facilitate consolidating some of these records.

Brantley: That would be great. If animal-cruelty investigators are aware of a case such as a sexual homicide in their community and they are also aware of any animal mutilation going on in the same area, I would encourage them to reach out to us.

Note: *Alan C. Brantley was interviewed by Dr Randall Lockwood and Ann Church. The Interview was originally published in* HSUS News *(Fall 1996) and is reproduced with the permission of Mr Brantley and the HSUS.*

18

Laws and Policy to Address the Link of Family Violence

JOAN E. SCHAFFNER

While the social science data supporting the link has been around for many years, the law has been slow to acknowledge it and even slower to capitalize upon it. The early animal cruelty laws were enacted to protect humans' interests directly – owners' interest in their property and society's interest in promoting morality.[1] More recently, the link between animal cruelty and human violence has provided the incentive for legislators and prosecutors to take animal cruelty seriously.[2] The laws criminalize behaviour that directly harms animals but in turn might lead to, or coincide with, violence against other humans. However, currently the law *independently* addresses animal abuse, domestic violence, child abuse, and elder abuse but does not directly target *the relationships among these abuses* and thus inadequately protects citizens from these crimes.

Why Law and Policy Should Directly Target the Link

It is time for the law and policy directly to target the link. By doing so, violence can be prevented and more effectively prosecuted. The complex relationship among animal abuse, spouse abuse, child abuse, and elder abuse create serious problems for victims. First, one act of violence often comprises multiple forms of abuse. For example, the abuser may abuse the family pet not only to harm the pet but to intimidate and/or psychologically harm other members of the family.[3] In this manner, the direct act of animal abuse is also an indirect form of spouse abuse, child abuse, and/or elder abuse. Second, the threat of one type of abuse may be used to silence the victim from reporting other abuses. For example, the abuser may threaten to kill the family pet if the child he has abused tells anyone about her own abuse.[4] Third, multiple abuses may delay or prevent the victim from escaping the abusive environment. For example, many victims of spouse abuse/domestic violence refuse to leave an abusive home because they are unable to take their pet and fear that the abuser will harm or kill their pet in retaliation if they leave.[5] Fourth, the multiple abuses may create liability for the victim. For example, a mother who is a victim of domestic violence and does not leave the home may find herself guilty of child neglect and at risk of losing her child.[6] The victim is in a no-win situation, the pet may be killed if she leaves but her child may be taken from her if she does not leave. Fifth, a victim of abuse often feels responsible for her own abuse and guilt for not being able to protect other family members from abuse.[7] For example, the victim of spouse abuse may be reluctant to discuss her own abuse and feel additional pain from witnessing the suffering of her pet.

The law can and should help these victims rather than create roadblocks to safety. With laws that directly target the link, victims can seek safety more easily, additional violence can be prevented, and prosecution of the abuser enhanced.

How Law and Policy Can Directly Target the Link

The law can target and capitalize upon the link between animal abuse and human violence at every step along the cycle of violence – from before the abuse starts through sanction and rehabilitation after the abuser is found guilty. The District of Columbia (DC) has recently introduced comprehensive legislation to reform the District's animal welfare and cruelty statutes – the Animal Protection Amendment Act of 2007.[8] Several provisions of the APAA specifically target the link to accomplish these goals. Other reforms directed at the courts or federal entities are also necessary to complete the legal reform. By recognizing the link, law and policy properly implemented can (1) prevent all forms of abuse through humane education, (2) prevent human abuse though effective animal cruelty laws, (3) detect abuse earlier through reporting, (4) enhance protection of family abuse victims through comprehensive protective orders and safe havens, (5) facilitate prosecution of the abuser through evidentiary rules, and (6) avoid further abuse through appropriate sanctions.

Teach Compassion

Humane education programmes in schools teach compassion for all living beings from an early age and may prevent a child from becoming violent.[9] Characteristics taught through a humane education programme include 'respect for others, responsibility, honesty, kindness and compassion'.[10] Several states mandate or encourage humane education. For example, New York requires in elementary schools 'the humane treatment and protection of animals and the importance of the part they play in the economy of nature as well as the necessity of controlling the proliferation of animals which are subsequently abandoned and caused to suffer extreme cruelty'.[11] California mandates that teachers 'endeavor to impress upon the minds of pupils . . . kindness toward domestic pets and the humane treatment of living creatures'.[12]

While humane education may appear to be a non-essential aspect of public education it addresses a critical component of childhood development – compassion.

Prevent Human Abuse through Effective Animal Cruelty Laws

Devoting resources to legislate effectively against and prosecute animal cruelty can prevent future violence towards human victims, since animal cruelty is often the first step towards violence against humans.

First, the legislature must enact adequate animal cruelty laws that properly indicate the seriousness of the crime. Forty-three states, the District of Columbia, Puerto Rico, and the Virgin Islands define certain types of animal cruelty as a felony offence.[13] Acts of animal cruelty in the District include knowingly overloading, torturing, depriving of necessary sustenance, cruelly chaining, or mutilating an animal.[14] If the offender 'with the intent to commit serious bodily injury or death to an animal . . . under circumstances manifesting extreme indifference to animal life, commits any of the[se] acts or omissions . . . which results in serious bodily injury or death to the animal' the offender is charged with a felony and 'shall be punished by imprisonment not exceeding 5 years, or by a fine not exceeding $25,000, or both'.[15] To reflect the seriousness of the offence properly, the law should impose a minimum sentence.

Second, prosecutors must aggressively enforce animal cruelty laws by prosecuting animal cruelty cases to the fullest extent of the law. If the legislature signals the seriousness of the crime adequately through the laws and sanctions, prosecutors will have greater incentive to devote adequate resources to these cases.

Finally, the law should grant judges the authority to impose more creative sentences to help rehabilitate the offender. Twenty-eight states include psychological counselling for those convicted of animal cruelty.[16] In particular, the APAA states that 'the court may order a person convicted of animal cruelty to participate in an animal cruelty prevention program'.[17] One such programme is the AniCare Model.[18] This model is the first professionally developed psychological intervention programme for adult animal abusers. The model 'uses a cognitive-behavioral approach with direct interventions emphasizing the client's need to acknowledge accountability for his or her behavior'.[19] The developers have also created the AniCare Child Model for children who abuse animals.[20] Additionally, the court should monitor attendance to improve the effectiveness of the programme.

Detect Abuse Earlier

There are several ways in which the law may capitalize upon the inter-related nature of animal abuse and human violence to detect abuse earlier. First, information concerning incidents of animal cruelty must be gathered and maintained in an accessible database for analysis.[21] Although every state collects data on incidents of animal cruelty, the national database maintained by the FBI, the Uniform Crime Reporting Program (UCR) does not segregate this information from other crimes.[22] As a result, no statistical evidence of the incidents of animal cruelty is available in the US. The solution to this problem is simple – create a separate category for animal cruelty data within the UCR.[23]

Second, perhaps the most direct method for capitalizing on the link is to mandate direct reporting and cross-reporting among social service agencies responsible for investigating and reporting family abuses in order to detect family abuse before it escalates.[24] Mandated direct reporting of suspect child abuse by physicians, teachers, and other professionals is common.[25] Five states include animal control officers among the professionals required to report suspected child abuse and neglect.[26] Some have discussed extending this requirement to veterinarians given the demonstrated link between child abuse and animal abuse within the family.[27]

Several states require or encourage veterinarians to report suspected animal abuse to humane enforcement.[28] Issues of confidentiality and privilege may arise when veterinarians report abuse. States that mandate reporting also protect the confidentiality of the informing veterinarian.[29] Further, while there is no common law veterinarian-client privilege, some states statutorily require that veterinarians keep their client information confidential.[30] Since both mandated reporting of suspected animal abuse and confidentiality of client information are statutorily created there is likely no conflict between these competing duties for veterinarians.

The APAA does not contain a mandatory reporting requirement for veterinarians because of the possible effect of deterring the abusers (or their family) from seeking medical attention for their injured pet. Unfortunately it is unclear whether the benefit of mandated reporting would outweigh the cost of avoiding medical help out of fear of retribution. While the same argument was made for mandated reporting of child abuse, no serious problem has been detected in the child abuse context. However, it is more likely to occur with pets. Abusers (or their family) in a child abuse case would be more likely to seek medical attention for their child when necessary and risk prosecution than in an animal abuse case. While veterinary reporting is certainly a viable option, it was not proposed in DC.

Cross-reporting among the respective agencies can enhance early detection of family abuse; however, no state currently mandates two-way reporting.[31] Child and adult protective services workers and animal cruelty officers visit homes frequently investigating complaints of abuse; however, they rarely communicate with each other. Since it has been shown that where there is one form of family abuse, it is likely that there are others, these professionals should work together to identify multiple abuses in the home.

The APAA imposes cross-reporting. When a humane officer investigating animal cruelty in the home reasonably suspects child or elder abuse, the officer is to report the suspicion and grounds therefore to the appropriate agency and vice versa.[32] The bill adds an additional reporting requirement, an animal presence report, for child or adult protective service investigators when they observe an animal in the home.[33] This second report is not treated by the Washington Humane Society (WHS), the entity responsible for enforcing the District's animal cruelty laws, as a complaint of animal abuse but rather as a warning to be alert to possible animal abuse in that home. The anticipated need for the animal presence report is based upon the assumption that the weakest member of the family, the pet, is the most vulnerable and thus the more likely target to be a victim of abuse if other abuses are also present. Moreover, the abuser may be abusing the pet to intimidate or control the child, spouse, or elder whose abuse is being investigated even if outward signs of animal abuse are not detected.

Enhance Protection of Family Victims

Protecting victims of family abuse is paramount. Capitalizing on the link can facilitate the early securement of an intrafamily offence protective order by authorizing courts to award protective orders upon a showing of cruelty against the family pet.[34] In DC, an 'intrafamily offence' is defined as a criminal act committed by an offender upon a person to whom the offender is related or with whom the offender shares a mutual residence or maintains a romantic relationship.[35] By definition, an intrafamily offence involves only human members of the family. However, by recognizing that abuse of the family pet is often used to emotionally abuse a human family member, the APAA authorizes the judge to grant a protective order if, after a hearing, there is good cause to believe that the alleged abuser has committed or is threatening to commit animal cruelty against the household pet with the effect of emotionally or physically injuring a human family member.[36] This provision is designed to provide earlier protection for all family members before the abuse escalates to physical violence against a human family member, and to facilitate the securement of a protective order if the adult victims of domestic violence are more willing to report their pet's abuse than their own physical abuse.

The protective order, however, is merely the first step to providing comprehensive protection for all family victims. Three additional components must be in place: (1) women's shelters and/or social services agencies must expand intake information to identify when protection is needed for a family pet; (2) courts must be given express authority to issue a protective order to direct the care, custody, or control of a companion animal residing in the home; (3) there must be a safe haven created for all family members by designating at least one human shelter as 'pet friendly' to maintain family unity during the transition and/or by coordinating with veterinarians and local shelters to provide shelter for the family pet until the family can be reunited.

The District is working to achieve all three. First, animal welfare advocates and the DC Coalition Against Domestic Violence are working to improve communication. Because victims of domestic violence often delay leaving an abusive home because they do not want to leave their pet behind, identifying women with pets in need of shelter and informing them of options available to protect their pet is crucial. Specifically, intake forms should include questions about the family pet.[37] Second, the APAA gives authority to judges when issuing an intrafamily protective order to direct 'the care, custody or control of a common household pet . . . owned, possessed, leased, kept or held by the respondent, complainant, or a minor child'.[38] Anyone in violation of such order 'shall be chargeable with a misdemeanor and upon conviction shall be punished by a fine not exceeding $1,000 or by imprisonment for not more than 180 days, or both'.[39] Finally, the Washington Humane Society offers safe haven for the pets of victims of domestic abuse.[40] Interestingly, in 2002 the Shelter for Abused Women and Children in Naples, Florida, opened its new family violence shelter allowing shelter for family pets as well.[41] While it is rare for a human shelter to allow pets given the potential for health and safety problems, allowing the family to remain united during this time can significantly help all victims of the family abuse, especially the children.

Facilitate Prosecution of Abuse

Proving guilt of the abuser can be difficult under any circumstance, given the standard of proof in a criminal case is 'beyond a reasonable doubt' and motive and/or intent often lack objective evidence. However, recognizing the relevance of one form of family abuse to another during trial, and allowing introduction of evidence of these related abuses will facilitate prosecution of the offender.[42] The rules of evidence in both criminal and civil trials limit evidence of other bad acts against the offender.[43] Specifically, the rules disallow such evidence 'to prove the character of a person or to show that the person acted in conformity therewith'[44] but allow it 'as proof of motive, opportunity, intent, preparation, plan, knowledge, identity, or absence of mistake or accident'[45] at the discretion of the trial judge. 'The evidence must be relevant to an issue other than the defendant's propensity to commit the crime charged, the other act must be similar enough and close enough in time to be relevant, there must be sufficient evidence that the defendant committed the similar act, and the probative value of the evidence must not be substantially outweighed by the danger of unfair prejudice'.[46]

A review of the published cases uncovered only two cases in which the court directly addressed the propriety of introducing evidence of animal abuse in a case involving human abuse.[47] Both cases involved charges of sexual abuse in the home where the defendant abused an animal in front of the victim.[48] The courts allowed the evidence in only as proof of the victim's state of mind – to prove that she was afraid of her abuser and/or to explain why she never reported all of the incidents of abuse to others[49] – or to impeach the credibility of the defendant after he denied doing anything in front of the victim to intimidate her.[50] The court expressly determined that evidence of animal abuse by the defendant not performed in the presence of the victim would be inadmissible.[51]

Because these courts were introducing the evidence of animal abuse as proof of the victim's state of mind, it is arguably correct to require that the abuse take place in the victim's presence. However, one could argue that proof of the victim's knowledge of the pet's abuse by the abuser and/or threats of abuse of the family pet by the abuser if proven should also be admissible. Moreover, given the link between animal abuse and spouse, child, or elder abuse in the home, the relevance of pet abuse should be sufficient to outweigh its prejudicial effect under 404(b) in order to establish identity, intent, and/or motive of the abuser in abusing the human victim.[52]

Avoid Further Abuse through Sanction

Finally, sanctions against the abuser that directly address the link complete the cycle. First, in addition to requiring that the owner forfeit an animal that he has abused, the APAA adds that: 'The court may order the defendant not to own or possess an animal for any period of time'.[53] While the offender is still capable of abusing others' animals or humans if determined to do so, at least one form of family abuse is removed from his arsenal.

Second, when the family dissolves, important issues of child custody and visitation are raised. By recognizing that all abuse in the family is related and thus relevant to these issues, the court should allow evidence of animal abuse of the family pet by the offender in order to make a better-informed determination of custody or visitation rights of the offender.[54] The issues of relevance are similar to those discussed above in the criminal trial context.

Notes

1 See Margit Livingston, 'Desecrating the ark: Animal abuse and the law's role in prevention', *Iowa Law Review* 87, 1 (2001): 21–28; Bernard Rollin, 'An ethicist's commentary on whether veterinarians should report cruelty', in R. Lockwood and F. R. Ascione (eds), *Cruelty to animals and interpersonal violence: Readings in research and application* (West Lafayette, IN: Purdue University Press, 1998), p. 413.

2 See Joseph Sauder, 'Enacting and enforcing felony cruelty laws to prevent violence against humans', *Animal Law* 1 (2000), p. 6.

3 Jennifer Robbins, 'Recognizing the relationship between domestic violence and animal abuse: Recommendations for change to the Texas legislature', *Texas Journal of Women and the Law* 16 (2006), p. 129, citing Carol Adams, 'Women battering and harm to animals', in C. Adams and J. Donovan (eds), *Animals and women* (Durham, NC: Duke University Press, 1995), pp. 55, 62.

4 *Ibid.*

5 See Dianna J. Gentry, 'Including companion animals in protective orders: Curtailing the reach of domestic violence', *Yale Journal of Law and Feminism* 97 (2001), p. 13.

6 See Nicholson v. Scoppetta, 3 N.Y.3d 357, 820 N.E.2d 840 (2004). In this class action on behalf of mothers and their children challenging the constitutionality of New York City's policy of finding child neglect and removing children from their mothers' custody solely on ground that the mothers had failed to prevent children

from witnessing domestic violence, the court held that (1) allowing child to witness domestic abuse is insufficient, without more, to satisfy statutory definition of 'neglected child'; and (2) emotional injury from witnessing domestic violence can justify removal of the child, but does not, by itself, give rise to a presumption of injury.

7   See Judge Roger Dutson, 'Domestic violence', *Utah Bar Journal* 7 (1994), p. 43.

8   DC Council Bill 17–0089 (introduced 6 February 2007, hearings held 6 June 2007, referred to Committees on Health and Public Safety and the Judiciary) [hereinafter APAA]. As the Co-Director of the GW Animal Welfare Project, I worked with Professor, and now DC Council member, Mary Cheh and our students on this legislation. Council member Cheh introduced the legislation in February 2007 and hearings were held June 2007. The legislation is slated to be voted upon by the Council in July 2008. Several amendments have been made to the bill and where appropriate are incorporated here. All citations are to the June 10, 2008 Committee Print version of the Bill.

9   See Meena Alagappan, 'Revitalizing interest in humane education', ABA-TIPS, *Animal Law Committee Newsletter* (Spring 2007): 8–10; World Animal Net, *The need for humane education*, at http://www.worldanimal.net/hme-need.html. Several programmes are devoted to humane education – see, for example, Humane Education Advocates Reaching Teachers (HEART) at http://www.teachhumane. org/; Humane Education Programs at http://www.humaneedu.com; Institute for Humane Education at http://www.humaneeducation.org; The National Humane Education Society at http://www.nhes.org/; National Association for Humane and Environmental Education at http://www.nahee.org/.

10   Lynda Antoncic, 'A new era in humane education: How troubling youth trends and calls for character education are breathing new life into efforts to educate our youth about the value of all life', *Animal Law* 9 (2003), pp. 183, 189.

11   NY Educ. Law § 809.

12   West's Ann. Cal. Educ. Code § 233.5.

13   HSUS Fact Sheet, *State Animal Anti-cruelty Law Provisions* (June 2007): hsus.org/web-files/PDF/state_cruelty_chart.pdf.

14   DC Code § 22–1001(a).

15   DC Code § 22–1001(d).

16   HSUS Fact Sheet (see note 14).

17   APAA § 101(b).

18   See Society & Animals Forum web site at http://www.psyeta.org/AniCare.htm for a description of the model.

19   *Ibid.*

20   *Ibid.*

21   For discussion of the early FBI uniform crime reporting programme, see Marvin Wolfgang, 'Uniform crime reports: A critical appraisal', *University of Pennsylvania Law Review* 11 (1963), p. 708.

22   Naseem Stecker, *Domestic violence and the animal cruelty connection*, 83 Sep-Mich. B. J. (2004) (citing Dr Mary Lou Randour).

23   See House Report 108–576, Dept. Commerce, Justice, and State, The Judiciary and Related Agencies Appropriations Bill, Fiscal Year 2005, 108th Congress, to Accompany H.R. 4754.

24   Phil Arkow, 'The correlations between cruelty to animals and child abuse and the implications for veterinary medicine', in R. Lockwood and F. R. Ascione (eds),

Cruelty to animals and interpersonal violence, p. 409 (discussing the implications for veterinarians to report child abuse). See also, for example, Cal. Penal Code § 11166(a) (West 1999); Conn. Gen. Stat. § 46b-129(a) (1995); see also 'First strike: The connection between animal cruelty and human violence', Humane Society of the United States, at http://www.hsus.org/hsus_field/first_strike_the connection_between_ animal_cruelty_and_human_violence/.

25   Arkow, 'The correlations', p. 409.

26   Mary Lou Randour and Howard Davidson, *A common bond: Maltreated children and animals in the home* (Englewood, CO: American Humane Society, 2007) p. 16 (the five states are California, Colorado, Indiana, Maine, and Ohio).

27   Arkow, 'The correlations', p. 409.

28   AVMA, State Legislative Resources, 'Required reporting of animal abuse for veterinarians', available at http://www.avma.org/advocacy/state/issues/sr_animal_abuse. asp; see also Rollin, 'An ethicist's commentary', p. 413.

29   Heather Winters, 'Updating Ohio's animal cruelty statute: How human interests are advanced', *Capital University Law Review* 29 (2002), pp. 857, 867.

30   Rebecca Huss, 'Valuation in veterinary malpractice', *Loyola University Chicago Law Journal* 35 (2004), pp. 79, 490; see also Harold W. Hannah, 'Communications, privilege, and the veterinarian', *Journal of American Veterinary Medical Association* 219 (2001), p. 32.

31   See for example Cal. Penal Code § 11166(a) (West 1999) (animal control officers must report suspected child abuse); Tenn. C.A. § 38–1–402 (protective services agency workers must report suspected animal abuse).

32   APAA § 113.

33   APAA § 101.

34   See Robbins, 'Recognizing the relationship', p. 138.

35   DC Code § 16–1001(5).

36   APAA § 115.

37   See Frank R. Ascione, *Safe havens for pets: Guidelines for programs sheltering pets for women who are battered* (Logan, UT: Utah State University Press, 2000).

38   APAA § 115. The first states to enact such legislation in 2006 were Vermont, Maine, and New York. See Vermont Bill H.0373 § 4; Maine Bill LD 1881 (HP 1321) § 12; New York Bill 10767A. See Gentry, 'Including companion animals', p. 12 .

39   DC Code §16–1005(g).

40   *Ibid.*; see also http://www.washhumane.org/programs.htm (WHS Safe Haven Program). For a directory of safe haven programs in the US see Humane Society of the United States web site at http://www.hsus.org/acf/cruelty/publiced/safe _havens_for_animals_/safe_havens_directory.html.

41   Allie Phillips, 'The dynamics between animal abuse, domestic violence and child abuse: How pets can help abused children', 38 OCT Prosecutor 22, 28 n. 11 (Sept./Oct. 2004).

42   See Angela Campbell, 'The admissibility of evidence of animal abuse in criminal trials for child and domestic abuse', *The Boston College Law Review* 43 (2002), p. 463.

43   *U.S. v. Curtin*, 489 F.3d 935, 944 (9th Cir. 2007).

44   Fed R Evid. 404(b).

45   *Ibid.*

46   *U.S. v. Hurn*, 2007 WL 2215765 at *2.

47   *People v. Singleton*, 2002 WL 31022398 (Cal.App. 4 Dist.); *State v. Thompson*, 533

S.E.2d 834 (Ct app NC 2000); *see also State v. Pugsley*, 911 P.2d 761, 773 (Idaho app. 1995); State v. Foster, 915 P.2d 567, 571 (Wash. App. 1996) (mentioning animal abuse in case of human abuse but no evidentiary analysis).

48 Singleton, 2002 WL at *1–2, 15, Thompson, 533 S.E.2d at 302, 305.

49 Thompson, 533 S.E.2d at 305.

50 Singleton, 2002 WL at *15.

51 Thompson, 533 S.E.2d at 305–06.

52 See Campbell, 'The admissibility of evidence'.

53 APAA § 101(b). Several States currently address future ownership of pets by convicted animal abusers. See, for example, 11 Del. C § 1325(c) (prohibited from owning animal for 5 years after misdemeanour conviction, and 15 years for felony conviction).

54 Campbell, 'The admissibility of evidence', p. 482; Melissa Trollinger, 'The link among animal abuse, child abuse, and domestic violence', *University of Colorado Law Review* (September 2001), pp. 29, 31.

Dealing with Animal Offenders

ANGUS NURSE

Discussions of animal cruelty and human violence frequently focus on the abuse of domestic animals, yet the United Kingdom also has a persistent problem of animal abuse involving wildlife. Crimes such as bird of prey persecution, the killing and trapping of animals (such as badgers) for sport, and hare coursing continue alongside other animal abuse activities like dog-fighting. A variety of animal and wildlife protection legislation is on the statute books in the UK, but these problems still persist.

The focus of this paper is those crimes involving illegal persecution, violence, and abuse of animals, rather than the trade in wildlife often discussed as wildlife crime. The term 'animal abuse' is used throughout this paper to describe these crimes, one key element of which is that some form of violence or injury to the animals involved is inevitable. Analysis of published material relating to such crimes in the UK reveals that the crimes attract particular types of offender (mostly male and mostly adult). The harm caused to animals is a significant factor in committing the offence and shows a tendency towards or tolerance of violence inflicted on animals by the offender. Yet for the most part, wildlife crime is dealt with outside mainstream criminal justice and offenders are dealt with solely as wildlife offenders rather than as (potentially) violent offenders.

The Legislative Background

Much animal protection and wildlife legislation has been developed as a result of the efforts of NGOs, from a moral rather than a criminal justice perspective. In part this determines the importance (or lack thereof) attached to animal abuse legislation by successive governments, leading to the enforcement of such legislation being considered less as a criminal justice issue and more as an environmental or animal welfare one.

Early attempts to prevent specific acts of cruelty to animals failed. Radford explains that the importance of Thomas Erskine's 1809 Animal Cruelty Bill was that it aimed to provide general protection for animals rather than seeking to ban specific activities like animal baiting which were legal and widespread. The Bill 'sought to make it a misdemeanour for any person, including the owner, maliciously to wound or with wanton cruelty to beat or otherwise abuse any horse, mare, ass, ox, sheep or swine'.[1] Erskine's Bill failed and it was more than ten years before the first successful attempt to introduce animal protection legislation in the form of a Bill to prevent cruelty to cattle, which received the Royal Assent in June 1822.

Since these early efforts various wildlife and animal protection legislations have been enacted. Criminal justice practitioners dealing with animal abuse crimes in the UK today have to negotiate a complicated legislative regime often containing different powers and sentencing provisions. There is no single piece of legislation protecting all animals in the United Kingdom (although the Animal Welfare Act 2006 which came into force in April 2007 contains general provisions preventing cruelty to animals and providing that animals' welfare needs must be met). Instead, legislation has been enacted at species level with such pieces of legislation as the Protection of Badgers Act 1992 and the Deer Act 1991, protecting individual species and defining specific forms of animal abuse as offences. There is however general legislation protecting a wide range of wild animals and mammals, such as the Wildlife and Countryside Act 1981 and the Wild Mammals (Protection) Act 1996. These pieces of legislation also specify some prohibited actions in relation to animals, creating specific offences in relation to some acts such as the use of self-locking snares or particular types of trap.

Animal Abuse Offences in the UK Today

A range of different animal abuse crimes are committed in the UK every year despite the legal protection afforded to wildlife. For example, the Protection of Badgers Act 1992 makes it an offence to kill, injure or take a badger or to attempt to do so. It is also an offence cruelly to ill-treat a badger, to interfere with a badger sett or to sell – or offer for sale – a badger. Yet badger crime persists. Hertfordshire Police provide the following explanation of badger crime:

> Every badger and every sett is protected by law but badgers are still vulnerable to illegal snaring, gassing and badger baiting.
>
> Badgers are dug out from their setts and taken away for fights with dogs. This extremely cruel activity causes serious injuries to dogs as well as the deaths of many badgers. It has been illegal since 1835 but appears to be on the increase and in some parts of the country the badger has been wiped out.[2]

The Badger Trust (formerly the National Federation of Badger Groups) has reported an estimated 10,000 badgers killed every year by badger baiting and digging, a figure widely accepted by a range of NGOs. In June 2002 the Trust also published a report that stated that 'a large number of badgers are snared in Britain, despite this being illegal. In addition, an analysis of snaring incidents dealt with by the RSPCA showed that of 246 animals found caught in snares, 103 were badgers'.[3]

The RSPCA's Annual Review confirms that dog-fighting, illegal hunting, badger baiting, and bird trapping all featured in 2006. The Society states that 'dog-fighting is still a major issue for the team with two large-scale cases ongoing in the West Midlands area. Forty-nine American pit bull terrier type dogs were seized in these cases alone with 41 defendants to be brought before the courts'.[4]

Although illegal in Britain since 1893 (1895 in Scotland), dog-fighting continues in secrecy today. Dog fights are highly organized events with their own sub-culture attached to them. Fights are carefully organized with bets placed on the outcome of the events by supporters and spectators. Case reports from both the UK and the US suggests that large sums of money are placed in the bets, with this illegal gambling being an integral part of the activity and the culture that surrounds it. ABC News reported that 'dogs with strong pedigrees can sell for as much as $10,000, and purses from betting on dog fights can be as high as $100,000 for the winners'.[5] Operation Gazpacho, a three-year nationwide investigation into illegal dog-fighting in the UK, found evidence of dog-fighting rings.[6]

Significant numbers of birds and animals are also killed as a result of illegal predator control, sometimes connected to game rearing. The League Against Cruel Sports' (LACS) report *The Killing Game* provides details of the use of illegal snares in the UK and the illegal persecution of birds of prey mostly by gamekeepers.

The Extent of Animal Crime in the Contemporary UK

However, the level of animal abuse crime in the UK is difficult to quantify. Much of the detailed information on the number of offences is still collated by NGOs with figures published in various forms including numbers of reported offences, actual offences, numbers of convictions, and number of defendants, making it difficult to make comparisons or establish the exact amount of animal abuse crime committed each year. However, the available data confirms that a number of crimes still take place annually, resulting in the illegal killing, taking, possession and exploitation of significant numbers of UK wildlife.

Figures produced by the RSPCA in their annual report show that the Society investigated 110,841 cruelty complaints in 2005. The Society's figures explain that there were 2,071 convictions, involving 1,013 defendants. The figures also show that there were a total of thirty-one prison and suspended sentences imposed on conviction in 2005, with a total of seven hundred and forty-nine banning orders imposed. The SSPCA report for 2006 shows a total of 9,594 investigations or abandonments in Scotland during 2006 compared with 8,206 in 2005 and seventy-four cases dealt with by the courts (compared with forty-five in 2005).[7] The figures demonstrate a range of different offence types including strictly animal welfare offences, such as neglect, but also crimes with a more serious level of criminal intent such as badger digging or cock fighting.

RSPB figures for bird of prey persecution in Scotland in 2006 describe it as 'the worst recorded for at least 20 years' with 98 reported cases of poisoning activity 42 of which were 'confirmed as pesticide abuse killing or threatening raptors'.[8]

Criminal Justice Policy on Animal Abuse Offences

Criminal justice policy on animal abuse offences is predominantly based on a law enforcement perspective of detection and punishment (by way of prosecution). It is an area where the involvement of voluntary organizations is significant. The RSPB and RSPCA have dedicated investigation sections, with other NGOs also carrying out investigations or campaigning work. In the case of the RSPCA (and its Scottish equivalent the SSPCA) a uniformed inspectorate responds to animal welfare and wildlife crime reports made by members of the public and the RSPCA's plainclothes Special Operations Unit (SOU) investigates much of the serious and organized animal crime.

The UK is still far short of having animal abuse and wildlife crime accepted as part of mainstream criminal justice. Most police forces now have a Wildlife Crime Officer (WCO), with responsibility for crimes including dog-fighting and badger baiting. However, the post is often a part-time or voluntary one, with officers taking on animal abuse enquiries in addition to their other duties. In written evidence to the Parliamentary Select Committee on Environmental Audit in March 2004, Richard Brunstrum, Chief Constable of North Wales Police stated that 'A number of forces (17) have full-time wildlife crime officers, of those 11 utilise police officers, 3 utilise support staff and 3 utilise police officers who have other duties although they spend a substantial part of their duties addressing wildlife crime. Recent years has seen an increase in the number of forces utilising full time wildlife crime officers'.[9]

Mr Brunstrum's evidence also confirmed, however, that the appointments of WCOs can depend on the views of chief police officers and that such posts may not be permanent fixtures. At the time of his evidence some new WCO posts had been created (South Wales Police) but others had been lost (e.g., Thames Valley and Lancashire Police). It was not until March 2005 that Lothian and Borders Police became 'the first police force in Scotland to appoint a full time police officer to combat wildlife crime'.[10]

However, the wildlife intelligence function of the National Criminal Intelligence Service (NCIS) was developed in October 2006 when the National Wildlife Crime Unit (NWCU) was launched by the Department for the Environment, Food and Rural Affairs (DEFRA). The NWCU is hosted by Lothian and Borders Police and gathers intelligence on national wildlife crime to provide analytical and investigative support to the individual police forces and customs officers in the UK. Enforcement of individual cases remains the responsibility of individual forces.

Deterrence is often cited as the main objective in criminal justice and sentencing policies and it is the central focus of enforcement activity in animal abuse crimes. Cavadino and Dignan explain that 'deterrence is the simple idea that the incidence of crime is reduced because of people's fear or apprehension of the punishment they may receive if they offend'.[11] Deterrence may be split into individual or general deterrence. For the individual caught and punished for a crime, theoretically he will find the punishment so unpleasant that he is determined not to repeat it and resolves to lead a law-abiding life from that point onwards. If individual deterrence worked effectively we would expect to see low reconviction rates among those offenders that have served prison sentences. However, Home Office figures demonstrate that reconviction rates are routinely in excess of 50 per cent and a Home Office publication in 2005 explained that 'overall, 61 per cent of all prisoners discharged in the first two quarters of 2001 were reconvicted for a standard list offence within two years of their discharge'.[12]

It can be argued that prison regimes need to be made tough and austere in order to make the punishment sufficiently unpleasant that an offender would not wish to repeat it. This was, however, the intention of the 'short, sharp, shock' detention centres of the 1980s, yet there is no evidence that they were any more successful in achieving lower reconviction rates.[13] The lack of success in using prison as a solution to other forms of crime, combined with the continual crisis of a lack of prison places casts doubt on the likelihood of prison and custodial sentences as a solution to animal abuse. If the likelihood of receiving a prison sentence in drug cases, for example, has failed to eradicate or significantly reduce drug crime, why should it reduce animal crime?

General deterrence occurs when the general public is stopped from committing crime because they are aware of the possibility of punishment. Publicity given to sentencing is essential in establishing general deterrence, as the public must be encouraged to believe that punishment automatically follows the commission of a crime. There are, of course, difficulties in evaluating the effectiveness of deterrence because it is impossible to measure and identify those potential offenders who do not commit an offence for fear of punishment. Lilly, Cullen, and Ball explain that 'unfortunately, there is little evidence that incarceration deters and a great deal of evidence that it exacerbates the problem'.[14]

One problem with deterrence theory is the assumption that offenders are rational and responsible individuals who calculate the risks of offending before deciding whether to commit an offence. Animal abuse offences often attract publicity at both national and local levels, although not necessarily in the level of detail that would allow an offender to effectively calculate the risk. However, it could be argued that 'a burglar sufficiently well-informed to have read the sentencing reports will also have read the criminological literature which tells him that the police detection and clear-up rate for burglary is less than 15 per cent'.[15] While it is unlikely that offenders conduct a full assessment of their offending behaviour before the commission of an offence, the part-time nature of wildlife policing, the stretched resources of NGOs, and the likelihood of a low-level sentence by the courts might make committing the offence a viable proposition.

If nothing else, the law enforcement approach provides for the incarceration of the offender at the end of the process. Despite problems of re-offending and the perceived limited effectiveness of prison regimes in addressing this, incarceration of offenders at least prevents them from committing offences for a set period of time (i.e., while in prison). Any serious attempt to prevent animal abuse offences must consider not just the detection, apprehension, and punishment of offenders but also the reasons why these crimes are committed, mechanisms for preventing crimes from being committed in the first place, and measures to prevent re-offending.

The Causes of Animal Abuse Offences

One difficulty inherent in dealing with the types of animal abuse offenders discussed in this paper is the presumption that a single approach (e.g., deterrence, custodial sentences) will work with all offenders. This view is not supported by analysis of the different types of offence committed, the behaviour of offenders, or the reasons why the offences are committed. The evidence of criminological theory is that the rationality of the offender is just one of a series of complex reasons why crime is committed; animal abuse policies should recognize this fact.

Animal abuse crime is not closely monitored by the criminal justice agencies in the UK and much enforcement action is reactive. Nor has it been the subject of intensive crime prevention or target hardening initiatives in the way that other objects of criminal activity have been. An offender who decides to steal cars, for example, has to contend with such things as alarms, immobilizers, theft registers, and the likelihood that the owner will immediately inform the police and insurance companies of the theft. In addition, the fact that cars have been increasingly designed to prevent theft and each individual car can be identified through number plates, chassis numbers, and other markings means that car theft carries with it some element of risk both in the act of taking the car and in the subsequent sale or disposal of the vehicle. By contrast, badger setts are not routinely monitored by statutory agencies but mainly by conservationists and volunteers from badger groups. With the exception of those setts which are monitored or where members of the public might accidentally encounter activities, damage to setts or the removal of badgers for 'sporting' activities is not likely to be noticed immediately and the police are not likely to be notified of the incident. While there may be a police response in the event of 'organized' criminal activity involving badgers, the primary responsibility for investigation and detection of such offences is often accepted by an NGO, the RSPCA. Such a crime, therefore, represents a soft option for the offender wishing to pursue his 'sport'.

Sutherland (1883–1950) developed the *differential association* theory to explain how criminal behaviour is learned and occurs through associations in intimate personal groups.[16] Where the associations lead to the individual accepting that the rules of society either need not or should not be obeyed, then crime is the result. For example, new gamekeepers may understand that self-locking snares and the use of poisoned baits are illegal. But if they are in a close-knit community where this form of illegal predator control is routinely practised or encouraged and violence against animals (in the form of killing of species considered to be competitors for game birds) is accepted, it may occur. Where such activities form part of their training and operational practices on an estate, it is likely that they will consider the activity to be an acceptable or necessary part of survival. Sutherland's theory provides a compelling explanation for how individuals learn and accept new and more sophisticated techniques for committing crime.

Lea and Young use the term 'relative deprivation' to explain one of the major causes of crime. They explain that 'relative deprivation is the excess of expectations over opportunities' meaning that where relative deprivation exists in conjunction with other factors criminal behaviour is likely to occur.[17] A person may experience relative deprivation yet be in a situation where other factors prevent him from turning to crime. On the other hand, the work of criminologists (such as the Chicago School researchers) suggests that crime will occur in environments where the community fails to supervise its inhabitants properly – for example, where it is understood that young men may be involved in dog-fighting, badger digging, or illegal predator control, but the community itself does not see the activity as being worthy of official attention.

While some offenders may be 'traditional offenders' seeking an easy source of direct financial gain or acting in an opportunistic manner, this does not hold true for many others. For some offenders crime is an expression of masculinity while for others their offending behaviour can be rooted in cultural and social factors and the community to which they belong. Any of these reasons or a combination of them can explain animal abuse crime.

A considerable amount of research has been conducted on crimes of masculinities and some of this considers animal abuse.[18] Fred Hawley from Louisiana State University researched cockfighting and cockfighting gangs in America. He explains that 'cockfighting can be said to have a mythos centered on the purported behaviour and character of the gamecock itself. Cocks are seen as emblems of bravery and resistance in the face of insurmountable odds'.[19] Hawley argues that the fighting involved is 'an affirmation of masculine identity in an increasingly complex and diverse era'.[20] The fighting spirit of the birds involved has great symbolic significance to those that Hawley studied. This is also true of dog-fighting in which the fighting spirit of the dog and even its ability to take punishment are prized by those involved. This indicates a type of offender not motivated solely by financial gain, but by other factors as well.

Such offences are seldom committed by lone individuals and a further motivator is the exercise of power allied to sport or entertainment; a link might also be made with organized crime and a sense of belonging. Examples include badger digging and badger baiting, cockfighting and dog-fighting, as well as some crimes that involve the 'sporting' killing or taking of wildlife. Offenders involved in such crimes are almost always male and in dealing with such offences the relationship between the members of the groups is relevant to the commission of offences. The 'secret society' element of certain crimes results in a situation where the community encourages crime and violence. Hawley identifies the significance of male bonding in carrying out certain activities. The banding together of men from the margins of society, for whom issues of belonging, male pride, and achievement are important, results in a situation where new offenders are integrated into the community. Hawley explained that:

> young men are taken under the wing of an older relative or father, and taught all aspects of chicken care and lore pertaining to the sport. Females are generally not significant players in this macho milieu, though a liberated daughter or paramour may take part in a 'powder puff' derby, a competition in which only women pit and handle the birds. This is male activity that takes place in 'male space', perhaps like the ancient Greek gymnasia, but without the homoerotic elements. In any event, discipline, if not character is certainly instilled by the constant care that domestic fowl demand.[21]

Forsyth and Evans made similar findings in researching dog-fighting in the United States.[22] They concluded that an appeal to higher loyalties and an attachment to smaller groups took precedence over attachment to society for the dog-men, with dog-fighting having great cultural significance for them.

The Rationalization of Animal Abuse Offenders

Those using animals as a means for financial gain have fairly straightforward rationalizations for their activities. The wildlife is a resource to be used and if they did not use it other people would. It has also often been argued that the crimes are victimless crimes and nobody suffers as a result of the offences that are committed. These offenders see their actions as, at best, minor crimes or crimes of a technical nature. They do not accept their offences as being serious crime that requires the attention of the criminal justice agencies.

Offenders committing crimes within the context of a 'sport', a community or group experience, often cite arguments based on historical precedent or tradition. Hawley observed that:

> Cockfighters often resort to arguments based on pseudo-psychological notions: the birds feel no pain. Some allow that perhaps the birds might feel pain but if they do it is of a qualitatively different order than that perceived by higher forms of animals. 'They (chickens) have completely different nerves [nervous systems] than people do', several informants vouchsafed. Cockfighters remain unmoved by contrary scholarship and are bemused and increasingly angered by the negative image that their pastime has in the popular imagination. They are especially incensed by the activities of People for the Ethical Treatment of Animals and other advocacy groups whom they view as effete intellectuals and kooks, of whom the best that can be said is that 'they just don't understand' what the activity entails to the enthusiast.[23]

Similar arguments occur in the UK concerning hunting with dogs. The conflicting arguments of the pro-ban and pro-hunt lobbies have been characterized as 'town versus country'. Resistance to legislation banning hunting with dogs employed arguments that emphasize the traditional nature of hunting and that legislation to ban hunting with dogs was simply interference from Whitehall in the ways of the countryside. Opponents of a ban argued that hunted animals feel no pain, that it is a perfectly natural activity, and that hunting is a necessary and effective method of predator control that people from 'the towns' simply don't understand.

Even after legislation to ban hunting with dogs was introduced its proponents continue to argue that the legislation was unjust (and unlawful) interference in what they considered to be legitimate sport. The arguments put forward by those involved are similar to the arguments put forward by cockfighters, badger baiters, and badger diggers. While this is not to suggest that the activities are the same in any legal sense, the rationalizations given are those of denial, unwarranted intervention by legislators, and a lack of understanding on the part of those that seek to ban the activity.

Offenders who commit animal abuse crimes as part of their employment also have a distinct set of rationalizations for their activities and any attention paid to them by the criminal justice agencies. In terms of rationalization, these offenders do not readily accept that their activities amount to criminal behaviour and use techniques of avoidance, denial, displacement of blame and challenges to the legitimacy of enforcers to explain away their actions. Much like those who are caught speeding by traffic enforcement cameras challenge the legitimacy of the cameras, the fines imposed or argue that cameras are simply a revenue-raising device, offenders dispute that their activities should fall within the remit of the criminal law.

Dealing with Animal Offenders

For those offenders committing animal abuse crime for profit, financial penalties may work as a means of negating any benefit they derive from their activity but the same approach is unlikely to work in other cases.

For those involved in animal abuse crimes as part of their employment (e.g., in game rearing areas or to protect fisheries), it is the nature of the employment that is the source of their offending behaviour. Any approach to these offenders must include pressure on and penalties for the employer as well as action which dictates that the risk of losing that employment is a real possibility. In many cases the current legislative regime does not provide for culpability of landowners/employers for the actions of their staff, and countryside and game industry employees do not suffer the stigma of other offenders on conviction. As a practical means of dealing with these offenders this position should be altered so that conviction of an animal abuse crime carries with it the threat of lost employment in the countryside, game rearing and fisheries or field sports industries as well as significant penalties for the employer. Action aimed at developing a cultural shift is also required so that animal abuse crimes (and the associated violence) are no longer tolerated by the immediate community and are demonstrably unacceptable within each industry.

For offenders whose activities are a product of masculinity and linked to a wider social involvement in marginal activities, the effectiveness of prison or high fines is also questionable. Much like gang members in the inner-city US, those involved in organized crime or youths who see ASBOs as a badge of honour (Youth Justice Board and BBC News, November 2006),[24] offenders may come to see prison as simply an occupational hazard as well as being a reinforcement of their male identity and confirmation of society's lack of understanding of their needs and culture. The violent nature of the offences is a factor and offenders should be considered not just as those who engage in wildlife or animal crime but as those involved in violent activity within a distinct sub-culture. While they may be temporarily incapacitated by prison, the community is forgiving and accepting of their behaviour, so there is no incentive to change. For these types of offender, situational crime prevention should be attempted, as well as a real attempt at rehabilitation alongside the traditional law enforcement approach of detection and prosecution.

Conclusions

Criminal justice policy should consider each different type of animal abuse offender rather than treating all offenders the same and employing a purely punitive regime heavily reliant on fines or custodial sentences. This is unlikely to be effective given what is known from mainstream criminology and from examining the types of offences committed within the UK.

Criminological theory and past experience of implementing criminal justice policies shows that there is no single cause of crime. Some crimes have a basis in individual or group criminal activity and behaviour, while a range of social conditions such as poverty, relative deprivation, and tradition can also cause some crime. However there is no definitive explanation for all crime and so policy on animal abuse crimes needs to consider the different causes of these crimes in order to determine where resources should be concentrated, and the precise policies needed to prevent or reduce crime.

Animal abuse offenders do not all share the same motivations or operate within similar communities or control mechanisms. This being the case, there is little point in treating all offenders as if they were the same – a blanket approach to dealing with offenders is unlikely to be successful. While fines and custodial sentences may deter and temporarily incapacitate some offenders, this does little to prevent new offenders from emerging each year or to address the conditions within certain communities or occupations which allow animal abuse offences to become an accepted part of the cultural or operational practices.

Any concerted attempt at reducing animal abuse offending requires resources allocated to crime prevention and exploring alternatives to custody. While there may be a proportion of these offences that can be prevented by crime prevention initiatives, it is unlikely that sufficient resources can be allocated to achieve this on any meaningful scale and so rehabilitative or diversionary measures may also be needed to prevent further offending. The violent nature of the offences also needs to be considered and it is of concern that offenders are treated in isolation as 'wildlife offenders' rather than as 'mainstream' violent offenders.

Notes

1   Mike Radford, *Animal welfare law in Britain* (Oxford: Oxford University Press, 2001), p. 37.

2   Hertfordshire Constabulary, *Justice for our wildlife* (Hertfordshire: Hertfordshire Constabulary, 1998), p. 2.

3   National Federation of Badger Groups, *The effect on badgers of hunting with dogs: A briefing paper by the National Federation of Badger Groups* (London: NFBG, 2002), p. 2.

4   Royal Society for the Prevention of Cruelty to Animals, *Annual Review 2006* (Horsham: RSPCA, 2007).

5   Dean Schabner, 'Arrest called break in dog fight effort' [sic], ABC News, 29 April 2003.

6   H. Carter, 'Man jailed after admitting dogfights', *The Guardian*, 17 May 2005; see http://www.guardian.co.uk/uk/2005/may/17/animalwelfare.world.

7   Scottish Society for the Prevention of Cruelty to Animals, *Annual Report 2006* (Edinburgh: SSPCA, 2007), p. 13.

8   Royal Society for the Protection of Birds, *Persecution: A review of bird of prey persecution in Scotland in 2006* (Edinburgh: RSPB, 2007), pp. 10, 14.

9   House of Commons, *Select committee on environmental audit: Twelfth report* (London: House of Commons, 2004).

10 Lothian and Borders Police, *First dedicated police wildlife crime officer, Lothian and Borders Police* (Edinburgh: Lothian and Borders Police, 2005).

11 Michael Cavadino and James Dignan, *The penal system: An introduction* (London: Sage, 1994), p. 33.

12 Rachel Councell, *Offender management caseload statistics 2004* (London: Home Office, 2005), p. 133.

13 Cavadino and Dignan, *The penal system*, p. 34.

14 J. Robert Lilly, Francis T. Cullen, and Richard A. Ball, *Criminological theory: Context and consequences* (London: Sage, 1995), p. 223.

15 Eric Stockdale and Silvia Casale (eds), *Criminal justice under stress* (London: Blackstone, 1992), p. 123.

16 George B. Vold, and Thomas J. Bernard, *Theoretical criminology* (Oxford: Oxford University Press, 1986).

17 John Lea and Jock Young, *What is to be done about law and order?*, revised edn (London: Pluto Press, 1993), p. 218.

18 See Tim Newburn and Elizabeth Stanko, *Just boys doing business? Men, masculinities and crime* (London: Routledge, 1994); Richard Collier, *Masculinities, crime and criminology: Men, heterosexuality and the criminal(ised) other* (London: Sage, 1998), and Anne Cossins, *Masculinities, sexualities and child sexual abuse* (Kluwer Law International, 2000).

19 Fred Hawley, 'The moral and conceptual universe of cockfighters: Symbolism and rationalization', *Society & Animals* 1, 2 (1993).

20 *Ibid.*, p. 3.

21 *Ibid.*, p. 5.

22 Craig J. Forsyth and Rhonda D. Evans, 'Dogmen: The rationalization of deviance', *Society & Animals* 6, 3 (1998).

23 Hawley, 'The moral and conceptual universe of cockfighters', p. 5.

24 BBC News, *ASBOs viewed as badge of honour*, 2 November 2006, http://news.bbc.co.uk/1/hi/uk/6107028.stm.

CHAPTER

20

Implications for Criminal Law, Sentencing Policy and Practice

MARTIN WASIK

Is there a relationship between a person's history of offences committed against animals and a propensity on their part to go on to commit violence against human beings? Other chapters have examined the available empirical evidence[1] and tested this hypothesis. My purpose is rather different. It is to consider in what ways that relationship, *if* established, could impinge on the practical operation of criminal law, sentencing policy and practice. The paper is written from the perspective of a lawyer who is both an academic and a practitioner in the criminal courts. The focus is on the legal system of England and Wales.

It is fair to say that, despite significant academic work exploring the link between cruelty to animals and violence against human beings,[2] this issue has not been explored in reported decisions of the higher courts. Nearly all cases of cruelty to animals are dealt with in the magistrates' courts, where decisions are unreported. When examples of animal cruelty appear in Crown Court cases, the element of cruelty is inevitably regarded as subsidiary to the main offence perpetrated against a human victim. Animals are not infrequently additional casualties in an offender's action against the intended human target. An example is *West*,[3] where the defendant, who had a grudge against the owner of a riding school, started a fire which got out of control, causing the deaths of ten horses. The sentence of seven years' imprisonment was upheld by the Court of Appeal, with Waterhouse J. referring to 'the understandable sense of public outrage' at what had happened. Another example is *McGregor*,[4] reported as a successful prosecution appeal against an unduly lenient sentence. The defendant pleaded guilty to arson being reckless as to whether life[5] would be endangered. In a jealous rage against his girlfriend he set light to some of her clothes in the bedroom of their terraced house. He then attacked and maimed the girlfriend's dog, a nine-month-old cocker spaniel, with a sledgehammer, locked the door and left the fire to burn. The defendant pleaded guilty at the Crown Court to the charge of arson being reckless whether life was endangered, having already pleaded guilty at the magistrates' court to the two summary offences of criminal damage (relating to the clothes), and cruelty to an animal. The dog was so badly injured it had to be put down. The judge imposed a probation order for twelve months in relation to these offences, but on appeal the sentence was increased by the Court of Appeal to one of two years' imprisonment.

A Matter of Evidence

Despite the intuitive plausibility of a link between animal abuse and human violence, the criminal courts would be reluctant to accept evidence of a link without a high threshold of agreement as to its veracity and reliability.[6] Poor quality expert evidence contributed to a number of notorious miscarriage of justice cases in the 1970s. A high threshold of reliability has been reflected in the United States in the famous *Frye*[7] test and, if anything, criminal courts in this country have been even more circumspect. It is true that DNA evidence has now come to be widely accepted and relied upon as powerful evidence pointing to guilt, despite the occasional trial in which the evidence has been flawed or presented in a misleading way. But DNA evidence is based upon natural science. When it comes to evidence from psychologists and psychiatrists, lawyers have always been sceptical, preferring, wherever possible, to say that human behaviour is something which in the vast majority of cases can readily be understood by a jury, without expert help.[8] There are occasional exceptions, where an insight from psychology or psychiatry can come to be accepted by the criminal courts, perhaps even in advance of widespread acceptance outside the law. One such example is 'battered women's syndrome', now accepted by the Court of Appeal as tending to account for circumstances in which a woman's apparently premeditated killing of her partner might properly be characterized as manslaughter, rather than murder, because of the context of domestic violence and abuse within which the killing took place.[9]

Relevant at Trial or to Sentence?

All of the above examples relate to the admissibility of evidence in the course of a criminal trial, to assist in determining guilt or innocence. They all relate to evidence relevant to the offence charged. If it could be shown that there was a link between a history of animal abuse and future violent offending, such evidence could only be admitted at trial by adducing evidence of relevant previous convictions of the defendant. Before the changes made by the Criminal Justice Act 2003 the circumstances in which a jury could hear about the defendant's previous convictions were very limited. Since the Act there has been some relaxation of the rules, but tests are still quite strict, requiring that evidence of bad character falls within a specific statutory permission or 'gateway'. The prosecution may argue that the defendant has a 'propensity' to commit offences of the kind charged, but this is always subject to a judicial discretion to exclude the evidence if it would have an adverse effect on the fairness of the proceedings.[10] There is little prospect of the prosecution being permitted by the judge to lead evidence of the defendant's previous convictions of animal abuse on a charge of, say, assault against a child, not least because these will of necessity be offences of a *different* kind.[11] This leads to the conclusion that, if the evidence is to be brought to bear at a criminal trial, it must do so at the sentencing stage.

The criminal trial falls into two distinct parts, trial and sentence. In practice, in many cases there is in fact no first part, because the offender chooses to plead guilty. There are major procedural differences between the two stages.[12] The trial is marked by adversarial proceedings, rigorous examination and cross-examination of witnesses giving oral testimony, all subject to strict rules of relevance and admissibility, where the judge assumes a neutral umpiring role, asks few if any questions, and provides a fair and balanced summing up for the jury when they retire to consider their verdict.[13] At the sentencing stage proceedings are no longer adversarial, there are few if any witnesses, the rules of evidence are relaxed, and the judge assumes a central role, inquiring into all aspects of the offender's background and circumstances, considering written reports, and imposing sentence. This is the stage, it would appear, at which evidence could be aired of a link between the defendant's past abuse of animals, and the risk of future violence which he may present.

Sentencing Dangerous Offenders

When the court comes to impose sentence it retains a fair measure of discretion over the decision, but nowadays is guided by the statutory purposes of sentencing,[14] other statutory rules, sentencing guidelines, and previous sentencing decisions of the Court of Appeal. Of particular importance in the present context are the statutory provisions in the Criminal Justice Act 2003 dealing with so-called 'dangerous' violent or sexual offenders. For these offenders the court, rather than sentencing on a 'backward-looking' basis and imposing a punishment broadly commensurate with the seriousness of the offence, must instead sentence on a 'forward-looking' basis, passing a sentence which is designed to reflect the degree of risk of serious future offending which the offender represents. It is necessary to explain these provisions in a little more detail here, but fortunately not to enter into the full complexity of the legislative scheme.[15] If an offender aged eighteen or over is convicted of a *serious specified violent or sexual offence* (which means a violent or sexual offence listed in the statute, and one which carries a maximum penalty of at least ten years, including those which carry life imprisonment) and the court is 'of the opinion that there is a significant risk to members of the public of serious harm occasioned by the commission by him of further specified offences',[16] then the court must impose a life sentence if the offence carries life as its maximum, or a sentence of imprisonment for public protection if the offence does not carry life.

It will be seen that Parliament has couched these sentencing arrangements in mandatory terms – if the relevant matters are established the court *must* impose one of these two sentences. There is, however, still some room for manoeuvre – the judge might find, on all the evidence, that there is no *significant* risk of serious harm, or no significant risk of *serious* harm of the offender committing further violent or sexual offences. The Court of Appeal, in the leading case of *Lang*,[17] said that an exercise of judgement on the part of the sentencer is always required here. If a life sentence or a sentence of imprisonment for public protection is passed by the court, it is required to fix a *minimum* period which must be served in full by the offender before he becomes eligible to be considered for early release. At the expiry of that period the Parole Board will begin the process of assessing whether, or at what stage, the risk posed by the offender has diminished such that he is safe to be released. This is entirely a matter for the Parole Board, and if the offender continues to represent a risk of the magnitude described he will not be released. Most offenders will be released at some point in their sentence, but these sentences are indeterminate and may result in the offender being detained for the rest of his natural life.

How Could Evidence of the Relationship Come Before the Court?

When the court comes to impose sentence, it will have regard to a number of sources of information – the offender's criminal record, reports (including a pre-sentence report and, if appropriate, a medical report), and a plea in mitigation. These are now considered in turn, both in general terms and particularly in the context of the sentencing of 'dangerous' offenders.

(i) The Criminal Record

The first of these is the offender's criminal record. The judge will have been in possession of the list of previous convictions from the start of the trial. Lay justices will not have seen the list until it is handed to them at the start of the sentencing process. The prosecution lawyer will start the sentencing process by outlining the facts of the offence (unless there has just been a trial, in which case this is not necessary) and will then run through the previous convictions. The record will have a brief entry relating to each previous conviction, and previous caution, indicating legal category of offence, date and court in which tried and sentenced, sentence imposed, and (if relevant) date of release from custody. Previous convictions are normally to be taken as aggravating the seriousness of the most recent offence.[18] Any previous convictions relating to animal abuse should, in principle, be clear from the record. Prosecutions for offences involving cruelty to protected animals[19] are brought by the RSPCA rather than by the Crown Prosecution Service.[20] The policy of the RSPCA is to prosecute only as a last resort, preferring wherever possible to advise, warn, or if appropriate, re-home animals at threat with the owner's agreement.[21] If a prosecution is brought, it will now usually be under section four of the Animal Welfare Act 2006 (which in 2007 replaced section one of the Protection of Animals Act 1911). The offence can only be heard in the magistrates' court. The sentencing guidelines for the offence[22] indicate that magistrates should consider a community penalty in a case where the offender has disputed guilt, but most cases are dealt with by a financial penalty, sometimes accompanied by an order disqualifying the offender from keeping animals of the type involved, or animals more generally, for an appropriate period of time. Aggravating features mentioned in the guidelines include 'offender in position of special responsibility, adult involves children in offending, offender ignored advice/warnings, serious injury or death, and use of weapon'. Prison sentences are available for this offence, up to a maximum of six months, but are relatively uncommon.[23]

If an offender has committed such an offence in the past, and has been convicted or cautioned for it, it should appear on his criminal record. It goes without saying, of course, that the great majority of instances of animal abuse will not have been reported, still less prosecuted or resulted in conviction. The record will not normally carry further details of the circumstances of past offences, but in the Crown Court there should be attached to the list of previous convictions a short summary of the facts of the last three convictions which seem particularly relevant by virtue of their similarity and/or proximity in time to the current offence.[24] It might be thought that, if there was an established link between past offences of animal abuse and future risk of violence, the prosecutor could address the judge as to that link, especially where the 'dangerous' offender sentencing provisions were applicable. The traditional role of the English prosecutor on sentencing has, however, been rather restricted. Unlike the position in the United States, the prosecutor in England and Wales has been required to adopt a neutral stance on sentence,[25] beyond ensuring that the judge is made aware of the victim personal statement, any guideline sentencing case and is aware (if appropriate) that the 'dangerous' offender sentencing provisions are applicable to the case.[26] In recent years the prosecutor's role has been developing and, with the encouragement of the senior judiciary, is becoming somewhat more active at the sentencing stage. The Code for Crown Prosecutors now indicates that the prosecutor should, amongst other matters, 'draw the court's attention to any aggravating or mitigating factors disclosed by the prosecution case'. As we have seen, previous convictions of the defendant are regarded as aggravating the current offence and so, in principle, a prosecutor might now be able to advance the importance of the link between the offender's offending history, the nature of the current offence, and the risk that he may represent in future.

(ii) The Pre-sentence Report

The next piece of information before the sentencing court will be in the form of a pre-sentence report. Such a report is not mandatory, but would almost always be required if the offender had been convicted of an offence involving significant violence. The report will contain a range of information about the background and circumstances of the offender and his attitude to the offence committed. If the dangerous offender provisions are in play, the pre-sentence report must carry a section which deals with the issue of risk.[27] The risk assessment is generated by way of a programme called OASys, the Offender Assessment System, developed by the probation service and in operation nationally.[28]

OASys requires the probation officer producing the report to input data into twelve separate fields (such as offending information, lifestyle and associates, drug misuse, alcohol misuse, emotional well-being, thinking, and behaviour), each of which carries a numerical weighting depending on the research evidence as to its predictiveness of reconviction. Completion of the sections generates a numerical risk score. There is also an optional self-assessment form which provides the offender's own perspective on his offending behaviour. Completion of the form may alert the officer to the need for additional and more specific assessment, such as violent offender assessment, mental health assessment, or dangerous and severe personality assessment. OASys is designed to address specific risks, including harm to the public, harm to known adults, and harm to children. Levels of risk of serious harm are generated, which range from low, through medium and high, to very high. If the offender falls within the upper two categories the pre-sentence report will conclude with a risk management plan for consideration by the sentencer.

The Court of Appeal has made it clear that the risk analysis in the pre-sentence report will often be crucial when sentencing a dangerous offender, but the decision whether or not to impose such a sentence remains one for the court and the sentencer may disagree with the assessment, but would certainly be expected to explain the decision to take a different view. If the judge is thinking of taking a different line from the report, both prosecution and defence counsel should be given an opportunity to address the court on the issue of dangerousness,[29] but it would be unusual to subject the report writer to questioning in court. Currently there is no specific recognition within the OASys scheme of the significance of past offences of animal abuse when a report is being prepared on a violent offender. It would seem that this is an important potential way in which the connection could have a practical impact on pre-sentence report risk assessments and hence on sentencing outcomes. The completion of the OASys fields, and the associated interviewing of the defendant, might bring to light information about past offending against animals which might not be apparent from the list of previous convictions.[30]

(iii) The Psychiatric Report

Sometimes, in addition to the pre-sentence report, there will be a medical (or psychiatric) report. This issue of the offender's mental well-being might have been raised before the trial, on the question whether he was fit to be tried, or during the trial, such as where a defence of insanity, automatism or diminished responsibility has been in issue. Or the question may arise purely at sentence, such as where the offender has pleaded guilty but there is reason to think that a medical disposal may be more appropriate than a punitive sentence. The defence may request such a report, or the court may do so on its own initiative, to inform the sentencing decision. Statute requires that a medical report be obtained in any case in which the defendant is or appears to be mentally disturbed.[31] In *Lang* the Court of Appeal said that a medical report would clearly be appropriate in some public protection cases.

The report must be prepared by a person approved[32] by virtue of their special experience in the diagnosis and treatment of mental disorder. The content of a psychiatric report is subject to guidelines[33] which state that such a report should include (i) the data on which the report is based, (ii) how this relates to the opinion given, (iii) factors relating to the presence of mental disorder that may affect the risk that the offender poses to himself/herself or others, (iv) factors relating to the presence of mental disorder that may affect the risk of re-offending, (v) if admission to hospital is recommended what, if any, special treatment or security is needed and how this would be addressed, and (vi) where no medical proposal is made, advice on management may be appropriate.

Guidance to the criminal courts from the National Offender Management Service (NOMS) in the *Probation Bench Handbook* states that it is always helpful if the court specifies what is required in the report, such as the relationship between the mental disorder and the offending, risk to self and/or others, and an opinion on what disposal would address the disorder and assist in reducing offending. If a custodial sentence is likely, the court should ask the report writer to address the likely impact of such a sentence on the offender and any available treatments. If the offence is a specified violent offence or specified sexual offence which might attract a public protection sentence then the court should ask for an assessment of the risk to the public of serious harm by the commission of further such offences by the offender. If the offender is on bail awaiting sentence the probation service will act as commissioning agents for the report, and if the offender is in custody awaiting sentence the prison will be responsible for arranging the report. The court must send a clear instruction to the prison that a psychiatric report has been ordered.

Reasons for ordering a report will derive from the trial, if there has been one (often there will have been a plea of guilty), the prosecution statement of the facts of the offence, the nature of the offender's record, especially where that raises concern about risk to the public, the nature of instant offence (such as manslaughter by diminished responsibility, or arson,[34] which are long-recognized trigger offences for ordering a report), or the offender's eligibility for particular forms of sentence, such as a community order with a mental health treatment requirement, a public protection sentence, or a hospital order or guardianship order.

If the offender has a history of animal abuse, whether or not associated with previous convictions for that behaviour, the report writer might well wish to draw attention to it and to any established link between such conduct in the past and the risk of violence in the future. Cruelty to animals is included in the symptom list for 'conduct disorder' in the *Diagnostic and statistical manual of mental disorders*.[35] 'Conduct disorder' is defined as 'a repetitive and persistent pattern of behaviour in which the basic rights of others or major age-appropriate societal norms or rules are violated' and requires that at least three of fifteen separate symptoms have been present during the last year – these symptoms include 'deceitfulness or theft', 'destruction of property', and 'aggression to people and animals'. The other authoritative manual is the *Classification of mental and behavioural disorders: Clinical descriptions and diagnostic guidelines*.[36] Here, 'conduct disorders' are said to be disorders characterized by a repetitive and persistent pattern of dissocial, aggressive, or defiant conduct. Amongst the examples of behaviours on which the diagnosis is based are 'cruelty to other people or animals, destructiveness to property, fire-raising, stealing, repeated lying', and so on. It appears that follow-up studies of conduct-disordered children have shown a high incidence of antisocial personality disorder, affective illnesses, and chronic criminal behaviour in later life.[37]

Such information could be provided in a psychiatric report to the court, in support of the argument that an offender with a previous history of animal abuse presents a risk of continuing (and perhaps escalating) criminal behaviour. It is important, however, to recall the relevant words of the provision on dangerous offenders – the court must be clear that the offender represents 'a serious risk to members of the public of serious harm occasioned by the commission by him of further specified offences'. The issue is whether the psychiatric evidence, taken alone or in conjunction with all the other relevant information, can justify that conclusion.[38]

Conclusions

(1) If there is indeed a significant relationship between an offender's history of abuse of animals and their future violence towards human beings, this issue is much more likely to be relevant to sentencing rather than to the determination of guilt or innocence.

(2) The traditionally restricted role of the English prosecutor at the sentencing stage means that it may not be possible for evidence of this

relationship to be advanced effectively by the prosecution at the sentencing stage.

(3) The relationship could have some practical impact on sentencing by being incorporated within the probation service's OASys tool for risk assessment. This would mean that questions about the offender's past abuse of animals would have to be asked during preparation of the report. This could gather information not readily apparent from the offender's previous convictions. Inclusion of the information in OASys, as relevant to risk of re-offending, would affect the re-offending prediction score and hence impinge on sentencing outcomes.

(4) It is possible that the relationship could be placed before a judge in a psychiatric report prepared to assist the court at the sentencing stage. The definition of conduct disorder in both the *DSM-IV* and the ICD-10 refers to cruelty to animals as one among a number of symptoms of a conduct disorder, which itself seems to be a persistent form of antisocial behaviour. If the report writer felt that such past behaviour was significant in the determination of risk, it would be certainly appropriate to refer to it in the report.

Notes

1   See F. R. Ascione, *Children and animals: Exploring the roots of kindness and cruelty* (West Lafayette, IN: Purdue University Press, 2005); R. Lockwood and F. R. Ascione (eds), *Cruelty to animals and interpersonal violence: Readings in research and application* (West Lafayette, IN: Purdue University Press, 1997).

2   See, for example, A. Arluke, J. Levin, C. Luke and F. R. Ascione, 'The relationship of animal abuse to violence and other forms of antisocial behaviour', *Journal of Interpersonal Violence* 14 (1999), p. 963; L. Bell, 'Abusing children – abusing animals', *Journal of Social Work* 1 (2001), p. 223; N. C. Sweeney, 'Animals and children caught in a cycle of cruelty', *Justice of the Peace* 168 (2004), p. 224.

3   (1991) 13 Cr App R (S) 70.

4   *Attorney-General's Reference (No 61 of 1996) (Thomas Hunter McGregor)* [1997] 2 Cr App R (S) 316.

5   Life, in this context means human, rather than animal, life. It is normal to specify in the indictment the name of at least one person whose life was, according to the prosecution, endangered.

6   M. Redmayne, *Expert evidence and criminal justice* (Oxford: Oxford University Press, 2001).

7   *Frye v. United States* 2903 F. 1013 (1923), generating a rule excluding expert evidence based on a new scientific discovery or technique, until that discovery or technique has gained general acceptance in the scientific community. The test has been relaxed somewhat in Federal courts by *Daubert v. Merrell Dow Pharmaceuticals, Inc.* 113 S Ct 27886 (1993).

8   *Turner* (1975) 61 Cr App R 67, considered in detail by Redmayne, *Expert evidence*, chapter 6.

9   The Court of Appeal in *Ahluwahlia* [1992] 4 All ER 889, after a re-trial, accepted that such condition could amount to diminished responsibility under the terms of the Homicide Act 1957, s.2. See also *Hobson* [1998] 1 Cr App R 31.

10 Criminal Justice Act 2003, ss.98–110.

11 The only possible exception would be where the circumstances surrounding the past offence and the current charge were both closely similar and highly unusual. The clear inference that the same person committed both crimes might justify admissibility of the past animal-related offence (see *Hanson* [2005] 1 WLR 3169).

12 J. Shapland, *Between conviction and sentence* (London: Routledge, 1981).

13 In a summary trial the magistrates both oversee the trial and determine guilt or innocence, but that issue is beyond the scope of this paper.

14 Criminal Justice Act 2003, s.142(1).

15 The following account omits references to sentences for offenders under 18, extended sentences for those aged 18 and over, and various powers of the courts to adjust licence length and requirements for such offenders on release. A comprehensive guide is provided by the Sentencing Guidelines Council, *Dangerous offenders: Guide for sentencers and practitioners*, 2007.

16 Criminal Justice Act 2003, s.225(1).

17 [2006] 2 All ER 410.

18 Criminal Justice Act 2003, s.143(2).

19 Under the Animal Welfare Act 2006.

20 Prosecution by a local authority is also possible: see 2006 Act, s.30.

21 M. Radford, *Animal welfare law in Britain: Regulation and responsibility* (Oxford: Oxford University Press, 2001), Part F.

22 *Magistrates' courts sentencing guidelines* (London: Sentencing Guidelines Council, 2008), p. 22.

23 Anthony and Berryman's *Magistrates' courts guide* (annual edition), Lexis-Nexis Butterworths, advises (at A[17.16]) that 'Magistrates should . . . be careful to maintain some relationship with penalties for assaulting persons, lest a criticism may be sustained that a more serious view has been taken of cruelty to an animal than cruelty to a human being'.

24 Consolidated Criminal Practice Direction, III.27: Antecedents. The whole document is set out in *Blackstone's criminal practice* (Oxford: Oxford University Press, 2007), Appendix 7.

25 The Code of Conduct of the Bar states that the prosecutor 'should not attempt by advocacy to influence the court in regard to sentence'.

26 *Code for Crown Prosecutors* (2004).

27 As required by the National Probation Service's *Guide for sentences of public protection* (London: NPS, 2005).

28 The following section draws upon the National Probation Service's *Probation bench handbook* (London: National Offender Management Service, Edition Two, August 2007, Appendix 1). See now the National Offender Management Service, *OASys Manual v2 with Revised Chapter 8*, 2006.

29 *Lang* [17(ii)].

30 Ascione refers to a number of studies involving interviews of convicted violent offenders revealing apparently high rates of commission of animal cruelty. See *Children and animals*, pp. 91–95.

31 Criminal Justice Act 2003, s.157 (1) and (2) – although, mysteriously, the court may dispense with the report if it considers that one is 'unnecessary'.

32 Under the Mental Health Act 1983, s.12.

33 *Code of practice to the Mental Health Act 1983* (London: Department of Health, 1999).

34 *Calladine, The Times*, 3 December 1975, a principle often referred to in later cases.
35 *The DSM-IV* (Arlington, VA: American Psychiatric Association, 1994). See Ascione, *Children and animals*, p. 95.
36 ICD-10 (World Health Organization, Geneva, 1992).
37 See R. Loeber, D. P. Farrington and D. A. Waschbusch, 'Serious and violent juvenile offenders', in R. Loeber and D. P. Farrington, *Serious and violent juvenile offenders: Risk factors and successful interventions* (Thousand Oaks, CA: Sage Publications, 1998), p. 13, and Ascione, *Children and animals*, chapter 7.
38 Thanks are due to my Keele colleague Tony Hobbs for assistance with this final section.

PART
VII

Prevention and Professional Obligations

Part VII addresses the issues surrounding the role of professionals in providing effective detection, identification, and reporting of cases of abuse.

Ian Robertson (*A Legal Duty to Report Suspected Animal Abuse – Are Veterinarians Ready?*) highlights how the UK's Animal Welfare Act of 2006 imposes duties of care on animal caregivers, but that 'effective enforcement of these duties, powers, and penalties' depends upon 'efficient and effective identification and reporting of suspected cases of animal abuse'. Veterinarians are broadly recognized as the first point of call for animal health issues, and there is already an ethical duty to report for veterinarians who are registered with the Royal College of Veterinary Surgeons. But that ethical duty may not, for a range of reasons, be sufficient – only a mandatory legal duty to report removes the 'moral dilemma' that many veterinarians experience. Robertson concludes that 'a legislative mandatory veterinary duty to report' is the 'logical' way of fulfilling the veterinary profession's obligation to counter abuse.

From a US perspective, Corey C. Montoya and Catherine A. Miller (*The Role of Veterinarians and Other Animal Welfare Workers in the Reporting of Suspected Child Abuse*) highlight the potential significance of veterinarians and others in reporting suspected abuse of children.

Given the close relationship between animal and child abuse, both historically and empirically, Montoya and Miller conclude that 'animal welfare workers have a valuable and unique opportunity to be proactive in cases of child abuse'. This is an important part of ending the 'cycle of animal abuse, child abuse, and interpersonal abuse that may otherwise continue to affect all those involved, human and animal'.

Dawn Hawksworth and Rachel Balen (*Animal Cruelty and Child Welfare – The Health Visitor's Perspective*) provide first-hand evidence from a UK perspective of the link between patterns of child and animal neglect. One of the authors relates from her professional work three compelling cases that expose common patterns of neglect with regard to both children and the companion animals within the respective households. However, they explain, 'within the commonly used [Government approved] Frameworks [for assessment] . . . it is not possible to identify material relating to the harming of animals that would inform assessment and planning'. There is a need for cross-reporting, multi-agency practice, and information sharing in order that the issue of abuse – to children and animals alike – is fully addressed by professionals.

A Legal Duty to Report Suspected Animal Abuse: Are Veterinarians Ready?

IAN ROBERTSON

The law is foundational to any and all proposed changes or developments with respect to the issue of human violence and animal abuse, because any and all proposed initiatives can only be implemented if they are *lawful* initiatives. Consequently, whether discussions consider ethical or social perspectives, rights debates, definitions, policies or practices, or any other view regarding the relationship between human violence and animal abuse, the law must be a fundamental part of all such discussions.

The association of animal abuse with domestic violence has been well documented. Animal abuse has been recognized as an indicator of a potentially aggressive and antisocial demeanour that may begin with animals, and progress into violence against humans, including family members. The recently enacted Animal Welfare Act 2006 therefore has important implications in safeguarding animal and human victims alike. The Act builds on anti-cruelty concepts contained within earlier legislation, and imposes positive duties of care on animal caregivers, broadly referred to as the five freedoms. The Act also increases powers of search and seizure by authorities, and increases penalties for breaches of duties and obligations under the Act. Effective enforcement of these duties, powers, and penalties are dependent, however, on efficient and effective identification and reporting of suspected cases of animal abuse.

Veterinarians are broadly recognized within society as a first point of call for animal health issues, and are one of a number of professionals who may see or hear things during the course of their professional activity which may arouse suspicion of animal abuse, domestic violence, or child abuse. It logically follows that veterinarians play an important role in the efficient and effective identification and reporting of suspected animal abuse cases. In view of the fact that some individuals convicted of criminal assault have been documented to have inflicted injuries on animals prior to engaging in physical assaults on people, efficient reporting is important to the welfare of humans and animals alike. In recognition of this fact, some American states[1] have already made it mandatory for veterinarians to report animal abuse to a designated agency. A similar requirement is now required in parts of Canada. These legislative developments regarding the veterinarian's role in the management of cases involving suspected animal abuse raise the question of whether a similar mandatory duty to report should be applied to veterinarians in England.[2]

There is an existing ethical duty for veterinarians who are registered with the Royal College of Veterinary Surgeons,[3] which directs the course of action a veterinarian should take if presented with a case of suspected animal abuse.[4] Member veterinarians are advised to include non-accidental injury in their differential diagnosis when presented with an injured animal whose clinical signs cannot be attributed to the history provided by the client. Depending on the level of appropriateness, the veterinarian is further advised either to attempt to discuss the matter with the client, or to contact the relevant authorities.

The current duty is an ethical duty only. While not minimizing the significance of an ethical duty, an ethical responsibility is significantly different from a legislative requirement. A legal duty may be viewed as extending what a veterinarian 'should' ethically do as judged by the profession's authorities, to what a veterinarian 'must' do, as judged by the profession *and* the courts. A legal mandatory obligation on a veterinarian to report suspected cases of animal abuse, arguably also infers a legal liability for *not* reporting a suspected case of animal abuse. Although studies have confirmed that veterinarians do see cases of suspected animal or child abuse, studies have also shown that they are divided on whether they should be required by law to report those suspicions.[5] Whether veterinarians believe they should be mandated to report or not, the fact remains that veterinarians are uniquely placed to identify and report suspected cases of animal abuse. Furthermore, there are strong arguments supporting the idea that a properly constructed statutory requirement attached to the unique role of the veterinarian has significant advantages, both for veterinarians and victims.

In reading this paper, it is helpful to be clear on three points. Firstly, there is already an *existing* ethical duty on veterinarians[6] directing how they should deal with a case of suspected animal abuse.[7] Secondly, this duty applies to *all* veterinarians registered with the RCVS.[8] Points one and two mean that the question being addressed is not 'if' there should be a duty in respect of reporting animal abuse because, obviously, that decision has already been made. Instead the question focuses on *how* implementation of a *mandatory legal duty to report improves compliance with this duty.* The third point is a reminder about the purpose of the duty itself. Whether or not victims of abuse, animals or people, receive the appropriate help and care, may depend significantly on the attending veterinarian's competence and actions – or lack thereof.

Following the lead of other jurisdictions where legislatures and veterinary bodies have recognized the advantages of having a legal mandate to report, and subsequently legislated the duty, this paper proposes that it is timely to consider applying the same duty to veterinarians in England. Specifically, this paper considers, in three parts, whether or not veterinarians are ready for a mandatory duty to report: firstly, by examining the education currently provided to veterinarians on the issue of human violence and animal abuse; secondly by examining the current structure for reporting; and thirdly by considering the advantages, particularly to the veterinarian, of adding a legal duty to the existing ethical duty.

Education and Training

All veterinarians registered with the Royal College of Veterinary Surgeons (RCVS) already have an *existing* ethical duty which directs how a veterinarian should deal with a case of suspected animal abuse.[9] If a duty of any kind is imposed on veterinarians, then it logically follows that the veterinarians should have received sufficient education and assessment on the subject, and procedures should be established to enable and confirm that the veterinarians are able to fulfil their obligations. Accordingly, the very existence of the current ethical duty regarding suspected animal abuse arguably implies that all veterinarians are sufficiently trained to differentiate between cases of accident, disease, or possible abuse. It is further implied that veterinarians understand the responsibilities, procedures, and application of the duty itself; including, for example, the fact that veterinarians are not expected to confirm the abuse, but merely have to *suspect* that the presenting case may involve animal abuse for the duty to be activated.

With respect to the subject of veterinary education and training, one of the questions this paper raises is whether there is consistency of training and assessment of all veterinarians to ensure that, as a profession, they can indeed competently fulfil their responsibilities. For convenience it is useful to consider the training given to undergraduate veterinarians separately from postgraduates.

There are two important starting points in examining the undergraduate training provided in veterinary schools. Firstly, as stated above, is the fact that *all* veterinarians registered with the RCVS are expected to comply with the *existing* ethical duty regarding animal abuse.[10] Secondly, education regarding the subject is currently *not* a mandatory component of the undergraduate curriculum for veterinary schools under the jurisdiction of the RCVS. The fact that education on the subject is not mandatory may contribute to the significant inconsistency regarding the inclusion of the subject in undergraduate curricula and variance in the nature and degree of the training that is provided. With no central consensus on assessment of veterinary competency in this issue, it is therefore questionable whether veterinary schools under the jurisdiction of the RCVS are currently providing sufficient training and assessment in this subject to enable new graduate veterinarians to meet their existing ethical obligations upon registration.

Attention to this gap between education and imposed duty is likely to be one of the outcomes of implementing a mandatory legal duty to report. A *legal* obligation imputes the potential for greater involvement of the courts, in addition to the profession, in judging if a veterinarian has fulfilled his or her professional responsibilities. It is logical that in order to fulfil their duties, veterinarians would first need to be trained and assessed for competency in them. Accordingly, a legal mandatory duty would be likely to necessitate that training in this subject become *obligatory* in *all* veterinary schools, and that methods of *consistent assessment* be put in place. It is not a huge leap of logic to recognize the relevance of this development to ensuring that graduating veterinarians can competently fulfil their pivotal roles in highlighting the links associated with the issue of human violence and animal abuse.

The current education status of postgraduates with respect to this issue appears equally inconsistent and, arguably, inadequate. This may be due, in part, to the fact that recognition of potential links between human violence and animal abuse has been a relatively recent development. Consequently, many of today's practising veterinarians are likely to have received little or no education on the subject.

Although Continuing Professional Development (CPD) is a mandatory requirement for veterinarians registered with the RCVS, it is the opinion of some education providers that getting veterinarians voluntarily to attend CPD on this subject would be problematic. The reason for this is the perception that veterinarians are more interested in CPD that provides skills in subjects that are more financially rewarding.

The obvious problem is that the obligations concerning suspected animal abuse apply to *all* registered veterinarians; but there is no matching requirement for assessed education that ensures *all* registered veterinarians are sufficiently competent to fulfil the duties expected of them.

Compulsory CPD on the subject of the human–animal relationship and relevant professional duties is likely to be a result of applying a legal mandatory duty to report. Compulsory CPD provides a potential solution for rectifying gaps that may have occurred in veterinary undergraduate training. Obviously the gap between assessed training and an imposed ethical duty is already a cause for concern. However, continuation of this situation in the face of a *legal* duty would appear particularly problematic, because individuals are commonly expected to comply with the law irrespective of whether they know about the law or not – 'ignorance of the law is no excuse'.

The implementation of compulsory CPD is likely to be a significant step toward ensuring all existing postgraduate veterinarians are competent in recognizing suspected animal abuse, and familiar with their relevant reporting obligations.

Remember, at this point, that this discussion considers how the addition of a legal mandatory duty to the existing ethical duty might assist the veterinarians and, in turn, assist the potential victims affected by a veterinarian's action, or lack thereof.

Identifying or suspecting animal abuse, and reporting it, are two separate issues. It follows that efficient reporting requires more than simply instigating a central training and assessment programme for undergraduate and post-graduate veterinarians. Efficient reporting requires that the existing system for reporting is also examined.

Changes to Rectify a Problematic Ethical Duty

The current ethical duty begins by stating that, 'When a veterinary surgeon is presented with an injured animal whose clinical signs cannot be attributed to the history provided by the client, s/he should include non-accidental injury in their differential diagnosis'.[11] At first glance this may seem very straightforward; however, appropriate training and skills are arguably necessary to fulfil this duty effectively and considerately. Furthermore, and as illustrated above, the current lack of consistency in education and assessment – for undergraduates and postgraduates alike – is arguably in direct conflict with the ethical duty imposed.

The ethical duty continues by requiring the veterinarian to make professional judgements about issues, including the seriousness of the circumstances,[12] confidential information, reasonable grounds, public interest, and client confidentiality.[13] Although such considerations are framed within an ethical duty, these terms are all requirements that may have potential, and significant, legal consequences for the veterinarian individually, and for the veterinary practice.

The ethical duty, for example, directs that, 'In the first instance, in appropriate cases, the veterinary surgeon should attempt to discuss his/her concerns with the client'. In referring to 'appropriate' circumstances, the directive arguably acknowledges that there may well be inappropriate circumstances – and the veterinarian is expected to make a subjective judgment to differentiate between these two situations. The ethical duty continues: 'In cases where this would not be appropriate or where the client's reaction increases rather than allays concerns, the veterinary surgeon should contact the relevant authorities'. Veterinarians may have been trained and assessed to levels of competencies in animal health; however, the practise of veterinary medicine is not restricted to interactions with animals: it inherently involves people. While this may appear to be stating the obvious, it is important to acknowledge that the effectiveness of communication between people is highly influenced by a multitude of factors, including, for example, client interests and the people skills of the attending professional.

Like all other professions, veterinarians may vary in their abilities, confidence, and concerns in applying their duties. Furthermore, there may also be direct conflicts of interest. Remembering that the ethical duty applies to all registered veterinarians, one might consider the potential conflicts that could arise in, for example, a case where a woman brings a dog suffering as a result of a fresh and serious burn in to the veterinary hospital. The woman was an established client of the practice, owned many animals, and consistently spent a very significant amount of money at the practice. Relevant to this discussion is the fact that the burn on the dogs back was in the shape of a household iron, and the owner stated that her angry son had intentionally inflicted it on the dog. There are obviously a number of issues in this fact pattern; however, the question is: is it possible that there may have been a range of differing responses from the attending veterinarian in respect of the duty to report? For example, could the decision to report, or not, potentially be influenced by whether the attending veterinarian owned the practice, or was a senior veterinarian[14] with no financial interest in the practice, or a new graduate?[15] Importantly, the question is *not* 'should' the response be the same, but 'could' the response be different? Interpreting the fact pattern and question posed as querying the trust or confidence in veterinarians and their ability to deal with ethical and legal questions entirely misses the point that consistent compliance and application is the central issue. Simple logic clearly indicates that veterinarians' responses may be influenced by their personal perspectives and understanding. This is an important reality if, for example, a disciplinary committee is faced with the task of assessing a veterinarian's compliance with an imposed duty, where the veterinarian is forced to make a number of subjective judgments. Obviously, the veterinarian's responses to the scenario presented above may or may not be appropriate, but the point is that a mandatory duty would mean that in the event that a case of suspected animal abuse is presented, the veterinarian must report it for trained adjudicators to assess.

Clarifying this further, research has confirmed that veterinarians have seen suspected animal abuse, and possible child abuse, but the central question to efficient reporting of animal abuse by veterinarians considers what percentage of veterinarians, having suspected animal abuse or child abuse, have reported it? At least one study has shown that an ethical duty to report may not be sufficient to motivate veterinarians to report suspicions of animal abuse.[16] A mandatory duty to report arguably simplifies the veterinarian's decision process significantly from a series of subjective judgments to one of 'if abuse is suspected, then it must be reported'. This, in turn, has important relevance for the veterinarian, and all those whose lives are affected by issues of animal abuse and related human violence.

A Mandatory Legal Duty to Report Removes the 'Moral Dilemma'

Although veterinarians are not specifically trained in human medicine or mental health, in the course of their professional duties they are likely to come across situations where the circumstances arouse concern for the well-being of the animal under their care. Veterinarians have expressed concerns regarding the potential ethical, legal, and economic outcomes that could follow if suspected abuse was reported.

These concerns have included,[17] for example, anxieties about personal safety, loss of business, and conflicts with client confidentiality.[18] From a professional perspective, the RCVS has indicated that the over-riding duty is in the public interest in protecting the animal, rather than the professional obligation to maintain client confidentiality. In spite of this directive, veterinarians are likely to face the same dilemmas as their counterparts in human medicine.[19]

With a view to simplifying the process for the veterinarian in their role with this issue, and maximizing the efficiency of the reporting process, Bernard E. Rollin succinctly and effectively states the value to the veterinarian of implementing a legislative mandatory duty:

> *Making veterinarians mandatory reporters of cruelty is very helpful to practitioners who suspect cruelty. It removes the moral dilemma of whether to report or not,* as in similar legislation for human physicians and other health-care providers in the case of child abuse.[20]

Enacting a mandatory legal duty to report activates a cascade of considerations for potential development. Pragmatic solutions would necessitate attention to the issue of providing consistent training and assessment to undergraduates and postgraduates alike. Mandatory inclusion of the subject in the undergraduate courses, and compulsory CPD courses to postgraduates offer potential solutions to any existing educational deficit. CPD for postgraduates might, for example, be implemented as part of a mandatory time-bound CPD programme for all veterinarians,[21] or as a pre-requisite to establishing a veterinary practice or registration at an accredited veterinary hospital. Further research of the barriers facing veterinarians in England, and legal research critically examining mandatory reporting laws in other jurisdictions, will be necessary to implement practical and effective legislation. Attention to issues of training and assessment of veterinarians *and* veterinary nurses, considerations of common liability, hospital recording policies, and establishment of cross reporting systems, are examples of other issues that are likely to warrant consideration.

Conclusion

Effective enforcement of the Animal Welfare Act 2006, and related issues of non-accidental injury to animals, relies heavily on efficient detection and reporting of relevant cases. Detection and reporting are areas in which the veterinarian has a particularly important role. It is therefore necessary to assess how the veterinarians may be assisted, and if necessary, compelled, to fulfil this role and duty more efficiently and effectively.

Jurisdictions in other countries have recognized the advantages of implementing a mandatory *legal* duty on veterinarians to report cases of suspected animal abuse. This paper addresses the question of applying the same duty to veterinarians registered with the Royal College of Veterinary Surgeons.

Where animal abuse is concerned, achieving consistency and compliance with professional duties under the existing, solely ethical, duty is problematic. Establishing a mandatory duty to report will likely, in turn, require attention to ensure consistency in training, competence, and compliance of *all* veterinarians registered with the RCVS. Furthermore, the implementation of a legal duty to report simplifies the veterinarian's decision process, thereby removing dilemmas for veterinarians who may be uncertain whether to report or not.

Government and the veterinary profession have both indicated their commitment to addressing issues of animal welfare. Accordingly, a legislative mandatory veterinary duty to report suspected animal abuse is a logical and relevant consideration in assessing how the veterinarian, and the veterinary profession, can most efficiently fulfil their key role in the issue of human violence and animal abuse.[22]

Notes

1   Eight states (Arizona, California, Illinois, Kansas, Minnesota, Oregon, West Virginia, and Wisconsin) have laws that require veterinary reporting of animal cruelty. Furthermore, twenty-one states have enacted legislation to protect veterinarians from potential civil or criminal liability arising from reporting suspected animal cruelty, and four states provide immunity from liability for participating in cruelty investigations. See S. L. Babcock and J. D. Neihsl,, 'Requirements for mandatory reporting of animal cruelty', *Journal of the American Veterinary Medical Association* (2006), p. 228. Alabama and Maryland are additional states that have mandated veterinarians to report animal abuse.

2   Interestingly, at least two American states have mandated veterinarians to report child abuse. See T. Cappucci and S. Gbadamosi, 'Prevention of animal abuse: Reflections on a public health malady in recognizing and reporting animal abuse', in P. Olson (ed.), *A veterinarian's guide* (Englewood, CO: American Humane Association, 1997).

3   The Royal College is the regulatory body for veterinary surgeons in the United Kingdom (www.rcvs.org.uk).

4   *The guide to professional conduct* Part 3–Annexes.c. outlines veterinarians' duty regarding animal abuse and also provides directives with respect to cases of possible child abuse and domestic violence.

5   A survey in the USA indicated that 87 per cent of veterinarian respondents had treated abused patients, with 50 per cent of veterinarians treating one to three such patients per year. Twenty per cent of those surveyed stated they had worked with clients whom they suspected were themselves being abused. See R. Landau, 'The veterinarian's role in recognizing and reporting abuse', in F. R. Ascione and P. Arkow (eds), *Child abuse, domestic violence, and animal abuse: Linking the circles of compassion for prevention and intervention* (West Lafayette, IN: Purdue University Press, 1999), pp. 241–249; see also P. Arkow, 'The veterinarian's roles in preventing family violence: The experience of the human medical profession', www.animaltherapy.net.

A study completed in 2005 in New Zealand indicated that 63 per cent of veterinary respondents had seen cases of deliberate abuse in the previous five years, and 16 per cent of the respondents were aware of or suspected violence in the families of the abused animals. The survey respondents also indicated that 73 per cent were in favour of mandatory reporting of clear-cut cases of deliberate animal abuse. See V. Williams, 'Veterinarian animal abuse study', www.vets.org.nz/Publications/Vets@Work/2005/V@WDec2005.pdf.

A survey of British veterinarians reported that 91.3 per cent of veterinarians acknowledge non-accidental injury (NAI), and 48.3 per cent had either suspected or seen NAI. See H. M. C. Munro and M. V. Thrusfield, 'Battered pets: Features that raise suspicion of non-accidental injury', *Journal of Small Animal Practice* 42 (2001), pp. 218–226; H. M. C. Munro and M. V. Thrusfield, 'Battered pets: Non-accidental physical injuries found in dogs and cats', *Journal of Small Animal Practice* 42 (2001), pp. 279–290; H. M. C. Munro and M. V. Thrusfield, 'Battered pets: Sexual abuse', *Journal of Small Animal Practice* 42 (2001), pp. 333–337; and H. M. C. Munro and M. V. Thrusfield, 'Battered pets: Munchausen syndrome by proxy', *Journal of Small Animal Practice* 42 (2001), pp. 385–389.

6   References to 'veterinarian(s)' in this paper refer to qualified veterinarians who are registered members of the Royal College of Veterinary Surgeons.

7   See note 5.

8   *Ibid.*

9   *The guide to professional conduct* Part 3–Annexes.c., outlining the duty on veterinarians regarding animal abuse, also provides directives with respect to cases of possible child abuse and domestic violence.

10   *Ibid.*

11   *Ibid.*

12   *Ibid.* The duty states: 'If there is *suspicion* of animal abuse, as a result of examining an animal, *a veterinary surgeon should consider whether the circumstances are sufficiently serious to justify breaching the usual obligations of client confidentiality*' (italics added).

13   *Ibid.* The duty states: 'Such action should only be taken when the veterinary surgeon considers on reasonable grounds that either animals show signs of abuse or are at real and immediate risk of abuse - in effect where *the public interest in protecting an animal overrides the professional obligation to maintain client confidentiality*. A veterinary surgeon may contact the RCVS for advice before any confidential information is divulged' (italics added).

14   The term 'senior veterinarian' is used in this context to describe a veterinarian who has been in postgraduate clinical practice for a number of years.

15   Surveys have indicated that veterinarians have a range of concerns with regard to reporting suspected animal abuse. Fears of adverse economic impact, confidentiality concerns, and lack of adequate training have been listed among this list. These concerns arguably pose potential barriers to effective reporting. See P. Arkow, 'The veterinarian's roles'.

16   A survey of Michigan veterinarians revealed that 88 per cent felt they had seen non-accidental trauma in their patients, but only 27 per cent had ever filed a report. See L. B. Stol, Y. J. Johnson-Ifearulundu, and J. B. Kaneene, 'Attitudes of veterinarians, animal control directors, and county prosecutors in Michigan regarding enforcement of state cruelty legislation', *Journal of the American Veterinary Medical Association* 211 (1997), pp. 1521–1523.

17 These concerns have been expressed to the author during the course of his careers in veterinary medicine and law. This mirrors concerns expressed in legal studies addressing the issue of mandatory reporting of animal cruelty and abuse. See Babcock and Neihsl, 'Requirements for mandatory reporting'.

18 The existing RCVS duty states 'Such action should only be taken when the veterinary surgeon considers on reasonable grounds that either animals show signs of abuse or are at real and immediate risk of abuse – in effect where the public interest in protecting an animal overrides the professional obligation to maintain client confidentiality' (*The guide to professional conduct* Part 3–Annexes.c).

19 Several studies have shown that even with knowledge of the underlying cause of domestic violence trauma, many physicians fail to respond to cases involving physical violence. Reasons cited most frequently for this reluctance include close identification with their patients that precludes them from considering the possibility of domestic violence in their differential diagnosis; fear of offending patients by discussing areas seen as private; violation of the physician/patient relationship; the overwhelming roles asked of a professional complicated by the time constraints of a busy practice; risk of alienating or stigmatizing the family; personal, legal, and financial risks; discomfort with the role of 'policeman'; problems of defining abuse. These concerns arguably pose potential barriers to effective reporting. See Arkow, 'The veterinarian's roles'.

20 Bernard E. Rollin, 'Veterinary medical ethics', *Canadian Veterinary Journal* 48, 5 (2007), pp. 459–462 (italics added).

21 CPD is currently a mandatory requirement for all registered veterinarians with the RCVS. CPD courses assessing competency in the area of suspected animal abuse, child abuse and domestic violence could, for example, be a CPD module that veterinarians must complete in the first three to five years following graduation.

22 For further information on this subject visit www.animal-law.biz.

The Role of Veterinarians and Other Animal Welfare Workers in the Reporting of Suspected Child Abuse

COREY C. MONTOYA AND CATHERINE A. MILLER

Most US states require that doctors, police officers, and social workers report any suspected child abuse. Many states additionally require other professionals that regularly come into contact with children to report child abuse.[1] It makes sense that states would require those people who have regular contact with children to report their suspicions to the proper authorities. It also makes sense that some states require other professionals, such as film developers, to report abusive behaviour, because those workers may have an opportunity to witness child abuse. For example, film developers may encounter photographs of abusive situations such as child pornography. However, California, Colorado, Ohio, and Maine require that animal welfare workers or veterinarians report suspected child abuse. The purpose of this requirement is less clear than other mandated reporters. This chapter will look at the connection between animal abuse and child abuse and postulate reasons why animal welfare workers may be in a position to witness or suspect child abuse.

Child Abuse History

The American Society for the Prevention of Cruelty to Animals (ASPCA) was founded in 1866 by Henry Bergh and was focused on the welfare of animals, including companion animals, work animals, and animals raised for consumption. However, American laws related to the prevention of animal cruelty can be found as early as 1829.[2] Bergh was later involved in two monumental cases dealing with cruelty towards children. The first of these was the case of Emily Thompson in 1871. Bergh investigated the case of alleged abuse in his official capacity as head of the ASPCA, and Emily's foster mother was convicted. Unfortunately, Emily recanted her allegations of abuse and the sentence was suspended. In 1874 another case of child abuse, the infamous case of Mary Ellen Wilson, was brought to Bergh's attention, but this time he was much more reticent to act in an official capacity. Because the alleged abuse was occurring behind closed doors in her foster parents' tenement apartment, police could not intervene. Had it happened in public her parents could have been charged with abuse, but there were not yet any provisions in place for removing a child from an abusive home without actually seeing the abusive acts. Etta Wheeler, a church worker, learned of the child's situation from a concerned neighbour and was further convinced when, under the guise of inquiring about another neighbour, she observed the child and her injuries. She went to Bergh and implored him to help based on the fact that Mary Ellen was at least a member of the animal kingdom and therefore deserved protection. Bergh agreed to help as a private citizen and sent the ASPCA's lawyer, Elbridge Gerry, to investigate. Mr Gerry reported on Mary Ellen's condition to a judge and convinced the judge to order the child's removal from the home. Mary Ellen's foster mother was later charged with and convicted of assault.[3]

It is commonly believed that the first child abuse case was actually tried as a case of animal abuse. Although it is a widely held belief, the case of Mary Ellen in the 1870s did not mark the beginning of child abuse law and was not in any way connected to the prosecution of animal abuse. It is likely that this assumption was made because of the involvement of Henry Bergh, the president of the ASPCA. Bergh insisted throughout the trial that he was involved as a concerned citizen and not in an official capacity. However, the media attention brought on by the case did spur the creation of the New York Society for the Prevention of Cruelty to Children (NYSPCC) in 1874.[4] The same year saw the formation of the American Humane Association (AHA), which was founded with the primary goal of preventing cruelty towards animals and children.[5]

The Connection Between Animal Abuse and Child Abuse

Other chapters have examined the link between animal abuse and child abuse in some detail, but it is worth reminding ourselves of the some of the more important research in this area.

In a study done in 1983 DeViney *et al.* found that out of fifty-three pet-owning families that were being treated because of incidents of child abuse, 88 per cent reported animal abuse as well. In two-thirds of those cases the abuser had either injured or killed the family pet. The remaining one third of cases had been perpetrated by the children of the abuser. A similar study found that of families that had been reported to animal services for abusing cats and/or dogs, 80 per cent had also been reported to social services for suspected child abuse.[6] Crowell opined that children who live in an environment in which abuse of people or animals is common are likely to imitate that behaviour themselves and to view violence as commonplace.[7] Further, according to Gil, the child's abusive acts towards animals will often mimic their own abuse.[8] To these children, only animals and smaller children are more vulnerable, and so they play out their feelings of anger, helplessness, and frustration onto these natural victims. According to Friedrich *et al.*, 35 per cent of boys who were sexually abused had also abused animals, compared to only 5 per cent of boys who had not been sexually abused.[9] Duffield *et al.*[10] reported that out of three hundred children who had sexually abused other children approximately 20 per cent had also sexually abused animals. In their abuse, these children often treated the animals in the same manner that they treated their child victims, including planning the abuse and grooming the victim. Many of these children had also been seriously abused.

In 1971, Tapia conducted a study of children referred to the clinic at the University of Michigan Child Psychiatry Section. He identified eighteen cases in which the child was referred to the clinic either solely on account of cruelty to animals or because animal cruelty was one of a number of reasons for the referral. These cases spanned an eleven-year period and all were boys between the ages of five and fourteen. The animal cruelty was extreme and persistent. In sixteen of those eighteen cases, there was also violence directed at humans. Often this violence was also sadistic and extreme, including anally penetrating a three-year-old and attempting to smother an infant sibling. In his discussion of these cases Tapia mentioned that many of these boys were the victims of physical and/or sexual abuse, and many had also lived in situations that included domestic violence.[11] In a follow-up study six years later Tapia and Rigdon found that in many of the original cases the boys continued to act abusively towards animals, suggesting that animal abuse is not 'a phase', as previously suspected.[12] These two studies illustrate the connections among victimization, animal abuse, and cruelty towards other people, and also point out just how early this cycle can begin. Ascione found that parental reports of children acting abusively towards animals were seven times higher for boys who had been sexually abused and eight times higher for girls who had been sexually abused.[13]

The following quote illustrates the connection between victimization and animal abuse. It was written by Mary Wertsch in a book chronicling her life in a military family and with an abusive father.

> I'm ashamed to tell this . . . I remember bringing this dog in (the hallway) once, a small dog, and I remember shutting all of the doors to the hall so it had no escape, and getting a belt, and whipping this dog. Just whipping. And delighting in hearing the dog cry. I could cry now to think of it. What a terrible thing. But I remember doing it. Then I remember trying to hug the dog, trying to make the dog realize I really loved it.
>
> And I've never forgiven myself for that. But I also know that I had to do it for survival. I had to act it out . . .

> My brother used to be very cruel also . . . he used to throw bread out the window to attract the birds, and then kill them. Just like our father used to set us up and trap us.[14]

Sometimes, rather than using abuse to deal with their own abusive history, an abusive spouse will use animal abuse to intimidate or bully the domestic violence victim and/or the family. For example, in a book by Alexandra Artley,[15] a viciously abusive father and husband was upset with the family cat. He made his wife fill a container with water, stuffed the cat into a flour sack, and then stuffed the cat into the container. His children were called in to watch the 'lesson' their father was about to teach. Later his youngest daughter was forced to place a lid on the container and hold it as the cat attempted to escape.

State Statutes Regarding Mandated Reporting of Child Abuse

Every state has a list of people, identified by profession, who are legally required to report suspected child abuse. Commonly these include health care workers, social workers, law enforcement officials, and schoolteachers. Less often they include film developers, coaches, funeral directors, clergy, and others who may be in direct or indirect contact with children. Presently there are four states that have statutes mandating animal welfare workers, veterinarians, or humane agents to report suspected child abuse. These are Colorado, Maine, California, and Ohio. Some other states throw a much wider net and require all people to report suspected child abuse.[16]

Child abuse and neglect is defined on both a federal and a state level. The Child Abuse Prevention and Treatment Act (CAPTA, 2005) provides the minimum standards for states' individual definitions of child abuse and neglect. By CAPTA standards, child abuse and neglect is defined as, 'Any recent act or failure to act on the part of a parent of caretaker, which results in death, serious physical or emotional harm, sexual abuse, or exploitation, or an act or failure to act which presents an imminent risk of serious harm'.[17]

Colorado statutes dictate that any veterinarian, officer of the state bureau of animal protection, or animal control officer must report any situation in which he or she has reasonable cause to suspect that a child has been a victim of abuse or neglect, or who has observed situations or circumstances that the reporter believes would reasonably lead to abuse or neglect.[18] Maine requires only those humane agents employed by the Department of Agriculture, Food and Rural Resources, and working in a professional capacity, to file a report if there is reasonable cause for them to believe that a child has been or will be abused or neglected.[19] Humane agents employed by the Department of Agriculture, Food and Rural Resources are responsible for ensuring the humane and proper treatment of animals and for maintaining public health and safety as it relates to farm animals. According to the California Penal Child

Abuse and Neglect Reporting Act (2006),[20] animal control officers are mandated to report child abuse or neglect, defined as any physical injury (other than accidental injuries) caused by another person, sexual abuse, the wilful harming or injuring of a child, or the endangering of health of the child. This also includes unlawful corporal punishment.[21] Neglect is defined as the maltreatment of a child by a person who is responsible for that child's welfare and well-being. This includes both acts and omissions. Neglect is further divided into two categories, severe and general. Severe neglect is defined as a failure to protect a child from severe malnutrition or diagnosed non-organic failure to thrive, or allowing a child to remain in a situation in which their health is seriously endangered. General neglect is defined as the failure to provide adequate food, shelter, clothing, medical care, or supervision. In cases of general neglect no physical injury needs to have occurred.[22] In California an animal control officer is defined as any person employed for the purpose of enforcing animal control laws.[23] Ohio statute dictates that any agents of humane societies must report any suspected suffering or threat of suffering of child abuse or neglect.[24]

Each of the four states reviewed includes in their statute a definition of abuse and neglect that includes situations in which the child's health or well-being is compromised. The California Child Abuse and Neglect Reporting Act includes allowing a child to be placed in a situation in which their 'person or health is endangered' in their definition of abuse and neglect.[25] Maine statute defines child abuse or neglect as physical abuse, sexual abuse, exploitation, mental or emotional injury or impairment, the deprivation of basic needs, or failure to protect the child from these abuses.[26] This can be interpreted to include allowing a child to remain in a situation or environment that is unsafe or unhealthy. According to Colorado statute §19–1–103; 19–3–102, neglect includes a failure to provide proper parental care and allowing a child to remain in an environment that is injurious to his or her welfare. Ohio adopts a broad definition of neglect by saying that a neglected child lacks proper parental care because of the actions or faults of the parents.

Where to Look for Child Abuse

Although the connection between animal abuse and child abuse is strong, it is important to remember that signs of animal abuse do not directly indicate the presence of child abuse. The job of the animal welfare agent or mandated reporter is much more complicated than simply identifying possible animal abuse and knowing the connection that this type of abuse may have to child abuse. So how is it that veterinarians, animal control officers, and humane workers even become aware of child abuse? On the surface it seems that no abuser, or even abuse victim, would disclose child abuse to a person investigating or treating animal abuse. However, in a study done by Arkow, the researcher found cases in which the animal control officer was told about child abuse while investigating allegations of animal abuse.[27] Specifically, the animal care worker was interviewing neighbours because the Humane Society had received reports that a woman had been taping her dog's mouth shut to prevent it from barking. During the interview the neighbours reported that they had seen the same woman beating her children in the backyard.

Another way that animal welfare workers may become aware of child abuse is during the investigation of animal neglect and inhumane living conditions. In the case of Schambon v. Commonwealth[28] a dog warden responded to a case of suspected animal abuse. They found twenty dogs kept in an unventilated garage covered with inches of animal faeces, two walls in the house lined with caged cats, animal faeces covering the house, and a decomposing dog in the kitchen. Because of these conditions the four children who had been living in the home were removed and placed in foster care. In this case the investigation of animal cruelty led to the discovery of child neglect and endangerment. After the children were removed from the home they reported a number of instances of both physical and sexual abuse perpetrated by their parents and the parents were later found guilty of all charges.

Boat gave another example of how an animal's unsanitary living conditions can lead to abuse or neglect of children.[29] Animal control officers entered a home where a large number of turtles were being kept in cages. While there, a toddler was observed poking her fingers into turtle faeces and then placing her fingers into her mouth. The risk for contracting salmonella was substantial enough that the animal control officers determined that the children also needed assistance.

Cross-Reporting

Cross reporting encourages cooperation between agencies, and in cases of animal abuse and child abuse the most likely agencies to be involved are animal welfare agencies and child protection services. In this case, animal welfare officers would look for cases of child maltreatment when investigating animal cruelty or neglect, and child protection workers would note the condition of any animals when investigating child abuse or neglect. The amount of cooperation between agencies varies between reports. Boat suggested that there was a high level of cooperation between animal control, child protection services, and law enforcement.[30] She gave the example of a sheriff who went to a house to investigate a report of domestic violence. He found three pit bulls chained in the front yard. He became suspicious and returned with an animal control officer and a search warrant. At that visit they found behind the house the bodies of three dogs, thirty live dogs, and a dog-fighting ring. Child protection services were later called to investigate the welfare of the children living in the home.

Not all studies have found such a high level of cooperation in terms of cross-reporting. Zilney and Zilney examined a project to reunite Family and

Children's Services (FCS) and the Humane Society (HS) of Wellington County, Canada.[31] These two agencies had previously acted as one agency, but had separated in the early 1900s. In 2000 they reunited because of the known association between animal abuse and child abuse. This study was designed to determine the effectiveness and co-operation of the agents in terms of cross-reporting. The authors found that of 1,485 cases investigated by FCS between 2001 and 2002, 50 per cent were homes that included at least one animal. Of those seven hundred and forty-seven homes, FCS made sixteen (2.1 per cent) referrals to HS. Conversely, HS referred ten of their two hundred and forty-seven cases (10.6 per cent) to FCS. This higher number of referrals may be attributed to a higher level of caution when children were involved. On the other hand, the researchers pointed out obviously discrepant values between the workers of FCS and the workers of HS. They noted that the HS investigators were more invested in the project, while many FCS investigators had to be reminded of their commitment to participate and did not seem to take the project as seriously.

Conclusion

At first glance it may seem that the inclusion of veterinarians and other animal welfare agents as mandated reporters of child abuse was an arbitrary choice designed to include as many professionals as possible in order to get as many reports as possible. However, this review of the available literature has shown that animal welfare workers have a valuable and unique opportunity to be proactive in cases of child abuse. The connection between animal abuse and child abuse or domestic violence has been well documented. Further, there are numerous situations in which an animal care worker would be in a position to suspect that possible child abuse or neglect is occurring or likely to occur. In these cases, the worker needs only to remember his or her role as a mandated reporter in order to make a difference in that child's or family's life. The role of mandated reporter does not need to be an additional burden placed on the worker's shoulders, but rather something to note in his or her routine observations of an animal's condition or living environment. Further, as a mandated reporter, the worker does not need to feel powerless in helping the families of the animals that they have committed to serve. By reporting suspected child abuse, the veterinarian, animal control officer, or humane agent is doing his or her part to end the cycle of animal abuse, child abuse, and interpersonal abuse that may otherwise continue to affect all those involved, human and animal.

Notes

1   See Oklahoma statute §7103; Tennessee §37–1–403(a); Wyoming §14–3–205(a); Florida §39.201(1); National Clearinghouse on Child Abuse and Neglect Information [NCCANI], *Mandatory reporters of child abuse and neglect*, 2003, http://nccanch.acf.hhs.gov/general/legal/statutes/manda.pdf.

2   F. R. Ascione, *Children and animals: Exploring the roots of kindness and cruelty* (West Lafayette, IN: Purdue University Press, 2005).

3   *Ibid.*

4   S. Watkins, 'The Mary Ellen myth: Correcting child welfare history', *Social Work* 35 (1990), pp. 500–503.

5   Ascione, *Children and animals*.

6   J. Hutton, 'Animal abuse as a diagnostic approach in social work: A pilot study', in A. H. Katcher and A. Beck (eds), *New perspectives on our lives with companion animals* (Philadelphia: University of Pennsylvania Press, 1983).

7   S. Crowell, 'Animal cruelty as it relates to child abuse: Shedding light on a "hidden" problem', *Journal of Juvenile Law* 20 (1999).

8   E. Gil, 'Children and animals: A clinician's view', *The Animal's Agenda* 20 (1994).

9   W. Friedrich, A. Urquiza, and R. Beilke, 'Behavior problems in sexually abused young children', *Journal of Pediatric Psychology* 11 (1984): 47–57.

10 As cited in F. Becker and L. French, 'Making the links: Child abuse, animal cruelty and domestic violence', *Child Abuse Review* 13 (2004), pp. 399–414.

11 F. Tapia, 'Children who are cruel to animals', *Child Psychiatry and Human Development* 2 (1971), pp. 70–77.

12 J. Rigdon and F. Tapia, 'Children who are cruel to animals: A follow-up study', *Journal of Operational Psychiatry* 8 (1977), pp. 27–36.

13 Ascione, *Children and animals*.

14 M. Wertsch, *Military brats: Legacies of childhood inside the fortress* (New York: Harmony Books, 1991), p. 236.

15 As cited in Ascione, *Children and animals*.

16 Namely, Oklahoma statute §7103, Rhode Island §40–11–3(a), Tennessee §37–1–403 (a), Utah §62A-4a-403(1)-(3), Wyoming §14–3–205(a), Florida §39.201(1) (NCCANI, *Mandatory reporters*).

17 NCCANI, *Definitions of child abuse and neglect*, 2005, http://nccanch.acf.hhs. gov/general/legal/statutes/defineall.pdf, p. 1.

18 CO §19–3–304, 2006.

19 ME §4011–A, 2006.

20 California Child Abuse and Neglect Reporting Act 11165.7 (Leginfor.ca.gov 2006).

21 CA §11165.6, 2006.

22 CA §11165.2, 2006.

23 CA §11165.7 (31–A), 2006.

24 CA §2151.421(A) (1), 2006.

25 CA §11165.3, 2006.

26 Title 22 §4002.

27 As cited in Crowell, 'Animal cruelty'.

28 *Ibid.*

29 B. Boat, 'The relationship between violence to children and violence to animals: An ignored link?' *Journal of Interpersonal Violence* 10, 4 (1995): 229–235.

30 *Ibid.*

31 L. A. Zilney and M. Zilney, 'Reunification of child and animal welfare agencies: Cross-reporting of abuse in Wellington County, Ontario', *Child Welfare* 84, 1 (2005): 47–66.

23

Animal Cruelty and Child Welfare: The Health Visitor's Perspective

DAWN HAWKSWORTH AND RACHEL BALEN

Despite efforts to clarify and define core responsibilities, the role of the Health Visitor within the UK remains the subject of contentious current debate. Indeed, against a backdrop of enormous organizational change within the National Health Service, both at local and national level, the need to quantify services in the search for value for money remains high on the health and social care agenda.[1] However, while the monetary value of the Health Visiting service remains at present impossible to quantify, not least because long term health and social outcomes are difficult to measure, the value of this highly skilled member of the nursing profession's contribution to the public health role with children and families has recently been confirmed at government level.[2] Furthermore, the refocusing of responsibilities for the provision of Section 17 services to children and families in need, underpinned by the Children Act 2004, further strengthens the safeguarding role of Health Visitors and underlines the need to maintain the robust home-visiting context traditionally associated with the profession.

A pragmatic approach to risk assessment associated with the role necessitates an assessment of wider environmental issues and consideration of complex family dynamics. Although not within existing practice guidelines, our personal interest in animal welfare issues and moral values has undoubtedly influenced our approaches to this assessment process, and has led us to include the consideration of the care and treatment of animals within families.

Having close contact within the homes of often vulnerable families in a socially deprived area, one of us, as a practising health visitor, has observed direct cruelty to animals and has frequently witnessed signs that animals are suffering as a result of neglect. However, within the commonly used Framework for the Assessment of Children in Need and their Families,[3] and the more recent Common Assessment Framework,[4] it is not possible to identify material relating to the harming of animals that would inform assessment and planning. An extensive review of the relevant literature[5] reveals a lively debate focusing on a range of constructs that confirm the existence of an inter-relationship between animal cruelty and child abuse, specifically associated with family violence. In addition, concern is expressed within the literature that cruelty to animals by children has potential implications for future harmful behaviour.

At practice level within the UK, the paucity of policies, procedures, and training around this subject area reflects the finding that the vast majority of research has been conducted within the USA. Indeed, while relevant bodies such as the National Society for the Prevention of Cruelty to Children (NSPCC) and the Royal Society for the Prevention of Cruelty to Animals (RSPCA) are committed to raising awareness and influencing policy, the UK has produced little research evidence.

The emerging themes within the literature reveal a range of significant factors that suggest children may be at risk of significant harm in families that are also cruel to animals. For example, there is research evidence to support the view that animal and child abuse co-exists within dysfunctional families,[6] together with a body of evidence connecting emotionally harmful parenting styles with childhood animal cruelty.[7]

While sampling and data-gathering methods are frequently criticized,[8] there is sound evidence of a worrying trend connecting family violence with animal cruelty.[9] Furthermore, although less prominent within the literature, there is some evidence that draws attention to an equally concerning connection with sexual abuse,[10] highlighting the developmental impact on children of witnessing animal cruelty.[11]

In addition to the focus on the child and family, further themes emerge focusing on the predictive nature of childhood animal cruelty, revealing a more contentious debate, with many authors leaning heavily towards the serial killer link as evidence of a causal relationship.[12] However, while some authors dispute the connection between animal cruelty and later human violence,[13] a more convincing body of evidence exists suggesting a degree of connection with some form of later harmful antisocial behaviour, including human violence, sexual offending, non-violent crime and vandalism.[14]

Further exploration of the possible underlying factors associated with future harmful behaviour uncovers evidence relating to desensitization[15] and, more frequently, intrinsic factors such as conduct disorder.[16] The contrasting opinions within the literature suggest, however, that this is an underdeveloped argument that would benefit from further investigation.

Personal practice experience reflects several elements of the themes from the literature and also serves to highlight the key issues relating to primary health and social care policy, multi-agency practice and training, and information sharing. The following discussion of three examples from the health visiting practice of one of the authors represents the common threads of joint human and animal suffering and highlights the implications of these experiences for frontline practitioners.

Family A

Family A consisted of two school-age children, one child under five years, a mother, father, and uncle. Educational staff had expressed concerns that the older children were extremely dirty, persistently infested with head lice, and were becoming withdrawn. School staff had made attempts to visit the family home, which was concealed away from public view, but had not gained entry, noting that dogs were tied up in a small garden littered with animal faeces. In response to these concerns the school nurse agreed to a joint visit with the family to assess home conditions and address the hygiene and lice problems affecting the children.

The outside of the property gave many clues as to the chronic neglect of both children and animals that was unveiled inside. Just as the school staff had experienced, we were greeted by a pit bull terrier, tied up on a short rope. The dog had no shelter, access to food or water and was surrounded by its own faeces. However, in contrast to the image it was perhaps intended to portray, this dog was quiet and miserable, responding enthusiastically to our friendly gestures.

The scene inside served to explain the presentation of the children at school and reflects the evidence emerging from research of the co-existence of child and animal suffering, particularly vulnerable children and domestic pets.[17] In addition to dogs, the family owned a severely malnourished and frightened cat, together with several fish. Animal faeces were not confined to the garden and contributed to an appalling risk of infection from a combination of human faeces, discarded used nappies, rotting left-over takeaway food, maggots and flies. The children slept in a single shared bed that was dirty, used a broken filthy toilet and had no access to hygiene products or dental care. On the initial visit to the house there was very little edible food available for the children and no evidence of food for the animals. Indeed, further assessment of the family revealed a diet of takeaway junk food, of which the left-over scraps were fed to the animals. The fish were also neglected and all later died.

While the mother showed embarrassment and a degree of remorse, the father's abusive and controlling behaviour was indicative of the evidence emerging from the literature relating to family violence and animal cruelty.[18] While the importance of identifying children at risk of harm within violent families has been consistently highlighted within UK safeguarding literature,[19] together with recent important practice guidance,[20] the need to consider the care of animals is not included.

Family violence is arguably covert in its nature, underlining the importance of recognizing factors which may prompt professionals to take action. As highlighted by this case, the image of the dog outside this family home not only mirrored the treatment of the children but also serves to highlight the importance of overcoming the barriers erected by abusive parents who use fighting dogs to intimidate and warn off professionals – although the dogs in this case were not dangerous, it was clear that the father intended to use them as a deterrent.

Following urgent multi-agency referrals involving child protection services and animal welfare organizations, the children in this case were placed on the child protection register. The cat was eventually re-homed and the welfare of the dog was closely monitored by animal welfare officers. Furthermore, in an attempt to recognize the relationship between the care of both children and animals within this family, the child protection plan also contained instructions for health and social care professionals to check for animal access to food and water, although the relevance of this to the welfare of the children was questioned by other health professionals not involved in the case.

These differences of opinions – '*not my role; someone else should do that; don't like dogs anyway*' – are typical of the varying attitudes of health and social care professionals towards the welfare of animals that we encounter in practice, highlighting the need for the inclusion of issues relating to joint human and animal suffering within child protection training. Research by Staley indicates that animal cruelty is more likely to be identified by experienced members of the multi-agency team, although our experiences from practice, highlighted by this case, suggest that individual beliefs and moral values are more likely to influence professionals' responses to animal cruelty.[21] To echo Arkow's viewpoint,[22] those involved with vulnerable families and animals at ground level are obvious targets for specific training on the links between animal cruelty and human suffering, not least because of their close contact but also, as proposed by Faver and Strand,[23] with the exception of animal welfare officers,[24] because practice culture has traditionally focused on human welfare, underlining the need to broaden viewpoints beyond a narrow single-agency focus.

The mutual suffering experienced by both children and animals and contrasting approaches of professionals are also common features of the experience of working closely with *Family B*. However, specific elements emerging from the family history of the mother also serve to highlight the modelling and social learning theories associated with the phenomenon.

Family B

Family B consisted of two young parents and a baby living in a small two-roomed property. Both parents had a degree of learning disability and although both had extended family living in nearby areas, the couple were, prior to the birth of their baby, ostensibly living independently of family support or external agencies. Having concealed the pregnancy and presented late to maternity services, a rapid multi-agency response resulted in an urgent child protection case conference and registration on to the child protection register.

An intense package of care was developed encompassing interventions from a range of professionals from health and social care, including parenting and psychological assessments. However, despite commendable efforts by all the professionals concerned, the significant risks to the baby from both physical and emotional harm resulted in removal and later adoption.

Initial discussions among all members of the child protection core group included some reference to the cats and kittens living at the property. The majority of concerns focused on the risks to the baby from either infection or injury from the cats, and from the poor general hygiene standard of the couple, made worse by the confined living space. However, the true picture of animal cruelty and the significance of this in terms of both risks to the baby and suffering of the cats emerged following more detailed assessment, facilitated through longer periods of home visiting and observation of direct animal cruelty such as throwing the kitten across the room and withholding food and water as the kitten had '*been naughty*'.

The differing perception of risk and value attached to the cats in this case represents a common feature of child protection assessments. For example, the evaluation by Parton *et al.* of thirty randomly selected case records serves to highlight the different interpretations of perceived risk in child protection work arising from a complex presentation of common factors.[25] Furthermore, the implications of a flawed assessment, hampered by the time frames dictated by UK legislation, are considered significant by Sheldrick.[26] Therefore, while animal welfare issues remain distinct from child welfare, issues in health and social care practice and joint human and animal suffering are not generally considered relevant, and it is not surprising that professionals under pressure fail to reach a consensus during the assessment process, further underlining the need for the inclusion of animal welfare issues within joint agency training.

Evidence emerging from the literature also suggests that the importance attached to animal cruelty within the assessment protocols of child and adolescent mental health services differs greatly in the UK.[27] However, the documented concern recorded by the psychologist in the case of *Family B*, who also witnessed direct physical cruelty to the cats, undoubtedly influenced later care proceedings leading to the subsequent removal and adoption of this baby, suggesting an encouraging awareness of the relevant issues from not only this agency but also those involved at judicial level during care proceedings.

As with *Family A*, the welfare of the cats in this case was addressed through liaison with animal welfare officers. However, this example of multi-agency collaboration also uncovered valuable insight into the mother's own childhood, leading to greater understanding of her behaviour. For example, it was revealed that the mother had been known to animal welfare officers since her childhood. Similarly, her father was known to the agency for the neglect and cruel treatment of cats.

The search for predictive behaviour and causal relationships has become increasingly important within child protection research[28] and features prominently within the literature pertaining to a progression or graduation theory associated with animal cruelty. However, closer inspection of the evidence reveals a lively debate around the exact causal nature of this relationship, suggesting that although researchers have attempted to demonstrate a link, the exact nature of this association remains unclear.[29] While a critical view exists suggesting that the largely prognostic theme within the literature is based on nothing more than quasi-scientific presentation,[30] the rigorous research by Kellert and Felthous,[31] although dated, demonstrates the clear empirical association between childhood animal cruelty and later human violence reflected by this case.

As emphasized by Haden and Scarpa,[32] the aetiology of childhood animal cruelty, as with all human behaviour, is complex and multi-dimensional. The role and behaviour of parents are not surprisingly critical and have emerged as a consistent theme within the literature. For example, Currie sampled forty-seven victims of domestic violence where animal cruelty was a factor, and concluded that the children exposed to the animal cruelty were more likely to be cruel to animals due to the powerful role modelling of their parents.[33] Similarly, the findings of Duncan *et al.* suggest that cruel and abusive behaviours witnessed at home directly influence the animal cruelty perpetrated by children.[34]

It would seem almost common sense to assume that the mother in this case learned harmful behaviour from her father; indeed the impact of role-modelling is repeatedly referred to in the literature.[35] However, closer examination of parenting styles, attachment theories and coercive control, as illustrated by Print and Erooga,[36] facilitates an understanding of how, for some children, abusive environments interfere with the normal developmental trajectory. Studies highlighting statistical significance associated with witnessing animal cruelty and childhood animal cruelty serve to emphasize the modelling theory.[37] Furthermore, according to Lacroix,[38] children who are brought up in homes where animals are abused learn to gain compliance through aggression, which interferes with the development of concern for the well-being of others or empathy. The mother in this case was typical of this theory, which emphasizes the importance of not only recognizing the interrelationship of human/animal cruelty but also the importance of timely inter-agency information-sharing.

Family C

The importance of accurate interagency cross-reporting was also a prominent feature of the issues surrounding *Family C*, and serves as a stark reminder of the potential risks to both children and animals when professionals fail to share important information. *Family C* lived on a housing estate renowned for its high levels of deprivation, which at the time included some of the highest figures of reported crime, drug offences and vandalism in the area. Indeed, the family were also well known to the police for their criminal activity. The birth of the sixth child prompted health visitor involvement and represented a first significant experience of multi-agency practice involving animal welfare officers.

Initial visits to the family drew attention to the worrying pattern of neglectful parenting and animal cruelty often encountered when working with vulnerable families. The children were quiet and unkempt, and shared cramped, dirty home conditions with a large number of dogs who were kept mainly out of sight but could be heard whimpering in other rooms. Liaison with the school nurse revealed that unsatisfactory school attendance had been an area of concern for many years. Indeed, further assessment suggested that the children were often kept at home and expected to care for both their siblings and their mother, a pattern of behaviour observed during visits. In response to concerns, the family were offered support and assistance from education, health, and social services, which later resulted in registration on the child protection register following disclosure of physical abuse from one of the older children. However, the neglect of several dogs within the home and failure to treat an infected burn on one animal gave many clues as to the true picture of historical child and animal cruelty that emerged at a later date.

The interrelationship of animal cruelty, child abuse, and other criminal activity within this family reflects findings from a different angle of research within the literature. For example, Beirne[39] suggests that the subject of abused animals is becoming increasingly more pertinent as scientists attempt to apply both ecological and ethological principles to criminology research, although it is emphasized that this shift in focus represents only minor changes and numbers of studies remain low. An early study acknowledges the wider criminal associations with animal cruelty by the inclusion of a non-violent criminal sample alongside a violent sample and non-criminal sample, although findings from this study suggest only a modest relationship.[40]

Further inferences to harmful behaviour are outlined by Henry, who sampled two hundred and six college students, concluding that those students who had either engaged in or observed animal cruelty were more likely to have participated in a variety of delinquent behaviours.[41] This phenomenon was also researched by Coston and Protz who, in an attempt to avoid self-reporting bias, meticulously examined the data of nine hundred and fifty-eight animal cruelty records, demonstrating that, for this sample, seven hundred and eighty-five other emergency calls were also made in the previous two years, suggesting a strong association with other antisocial behaviour.[42]

This theme is also reflected in the rigorous examination of one hundred and fifty-three criminal records by Arluke *et al.*,[43] suggesting that a narrow focus on the violence variable belies more complex factors that may be linked to other socially unacceptable behaviour. For example, using antisocial behaviour as the dependent variable, Arluke *et al.* found that 70 per cent of the animal cruelty (AC) group also committed at least one other offence, compared with only 22 per cent of the control sample. The AC group were also four times more likely to have been arrested for property crimes, 3.5 times more likely to be involved with drugs, and 3.5 times more likely to have been arrested for disorderly behaviour.

The types of crimes referred to in this research reflect the lifestyle choices of *Family C*, highlighting not only the challenges of working with such families but also the need to seek information from a wider network of agencies. For example, a referral to animal welfare officers in this case resulted in the discovery that the family were in fact banned from keeping dogs following a previous prosecution for cruelty. However, although *Family C* had two children at the time of this prosecution, child welfare agencies had not been informed, indicating both a lack of awareness and of cross-reporting guidance at that time.

Current UK health and social care policies, developed following the Laming Report,[44] have necessitated a more co-ordinated multi-agency response to child welfare concerns. However, the most recent government guidance on this approach does not represent an entirely new concept,[45] as the reality of 'working together' has taken on a number of forms over recent years, encompassing a range of collaborative terms that are often used interchangeably.[46]

An emphasis on collaborative efforts, aimed at identifying and assisting families where animal cruelty is suspected, should therefore feature prominently in training. Indeed, as emphasized by Tiffin and Kaplan,[47] it is acknowledged that in practice, families with children who exhibit high risk behaviours, such as animal cruelty, are often hard to reach, further underlining the importance of inter-agency communication and information sharing. However, it is noteworthy that the proposed solution to fragmented practice, currently being rolled out in the UK,[48] does not contain a reference to information sharing with animal welfare agencies. Furthermore, despite containing very detailed guidance on specific dimensions that draw parallels with themes highlighted in the literature – development and behaviour of the child; parents' capacity; family and environment – the subject of animal cruelty is not mentioned in the document.

The evidence in the literature of an established cross-reporting system between human and animal welfare agencies in the USA reflects a greater societal and cultural awareness of the significance of animal cruelty, borne out of a sustained effort among almost one hundred health and social services, veterinary and humane collaborations.[49]

Joint working initiatives in the UK around the subject of animal and human welfare have received brief attention,[50] although recent efforts from the Links Group have served to raise the profile of information sharing around domestic violence and animal cruelty.[51] It could also be argued that the differences in mandatory reporting legislation, evident in parts of America such as California, San Diego, Maine, and Maryland[52] only serve to illuminate the vast differences between UK and US practice. Similarly, with the exception of the NSPCC,[53] the majority of training material reflects US policy and legislation,[54] highlighting the potential lack of transferability of this material.

Nevertheless, together with the case of *Family C*, several examples in the literature serve to highlight both the benefits and pitfalls associated with cross-reporting, suggesting that in spite of technical difficulties, it is worth pursuing a multi-agency approach to training around these issues.[55] Indeed, all three cases discussed in this paper share common features that highlight the need for a wide range of professionals encountering vulnerable children and animals to look beyond a narrow single-agency focus in response to the evidence emerging from research. Similarly, although not addressed in this paper, the contact by animal welfare agencies with vulnerable adults, such as older people or those with mental health problems, is clearly also an important consideration.

The format of child protection training in the UK acknowledges the benefits of a multi-agency focus, enabling those involved to share experiences and gain insight into different roles. The evidence of an interrelationship between animal cruelty, child abuse, family violence, and later harmful behaviour emerging from the literature signals an urgent need for the inclusion of animal welfare agencies within those programmes. The technical and logistical aspects of multi-agency training are, not surprisingly, complex. However, the appalling suffering highlighted by the three case examples discussed in this paper underlines the moral and ethical importance of pursuing what is clearly a significant safeguarding issue in the interests of humans and animals alike.

Notes

1   AMICUS/CPHVA, Campaigning résumé, May 2006, 'Health Visiting jobs meltdown', www.amicustheunion.org/docs.

2   R. Lowe, 'Facing the future: A review of the role of Health Visitors' (2007), www.dh.gov.uk/cno.

3   DFES, Framework for the assessment of children in need and their families (London: HMSO, 2000).

4   DFES, *Every child matters – The common assessment framework for children and young people: Practitioners guide. Integrated working to improve outcomes for children and young people* (London: TSO, 2006).

5   D. L. Hawksworth, *Animal cruelty: A relationship with child abuse, family violence and later harmful behaviour*, MA Dissertation (University of Huddersfield, 2007).

6   E. DeViney, J. Dickert, and R. Lockwood, 'The care of pets within child abusing families', *International Journal of the Study of Animal Problems* 4 (1983): 321–329; A. Duncan, J. C. Thomas, and C. Miller, 'Significance of family risk factors in development of childhood animal cruelty in adolescent boys with conduct problems', *Journal of Family Violence* 20, 4 (2005): 235–239.

7   C. P. Flynn, 'Exploring the link between corporal punishment and children's cruelty to animals', *Journal of Marriage and the Family* 61, 4 (1999): 971–981; C. D. Raupp, 'Treasuring, trashing or terrorizing: Adult outcomes of childhood socialization about companion animals', *Society & Animals* 7, 2 (1999): 141–159; S. Verlinden, M. Herson, and J. Thomas, 'Risk factors in school shootings', *Clinical Psychology Review* 20, 1 (2000): 3–56; F. R. Ascione, C. V. Webber, and D. S. Wood, 'The abuse of animals and domestic violence: A national survey of shelters for women who are battered', *Society & Animals* 5, 3 (1997), www.psyeta.org/sa/sa5.3/Ascione.html; L.

A. Zilney and M. Zilney, 'Reunification of child and animal welfare agencies: Cross-reporting of abuse in Wellington County, Ontario', *Child Welfare* 84, 1 (2005): 47–66.

8 D. Solot, 'Untangling the animal abuse web', *Society & Animals* 5, 3 (1997), www.psyeta.org; C. Miller, 'Childhood animal cruelty and interpersonal violence', *Clinical Psychology Review* 21, 5 (2001): 735–749; M. R. Dadds, C. M. Turner, and J. McAloon, 'Developmental links between cruelty to animals and human violence', *The Australian and New Zealand Journal of Criminology* 35, 3 (2002): 363–382; H. Piper, 'The linkage of animal abuse with interpersonal violence: A sheep in wolf's clothing?' *Journal of Social Work* 3, 2 (2003): 161–177; P. Tiffin and C. Kaplan, 'Dangerous children: Assessment and management of risk', *Child and Adolescent Mental Health* 9, 2 (2004): 56–64; H. Piper and S. Myers, 'Forging the links: (De) constructing chains of behaviours', *Child Abuse Review* 15 (2006): 178–187.

9 R. A. Prenky and D. L. Carter, 'The predictive value of the triad for sex offenders', *Behavioural Sciences and the Law* 2, 3 (1984): 341–354; Ascione *et al.*, 'The abuse of animals and domestic violence'; J. A. Quinslisk, 'Animal abuse and family violence', in F. R. Ascione and P. Arkow (eds), *Child abuse, domestic violence, and animal cruelty: Linking the circles of compassion for prevention and intervention* (West Lafayette, IN: Purdue University Press, 1999); P. Carlisle-Frank, J. M. Frank, and L. Nielson, 'Selective battering of the family pet', *Anthrozoös* 17, 1 (2004): 26–42; C. L. Currie, 'Animal cruelty by children exposed to domestic violence', *Child Abuse and Neglect* 30, 4 (2006): 425–435.

10 G. Duffield, A. Hassiotis, and E. Vizard, 'Zoophilia in young sexual abusers', *The Journal of Forensic Psychiatry* 9, 2 (1998): 294–304; F. R. Ascione, N. N. Friedrich, J. Heath, and K. Hayashi, 'Cruelty to animals in normative, sexually abused, and outpatient psychiatric samples of 6- to 12-year-old children: Relations to maltreatment and exposure to domestic violence', *Anthrozoös* 17, 3 (2003): 194–212.

11 C. A. Lacroix, 'Another weapon for combating family violence – prevention of animal abuse', in F. R. Ascione and P. Arkow (eds), *Child abuse, domestic violence and animal cruelty*; Quinslisk, 'Animal abuse'; Raupp, 'Treasuring'; B. C. Henry, 'The relationship between animal cruelty, delinquency and attitudes towards the treatment of animals', *Society & Animals* 12, 3 (2004): 185–207.

12 P. Arkow, 'The correlations between cruelty to animals and child abuse and the implications for veterinary medicine', *Canadian Veterinary Journal* 33, 8 (1992): 518–521; R. De Angelis, 'The vicious circle', *Animal Guardian* 11, 3 (1998), 8–10; M. Merritt, 'Study links child and animal abuse', *Scotland on Sunday*, 28 June 1998, www.proquest.umi.com/pqdweb?index; J. Hardy, 'Man's best friend: Killers start with pet torture say experts', *The Mirror*, 6 August 2001, www.proquest.umi.com/pqdweb?index; Verlinden *et al.*, 'Risk factors'; N. C. Sweeney, 'Animals and children caught up in a cycle of cruelty', *Justice of the Peace* 13 (March 2004), p. 224.

13 K. S. Miller and J. F. Knutson, 'Reports of severe physical punishment and exposure to animal cruelty by inmates convicted of felonies and by university students', *Child Abuse and Neglect* 21, 1 (1997): 59–82; S. E. Tallichet, C. Hensley, and S. D. Singer, 'Unravelling the methods of childhood and adolescent cruelty to nonhuman animals', *Society & Animals* 13, 2 (2005), 91–107.

14 A. R. Felthous, 'Aggression against cats, dogs and people', *Child Psychiatry and Human Development* 10, 3 (1980): 169–177; S. R. Kellert amd A. R. Felthous, 'Childhood cruelty towards animals among criminals and non-criminals', *Human*

Relations 38 (1985): 1113–1129; D. Tingle, G. W. Barnard, L. Robbins, G. Newman, and D. Hutchinson, 'Childhood and adolescent characteristics of paedophiles and rapists', *International Journal of Law and Psychiatry* 9 (1986): 103–116; A. R. Felthous and S. R. Kellert, 'Childhood cruelty to animals and later aggression against people: A review', *American Journal of Psychiatry* 144, 6 (1987): 710–717; Miller and Knutson, 'Reports'; C. T. M. Coston and B. M. Protz, 'Kill your dog, beat your wife, screw your neighbour's kids, rob a bank? A cursory look at an individual's vat of social chaos resulting from deviance', *Free Inquiry in Creative Sociology* 26, 2 (1998): 153–158; A. Arluke, J. Levin, C. Luke and F. R. Ascione, 'The relationship of animal abuse to other forms of antisocial behaviour', *Journal of Interpersonal Violence* 14 (1999): 963–975; L. Merz-Perez, K. M. Heide, and I. J. Silverman, 'Childhood animal cruelty and subsequent violence against humans', *International Journal of Offender Therapy and Comparative Criminology* 45, 5 (2001): 556–573; W. Flemming, B. Jory, and D. L. Burton, 'Characteristics of juvenile offenders admitting to sexual activity with nonhuman animals', *Society & Animals* 10, 1 (2002), www.psyeta.org/sa/sa10.1/flemming.shtml; C. P. Flynn, 'Hunting and illegal violence against humans and other animals: Exploring the relationship', *Society & Animals* 10, 2 (2002), www.psyeta.org; K. R. Beyer and J. O. Beasley, 'Non-family child abductors who murder their victims: Offender demographics from interviews with incarcerated offenders', *Journal of Interpersonal Violence* 18, 10 (2003): 1167–1188; B. C. Henry, 'Exposure to animal abuse and group context: Two factors affecting participation in animal abuse', *Anthrozoös* 17, 4 (2004): 290–305; M. Muscari, 'Juvenile animal abuse: Practice and policy implications for PNP's', *Journal of Pediatric Health Care* 18, 1 (2004): 15–21.

15 F. R. Ascione, 'Children who are cruel to animals: A review of research and implications for developmental psychopathology', *Anthrozoös* 1, 4 (1993): 226–247; P. Beirne, 'From animal abuse to interhuman violence? A critical review of the progression thesis', *Society & Animals* 12, 1 (2003), www.psyeta.org/sa/sa12.1/beirne.shtml.

16 J. Kelso and M. A. Stewart, 'Factors which predict the persistence of aggressive conduct disorder', *Journal of Child Psychology and Psychiatry* 27, 1 (1986): 77–86; Duffield *et al.*, 'Zoophilia'; F. R. Ascione, 'The abuse of animals and interpersonal violence – making the connection', in F. R. Ascione and P. Arkow (eds), *Child abuse, domestic violence and animal cruelty*; B. W. Boat, 'Abuse of children and abuse of animals: Using the links to inform child assessment and protection', in F. R. Ascione and P. Arkow (eds), *Child abuse, domestic violence and animal cruelty*.

17 Ascione, 'The relationship of animal abuse'.

18 Ascione *et al.*, 'The abuse of animals and domestic violence'; Carlisle-Frank *et al.*, 'Selective battering'.

19 DFES, 'Framework for assessment'; R. Sinclair and R. Bullock, 'Learning from past experiences: A review of serious case reviews', (2002), www.doh.gov.uk/qualityprotects.

20 DFES, *Working together to safeguard children: A guide to interagency working to safeguard and promote the welfare of children* (London: TSO, 2006).

21 C. Staley, *Child and animal maltreatment: A local study of multi-agency staff knowledge, experience and perceptions of the links between child and animal abuse*, MA Dissertation, University of Huddersfield, 2006.

22 P. Arkow, 'The evolution of animal welfare as a human welfare concern', in F. R. Ascione and P. Arkow (eds), *Child abuse, domestic violence and animal cruelty*.

23 C. A. Faver and E. B. Strand, 'Domestic violence and animal cruelty: untangling the web of abuse' *Journal of Social Work Education* 39, 2 (2003): 237–253.

24 A. Arluke and C. Luke, 'Physical cruelty towards animals in Massachusetts', *Society & Animals* 5 (1997): 195–204; M. Allen, B. Gallagher, and B. Jones, 'Domestic violence and the abuse of pets: Researching the link and its implications in Ireland', *Practice* 18, 3 (2006): 167–181.

25 N. Parton, D. Thorpe, and C. Wattam, *Child protection: Risk and the moral order* (London: Macmillan, 1997).

26 C. Sheldrick, 'Practitioner Review: The assessment and management of risk in adolescents', *Journal of Child Psychology and Psychiatry* 40, 4 (1999): 507–518.

27 L. Bell, 'Abusing animals – abusing children', *Journal of Social Work* 1, 2 (2001): 223–234.

28 Parton *et al.*, 'Child protection'.

29 Lacroix, 'Another weapon'; A. Duncan and C. Miller, 'The impact of an abusive family context on childhood animal cruelty and adult violence', *Aggression and Violent Behaviour* 7, 4 (2002): 365–383; Dadds *et al.*, 'Developmental links'; M. R. Dadds, C. Whiting, P. Bunn, J. A. Fraser, J. H. Charson, and A. Pirola-Merlo, 'Measurement of cruelty in children: The cruelty to animals inventory', *Journal of Abnormal Child Psychology* 32 (2004): 321–334.

30 Piper, 'The linkage of animal abuse'.

31 Kellert and Felthous, 'Childhood cruelty'.

32 S. C. Haden and A. Scarpa, 'Childhood animal cruelty: A review of research, assessment and therapeutic issues', *The Forensic Examiner* 14, 2 (2005): 23–32.

33 Currie, 'Animal cruelty'.

34 Duncal *et al.*, 'Significance of family risk factors'.

35 S. Zawistowski, 'The legacy of Mary Ellen', *ASPCA Animal Watch*, Fall/Winter 1992, 1–6; R. Agnew, 'The causes of animal abuse: Psychological analysis', *Theoretical Criminology* 2, 2 (1998): 177–209; C. P. Flynn, 'Acknowledging the zoological connection: A sociological analysis of animal cruelty', *Society & Animals* 9, 1 (2001): 71–87; Muscari, 'Juvenile animal abuse'.

36 B. Print and M. Erooga, 'Young people who sexually abuse: Implications for assessment', in J. Horwath (ed), *The child's world: Assessing children in need* (London: Jessica Kingsley Publishers, 2001).

37 Quinslisk, 'Animal abuse'; Henry, 'The relationship between animal cruelty'.

38 Lacroix, 'Another weapon'.

39 P. Beirne, 'For a non-speciesist criminology: Animal abuse as an object of study', *Criminology* 37, 1 (1998): 117–148.

40 Kellert and Felthous, 'Childhood cruelty'.

41 Henry, 'Exposure to animal abuse'.

42 Coston and Protz, 'Kill your dog'.

43 Arluke *et al.*, 'The relationship of animal abuse'.

44 Lord Laming, *The Victoria Climbie inquiry: Report of an inquiry by Lord Laming* (London: HMSO, 2003).

45 DFES, *Working together*.

46 R. Gardner, 'Working together to improve children's life chances: The challenge of interagency collaboration', in J. Weinstein, C. Whittington, and T. Leiba, *Collaboration in social work practice* (London: Jessica Kingsley Publishers, 2003).

47 Tiffin and Kaplan, 'Dangerous children'.

48 DFES, *Every child matters*.

49 Ascione, 'The abuse of animals'; N. R. Fawcett, E. Gullone, and J. Johnson, 'Domestic violence and animal abuse: Encouraging collaborative relations between animal welfare and human welfare agencies in Australia', *Inpsych: The Bulletin of the Australian Psychological Society* 24, 2 (2002): 36–38; C. Maclennan, *First Strike targets links between animal and child abuse*, 2007, www.animalliberationfront. com/philosophy/abuseLinked.

50 BBC News, 'Child abuse and cruelty "linked"', 12 February 2001: www.bbc.co.uk/1/hi/1165768.stm; Guardian Unlimited, 'A safe house for animals: Special report Animal Rights' March 2003, www.guardian.co.uk/animalrights/ story; NSPCC, 'NSPCC and RSPCA join forces to tackle violence within family', 2003, www.nspcc.org.uk/html/home/ information.

51 J. Silk, 'Animal cruelty clue to domestic violence', *Care and Health News*, 2007, www.careandhealth.com/pages/story.

52 Doris Day Animal Foundation, *The violence connection: An examination of the link between animal abuse and other violent crimes* (Washington DC: Doris Day Animal Foundation, 2004), www.ddaf.org.

53 NSPCC, 'Understanding the links: child abuse, animal abuse, and domestic violence', 2005, www.nspcc.org.uk/inform.

54 American Humane Association, *A training guide for recognizing and reporting child abuse for animal control officers and humane investigators* (Englewood, CO: American Humane Association, 1995); American Humane Association, *The next step: Exploring the link between violence to people and animals*, 2007, www.americanhumane.org; P. Arkow, 'Canadian and Florida groups actively working on the link', *Latham Letter* (2001), p. 14, www.latham.org; P. Arkow, 'New training materials help professionals recognise non-accidental animal injury', *Latham Letter* (2003), pp. 11–13, www.latham.org; Humane Society for the United States, *Animal cruelty and family violence: Making the connection*, 2004, www.hsus.org/hsus-field/first-strike; Humane Society for the United States, *Frequently asked questions about animal cruelty*, 2006, www.hsus.org/hsus-field/first-strike.

55 C. J. Adams, 'Bringing peace home: A feminist philosophical perspective on the abuse of women, children and pet animals', *Hypatia* 9, 2 (1994): 63–84; Boat, 'Abuse of children'; C. Ponder and R. Lockwood, 'Programs educate law enforcement on link between animal cruelty and domestic violence', *The Police Chief* (November 2000): 31–36.

PART

VIII

The Abuse of Wild Animals

The book has been predominantly concerned with the links between human violence and domestic or companion animal abuse. That is not surprising since this is the area in which there has been most research. But of course that leaves to one side the abuse of wild, free-ranging animals, which is often both legal and socially condoned. Although the work in this field is not as substantial, it is clearly an important under-researched area that cries out for further attention. I have therefore decided to conclude the book with a selection in **Part VIII** of some pioneering papers addressing this lacuna, focusing on examples from the UK, the US, and Japan.

Nicola Taylor and Tania Signal (*Overview of Research*) provide a brief account of the literature. Pointing out that 'little attention has been paid to activities where deliberate animal harm is socially sanctioned', they nevertheless find suggestive leads in the research on hunting in partic-ular. Subsequent papers also focus on hunting and the possibility of abuse.

John Cooper (*Hunting as an Abusive Sub-culture*) focuses on the now illegal 'sport' of hunting with dogs in the UK. His main concern is with the institutionalized ethos of violence that hunting can represent, and its possible contribution to a wider abusive culture. He examines the work by scholars and legal authorities, and specifically cites reports of harassment, destruction of companion animals, and assaults on hunt monitors.

Priscilla Cohn and myself (*Hunting as a Morally Suspect Activity*) take this further by considering the grounds for supposing that hunting (specifically deer-hunting in the US) harms both the hunted and the hunter. We ask how reasonable it is to confine the link to domestic animals, and maintain that, 'There is no indication in the current literature that legality as such and in itself is an observed boundary when it comes to abusive treatment. Why then should we suppose that hunting cruelty – rather than say the abuse of children – is exempt from the patterns of abuse that we may detect elsewhere?' We consider, *inter alia*, evidence from self-reports of hunters, and discuss the long philosophical and theological tradition that links cruelty to animals with violence to humans. Taken together these two essays offer a distinct contrast, since one outlines some of the much-needed raw data, and the other builds on the data to develop a philosophical argument.

Thomas I. White (*Dolphin Drive Hunts and the Socratic Dictum: 'Vice harms the doer'*) turns to the hunting of dolphins in 'drive hunts' in Japan. Applying the Socratic dictum that 'vice harms the doer', White suggests that the defences offered for the hunts indicate intellectual vacuity. 'My central claim', he writes, 'is that the unethical treatment of dolphins produces precisely the sort of harm in the personality that Socrates describes – a weakened intellect that simply serves some desire'. Socrates held that the consequence of vice is that 'a desire for something grows so strong that satisfying it is more important than perceiving reality accurately, dealing with uncomfortable truths about a situation and respecting the canons of logic'. This putative 'damage', he claims, is evident in the justifications offered in defence of the drive hunts.

All the contributors to this final section would agree that further research is essential in order to document the claim that hunting specifically harms the hunters themselves. It has yet to be seen whether the academic community will devote time and resources to this hitherto insufficiently explored topic.

Overview of Research

NICOLA TAYLOR AND TANIA SIGNAL

If we accept that our attitudes towards animals may in some way affect our attitudes towards humans, then that opens the doors to many possibilities. For example, attitudes towards animals may be used in clinical settings to identify potentially problematic behaviour. Additionally, animal abuse itself, when detected, should be seen as a red flag indicating the need for further investigation. This is particularly the case with companion animal abuse, which may well indicate other forms of human abuse within the family unit.

The research so far goes some way to illustrate the importance that empathy and attitudes to animals may play in terms of the human–animal abuse thesis. That is, there is a point of convergence between empathy, attitudes towards animals, and individual propensity towards aggression or violence directed at both human and non-human animals. Much of the research to date has addressed this within the framework of family and/or interpersonal violence, where the deliberate harm of animals tends to be seen as symptomatic of other problems.

However, little attention has been paid to activities where deliberate animal harm is socially sanctioned and/or accepted, such as hunting or working within slaughterhouses.[1] It is not enough simply to address the issues raised by the human–animal abuse thesis on an individual, case-by-case level. There remains a need to analyze these issues within a wider framework which sees such links as indicative of an institutionalized attitude which condones – and indeed implicitly supports – violence towards disenfranchised 'others'.[2] Whilst there may be numerous examples of institutionalized violence toward humans available (e.g., domestic violence and child abuse), examples of institutionalized violence towards animals are not as well documented nor researched by the social sciences. Thus, any potential implications these kinds of activities may have for empathy levels and the concomitant human–animal abuse link have been neglected.

In the last twenty years or so, the issue of human relationships with the natural environment has received increasing attention. Accordingly, the focus of debate around hunting has broadened to include not only philosophical considerations of the 'moral' standing of hunting, but also to a consideration of the utility of hunting as a wildlife management strategy.[3]

To date much of the research around potential interactions among hunting, attitudes towards animals, empathy, and the potential for violence has tended to be conducted either with student populations[4] or based on archival research (e.g., applications for hunting licenses), and is predominantly North American in origin. For example, Clifton found a positive correlation between the number of hunting licenses issued and prevalence rates of violent crimes, including child abuse, in two states in America.[5] However, very little research has been conducted on these issues with hunters themselves. Where hunters have been directly involved it has tended to be from a wildlife or natural resource management perspective.[6]

Flynn investigated the relationship among personal experience of hunting (or hunting socialization), empathy, and illegal violence directed at humans and other animals.[7] He reported that students with a personal experience of hunting were approximately twice as likely to have engaged in deliberate animal abuse (of non-target species). Additionally, hunters were more than twice as likely as non-hunters to have damaged or destroyed property in the last twelve months. While Flynn reported that hunters tended to express less cognitive empathy than non-hunters, he urged caution in the interpretation of the findings due to the use of a student sample and suggested that in the future a more longitudinal approach would be of benefit.

Although the above research did report interrelations between hunting and either empathy or past occurrences of antisocial behaviour,[8] other research has failed to find any significant relationships.[9] Much of this ambivalence may result from flawed methodology and/or poor definition of the terms 'hunting' and 'cruelty/abuse'. For example, defining 'animal abuse' to a population who engages in routine deliberate animal harm (i.e., hunting) and employs a utilitarian discourse surrounding the necessity of culling wild animals has proved to be problematic.[10]

Defining hunting may be just as fraught with difficulty. Presenting hunting as 'for sport' or 'for food' has been shown to directly affect public attitudes towards, and acceptance of, hunting. That is, when hunting is defined as being 'for food', public opposition decreases; when characterized as being 'for sport', public opposition increases.[11] Generally speaking, research, of predominantly North American origin, shows that 10 per cent of the general public oppose hunting under all circumstances, 10 per cent support hunting in all circumstances, while 80 per cent neither strongly support nor oppose hunting.[12] In contrast, when the definition of hunting used specifies 'for trophy', opposition increases to nearly one hundred per cent.[13]

However, regardless of issues of definition, certain variables remain consistent in their influence on individual attitudes towards hunting. In both Europe and North America, for example, urban dwellers have been shown to be less accepting of hunting per se than rural dwellers.[14] Research consistently demonstrates a link between rural culture and a utilitarian orientation towards both nature and wildlife.[15] Furthermore, international research also demonstrates that a utilitarian attitude directly impacts upon the attitudes towards the treatment of animals.[16] Logically, by association this may have implications for human-directed empathy and propensity towards interpersonal violence. This is clearly an area that warrants further investigation.

The most consistent variable shown to influence attitudes towards hunting specifically, and towards animals more generally, is gender, with males tending to self-report less animal-welfare orientated attitudes[17] and a higher level of engagement in hunting.[18] Males also consistently score lower on measures of human-directed empathy[19] and have been found to have higher levels of physical aggression than women.[20] It has been suggested that this is due in no small part to socialization processes which place a premium on dominance and aggression for males.[21] This has led to some authors drawing links between a culture of hegemonic masculinity and the culture of hunting.[22] Proponents of this theory argue that the discourses surrounding hunting re-affirm stereotypical ideas concerning predatory masculinity and sexuality. Cartmill suggests that hunting is one avenue which men may take in order to affirm their virility, and thus hunting can be seen as sexual in nature. He goes further to suggest that hunting is, for some, a seasonal activity whereby ties to the land and ancestral traditions can be renewed and reaffirmed. Thus he concludes that for some men hunting 'affirms their identity as men'.[23]

Luke argues that in the discourses commonly used by hunters themselves, hunting is seen as an extension of traditional masculinity. This effectively removes hunting from the realms of moral consideration by constructing it as a 'natural' activity that is fundamentally linked to the expression of masculinity. That is, the construction of hunting as an expression of innate 'drives' presents it as being 'natural' and thus unalterable and inherently acceptable.[24] These arguments suggest that hunting practices and their attendant masculinity are caught up in a culture of coercion and control where 'man' must prove 'his' dominance over nature.[25]

While contributing considerably to the debate on hunting, such analyses have not specifically addressed the link between hunting and other forms of violence more generally. They point to a link between masculinity and hunting and an attendant link between masculinity and aggression but this area still remains relatively uncharted. Not only does hunting involve the killing/deliberate harm of animals, which in itself may be problematic given the links between violence against animals and violence against humans; other, related aspects of hunting and hunting culture may also increase the likelihood of violence or aggression and other antisocial behaviours. For example, research has shown that the mere presence of a weapon, in particular a firearm, leads to elevated aggression levels.[26]

Whatever the discourse or the politics of the situation, the fact remains that hunting, by definition, involves the deliberate killing and/or harm of an animal. Given what is already known about the links between attitudes towards animals, empathy, and human-directed aggression or violence, the issue of hunting begs further analysis in this respect. The majority of research to date into this connection addresses 'illegal' or 'illicit' forms of animal harm where, in fact, it may be that socially sanctioned forms of animal violence (such as hunting and wildlife 'culling' by members of the public) are more problematic and possibly more insidious due to their 'normalized' status. Thus, recent initiatives within parts of Australia where town councils offer incentives to members of the public to engage in deliberate harm to 'inconvenient' animals by, for example, offering a financial bounty for feral cat pelts, is at best negligent and at worst promotes the very type of harm to animals that research has shown as a risk factor for interpersonal violence. Arguably, such acts serve to normalize and legitimize violence towards animals which, as this chapter has shown, deserves serious consideration from both animal- and human-welfare perspectives. One thing which is clear is that this issue is multi-faceted and far from simple, and thus deserves further analysis, particularly in light of the emerging links between the treatment of animals and the treatment of humans. Moreover, the effect of institutionalized animal cruelty deserves far more attention, in part because it has previously been neglected, but also due to its insidious nature, which lends it superficial legitimacy and acceptance within the wider community.

Notes

1 For notable exception of the latter see, for example, T. Grandin, 'Behavior of slaughter plant and auction employees toward the animal', *Anthrozoös* 1 (1988): 205–213.

2 See, for example, M. Kheel, 'License to kill: An ecofeminist critique of hunters' discourse', in C. Adams and J. Donovan (eds), *Animals and women: Feminist theoretical explanations* (Durham NC: Duke University Press, 1995), pp. 85–125.

3 For example, H. C. Zinn, M. J. Manfredo, and S. C. Barro, 'Patterns of wildlife value orientations in hunters' families', *Human Dimensions of Wildlife* 7 (2002): 147–162.

4 For example, C. P. Flynn, 'Hunting and illegal violence against humans and other animals: Exploring the relationship', *Society & Animals* 10, 2 (2002): 137–154.

5 M. Clifton, 'Ohio data confirms hunting/child abuse link', *Animal People* 3, 9 (1994), pp. 1, 8–9.

6 T. A. Heberlein and G. Ericsson, 'Ties to the countryside: Accounting for urbanites attitudes towards hunting, wolves, and wildlife', *Human Dimensions of Wildlife* 10 (2005): 213–227; Zinn *et al.*, 'Patterns of wildlife'.

7 Flynn, 'Hunting and illegal violence'.

8 *Ibid.*; Clifton, 'Ohio data'.

9 H. E. Adair, 'The correlation between hunting and crime: A comment', *Society & Animals* 3 (1995): 189–195.

10 See Flynn, 'Hunting and illegal violence'.

11 J. M. Campbell and K. J. Mackay, 'Attitudinal and normative influences on support for hunting as a wildlife management strategy', *Human Dimensions of Wildlife* 8 (2003): 189–197.

12 J. A. Dicamillo, 'Focus groups as a tool for fish and wildlife management: A case study', *Wildlife Society Bulletin* 23 (1995): 616–620; Fleishman-Hillard Research

Inc., *Attitudes of the uncommitted middle towards wildlife management* (St Louis, MO: Fleishman-Hillard Research Inc., 1994).

13 Campbell and Mackay, 'Attitudinal and normative influences'.

14 Heberlein and Ericsson, 'Ties to the countryside'; R. C. Stedman, and T. A. Heberlein, 'Hunting and rural socialization: Contingent effects of the rural setting on hunting participation', *Rural Sociology* 66 (2002): 599–617; Zinn *et al.*, 'Patterns of wildlife'.

15 S. Kellert, 'American attitudes toward and knowledge of animals: An update', *International Journal for the Study of Animal Problems* 1, 2 (1980): 87–119.

16 T. Signal and N. Taylor, 'Attitudes to animals within the animal protection community compared to a normative community sample', *Society & Animals* 14, 3 (2006): 265–274; J. J. Vaske, M. P. Donnelly, D. R. Williams, and S. Jonker, 'Demographic influences on environmental value orientations and normative beliefs about national forest management', *Society and Natural Resources* 14 (2001): 761–776.

17 H. Herzog, N. Betchart, and R. Pittman, 'Sex role identity and attitudes toward animals', *Anthrozoös* 4, 3 (1991): 184–192; Signal and Taylor, 'Attitudes to animals'; N. Taylor and T. D. Signal, 'Empathy and attitudes towards animals', *Anthrozoös* 18, 1 (2005): 18–27.

18 Flynn, 'Hunting and illegal violence'.

19 G. J. Coman, B. J. Evans, and R. O. Stanley, 'Scores on the Interpersonal Reactivity Index: A sample of Australian medical students', *Psychological Reports* 62 (1988): 943–945; D. Warden and S. Mackinnon, 'Prosocial children, bullies and victims: An investigation of their sociometric status, empathy and social problem-solving strategies', *British Journal of Developmental Psychology* 21 (2003): 367–385.

20 See A. Fossati, C. Maffei, E. Acquarini, and A. Di Ceglie, 'Multigroup confirmatory component and factor analyses of the Italian version of the aggression questionnaire', *European Journal of Psychological Assessment* 19, 1 (2003): 54–65.

21 Flynn, 'Hunting and illegal violence'.

22 L. Kalof, A. Fitzgerald, and L. Baralt, 'Animals, women and weapons: Blurred sexual boundaries in the discourse of sport hunting', *Society & Animals* 12 (2004): 237–251; Kheel, 'License to kill'.

23 M. Cartmill, *A view to a death in the morning: Hunting and nature through history* (Cambridge, MA: Harvard University Press, 1993), p. 233.

24 B. Luke, 'Violent love: Hunting, heterosexuality, and the erotics of men's predation', *Feminist Studies* 24, 3 (1998): 627–655.

25 Kheel, 'License to kill'.

26 C. A. Anderson, A. J. Benjamin, and B. D. Bartholow, 'Does the gun pull the trigger? Automatic priming effects of weapon pictures and weapon names', *Psychological Science* 9 (1998): 308–314.

Hunting as an Abusive Sub-culture[1]

JOHN COOPER

It is properly a concern of law, and social policy-making, if hunting and other blood sports[2] are degrading to both the hunted and the hunter. As an illegal activity, hunting with dogs is especially interesting psychologically – what motivates persistent resort to law-breaking and, consequently, criminality? According to one neutral analysis, hunters 'differ greatly in terms of their attitudes, subjective norms, and perceptions of behavioural control, as well as wildlife-related values and values to life in general'.[3] Whereas the legality of hunting with dogs is now a dead debate in the UK,[4] hunters who still persist in offending should be identified as a pressing issue of concern.

Although both hunting and support for hunting have declined, there is still a core group that is committed to perpetuating hunting against the law. The protest against banning fox-hunting in Britain was attended by about 400,000 people, many of whom had committed to carry on hunting. The obvious inference is that those individuals were prepared to become offenders. While normative support for hunting – among the general public – has diminished in recent years, hunters constitute an important deviant sub-group.

Links between the abuse of animals and people have been the subject of empirical research studies for many years. But it should be acknowledged that some researchers have expressed scepticism regarding putative links as regards hunting. Clifton Flynn states that: '[w]ith regard to the link between hunting and violence, the limited evidence is mixed and inconclusive'.[5] Certainly, it is true that 'there is a need for solid, empirical research to address this question'.[6] However, Flynn also observes that '[t]he notion that . . . hunting may spill over into illegal violence is not new'.[7]

I

It is perhaps worth noting at the outset the change of moral sensibility about animals in the UK that has already shown itself in several important pieces of legislation. The Protection of Animals Act 1911 was amended by the Protection of Animals (Amendment) Act of 1988, which enabled a court to disqualify a person from having custody of an animal on a first conviction of cruelty, and to increase the penalties for offences relating to animal fights. The Animal Welfare Act 2006 (which came into force on 6 April 2007), imported a duty of care requirement as regards human interactions with animals. The statutory language of the 2006 Act is purposely cast as comprehensive and generous: s. 1(1) of the Act determines that 'animal' is to mean 'a vertebrate other than man'.[8] The Act therefore extends to the protection of all animals, domestic or wild, though there is a wild animal exclusion. Paragraph s. 1(4) of the 2006 Act states that:

> The power under subsection (3)(a) or (c) may only be exercised if the appropriate national authority is satisfied, on the basis of scientific evidence, that animals of the kind concerned are capable of experiencing pain or suffering.

What is constituted by 'scientific evidence' is a moot point that will become a live question of interpretation as the Act gains increasing ascendancy. Sufficiently reliable, coherent research findings, produced by regulated professionals and higher education institutions, may serve to activate the operation of subsection (3)(a). Academic interest in this area is experiencing a new impetus, and is set to gather pace. Accordingly, subject to research 'satisfying the national authority', certain research findings – which are sufficiently credible and robust – may promote the exercise of the power secured under subsection (3)(a). That the statutory language refers to intervention on the basis that animals of the kind concerned are *capable of* experiencing pain or suffering is highly relevant for these purposes. There is now ample evidence in peer-reviewed scientific journals that all mammals at least are capable of experiencing pain or suffering to a greater or lesser extent than we do.

It is becoming clear that the welfare and protection of animals must feature in any progressive programme of law reform – that humans themselves have a stake in anti-cruelty measures is increasingly accepted. As early as the eighteenth century, the jurist-philosopher Jeremy Bentham recognized the importance of marrying law reform designed to augment human quality of life with reform concerning the treatment of animals. 'A direct law against cruelty to animals', he wrote, 'would be an indirect law against cruelty towards men'.[9]

II

Traditionally, at least, hunting has been associated with the ruling or elite classes, as a means of exerting primacy and influence. Aggressive sweeping of the countryside was a way of asserting dominance, authority, even masculinity. Instrumental to this, a number of so-called 'game laws' were passed to facilitate the social function of sport for the élite, especially horse-racing and fox-hunting.[10]

Even today, an examination of the arguments advanced by the most vocal protesters of the ban on hunting proves instructive. They appear to embody a will to exercise control over the countryside, a territory they seem to see as their own, to the exclusion of competing interests of peace and protection for wildlife. The sequence of the arguments put forward is also telling. It is claimed that banning hunting would:

- outlaw a centuries-old lawful activity;
- constitute an unjustifiable restriction on pro-hunters' freedoms;
- result in significant job losses for people employed in hunting-related activities; and
- prevent effective management of fox numbers to the detriment of the farming industry and countryside.

Only the last two of these express wider concerns other than the hunters' own interests and enjoyment. Even then, the concerns registered are primarily put forward so as to maintain the *status quo* of institutions inextricably bound up with hunting. The first argument put forward – tradition – is simply untenable. A ritual or custom that causes suffering cannot be excused on grounds of habit or tradition, which is simply a means of self-preservation. The second, rights-based argument is nothing less than a sham. There is no such thing as a freedom to be cruel. Rabinder Singh QC, in an eloquent rehearsal of the Millian principle of self- and other-regarding action made it clear that:

> It is perfectly possible for a person to adopt the moral position that what others do in their private lives is a matter for them, so long as it does not harm others. That is in essence the position we take in modern free societies and that value is now enshrined in our law.[11]

Hunting is predicated on institutionalizing dominance. Billed as 'a natural way of the countryside', organizing hunts for sport is an unnatural and oppressive way to engage with wildlife. This interaction is obviously defective with respect to the animals being pursued. If one dog was pitted against one fox, and all the sets were open and unblocked, the fox would have a good chance of getting away. In contrast, fox-hunting is the practice of isolating one fox in order to play with and terrorize it, while running it breathlessly into the ground.

But it is also my concern that hunting may be a morally defective interaction with respect to the human beings who hunt, and others associated with or affected by hunting. Those who hunt with dogs are properly referred to as 'offenders' – both in the course of this chapter and as a label attaching more generally. The Hunting Act 2004, which made hare coursing, deer hunting, and the hunting of wild animals with dogs unlawful,[12] received Royal Assent in November 2004 (and came into force on 18 February 2005).[13] The last refuge sought by hunters fleeing from the operation of the law has consisted of questioning the validity of the Hunting Act and of the Parliament Act 1949. But the real concern and debate about hunting coalesces around the argument that hunting is cruel, not that it restricts individual freedom. Individual and group rights represent a balancing of competing considerations and claims: the courts have underscored the legitimacy of the approach taken by the Hunting Act 2004.

III

People who hunt may start doing so for the best of motives. People may become hunters because they are interested in wildlife from a naturalist's perspective. They like and value wildlife and hunting is, for them, the best way to get to see and understand wild creatures. Some people may read hunting magazines to learn specifically about tracking, finding, and observing wildlife. The big question is how and why, once enmeshed in the hunting culture, people lose sight of the impact on the animal, the potential for suffering by their quarry. My main concern is also with the institutionalized ethos of violence that hunting can represent, and its possible contribution to a wider abusive culture.

Confirmation of this concern is provided by the Court of Appeal, which recently had the opportunity to probe what is involved in the practice of hunting, and took the opportunity to describe it as:

> an ethically unacceptable 'blood sport'[,] which expression we understand to connote chasing an animal with hounds and exhausting it, and then, for foxes at least, having the hounds kill it often in an unacceptable manner; and this for sport.[14]

Shedding light on the psychology of hunting involves gaining insight into what kind of person – and group – chooses to engage in, and endorse, hunting as a blood sport. This is properly a concern falling within the ambit of criminal profiling. As a pattern of behaviour, it may demonstrate an ambivalent regard for wildlife, other people, and the law.

We are all semi-sophisticated in the new vocabulary of crime that includes genetic fingerprinting and offender profiling. The use of offender-profiling and clinical psychology in criminal investigations has now widely gained credence and currency.[15] Profiling a particular criminal for a particular crime is to do nothing more than attempt to 'get inside' that criminal's head, in order better to understand him or her, and the group of which they are a part. This provides for a better grasp of a criminal's *propensity* or disposition to commit a certain crime. Profiling has value because it shows certain offenders, and groups of offenders, to exhibit a degree of ambivalence towards other members of the community. This may impact on, and compromise, the safety and quality of life of individuals who live, or associate with, those offenders.

Consider, for example, some of the reported incidents of behaviour by hunters during the 2006–2007 season:

- *Rare breed birds panic as hunt hounds invade.* Nesting birds at the Falconry Centre . . . scattered their eggs and were injured flying around cages in panic as hounds from the . . . Hunt tore through on Saturday. Families with young children in pushchairs and toddlers screamed in terror as the pack of around 20 hounds bounded through the centre and neighbouring Arboretum Garden Centre. [The] founder of the Falconry Centre said staff were now anxiously monitoring birds and their eggs to see if the breeding programme for this year was ruined . . . 'It wasn't just the birds, we had between 30 and 40 visitors here at the time and they were horrified. The hounds just appeared out of nowhere'.[16]
- *Police Probe Hounds in Gardens Claim.* Police are investigating claims a pack of hounds ran through people's gardens . . . on Tuesday and killed a fox. Police were called to the . . . area shortly after 4 p.m. and found the dead fox in the garden of a property. An unnamed man who contacted the *Western Gazette* said residents had been horrified to see the hounds cross the river and race through people's gardens. 'There were about 30 dogs which were running loose, and cats, dogs and children were terrorized', he said. 'I know we live in a rural area, but you don't expect a pack of hounds to run through your garden. My wife was terrified'.[17]
- *Pregnant woman in fear of hunt dogs.* [The] . . . Hunt says it was following an artificially laid trail when two of its hounds ran into the garden of a home . . . [The local resident] claims she was laughed at by hunt members as she tried to save her two cats from the hounds in her garden. Neither [the local resident], who is pregnant, nor her cats suffered any injury. 'I called the police and I have logged a complaint, as the hunters had absolutely no regard or respect for myself and my property', she said. 'I have never seen a hunt so close to a residential area and I was concerned for my cats. Two great big hunting dogs came running on to my property, howling and barking. This scared me immensely, as these dogs are trained to kill'. [The local resident] said she asked hunt members several times to get their dogs off her property. She added, 'When I tried to scare the dogs off, they started to laugh at me. These people seem to think they own the countryside. I was very distressed as I didn't know where my cats were and I am pregnant as well, and worried that these dogs would either knock me over or worse. They continued to laugh at me and I ran into my house'.[18]
- *A leading hunt is being investigated by police after its hounds killed a fox in a pensioner's garden.* The . . . Hunt blamed the killing of a fox . . . on strong winds which blew the legal trail scent further away. But 78-year-old [local resident] said she watched in horror as she saw hounds crossing a neighbour's field and following a fox into her garden. 'They just tore into it. There was fur flying and some blood spattered up on the garage door.

I was really upset about it. It wasn't very pleasant. One of the huntswomen came up and said she was very sorry. I said: "Get them out of here."[19]

Of especial relevance is this letter published in a pro-hunting magazine, which illustrates the indifference of hunters:

I am a professional shooting instructor and an avid supporter of all country sports. While on holiday on Exmoor, we came across a hunt near Withypool. We were travelling down a typical Devon single-track lane with high banks. The lane had been blocked by supporters' vehicles, which were abandoned while the occupants stood on the bank watching the hunt. When I sounded my horn to get their attention, I was just glared at. After a while, some of the mounted field started to squeeze up the lane between the cars and the bank, one rider knocking my wing mirror in with his leg. Manners and consideration cost nothing. Why should I try to justify hunting to others if this is the attitude of people who hunt?[20]

And here are some other examples from the 2007–2008 season:

- *Horror as hounds savage pet terrier.* The heartbroken owners of a pet dog have spoken of their devastation after it was mauled in an attack by hounds last week. On Monday morning [a local resident] was walking his nine-month-old Jack Russell called Spike on its lead when it was pounced on by a 30-strong pack belonging to the . . . hunt. . . . A spokesman for the hunt said they had permission from the farm owner to be on the land but [local resident] said more controls needed to be introduced as it is a popular walking spot for dog owners . . . [21]
- *Hunting hound killed on road.* A pack of fox hounds caused traffic chaos as they ran across a busy dual carriageway on Saturday. One dog was hit by a vehicle and killed in the incident, which happened at about 1 p.m., on [a main road]. . . . The dogs, which form part of the . . . Beagle's pack . . . broke away from a trail hunt and ran across both sides of the carriageway into the path of moving traffic. It was 40 minutes before they were herded into a nearby field. A . . . Beagles spokesman said: 'The hounds were following a trail when a handful broke away from the hunt and ran towards the road. We tried to stop them before they reached the carriageway but some made it on to the road'.[22]
- *Grandson watched as hounds ripped fox apart.* A woman and her grandson have been left traumatized after a fox was torn to shreds by hunting hounds in their Worcestershire garden. [The woman] was with her five-year-old grandson at her home . . . when the hounds entered her garden. 'We were suddenly surrounded by a pack of very noisy and excited fox hounds tearing around our garden, trampling over flower beds, pushing through fencing and terrorizing my grandson who was lost among the pack of hounds', she said. The incident happened last Saturday when the

pack was flushing out a fox, which the hunt later planned to kill using a bird of prey – a practice still legal in Britain. But instead the hounds got hold of the fox and killed it, although the hunt has since said it was an accident. 'The hounds dragged it (the fox) out in our full view to be torn apart before our eyes', [the woman] said.[23]

The important thing to notice about these incidents is that they happened *after* the ban on hunting had come into force. That is, even after public disapproval was expressed through legislative change, hunts still continue to harass their local neighbours.

IV

Writing as a sociologist, K. Fukuda has looked closely at human–animal relationships, and offers an account of the arguments typically used to justify and defend hunting.[24] In terms of determining the criminal profiling of those who hunt, Fukuda's work merits close attention, based as it is on 'ethnographic information' generated by her field research. She has canvassed what is meant by cruelty, according to different groups (as 'described by their participants'[25]). How different groups perceive cruelty in different ways reveals a lack of any objective measurement. Fukuda 'examine[s] hunting and pet-keeping in a social context',[26] and 'suggest[s] that the definition of 'cruelty' is largely a product of social conditions',[27] which fuels one of the concerns expressed here, namely that cruelty is the result of a defective socialization. Fukuda identifies the obvious truth that:

> The actual and evident reason for people's participation in fox-hunting is that they enjoy it, although the content of [their] enjoyment has not been well discussed in public.[28]

Moreover, the blooding associated with hunting as 'sport' is part and parcel of that 'enjoyment'. A distinction is sometimes drawn, Fukuda notes, which hunters often themselves adopt, between 'two types of people who participate in fox-hunting: those who hunt to ride and those who ride to hunt'.[29] 'The latter define their enjoyment in hunting as observing interaction between foxes and hounds'.[30] Importantly, however, Fukuda disputes the notion of 'hunt to ride; indifferent to the kill', which many hunters put forward, exposing it as a sham justification: 'For many people who ride to hunt . . . the fox is an indispensable element of the sport'.[31]

Hunters themselves (inadvertently) offer empirical evidence to substantiate this observation, in deliberately downplaying the feasibility of scent trails – by focusing on the artificiality of this otherwise acceptable compromise. In neutral language, Fukuda attempts to make sense of what she terms 'the pleasure of hunting', noting that it appears particularly cruel because the way in which hunters appreciate the quality of animals is alienated both from the sentiment of the current animal protection movement and from most people's way of life.[32]

Fukuda maintains that the hunting mentality is an 'alienated' one, divorced from normative, balanced perceptions of what is unacceptable and base conduct. She suggests that what hunters do is a warping experience that involves both 'the inevitability of killing' and a 'fascination with the experience [that is] an outcome of the process'.[33]

The Court of Appeal, in 2006, specifically considered the claims that hunters make for hunting. The categories of interaction with animals the court canvassed were:

- pest control;
- sport and recreation;
- hunting as a way of life, and;
- hunting as an industry.

And the Court observed that

all of the types of hunting that are banned by the Hunting Act are seen by those who participate in them as a valuable form of sport and recreation. And all of the types of hunting share the common characteristic, important to the participants, of involving the chasing by hounds of a live quarry. That is why the still permitted alternative of drag hunting (where hounds and riders follow a pre-laid trail) is not acceptable to them, and in their view would not enable the present hunt structure to survive. As Baroness Mallalieu put it in paragraph 93 of her second witness statement: 'Drag hunting centres around the relationship between horse and rider whereas the appeal of fox hunting comes from the relationship between hound and huntsman'.[34]

The Court further considered, in paragraph thirty-eight of its judgment, what it referred to as 'Hunting as a way of life':

There is a good deal of evidence that for some of those who work in the hunting industry, and for some of those who participate in hunting, hunting is, as they put it in their evidence, a way of life. The Divisional Court considered this aspect of hunting in connexion with its analysis of the claims under art 8 of the ECHR [European Court of Human Rights], a matter to which we will have to return. *It was however satisfied that there were people, though it thought probably a small number, for whom hunting was more than just a sport or a source of employment.*[35]

Certain groups, of which hunters form just one kind, show a propensity to violence towards certain species of animal.[36] Hunting as an interaction with wildlife is wrong because (to utilize Kant's terminology about human beings) the animal is a *means* towards the hunter's own *end*. The interaction may be viewed as defective for that reason alone. Abuse of animals translates, at the level of forensic psychology, as a distinctly concerning lack of empathy for sentient creatures.[37]

V

The link between animal abuse and the abuse of people is, in part, borne out by studies that show how animal abusers may not differentiate between animals and humans, in their abusive treatment.[38] Feminists have argued that hunting is a form of violence and an example of male dominion and oppression.[39] This claim may be substantiated on the basis that most hunters (like animal abusers) are male, and hunting is an archetypal example of male socialization that focuses on dominance and aggression. Crucially, in this context, the socialization associated with hunting minimizes, or downgrades, empathy. Although anecdotally based, there is a putative link between battering female partners and hunting.[40] In turn, links to child abuse have been made, on an analysis of typically defective human–animal interactions and relationships.[41] Flynn observes that these research findings

> reinforc[e] this view of hunting as not only a recreational activity but also as an act of violence toward nonhuman animals that may be associated with other expressions of violence against humans and other animals.[42]

In support, consider these further incidents concerning hunters' activities with regard to those who monitor hunts during 2006–2007:

- January 2006: A hunt steward was given an £80 fixed penalty fine after using threatening behaviour towards a League hunt monitor.
- October 2006: A gamekeeper was found guilty of assault and threatening behaviour against a League worker in Cambridgeshire.
- October 2006: A hunt supporter was found guilty at Chichester Magistrates Court of assaulting an anti-hunt protester during a meet.
- August 2006: Lewes Crown Court fined hunt supporter £400 with £700 costs for an assault during the same incident.
- February 2007: A huntsman was ordered to pay £400 in costs, compensation, and a fine after assaulting a pensioner, while she was monitoring on behalf of the League.
- February 2007: A sixty-eight-year-old hunt supporter was given two police cautions by police after he drove his vehicle at a hunt monitor, shouted abuse, and then damaged her car door.

Again, it is worth remembering that these incidents happened after the hunting ban was in force. Monitoring hunt activity is of course an entirely legal activity, but even those people were subject to harassment or violence. And it is worth reminding ourselves that the above are not just reports but *proven* cases of abuse, intimidation, harassment and or assault.

One commentator has gone so far as to term hunting for sport 'legal violence'. Linda Colley, in *Britons: Forging the Nation 1707–1830*, maintains that the ceremonies associated with fox-hunting are akin to training for war.[43] Taylor also highlights the social divisions created by hunting, referring to 'the social symbolism that surrounds the chase'.[44] He likens hunters to outlaws, casting a foreboding, proprietorial shadow over the community: 'Hunts habitually trampled the crops of small rural proprietors, and made a virtue of these actions in their hunting songs'.[45]

A. H. Higginson, in *Foxhunting: Theory and practice*, elaborates on the kind of proprietorial chants that could be heard from the ranks of a meet, after a successful run:

> Oh, what were trampled pasture, and oh what was damaged wheat,
>
> . . .
>
> Oh, what were broken fences, what was stock all gone astray?
> There was stir and animation, the country-side was gay
> With all the pomp and glitter and pride of a hunting day![46]

This causing of so-called 'stir and animation' is a deliberate dumbing-down of hunting intrusions. (Unsurprisingly, Taylor observes that they caused most loss and disruption to poorer, less well-resourced members of the community.) Hunting, either by horse or while shooting, ultimately typified a close relationship to the land, which according to Jane Ridley (herself a historian as well as a hunter) perpetuated 'a proprietorship of traditional yeoman values'.[47] The sounding of the hunting horn is not dissimilar to a claimed authority, intended to denote power, seniority, rank, and servants. The wearing of markedly distinctive, particular clothing – as masters of the hunt wear, in the form of 'pinks' – may be seen as a kind of uniform or badge, again, intended to signify power, delineation, and masculinity. It was deliberately politicized,[48] and has a militaristic flavour:

> The panoply of uniforms and suggestion of a parade present in the hunt consolidated . . . traditional links with martial preparations for the battlefield. Moreover, there was an outline of the hierarchical order in the rigid precedence of master, kennelmen, whipper-in and earth-stopper.[49]

VI

As stated above, my main concern is with the institutionalized ethos of violence that hunting can represent, and its possible contribution to a wider abusive culture. We know that the hunted animal is frequently chased to exhaustion, outnumbered and surrounded by dogs who tear the animal to pieces. It is an understatement to say that it is not a peaceful death. That there is a great deal of violence directed toward the hunted animal, and that such animals suffer, is beyond question.

The concern of this chapter, however, is to examine the institutionalized violence that hunting exerts beyond the violence done to the hunted animals. First of all, the evidence shows that some hunters have little or no respect for the law, since they continue to hunt although hunting with hounds became illegal by an act of Parliament. Some hunters have asserted that they will continue to hunt whether hunting is legal or not. Incidentally, it should be noted that the violent behaviour of the hunters took place when hunting was legal and continues now that it is illegal. In particular, the evidence shows that property rights are sometimes disregarded as hunters trespass on private property. Furthermore, they either cannot control their dogs or do not attempt to do so. As a result, in at least one case, a dog ran onto a road and was killed by a passing car. These dogs, excitedly running in a pack, may maul or kill any other animal in their path – which may be someone's companion cat or dog – and in the process they often terrify the owner of the domestic animal who wants to protect his or her pet. Even more appalling is the violence directed by the hunters, and in one case even by a hunt steward, toward innocent bystanders or anyone who may try to monitor or observe their activity. Such people have been assaulted on more than one occasion.

What do these incidents show? They do not prove beyond all doubt that hunting contributes to a wider abusive culture, but there is a great deal of very suggestive anecdotal evidence that points in that direction. It should be noted that the evidence discussed in this chapter is not anecdotal in the sense that someone has said something that no one can verify. Indeed, some of the incidents described above are taken from legal reports that were thoroughly investigated and corroborated.

This descriptive information is only the first step in determining in a completely objective and scientific manner if, in fact, hunting leads to increased violence in the general culture. This information cries out for analysis: it is the raw data that must be systematized. We need to be able to answer questions such as: how often do hunters engage in violence? What is the precise nature of this violence? What percentage of hunters disregard the law? How often do hunters assault other people? How seriously are these people hurt? Are there other factors, such as hunters' ages, that influence the amount of violence? Is there enough consistent evidence that we can draw valid conclusions concerning the true nature of hunting? We must be able to answer such questions; we must have statistical findings if we are to determine with certainty the true nature of hunting, to know whether hunting does, in fact, lead to – and even encourage – violent and abusive behaviour.

Notes

1   This paper develops themes in the executive summary of evidence presented by the League Against Cruel Sports to the *Burns inquiry on hunting with dogs* (London: HMSO, 2000). One submission of the League was that 'The evidence . . . shows that hunting is closely associated with an abusive culture'. See http://www.defra.gov.uk/rural/hunting/inquiry/mainsections/huntingframe.htm.

2   The term 'blood sport' was first adopted by the reformer and humanitarian Henry Salt, to describe the inhumane treatment of animals for sport. See H. Salt (ed.), *Killing for sport* (London: George Bell and Sons, 1951), for an analysis of coursing, comparing stag and drag hunting, fox hunting, see also Salt's earlier book, *Animals' rights considered in relation to social progress* (originally published in 1892, reprinted by Open Gate Press, 1980).

3   J. Daigle, D. Hrubes, and I. Ajzen, 'A comparative study of beliefs, attitudes, and values among hunters, wildlife viewers, and other outdoor recreationists', *Human Dimensions of Wildlife* 7, 1 (2002): 1–19. The findings are neutral to the extent that they 'suggest that some activities are better suited than others to produce desired benefits for different types of individuals, and that outdoor recreationists need to be served in different ways to optimize the benefits they derive'. Research which has doubted the link between hunting and abuse of humans has conceded major limitations concerning the findings and research methods. For example, see C. P. Flynn, 'Hunting and illegal violence against humans and other animals: Exploring the relationship', *Society & Animals* 10, 2 (2002): 137–154.

4   The lawfulness of hunting is no longer seriously at issue, if indeed it ever was. The case of *R. v. Attorney-General* [2005] UKHL 56, [2005] 4 All ER 1253 was the final chapter in the legality debate. The courts had previously dismissed the constitutional challenge to the Hunting Act 2004. In both lower courts – the Queen's Bench Division, comprising of L.J. Maurice Kay and J. Collins, and the Court of Appeal, containing Lord Woolf, C.J. Phillips and L.J. May – declined to grant a declaration that either the Parliament Act 1949 or the Hunting Act 2004 were legally invalid. The House of Lords agreed, with L.J. Bingham giving the leading judgment. See T. Mullen, 'Reflections' on the case, *Legal Studies* 27, 1 (2007): 1–25. Mullen 'considers the question of whether the orthodox view of sovereignty is likely to be displaced in the foreseeable future by the view that Parliament's legislative power is subject to legal constraints'. He concludes that 'changes of this nature require the assent of the other institutions of government'.

5   H. E. Adair argues that 'the[se] . . . studies contain flawed methodology and, consequently, contribute little to determining the relationship between hunting and violence'. See 'The correlation between hunting and crime: A comment', *Society & Animals* 3, 2 (1995): 189–195. See also C. P. Flynn, 'Hunting and illegal violence', p. 138.

6   Flynn, 'Hunting and illegal violence', p. 139.

7   *Ibid.*

8   Perhaps with foresight to the different manifestations of abuse and corresponding protections that might be called for, s. 1(3) of the 2006 Act provides: 'The appropriate national authority may by regulations for all or any of the purposes of this Act – (a) extend the definition of "animal" so as to include invertebrates of any description; . . . (c) amend subsection (2) to extend the application of this Act to an animal from such earlier stage of its development as may be specified in the regulations'.

9 Jeremy Bentham, in *Indirect legislation*, chapter XIV, unpublished, University College London archives (UC).

10 For an excellent treatment of how the passing of the game laws secured the authority and place of the ruling or elite class, see S. Deuchar, *Sporting art in eighteenth-century England: A social and political history* (New Haven, CT: Yale University Press, 1988). A good overview is also found in P. Munsche, *Gentlemen and poachers: the English game laws, 1671–1831* (Cambridge: Cambridge University Press, 1981) and, anecdotally, D. Hay, 'Poaching and the game laws on Cannock Chase', in D. Hay, P. Linebaugh, and E. Thompson (eds), *Albion's fatal tree* (London: Penguin, 1975).

11 Human Rights Act 1998; See RSA journal, available at http://www.rsa.org.uk/journal/article.asp?articleID=717. Rabinder Singh QC represented the government in the case judicially reviewing the lawfulness of the Hunting Act 2004.

12 Hunting was already unlawful in Scotland at the time the English Hunting Act was passed, by virtue of the Protection of Wild Animals (Scotland) Act 2002, which was passed by the Scottish Parliament and received the Royal Assent on 15 March 2002. Broadly similar to, but not directly in parallel with, the Hunting Act, the validity of the Scottish statute has been unsuccessfully challenged on human rights grounds in Scottish courts (*Adams v. Scottish Ministers* [2002] UKHRR 1189 (Outer House) and [2004] SC 665: Scot CS 127 (Inner House).

13 The offences created by the Hunting Act are absolute. There is no provision equivalent to section 1 of the Protection of Animals Act 1911, where an element of some of the offences of cruelty to animals is that the offender causes the animal *unnecessary* suffering.

14 *R. v. Attorney General and others*, Court of Appeal (Civil Division) [2006] EWCA Civ. 817, para. 28.

15 The pioneer of offender profiling in the United Kingdom was Paul Britton, who has used criminal profiling in hundreds of high-profile police investigations since 1983.

16 *Cotswold Journal*, 1 March 2007.

17 *Western Gazette*, 22 February 2007.

18 *Malvern Gazette*, 2 February 2007.

19 *Western Daily Press*, 3 February 2007.

20 *Horse and Hound*, 19 April 2007.

21 *Western Gazette*, 4 November 2007.

22 *Western Morning News*, 10 March 2008.

23 *Worcester Evening News*, 29 December 2007.

24 K. Fukuda, 'Different views of animals and cruelty to animals: Cases in fox-hunting and pet-keeping in Britain', *Anthropology Today* 13, 5 (1997): 2–6. Perhaps lending further weight to the credentials of her research, Fukuda discloses the premise of her research as 'not to contribute to the moral judgement on hunting'.

25 *Ibid.*, p. 3.

26 *Ibid.*

27 *Ibid.*

28 *Ibid.*

29 *Ibid.*

30 *Ibid.*

31 *Ibid.*

32 *Ibid.*

33 *Ibid.*

34 *R. v. Attorney General and others*, Court of Appeal (Civil Division) [2006], [see p. 309 in text].

35 *R. v. Attorney General and others; R (on the application of Derwin and others) v. Attorney General and others*, Court of Appeal (Civil Division) [2006] EWCA Civ. 817, para. 35; emphasis added.

36 Generally, several studies report a variety of variables in attitudes towards the adequate treatment of animals, including upbringing, religious affiliation, sex, sex-roles, empathy, and personality. See J. Driscoll, 'Attitudes toward animal use', *Anthrozoös* 5 (1992): 32–39; A. Furnham, C. McManus, and D. Scott, 'Personality, empathy and attitudes to animal welfare', *Anthrozoös* 16 (2003): 135–146; G. G. Gallup and J. W. Beckstead, 'Attitudes toward animal research', *American Psychologist* (1988): 474–476; M. E. Hutchins and J. B. Armstrong, 'College students' attitudes toward animal use', *College Student Journal* 28 (1994): 258–266; R. Kimbal and J. P. Broida, 'Psychological profiles of students for and against vivisection using the Myers-Briggs Type Indicator', *Humane Innovations and Alternatives* 5 (1991): 232–235. Hunting is an example of a deficient learned response to interacting with wildlife. In particular, Hutchins and Armstrong (in 'College students' attitudes') found differences in attitudes towards animals between participants with urban versus rural upbringings, and men and women. By far the majority of hunters are men who claim hunting as 'a natural way to engage with the countryside', which would fit the template of what Hutchings and Armstrong posit as increased tendencies towards treating animals with violence.

37 See N. Taylor, and T. Signal, 'Empathy and attitudes towards animals', *Anthrozoös* 18, 1 (2005): 18–27; also J. Driscoll, 'Attitudes toward animal use'; and also A. Furnham, C. McManus, and D. Scott, 'Personality, empathy and attitudes to animal welfare'.

38 This failure to differentiate between poorly treating animals, and poorly treating humans, is clearly established in the empirical work of a number of sociologists and psychologists. In particular, see N. Taylor and T. Signal, 'Attitudes to animals: An indicator of interpersonal violence?' *Journal of the Home Economics Institute of Australia, Inc.* 11, 3 (2004): 9–12.

39 M. Kheel, 'License to kill: An ecofeminist critique of hunters' discourse', in C. J. Adams and J. Donovan (eds), *Animals and women: Feminist theoretical perspectives* (Durham, NC: Duke University Press, 1995), pp. 85–125, cited in C. P. Flynn, 'Hunting and illegal violence', p. 138.

40 *Ibid.*

41 N. Taylor, 'Child abuse, domestic violence and animal abuse: Considering the links', *Child Abuse Prevention Newsletter, Australian Institute of Family Studies* 12, 1 (2004): 16–18.

42 *Ibid.*

43 L. Colley, *Britons: Forging the nation 1707–1830* (New Haven, CT: Yale University Press, 1992), pp. 170–173.

44 N. Taylor, 'Child abuse', p. 41.

45 *Ibid.*

46 Quoted in A. H. Higginson, *Foxhunting: Theory and practice* (London: Collins, 1948), pp. 210–11, cited in Taylor, 'Child abuse', p. 41.

47 Jane Ridley, *Fox hunting* (London: Collins, 1990), pp. 78–80.

48 'As late as the 1860s the wearing of hunting pink by Lord George Bentinck and his followers was expressive of an unrepentant Toryism reluctant to concede ground to modernizers within the party' (Taylor, 'Child abuse', p. 33).

49 Taylor, 'Child abuse', p. 34. For a penetrating analysis of how attitudes among the hunting fraternity were in flux, see Keith Thomas, *Man and the natural world: Changing attitudes in England 1500–1800* (London: Penguin, 1983), pp. 60–165.

26

Hunting as a Morally Suspect Activity

PRISCILLA N. COHN AND ANDREW LINZEY

The purpose of our chapter is to suggest that hunting is a morally suspect activity. By 'hunting' in this context we mean sport hunting (sometimes called 'recreational hunting' or 'trophy hunting'), and we shall focus on deer hunting as practised in the USA, although our comments will obviously have relevance to a range of 'sporting' activities with animals. By 'morally suspect' we refer to an activity the moral basis of which is open to question. Our concern is that hunting may be suspect in the sense of harming both the animals involved *and* the people engaged in it.

I

That hunting is suspect in the sense of harming animals seems beyond doubt, so we shall concentrate on this aspect first. Much has been said and written about socially and culturally condemned abuse that is illegal, especially cruelty to companion animals, but it is also necessary to remind ourselves of animal cruelty that is socially or culturally condoned, even praised. Such cruelty is widespread and often passes unnoticed precisely because it is accepted by society; it is how things are done; it is assumed that the status quo is necessary although, of course, it is not.

What does 'socially or culturally condoned cruelty' mean? The definition of cruelty that Frank R. Ascione gives is useful if we simply drop the words 'socially unacceptable'. Cruelty is then simply the intentional 'behaviour that systematically causes unnecessary pain, suffering, or distress to and/or death of an animal'.[1]

Cruelty is often acceptable and approved by society when financial gain is involved. The cruelty laws in the US, for instance, do not apply to those animals classed as 'game'. But this classification is arbitrary and thus morally arbitrary. It is as if animals hunted as game refer to specific species that somehow are incapable of suffering or as if any suffering involved was necessary. For example, it would be considered cruel if, for your entertainment, you shot your dog with a razor-tipped arrow designed to cut through sinew and flesh, but it is deemed not cruel to do so to a deer: bow hunting is an acceptable recreation for many people. Obviously 'game' or wild animals are sentient creatures capable of experiencing pain and suffering. From a logical point of view, it makes little sense to exclude from our discussion – or laws – the pain and suffering of certain classes of animals just because some find it entertaining or amusing to chase them or shoot them.

The definition of cruelty given above refers to the notion of 'unnecessary' pain. Recreational hunting, as the name suggests, is a form of recreation or amusement. The common understanding of necessity involves something inevitable, unavoidable, or absolutely essential. The pain involved in recreational hunting is not necessary because hunting itself is not necessary. To hunt is deliberately to cause intense discomfort or death to satisfy nonessential – and indeed often frivolous – human desires. To exclude some animals from the definition of cruelty really means – to put it bluntly – that society disapproves of some instances of cruelty while it approves of others. It would appear that society believes there is good cruelty and bad cruelty.

Some may protest that hunters are not *intentionally* cruel, in that they do not set out (at least in all cases) to cause suffering. Some of them indeed would baulk at the very idea that they were involved in cruelty. But whatever their subjective mindset is, they intentionally kill and do so in a manner that is not normally humane (as we go on to show), so they act cruelly whether or not they think so or intend to do so.

Most people seem to think that hunting deer in particular is not cruel because the deer are shot and die instantaneously. Now we do not want to deny that in some, limited cases, that might be true. Leaving aside for the moment whether it can ever be justifiable to kill an animal simply for recreation, we accept that it is possible for an expert marksman to render an animal immediately unconscious. But that that is not automatically, evenly routinely, the case is shown by the accounts that hunters themselves give of their own activity. Many books on hunting give instructions on how hunters should follow a wounded deer to finish it off.

Consider the following statements provided by a guide to hunting:

- A gunshot to the rear legs cripples the animal and facilitates another shot.
- A deer that runs in a 'humped up' position and takes short strides has usually been hit.
- A wound in the rear will sometimes cause the deer to kick like a donkey in its panic.
- With a lung shot through both lungs, the deer will usually run no more than 80 yards. If only one lung was punctured, the deer can run 600 yards or more . . . deer wounded here leave lots of blood sign which is distinctively pink and frothy with bubbles.

- Liver shots allow deer to run 80 yards or so and take *about 5 minutes* to kill on average.
- Kidney shots usually send the deer 90 yards. They die *within 10 to 15 minutes* and leave a thin, dark blood trail.
- Gut shots mean that the deer seldom dies sooner than *15 to 16 hours* after hit.
- Gut-shot deer leave green and yellow in their blood trails.[2]

Of course, it does not automatically follow that movement after being shot, by itself, indicates that the animal is still either sensible and/or alive. There can be a variety of involuntary reflex actions after death, some of which may be distasteful to witness, but they happen *after* death. But even allowing for this, it is clear from the examples above that an extended period of suffering is envisaged.

Again, some might protest that the appearance of blood can indicate a swift kill. But what these examples show is that although vital organs may be hit, the deer does not die instantly; indeed, even when such vitals are hit, death can still be protracted. The blood trails show, not instantaneous death, but rather that the deer was still moving in an attempt to escape or seeking a place to hide. Even worse, a headshot that might facilitate a quick kill is not always recommended. The same author also discusses the shots that might ruin a trophy. He notes that '[t]he spine, the neck and two main arteries located here offer a good target. A neck mount might be blemished beyond repair for a perfect taxidermy job with this shot'. He also cautions a prospective hunter to

> Avoid head shots except when they are absolutely necessary. . . . Between the eyes is, of course, the brain shot, which will drop the deer quickly and also, with the wrong bullet, ruin a trophy quickly.[3]

Another example may suffice. In his book, *Deer and deer hunting: A guide for serious hunters*, Robert Wegner includes a chapter on crippling losses, that is deer that are left in the woods, some of which escape from the hunter after being critically wounded, and some of which survive. He presents more than fifty studies on this topic showing that the calculated crippling loss (as a percentage of the legal harvest left in the woods) range from a low of 2.9 to 10.9 in one study to thirty-five to one hundred and fifty per cent in another.[4] He quotes scientists who suggest that, 'Few hunters have the will power to resist shooting at deer that are beyond the effective killing range of their weapon, or that are moving too fast to be hit consistently in a vital spot'.[5]

Included at the end of Wegner's chapter are a number of statements concerning this problem by what he calls the '"leading members" of the deer hunting fraternity'. For instance, Wegner quotes Paul Brandreth who writes that

> too many hunters shoot at any part of the animal's body, instead of at a selected

point. . . . Hence the bloody trails, the cripples that succumb slowly under the hardships of the following winter . . . [6]

Similarly, Lawrence Koller deplores the lingering death inflicted on deer:

> fewer of these fine animals should be wounded to stagger off into swamps and thickets and die slowly and miserably, alone, without comfort, not knowing why; with festering wounds, tongue and throat slowly burning for water they cannot reach; with fever gradually consuming their great strength and vitality, and their blood slowly flowing to the forest floor, taking with it the final spark of vigour. These whitetail deer are warm blooded creatures, like ourselves. They must feel pain to much the same degree, perhaps even more, because of their extreme sensitivity.[7]

In short, while instantaneous death may be possible with either a gun or bow, it seems likely that a large proportion of deer will not die immediately and that some may suffer a lingering death. Their pain and suffering is described by the hunters themselves so it is difficult not to conclude that such a practice renders the animals liable to cruelty, as traditionally defined.

II

We now turn to whether, apart from the harm done to the animals, such activity also harms the hunters themselves. At first sight the suggestion might seem implausible. Millions of Americans hunt for sport. Recreational hunting is legal in all fifty states of the US and is, as we have already indicated, a socially condoned activity. How could such a well-entrenched activity of such longevity actually harm its practitioners?

We accept at the outset that there is no knockdown argument that justifies our suspicion. Indeed, there is a dearth of hard statistical and other evidence either way. But the question is, are there some considerations, however indirect or tangential, that make the suspicion at least reasonable?

The first consideration concerns the statistical link between illegal cruelty to, or abuse of, domestic animals and antisocial behaviour that has already been established and corroborated by a number of researchers in various fields. If that link is sound, we have to ask what rational grounds we could have for confining that link to domestic animals. How rational is it to assume that the abuser who abuses women and children will stop at family pets? In fact, we know that the cycle of violence that so often includes children, and women, also includes *all* family pets, both domestic and wild. There is no indication in the current literature that legality as such and in itself is an observed boundary when it comes to abusive treatment. Why then should we suppose that hunting cruelty – rather than, say, the abuse of children – is exempt from the patterns of abuse that we may detect elsewhere? While these logical considerations do not prove that hunting harms the hunter in the sense of robbing him or her (though it is usually 'him') of compassion and empathy, they may point to such a claim being reasonable, perhaps even likely.

We suggest that the apparent lack of hard evidence about the harm of hunting – from a human point of view – is glaringly due to the question not even being asked, and the connection hardly ever being considered. There is little, if any, data concerning hunting and extremes of antisocial behaviour – such as murder – and little data on lesser forms of violence – such as beating, hitting, shoving, and so on. Occasionally, in first person accounts, one finds that the perpetrator of cruelty is said to hunt.[8] A study by the La Crosse Community Coalition Against Violence (CCAV) involved 'a small sample of male participants in the local abuser treatment programme. Of the men surveyed, over 50 per cent said they were hunters and owned guns or rifles'.[9]

The original question remains: is it possible, or likely, that only illegal violence is related to antisocial behaviour and that socially accepted or legal violence is not? If illegal violence is not totally unlike legal violence, then from a logical point of view it would follow that activities involving legal violence, such as hunting, would also be linked to antisocial behaviour. Of course this position rests on an assumption concerning the similarity between legal and illegal violence, but is this not a reasonable conclusion, even a likely one?

III

The second consideration concerns the number of incidents in which those involved in antisocial behaviour – even murder – have themselves had a history of hunting. It is noteworthy that the fact that a particular murderer is also a hunter is revealed in the newspaper accounts of murder cited below, since reporters do not generally ask about hunting. Even more so is that this fact showed up so frequently in a random study involving only the murders that occurred or were written about in the period when the present essay was written. Consider the following examples (names and other means of identification have been removed):

13 November 2005, Pennsylvania. [An] 18 year old, pleaded guilty to two counts of first degree murder for killing both parents of his 14-year-old girlfriend. . . . The murder occurred after [his girl friend's] parents forbade him to continue to see their daughter. When [he] came to talk with [parents], either in his car or with him he had a .40 caliber Glock, a high-powered hunting rifle, and a hunting knife. The previous year he had posted 20 photographs on his blog, which he had labeled 'hunting 2004'. The blog was later removed. Some of the photographs show him posing with a deer he had shot, some of his friends with their kills, and one of him smiling as he guts a bloody deer.[10]

29 September 2006, Wisconsin. Many people observed [a] 16 year old, as he killed the principal of his school. A blog written during his trial by WISC-TV reporters

said he had 'hunted frequently' and 'relished hunting and fishing with his father'. At his trial, questions were raised about whether he should be tried as a juvenile or as an adult. According to newspaper reports, the county district attorney asserted that [he] asked a detective on the day of the shooting whether a felony would be cleansed from his record when he reached 18 'because he wanted to keep hunting'.[11]

6 October 2006, Pennsylvania. [A] 32 year old, walked into a one-room school. After releasing a pregnant woman and the male students, he tied up the 10 remaining young girls and then shot them. Accounts vary somewhat, but three girls died immediately, two more died overnight. The other girls were seriously wounded and hospitalized. Before the police could enter, he killed himself. According to the *Philadelphia Inquirer*, he had no previous police record and no record of violence. The same article stated that 'Guns were a cherished part of his lineage' and that 'his fall passion was deer hunting with both gun and bow'.[12]

14 October 2006, Iowa. [A] 22 year old, shot and killed his entire family: his father, mother and three younger sisters with a .22 caliber rifle. 'Both [of his parents] loved the outdoors, hunting and boating, and their four children shared those loves'.[13]

14 July 2007, Wyoming. Police found evidence that [a] 36 year old, 'an avid outdoorsman', and a trained sniper, shot his wife – from whom he was separated – in the head as she was singing in [a] restaurant. When police finally discovered where he was and approached him, he shot and killed himself. [He] was 'a big hunter' and in fact posted a photograph on the internet of himself with a deer he had killed; also posted was a photograph of his wife with the first elk she had shot apparently in 'happier times'.[14]

30 July 2007, Pennsylvania. [A] thirteen-year-old told authorities that she took her father's 12 gauge shotgun that he had taught her to use and shot him in the face, killing him while he was asleep. She said her father, who was 'an avid hunter', had been sexually abusing her since she was 7 years old. A neighbour said she heard the young girl screaming at night. It was also alleged that her 14-year-old brother was sexually abused by his father. Authorities reported that the house where they lived was in 'deplorable' conditions, filled with trash, fleas, and animal faeces. Four dogs, some of which were emaciated and lacking hair, four cats, some rabbits and other animals were removed from the house by animal control officers.[15]

10 September 2007, Missouri. The remains of the two children of [an] estranged couple . . . were recently found and identified by dental records. The children had been missing since their father picked them up for a weekend visit [in] 2004. [He] was convicted in 2006 of parental kidnapping with the intent to terrorize his ex-wife and sentenced to 38 years in prison. The bodies were found in an area near the Missouri River where [he] was known to hunt deer (or, according to an Associated Press release, 'to poach'). [He] was charged with two counts of first degree murder in 2007.[16]

Even more striking are those examples of where the murderer himself identifies killing a person with killing an animal, as is revealed in the confessions of two murderers. One serial killer described how he would take a prostitute to his remote hunting cabin, rape and torture her, and then release her giving her a head start before he hunted her down and killed her with a hunting knife or with a high-powered rifle. He said it was like 'going after a trophy Dall sheep or a grizzly bear'.[17] And another also compared the killing of a fellow student with the killing of an animal. In a documentary movie of his life, he said that he felt no different shooting his fellow student than he did shooting a bird.[18]

What can be concluded, if anything, from these reports that recent murderers were also 'avid hunters' or from the confessions of the murderers that connected their hunting with the killing of humans? It is, of course, notoriously difficult to isolate one factor as the cause when confronted with the complex web of abusive relations. A host of questions present themselves: was hunting only an example of the general aptitude towards violence exemplified by offenders? Did hunting magnify those pre-existing tendencies towards aggression? If so, what is the mechanism whereby hunting exacerbates propensities towards violence? Was hunting a cause or a symptom, or both? And wasn't the ready access to hunting weapons at least a clear factor in many of these events?

It may be easier to state what conclusions cannot be drawn. Clearly not every hunter murders people; indeed the vast majority of hunters do not murder people. With several million hunters in North America and many thousands of murders each year, one is bound to find that some hunters are involved in murders. We are certainly not talking about a simple relationship of cause and effect. Could we then assert that it is pure coincidence that a number of murderers were also hunters? The answer is that we do not know for sure. While it is within the realm of possibility, the ease and frequency with which we discover that rural murders involve hunters suggests that the notion of mere coincidence may be unlikely.

Reports of spousal or child abuse, as far as we are aware, do not identify the abuser as either a hunter or non-hunter. This lack of data means we have not collected evidence that might prove to be significant in establishing a link between hunting, as a socially acceptable form of animal cruelty, and human violence. A lack of information, however, does not prove that there is no relationship. The bottom line is that the question wasn't even asked, and that is the reason for the dearth of statistical evidence.

IV

The third consideration concerns the desensitization that is involved in frequent acts of killing or abuse. Is such desensitization towards animals likely to spill over into desensitization towards, or even tolerance of, human suffering? If that is true of illegal abuse, it is difficult to find the grounds for saying that such activities, even if commonplace and legal, should not also carry the same, or similar, adverse affects.

Some of the greatest thinkers throughout the ages have condemned animal abuse and discussed the damaging effect of cruelty on one's own humanity, as well as on society and the way in which we treat other people. St Augustine, for example, relates the story of a student of his, later to become a bishop, who accompanied some friends to the gladiatorial games. Augustine described the amphitheatre as 'seething with the lust for cruelty'. His young friend closed his eyes, determined to ignore the 'atrocities' taking place. Suddenly the crowd roared, and the young man opened his eyes to see what was happening:

> When he saw the blood, it was as though he had drunk a deep draught of savage poison. Instead of turning away, he fixed his eyes upon the scene and drank in all its frenzy. . . . He revelled in the wickedness of the fighting and was drunk with the fascination of bloodshed. . . . He grew hot with excitement, and when he left the arena, he carried away with him a diseased mind which would leave him no peace until he came back again . . . [19]

St Thomas Aquinas echoes the theme that cruelty to animals may lead to cruelty to humans. He writes that statements in Scripture against cruelty to animals are designed 'to turn the mind of man away from cruelty which might be used on other men, lest a person through practicing cruelty on brutes might go on to do the same to men'.[20] And St Thomas More specifically castigates hunters who 'seek pleasure from the slaughter and mutilation of some small helpless animal'. Utopians count hunting as 'unworthy of free men' and judge that the 'enjoyment in beholding deaths, even in beasts, comes from an inherently cruel disposition or from the habitual practice of cruelty in so brutal a pleasure'.[21]

Thinkers as diverse as Michel de Montaigne and John Locke also concur that cruelty is a dangerous trait. 'Natures that are bloodthirsty toward animals give proof of a natural propensity toward cruelty', says Montaigne, maintaining that the slaughter of animals in Rome only whetted the gladiators' appetite for killing fellow humans.[22] From observation, Locke concludes that children habituated to abuse animals are on a slippery slope to abusing humans because 'the custom of tormenting and killing of beasts will, by degrees, harden their minds even towards men; and they who delight in the suffering and destruction of inferior creatures, will not be apt to be very compassionate or benign to those of their own kind'.[23] And Immanuel Kant emphasizes the same point when considering Hogarth's engravings entitled 'The Stages of Cruelty' (1751). Hogarth 'shows how cruelty grows and develops. He shows the child's cruelty to animals, pinching the tail of a dog or a cat; he then depicts the grown man in his cart running over a child, and lastly the culmination of cruelty in murder. He thus brings home to us in a terrible fashion the rewards of cruelty'.[24]

Even José Ortega y Gasset, a contemporary Spanish thinker who glorifies bull fighting and wrote a book in praise of hunting, admits that the sight of blood is like a drug. Blood, for Ortega, is an essential part of the hunt. Because blood 'carries and symbolises life', when it is spilled it produces at first 'disgust and terror', but this is only a first impression. If the 'blood flows abundantly ... it intoxicates, excites, maddens both man and beast ... [since] Blood has unequalled orgiastic power'.[25] Ortega asserts that such 'intoxication aroused by the sight of blood' is one of the ingredients of a hunt without which 'the spirit of the hunt disappears'.[26] In this connection, he refers to both the Spanish bullfights and the ancient Roman games. For Ortega, all of this blood, from both the animals and the humans in the ancient games, as well as the blood of the tortured bull in the bullring, acts like a 'stupefying drug'. 'Stupefying' here means 'to make stupid', that is, lacking reason, or marked by unreasoned acting, rather than being 'dulled in feeling or sensation'. Hunting, for Ortega, is a 'return to Nature' or to Paleolithic man, to the proto-human, who hunted and who was part animal and part human, so to speak. When one hunts one is moved by 'instinct' and becomes like an animal (if animals cannot reason). Hunting 'is the only normal case in which the killing of one creature constitutes the delight of another'.[27] If so, then hunting certainly desensitizes, if not warps the individual involved.

Although different practices are referred to, it is striking that so many philosophers holding different, even opposing views in general, and from so many different historical periods, all maintain that cruelty to animals has a power to desensitize individuals and make them violent to other humans. The dramatic way that both Augustine and Ortega write about 'blood lust' applies equally to hunting. If the blood spurts and is 'maddening', it does not matter for our purposes if the blood is spilled in ancient or modern times, in hunting or in circuses, the point about its effect on the human onlooker remains.

Now it may be claimed that the consideration of desensitization, even if valid, works both ways. Hunters may be desensitized, but they may also be able to compartmentalize their feelings so that there is no real danger to human subjects. Whether this bifurcation is ever total, however, seems unlikely. Although some devoted hunters write about the pangs of sadness they experience when they wound or kill an animal, it is only a passing phenomenon. Ted Kerasote, for example, writes:

> Still I hesitate, for though I can lose myself in the hunting, I have never been able to stop thinking about its results ... that this being before me – who sees, who smells, who *knows* – will no longer be among us. ... And I don't know how to escape this incongruous pain out of which we grow, this unresolvable unfairness, other than saying that I would rather be caught in this lovely tragedy with those whom I love, than with those far away, whose death I cannot own ... [28]

And James A. Swan claims that

> the modern hunter is challenged not so much by fear as by overcoming guilt ...

There is a special fondness in our hearts for wild things, and a hunter must work through guilt feelings to be successful.[29]

Although Ortega claims that 'Death is essential because without it there is no authentic hunting', he also asserts that, 'Every good hunter is uneasy in the depth of his conscience when faced with the death he is about to inflict on the enchanting animal'.[30]

However, even when hunters write about the regret of killing a once vibrant animal, the feeling does not persist; it is not so strong that the hunter ceases to hunt or condemns hunting. Experienced hunters have learned to overcome this sadness, or to rationalize it away, so that it is typically a momentary or passing feeling. The fact that hunters can so easily extinguish what would seem to be a natural feeling of compassion is an indication of the psychological cost of hunting.

Most importantly of all, it is difficult to see how there is a significant difference between the diminished empathy of the hunter who kills animal after animal and the diminished empathy of the person who abuses his or her pets, spouse or children. It is the violence that is damaging psychologically – not whether it is legal or illegal – and it is the resultant lack of empathy that in turn is linked to domestic animal abuse and to antisocial behaviour.

V

As we said at the beginning, there is no absolute proof that hunting is linked to antisocial behaviour, but there are, we submit, considerations enough to give us pause. It is difficult to ask researchers and scholars to examine a practice that so many see as a harmless pastime or even as a valued tradition, but that is precisely what is necessary if we are really concerned with what well may be a possible well-spring of cruelty and aggression directed at both human and non-human animals. Whether our suspicions will be reinforced by empirical evidence, only time will tell. But we shall never know – with any degree of certainty – unless the question is put firmly on the academic agenda. What we know about the links between (largely domestic) animal abuse and human violence has only begun to occupy centre stage as the result of tenacious and persistent (and often costly) research, and even now we are far from having anything like complete answers to many questions, especially those concerning the precise nature of this link. We need new generations able to serve the cause of wild animals, as past researchers have served the cause of domestic ones.

Notes

1 F. R. Ascione, in F. R. Ascione and P. Arkow (eds), *Child abuse, domestic violence, and animal abuse: Linking the circles of compassion for prevention and intervention* (West Lafayette, IN: Purdue University Press, 1999), p. 51, citing his previous work, 'Children who are cruel to animals: A review of research and implications for developmental psychopathology', *Anthrozoös* 6 (1993): 226–47.

2   Gary Lawton Hargis, *Bambo: Whitetail deer hunting 101: A complete guide* (Fowlerville, MI: Wilderness Adventure Books, 1990), pp. 139–42, emphases added.

3   Hargis, *Bambo*, p. 138.

4   Robert Wegner, *Deer and deer hunting: A guide for serious hunters* (Harrisburg, PA: Stackpole Books, 1984), p. 239. In his second book, titled *Deer and deer hunting, Book 2: Strategies and tactics for the advanced hunter*, published in 1992, Wegner once again includes a chapter on crippling loss, although this time he refers to more recent studies, all of which involve bow hunting.

5   Wegner, *Deer and deer hunting*, p. 240.

6   Paul Brandreth, *Trails of enchantment* (New York: Watt, 1939), pp. 318ff; cited in Wegner, *Deer and deer hunting*, p. 244.

7   Lawrence Koller, *Shots at whitetails* (New York: Knopf, [1948] 1975), pp. 359ff; cited in Wegner, *Deer and deer hunting*, p. 240.

8   Ascione and Arkow, *Child abuse, domestic violence, and animal abuse*, p. 137.

9   *Ibid.*, p. 171.

10 The individual's blog was removed, but before this happened the Committee to Abolish Sport Hunting (C.A.S.H.) published the photographs in Anne Muller's article, 'DEC's Solution to world's ills: Lower the hunting age', *CASH Courier* Newsletter, Winter 2005. The photographs can be seen at http://www.all-creatures.org/cash/cc2005-w-dec.html.

11 See   http//editorialmatters.lee.net/articles/2007//12/11/stories/top-tories/9vnews. 18211; '[The individual] sentenced to life in prison', *Baraboo News Republic*, 7 May 2008.

12 *Philadelphia Inquirer*, 16 October 2006.

13 *The Gazette* (Cedar Rapids-Iowa City, IA), 18 October 2006; see also *The Gazette*, 16 October 2006.

14 See http://www.postchronicle.com/news/ original/article21292539.shtml.

15 See http://www.post-gazette.com/pg/07213/805918-55.stm.

16 'Bones found in shallow grave may be children kidnapped in 2004', Associated Press, 10 September 2007, and also 'Bones confirmed as missing MO kids', AP Press Release, 20 November 2007. Our thanks to Anne Muller for bringing some of the most recent hunter/murderer examples to our attention.

17 See http://www.crimelibrary.com/serial_killers/weird/robert_hansen/6.html.

18 From 'The killer within' directed by Macky Alston. The producer is Sandra M. Itkof, and the world premier was 13 September 2006; Philadelphia Film Festival, April 5–18 2007; see http://dsc.discovery.com/promo/killerwithin/; http://www. mdb.com/title/tt0497398/, and http://phillyfests.bside.com/2007/ ?mediaTab= filmDetails&_view=_filmdetails&filmId=15659537.

19 Augustine, *Confessions*, VI, 8.

20 Aquinas, *Summa contra gentiles*, III, 2, 112–13.

21 Thomas More, *Utopia*, trans. and ed. H. V. S. Ogden (New York: Appleton-Century-Crofts, Inc., 1949), p. 51.

22 Michel de Montaigne, 'Of cruelty' [1578–1580] in vol. 2 of *The complete essays of Montaigne*, trans. Donald M. Frame (New York: Garden City, 1960), p. 109.

23 Locke, 'Cruelty' in 'Some thoughts concerning education' [1693], in the *Works of John Locke in ten volumes*, 10th edn (London: 1801), p. 112; extract in Andrew Linzey and Paul A. B. Clarke (eds), *Animal rights: A historical anthology* (New York: Columbia University Press, 2004), p. 119.

24 Kant, 'Duties towards animals and spirits', in *Lectures on ethics, 1775–1780*, trans. Louis Infield (Indianapolis and Cambridge: Hackett Publishing Company, 1963), p. 240.

25 José Ortega y Gasset, *Meditations on hunting*, trans. Howard B. Wescot (New York: Charles Scribner's Sons, 1972), p. 91.

26 *Ibid.*, p. 95.

27 *Ibid.*, p. 92.

28 Kerasote also narrates how he follows an elk he had wounded: 'I climb over several fallen trees and find her lying not thirty feet away, her head turned over her left shoulder, great brown eyes utterly calm. My heart tears apart. I shoot and she drops her head. As she kicks her final shudders I go to her, sitting with my hip against her spine, my hand on her flank, feeling her warmth, her pulse, her life, changing states. She is enormous, and beautiful, and my throat constricts'. And then describes how he 'slit the hide on her belly . . . I open her peritoneum and go inside her up to my elbows. As I puncture her diaphragm, steam emerges around my shoulders with a gasp. Cutting away her heart, I feel hot blood bathe my arms . . . I discover a piece of meat on my finger. I put it in my mouth, chew it and swallow it. She tastes like warm, raw elk . . . I smile because I can feel saliva lubricating my mouth', all from *Bloodties: Nature, culture and the hunt* (New York: Kodansha International, 1993) pp. 245–247. If there is sympathy for the animal here, it appears to be quickly over-come by the taste of flesh.

29 James A. Swan, *In defense of hunting* (San Francisco: HarperCollins, 1995), p. 290.

30 Ortega y Gasset, *Meditations on hunting*, pp. 96, 88.

Dolphin Drive Hunts and the Socratic Dictum: 'Vice Harms the Doer'

THOMAS I. WHITE

Discussion of ethical issues related to human–dolphin interaction typically concentrates on the question of whether or not *dolphins* are harmed by the practices in question. The deaths and injuries of dolphins connected with human fishing are defended with claims that the species of dolphins affected aren't 'endangered' by the practices used. Captivity of dolphins in the entertainment industry is defended with assertions that the dolphins are treated 'humanely' and that they even form strong relationships with their trainers. This chapter, however, shifts the focus of discussion and explores the negative impact of ethically questionable human/dolphin interaction on *humans*. Applying the Socratic dictum that 'vice harms the doer', this paper details the harm to humans that results from a particularly notorious example of human abuse of dolphins – the Japanese 'drive hunts'. This chapter begins with a description of the drive hunts themselves, but my main concern is actually *the defences offered* for the hunts. My central claim is that the unethical treatment of dolphins produces precisely the sort of harm in the personality that Socrates describes – a weakened intellect that simply serves some desire. Socrates contends that the consequence of vice is that a desire for something grows so strong that satisfying it is more important than perceiving reality accurately, dealing with uncomfortable truths about a situation, and respecting the canons of logic. And this damage is evident in the defences of the drive hunts.

'Drive Hunts'

The Japanese 'drive hunts' take place annually from September through April.[1] Sanctioned by the government, the hunts occur mainly in the town of Taiji. Using noise or nets, fishermen drive hundreds of dolphins and other small cetaceans into shallow water. The cetaceans are killed in the water – slowly bleeding to death. Or, they are caught with a hook, hoisted out of the water by a rope tied around their flukes, and transported to a site where they can be killed out of public view. The hunts slaughter thousands of dolphins each year.

The dolphins were traditionally killed for their meat and blubber – although there is debate about how much meat is eaten by humans and how much goes to fertilizer and pet food. Recently, it has become apparent that the drive hunts have become a major source of captive dolphins for the aquarium industry.

The drive hunts have been roundly condemned by a variety of conservation and animal welfare groups.[2] The World Association of Zoos and Aquariums considers the hunts 'inhumane', has denounced the practice of collecting dolphins from the hunts for use in captivity, and has urged the Japanese government to stop the hunts.[3] The Scientific Committee of the International Whaling Commission has opposed the hunts since 1992.[4] Marine scientists, in particular, decry the practice. Diana Reiss, director of the marine mammal research programme at the New York Aquarium's Osborn Laboratories of Marine Science, characterizes the hunt as 'a brutal and inhumane practice that violates all standards for animal welfare'.[5]

For two years, a group of marine scientists met with Japanese government officials and presented findings about dolphin brain anatomy, intelligence, social behaviour, ecology, and physiology. When this failed to persuade the Japanese government to stop the hunts, a coalition of scientists launched a public campaign in November 2006.[6] The controversy will probably continue for years.

Why the Hunts are Wrong

From an ethical perspective, there is no question that the Japanese drive hunts are seriously wrong. I have argued elsewhere that the scientific evidence is now strong enough to support the claim that dolphins are, like humans, self-aware, intelligent beings with emotions, personalities, and the capacity to control their actions. Accordingly, dolphins should be regarded as 'non-human persons' and valued as *individuals*.[7] Even if dolphins were to die swiftly and painlessly in the hunts, their deaths would still be the moral equivalent of the murder of a human being. However, not only do these dolphins typically die in a slow and agonizing way, they also witness the similar deaths of those around them. Even dolphins who survive are likely to be traumatized by the event. This is quite clearly abuse and brutality.

Defences

Defences of two dimensions of the drive hunts are offered – the hunts themselves and the aquarium industry's involvement in them.

The hunts themselves

Although there is no "official" defence of the hunts, a reconstruction of the arguments put forth by various parties suggests that there are four elements to the defence: environmental, economic, cultural, and ethical.

- First, the hunts are said to be consistent with the sustainable use of marine resources.
- The economic defence surfaces in a couple of ways. The hunts are regulated by the Japanese government so that they are limited to areas where fishermen are struggling to get by. Cetaceans are also seen as competitors with humans for fish and squid. Fewer dolphins are said to mean more dependable and abundant catches.
- The cultural defence is grounded in the fact that the hunts originated in the fifteenth century and in the idea that there is a contemporary culinary culture of eating cetacean meat in Japan.
- Ethical objections to the hunts are rejected as ethnocentric, and the hunts are defended as being no more objectionable than hunting other wild animals.

The hunts as a source of captive dolphins

Defenses offered for using the hunts as a source of captive dolphins are typically humanitarian ones – saving dolphins who otherwise would be killed.

The harm resulting from the defences

There are so many flaws with the defences of the drive hunts that it would be easy to dismiss them as disingenuous rationalizations for self-interested behaviour. Yet despite the weakness of these arguments, I think that supporters genuinely believe them. And I think it is this fact that reveals the main *human* harm that proceeds from the drive hunts. That is, I contend that these apparently sincere defences of such obvious brutality against dolphins are the product of the kind of harm that Socrates believes is produced by vice – a weakened intellect.[8]

Socrates: Vice Harms the Doer

One of Socrates' most central – and most counter-intuitive – ideas is that 'vice harms the doer'.[9] That is, when we treat someone unethically, we actually hurt ourselves more than we hurt our victim. The ultimate reason to act ethically, then, is self-interest.

While this idea surfaces in a variety of dialogues, the best description of exactly how vice harms the doer is found in the *Gorgias*.[10] This dialogue ultimately tackles the question of the value of moral virtue. For the purposes of this paper, the most important part is the exchange between Socrates and Callicles.

Callicles is an intelligent, ambitious, young Athenian who is hungry for wealth and power. He is talented, educated, refined – but quite immoral. He contends that people who are bright and cunning should rule the city because they are superior to the rest of the citizenry. He argues that the strong should take whatever they want as long as they can get away with it, and indulge themselves in every kind of pleasure. He rejects fairness, equality, and moderation as conventional ideas of morality which he dismisses as ways that inferior people make virtues out of their own weaknesses and hold superior people in check. In Socrates' reply to Callicles, the philosopher identifies how Callicles has been harmed by his lack of scruples. Socrates claims that Callicles' desires have become so strong that they are not only the central, controlling element of his life, but they have also weakened his intellect.

Socrates points out that Callicles' mind is, in effect, in thrall to his desires. Socrates describes Callicles as someone enslaved by the idea of pleasing the two current loves of his life – one, a beautiful young man; the other, the Athenian public. And Callicles will say whatever he must to please them. Socrates remarks:

> Now I have noticed that in each instance, whatever your favorite says, however his opinions may go, for all your cleverness you are unable to contradict him, but constantly shift back and forth at his whim. If you are making a speech in the Assembly and the Athenian public disagrees, you change and say what it desires; and in the presence of the beautiful young son of Pyrilampes your experience is precisely similar. You are unable to resist the plans or the assertions of your favorite; and the result of this is that if anyone were to express surprise at what you say on various occasions under the influence of your loves, you would tell him, if you wanted to speak true, that unless your favorites can be prevented from speaking as they do, neither can you.[11]

Note that Socrates makes a point of saying that what Callicles *says* is influenced by his desires. That Callicles' very words are now aligned with his search for pleasure and not with his reason and the search for truth is a major sign that his intellect has been affected by the way he is living – a life Socrates no doubt considers far from virtuous.

It might first seem that Callicles is simply a clear-headed manipulator who is clever enough to tell people what they need to hear in order to get what he wants. However, Callicles' unwillingness to change his position to any degree throughout his subsequent, extended conversation with Socrates is the most powerful sign that vice has weakened his intellect. Even though Socrates reveals a number of contradictions in Callicles' position, for example, Callicles is convinced that he is right and that Socrates hasn't been able to show otherwise. Either Callicles' ability to think rationally has been weakened, or the pull to satisfy his desires has become so strong that his intellect has lost any independence. Callicles' intellect is no longer a faculty for perceiving reality and rational analysis. It now functions primarily to serve his desires.

Support for Socrates: Augustine and Maslow

While the idea that vice harms the doer is primarily associated with Socrates, it actually surfaces elsewhere in ways that provide support for Socrates' claim.

The most prominent parallel can probably be found in the early Christian thinker St Augustine, who seems to echo Socrates when he claims that the consequences of vice are 'ignorance' and 'difficulty'. In *On Free Choice of the Will*, Augustine writes:

> It is absolutely just punishment for sin that each man loses what he is unwilling to use rightly, when he could without any difficulty use it if he willed. Thus the man who does not act rightly although he knows what he ought to do, loses the power to know what is right; and whoever is unwilling to do right when he can, loses the power to do it when he wills to. In fact, two penalties – ignorance and difficulty – beset every sinful soul.[12]

Describing an intellect enslaved by desire, Augustine paints a picture that Socrates would probably think applicable to Callicles – or anyone harmed by vice:

> Desire dominates the mind, despoils it of the wealth of its virtue, and drags it, poor and needy, now this way and now that; now approving and even defending what is false as though it were true, now disapproving what it previously defended, and rushing on to other falsities; now refusing assent and fearing clear reasoning; now despairing of fully discovering the truth and clinging to the deep obscurities of stupidity; now struggling into the light of understanding and falling back again from weariness.[13]

Like Socrates, Augustine believes that one of the consequences of wrongdoing is a weakened intellect in a personality that is now dominated by want. Truth, consistency, and logic matter less than satisfying desire.

Another, more recent (and somewhat surprising) source of support for Socrates' ideas is the contemporary psychologist Abraham Maslow. Maslow doesn't directly claim that 'vice harms the doer', but his research on psychological health suggests something of a corollary. Maslow reports that the most emotionally healthy individuals demonstrate a strong allegiance to ethics that carries with it a superior ability to perceive reality.

Maslow observes that 'self-actualized' individuals tend to agree about matters of right and wrong. In fact, he suggests that because of this agreement, their 'value judgments' seem to be more objective than subjective. He writes that, 'at least in the group I studied they tended to agree about what was right and wrong, as if they were perceiving something real and extrahuman rather than comparing tastes that might be relative to the individual person'.[14]

Maslow suggests that this agreement on values actually proceeds from their superior ability to perceive reality. That is, because of what they know about the world (what *is* the case), they know what *ought* to be done. Maslow observes,

> This is where knowledge brings certainty of decision, action, choice and what to do, and therefore, strength of arm. This is very much like the situation with a surgeon or dentist. The surgeon opening up the abdomen and finding an inflamed appendix knows that it had better be cut out because if it bursts it will kill the person. This is an example of truth dictating what must be done, of the *is* dictating the *ought*.[15]

Elsewhere he puts it this way,

> [This kind of] cognition can lead to moral sureness and decisiveness in just about the same sense that the high IQ can lead to a clear perception of a complicated set of facts, or in about the same sense that a constitutionally sensitive aesthetic perceiver tends to see very clearly what color-blind people cannot see or what other people do not see. It makes no difference that one million color-blind people cannot see that the rug is colored green. They may think it is colored gray, but this will make no difference to the person who clearly, vividly, and unmistakably perceives the truth of the matter. . . . I believe that the average person can then be described as is-perceptive but ought-blind. The healthy person is more ought-perceptive.[16]

Maslow does not say that 'vice harms the doer'. But his ideas imply that vice is a trait of the emotionally *un*healthy, and that such individuals lack the superior cognitive abilities of the self-actualized. One of the traits of the 'ought-blind', then, is looking at the same facts as the 'ought-perceptive' and coming to a faulty conclusion about the ethical character of the actions in question.

How the Defenders of the Drive Hunts are Harmed

If I am right in thinking that we can apply the ideas of Socrates (and Augustine and Maslow) to the defenders of the Japanese drive hunts, we should be able to find evidence that suggests an intellect weakened and serving some desire. And, as I suggested earlier in this paper, I believe the evidence lies in the fact that defenders offer transparently weak arguments to support the drive hunts.

The arguments are weak on a number of fronts.

Factual issues

First, central factual claims advanced by the hunts' defenders can be challenged.

- Claim: There is a culinary culture of eating cetacean meat in Japan.
  - Challenge: Eating cetacean meat is actually in decline. Concerns about pollutant contamination – especially mercury contamination – have driven down the price of dolphin meat.[17] Market demand is so weak that the government has tried to stimulate demand by subsidizing the sale of whale meat to schools and hospitals.[18]
- Claim: Cetaceans are competitors with humans for fish and squid. Fewer cetaceans mean more dependable and abundant catches.
  - Challenge: A Humane Society study argues that 'even though marine mammals consume a large quantity of marine resources as a whole, there is likely relatively little actual competition between "them" and "us"'.[19] The study contends that the cause of the current global fisheries crisis is 'a long history of mismanagement of fisheries'.[20] There is also reason to believe that if there is a significant economic factor involved in stimulating the drive hunts, it has to do with a more recent demand for captive dolphins, not a more traditional demand for cetacean meat.[21]

The validity of ethics

A second significant weakness in the defences of the drive hunts surfaces in their rejection of ethical objections as ethnocentric.

In view of thousands of years of sophisticated ethical inquiry by thinkers from every culture, simply to dismiss legitimate ethical objections out of hand in this way is hardly persuasive. There is abundant scientific research on dolphins that supports profound ethical objections against the drive hunts. It is the hunts' defenders, not their critics, who advance ethnocentric and anthropocentric positions.

The relevance of scientific and ethical inquiry

Given such a failure to appreciate the nature and value of ethical inquiry, it should come as no surprise that another weakness in the arguments of the drive hunts' defenders is that they ignore the ethical implications of the scientific research demonstrating that dolphins have sophisticated cognitive and affective abilities. Dolphins are self-aware beings with emotions, personalities, strong social bonds, and the ability to think abstractly, to solve complex problems, to choose and plan their actions, and to communicate in a way that suggests thought. Dolphins qualify as 'non-human persons'.[22] The ethical implications of the scientific research are that dolphins are a some-*one*, not a some-*thing*. That is, dolphins are entitled to moral standing as *individuals* and deserve to be treated with appropriate respect for their rights and interests. That is, dolphins are not merely a marine resource to be used, even if in a 'sustainable' way. From an ethical perspective, to claim that dolphins are a 'marine resource' is no different from the position advanced by American slaveholders in the eighteenth century that slaves were 'property' not 'persons'.

The scientific research on dolphins' intellectual and emotional abilities suggests that the pain that dolphins in the drive hunts experience is likely equivalent to what humans would experience in a similar situation.

Consider this account of a typical drive hunt:

> After being driven into shallow coves, the fishermen kill the dolphins with crude methods, cutting their throats or stabbing them with spears. Unconsciousness and death are not always immediate, and some dolphins take many minutes to die, thrashing about violently as blood pours from their wounds. Some of the dolphins suffocate during the round-up and slaughter; getting caught in the nets, weakened and unable to swim from the shock and stress of capture. Many dolphins panic and crash into nets, boats, pier walls and each other. As a result of this struggle, the water turns red with the blood of the dying dolphins. Sometimes the whole drive hunt process can take days, with the animals trapped and frightened, their fate unknown to them.[23]

Being herded into the coves, hearing the sounds of other dolphins' distress, witnessing the deaths of members of their community, and waiting for one's own death would be terrifying enough. The main method of slaughter, however, means a dolphin slowly bleeds to death over about ten minutes, which is surely an agonizing way to die. Even escaping slaughter and being chosen for captivity doesn't mean a dolphin will survive. The stresses connected with transport and adaptation to a captive facility are so considerable that the risk of death remains. And while living in an aquarium is better than being slaughtered in a cove, life in captivity is likely less satisfying than life in the wild.[24]

Even the most sceptical interpretation of the scientific research would have to conclude that there is a strong possibility that dolphins killed and captured in the drive hunts suffer greatly. And there is certainly no more fundamental imperative in ethics than that if our actions may harm someone, we have a duty to refrain from doing them. In an uncertain situation, our obligation is to be certain that we do no harm.

Nonetheless, defenders of the drive hunts regularly ignore the scientific findings and their ethical implications.

Logical fallacies

Logically flawed responses also provide evidence of the sort of weakened intellect suggested by Socrates and Augustine. The grey whale hunts engaged in by the Makah native Americans are sometimes cited in defence of the Japanese drive hunts. However, the fact that a small group of Americans engages in the ethically indefensible (even if possibly legal) killing of grey whales is irrelevant to the scientific and ethical character of the drive hunts. Indeed, such an argument is a classic example of the logical fallacies *irrelevant reason* (*non sequitur*) and *two wrongs make a right* (*tu quoque*).[25]

Similar fallacies characterize other defences offered:

- The defence of the hunts as 'cultural activity' and the idea that eating cetacean meat is part of a 'culinary culture' are examples of the fallacy of *appeal to traditional wisdom*.[26]
- To cite the fact that the fishermen in the areas of the drive hunts are economically stressed is an *irrelevant reason* when the issue is as serious as justifying the killing of self-aware, intelligent beings.
- The defence of the hunts as being no more objectionable than hunting other wild animals combines two fallacies: *questionable comparison* and *two wrongs*.[27] There is a significant difference between the cognitive and affective abilities of dolphins and most other mammals, so lumping all 'wild animals' together is inaccurate. And even if other hunts produce the same amount of suffering in other animals that the drive hunts do in dolphins, this hardly justifies any of the suffering produced.
- The aquarium industry's ostensibly humanitarian argument that taking dolphins from the drive hunt saves the lives of dolphins who would otherwise be slaughtered is an example of the fallacy of *questionable premise*. The defence is based on the assumption that the hunts would take place and dolphins would be killed whether representatives from the industry were there or not. The premise is faulty because it ignores the fact that there is reason to believe that the industry's demand for captive dolphins is, in fact, the main factor that perpetuates the hunts and that, without the considerable economic incentives connected with selling dolphins for captivity, the hunts would have ended by now. [28]

Defences Taken as a Whole: Evidence of 'Vice Harms the Doer'

While each defence of the drive hunts is problematic on its own, when we look at all of the defences together, they form a striking collection of illogical thinking and self-serving statements that could not hope to persuade an impartial audience. In addition, they are often offered by highly educated individuals whom we would presume to be unusually intelligent.

Why, then, do we have such intelligent individuals offering defences of the drive hunts that an objective audience would find patently unpersuasive? I believe that the best explanation is that this is precisely the sort of harm that Socrates has in mind when he claims that vice harms the doer.

Socrates contends that the consequence of vice is that a desire for something grows so strong that satisfying it is more important than perceiving reality accurately, dealing with uncomfortable truths about a situation and respecting the canons of logic. With the drive hunts, different desires may motivate different individuals to defend the hunts (simply to do what one wants, to increase feelings of national pride, to make money, etc.). However, what the desires have in common is that they all have become so strong that they have weakened the force and role of the intellect in all of the defenders. Given the seriousness of the issue at hand – the life and death of self-aware beings – to ignore relevant scientific research and the ethical implications of such evidence, to advance plainly fallacious arguments and to believe that such weak reasoning is a legitimate and persuasive defence of the drive hunts must surely count as serious harm to one's intellect. As in the case of Callicles, either the defenders' ability to think rationally has been weakened, or the pull to satisfy their desires has become so strong that their intellect has lost any independence as a faculty for perceiving reality and rational analysis. And this is precisely the sort of harm Socrates would predict from unethical actions.

The Relationship to Human Violence

This chapter has described a significant example of harm to humans that stems from abuse to non-humans – the internal harm done to the defenders of the Japanese drive hunts of the sort predicted by Socrates' idea that 'vice harms the doer'. Unfortunately, the human harm that results from the drive hunts is not limited to the defenders. They only defend what others are doing in killing and capturing the dolphins involved. So it is fair to say that the principals also experience the same sort of harm

Moreover, the drive hunts are only one instance of the vast amount of ethically indefensible treatment of dolphins that daily takes place on the planet. Thousands of dolphins are killed or injured in connection with other human fishing practices, and hundreds of dolphins are kept in captive entertainment facilities. In each case, some individuals inflict the harm directly, some defend it and others are entertained by it. A strong desire of one sort or another either weakens or overpowers the intellect of the individuals involved so that they become blind to the ethically questionable nature of their own actions. Like the defenders of the drive hunts, they may rationalize their behaviour and truly believe that their actions produce more good than harm. Perhaps, as is true of many defenders of captivity, they even believe that their actions benefit dolphins. But it is fair to think that, if Socrates is right, each person has been harmed in a way that only increases the likelihood that he or she will become chronically calloused to a wider range of unethical behaviours among humans.

For example, much human violence is based on the belief that superficial differences – race, sex, sexual orientation, nationality, tribal membership, religious beliefs – signal that those who are 'different' are actually 'inferior'. Such differences, then, are regarded as justification for treating 'different' people however we choose to. The defences of unethical behaviours towards dolphins surely only reinforce the sad belief that 'different' means 'inferior'. There is little difference between dismissing as irrelevant the intellectual and emotional capacities of dolphins and killing them because they are members of an 'inferior' species and dismissing the intellectual and emotional capacities of a particular group of humans and killing or discriminating against them because they are members of an 'inferior' group.

Nonetheless, we humans have repeatedly demonstrated the capacity to recognize as equals beings whom we once saw as inferiors. I believe that humans currently stand in roughly the same relationship with dolphins as white Americans did to Black slaves two hundred years ago. During the last two centuries, science and culture were gradually able to transcend the racism that constrained them to see other people only as property. There is, then, reason to be hopeful that, eventually, our species will overcome the cultural, economic, and political forces that limit our perspective about other beings with whom we share the planet. It will take patience and persistence, but it is surely not too much to hope of a species that regards itself as 'intelligent'.

Notes

1   This paper's account of the drive hunts is based on: Courtney S. Vail and Denise Risch, *Driven by demand: Drive hunts in Japan and the involvement of the aquarium industry* (Chippenham, UK: Whale and Dolphin Conservation Society, 2006); Rick Weiss, 'Intelligence of dolphins cited in fight against hunt: Others see equal weight in the value of tradition', *Washington Post*, November 20 2006: A1; and Diana Reiss and Lori Marino, 'Japan's dolphin drive hunts from a scientific and animal welfare perspective', http://www.theoceanproject.org/actfordolphins/ scivi.html. I am particularly indebted to Professors Lori Marino and Diana Reiss for their generous assistance.

2   This includes the World Association of Zoos and Aquariums, the Associations of Zoos and Aquariums in the United States, the Scientific Committee of the International Whaling Commission, Earth Island Institute, the Whale and Dolphin Conservation Society, the World Society for the Protection of Animals, and the Humane Society of the United States.

3   The WAZA is the world's premier zoo and aquarium association and represents approximately 12,000 institutions.

4   'Report of the scientific committee', *Report of the International Whaling Commission* 43 (1993), p. 84.

5   Rick Weiss, 'Intelligence of dolphins cited in fight against hunt', *The Washington Post*, 20 November 2006: A1.

6   'Scientific statement against the Japanese dolphin drive hunts', http://www.theoceanproject.org/actfordolphins/statement.html.

7   Thomas I. White, *In defense of dolphins: The new moral frontier* (Oxford: Blackwell, 2007).

8   The individuals who would offer such defences are not themselves killing dolphins in the drive hunts. But the defenders' actions help the hunts continue, which makes them partially responsible for the hunts' deaths. Such ethically problematic behaviour, then, is apparently sufficient to produce the harm that Socrates contends is connected with wrongdoing.

9   'Socrates: Vice harms the doer', in Thomas I. White, *Discovering philosophy*, 2nd edn (Upper Saddle River, NJ: Pearson/Prentice-Hall, 2007).

10   This paper is based on the interpretation that Plato's *Gorgias* (unlike the later dialogues) represents genuinely Socratic ideas.

11   Plato, *Gorgias*, trans. W. C. Helmbold (Indianapolis, IN: Bobbs-Merrill, 1952), pp. 49–50 (481d-482a).

12   Augustine, *On free choice of the will*, trans. Anna S. Benjamin and L. H. Hackstaff (Indianapolis, IN: Bobbs-Merrill, 1964), p. 128.

13   Augustine, *On free choice of the will*, p. 22; translation altered.

14   A. H. Maslow, *The farther reaches of human nature* (New York: Penguin Books, 1971), p. 9.

15   Maslow, *Farther reaches of human nature*, p. 117.

16   Maslow, *Farther reaches of human nature*, p. 118.

17   Duncan Robertson writes, 'In the last few years the wholesale price of dolphin meat has dropped to just under £1 a kilo because pollution fears have turned Japanese consumers off tinned dolphins'. See 'Dolphin slaughter sparks embassy protest', *Daily Mail* (London), 18 September 2006.

18   Vail and Risch, *Driven by demand*, p. 13; Anthony Fiola, 'Reviving a taste for whale: Japan introduces meat to children as it fights moratorium', *The Washington Post*, 19 June 2005: A19.

19   Kristin Kaschner and Daniel Pauly, *Competition between marine mammals and fisheries: Food for thought* (Washington, DC: The Humane Society of the United States/The Humane Society International, 2004), p. 22.

20   Kaschner and Pauly, *Competition*, p. 3.

21   Vail and Risch, *Driven by demand*, pp. 15–16.

22   White, *In defense of dolphins*.

23   Vail and Risch, *Driven by demand*, p. 9.

24   The Whale and Dolphin Conservation Society, for example, maintains 'that it is impossible to accommodate [dolphins'] mental, physical and social needs in captivity and that it is cruel to confine them' (Vail and Risch, *Driven by demand*, p. 28). For my explanation of the unacceptability of captivity, see chapter 7 of *In defense of dolphins*.

25   Howard Kahane and Nancy Cavender, *Logic and contemporary rhetoric: The use of reason in everyday life*, 9th edn (Belmont, CA: Wadsworth/Thompson Learning, 2002), pp. 75–79.

26   *Ibid.*, pp. 77–78.

27   *Ibid.*, pp. 96–98.

28   *Ibid.*, p. 62. The Whale and Dolphin Conservation Society contends that 'as Japanese prefectures appeared to be on the verge of abandoning the hunts, the demand for live animals to supply a growing number of marine parks and aquaria is emerging as a primary motivating factor for the drive hunts to continue in Japan' (Vail and Risch, *Driven by demand*, p. 7; see also pp. 15–16).

Index

Compiled by

ALASTAIR AND SARAH HARDEN

abuse (animal)
    and advocacy against, 95–103, 196–8, 232, 246
    as aggressive displacement, 44–7, 149
    causes/motivations of, 28–9, 44–6, 243–6
    as criminal offence, 13–14, 46, 130, 190–9, 230, 238–48, 250–8
    definition of, 31, 43–44, 76, 184–5, 191–3
    emotional, 75–86
    as entertainment, 8, 28, 44, 318, 337
    feminist perspectives on, 117–19, 123, 310
    incendiary, 14, 18–20, 110, 146–7, 164, 250–1
    and intrinsic moral significance, 186–9
    legal committing of, 8–9, 156, 191, 196–7
    as legally victimless, 192–3
    measuring, 16–17
    and morality, 6, 173–4, 184–9, 228, 317–26, 332
    and other criminal/antisocial behaviour, 17–19, 53–4, 145–59, 164–6, 193–5
    as pathological symptom, 15, 116, 121, 146
    and remorse, 16, 108–9, 283
    as risk indicator, 26, 48, 127, 130, 223–4, 252
    sexual, 4, 19, 27, 34, 76, 107, 119, 233, 275, 282
    socially condoned, 28, 297, 300, 317–26
    and speciesism, 6, 15, 44, 173, 175–82, 190–1, 198
    as retaliation/revenge, 28, 44, 229
    theories of, 28–9, 185–6
    torture, 2, 14, 18–20, 165–7, 169, 190, 207–9, 223–5, 325
    (see also neglect; see also under children)
abuse (human)
    child, 4, 13, 26–31, 33–34, 39–41, 45–7, 55, 69–70, 75–86, 99, 130–7, 145, 148–9, 154–8, 228, 231, 263–4, 273–9, 281–9, 298, 310, 323
    disabled, 101
    emotional/psychological, 38, 43–4, 50,
        75–86, 118, 132, 145, 150, 154–8, 158, 204, 207, 228
    elder, 13, 27–8, 30–1, 101, 228, 230–1, 234
    prevention of, 29–31, 85, 146, 177, 274–6
    sexual, 4, 75, 77, 81–2, 110, 131, 150, 154–8, 233, 275–8, 282
    (see also under abuse (animal); children; violence)
aggression, theories of, 38–44
aggressive psychiatric patients (APP), 132
alcoholism, 47, 66, 145, 148–9, 154–5, 158
Alzheimer's Disease, 187
American Society for the Prevention of Cruelty to Animals (ASPCA), 84, 97–9, 273–4, 292n.35
AniCare Model, 230, 235n.18
Animal-Assisted Activities (AAA), 126, 135, 137
Animal-Assisted Therapy (AAT), 126–7, 135, 137
animal experimentation
    as abuse, 202
    behavioural, 64, 68, 78, 81–2, 84
anthropocentrism, 6, 116, 121, 134–5, 336
    (see also speciesism; abuse (animal) and speciesism)
Antisocial Personality Disorder, 31, 49, 70, 146, 257
anxiety, 39, 49, 62, 75, 79–81, 83–4, 118, 134, 136
apes, 178, 219n.57
aquaria, 330–8
Aristotle, 175–7, 209, 215
arson, 250–1, 257 (see also abuse (animal), incendiary)
Artemis Intake Questionnaire, 111
Artley, Alexandra, 276
Ascione, Frank, 14–17, 25–7, 33–4, 43–4, 52–3, 85, 106–12, 117, 127, 130–2, 135, 164, 258n.1, 275, 317
Augustine, St, 176, 215, 324–5, 333–4, 336
Australia
    and asylum seekers, 43
    mass murder in, 17

Australia *(continued)*
  Sex Offender Treatment and Assessment
    Programme, 149

The Badger Trust, 239–40
badgers, 222, 238–40, 243–4, 246
bed-wetting *(see* enuresis)
Bell, Mary, 19
Bentham, Jeremy, 303
Berdella, Robert, 165
Bergh, Henry, 97, 99, 273–4
bestiality, 19, 35n.24, 165–6, 290n.10,
    291n.16 *(see also* abuse (animal),
    sexual)
bifurcation, 6–7, 325
Bill of Rights (England, 1688), 175–6
birds, 215, 240, 244, 306–8
  abuse of, 19, 165, 169, 210, 276, 323
  and consciousness/empathy, 69, 178
    (see also cock-fighting)
Boat, B.W., 16, 113n.8, 160n.15, 278
borderline personality disorder, 80
Brady, Ian, 18
British Veterinary Nursing Association, 5
Bryant, Clifford, 116
Bryant, Martin, 18
Bulger, James, 19
bull-fighting, 325
Bundy, Ted, 224
Buxton, Fowell, 3, 104n.14

California Child Abuse and Neglect
    Reporting Act, 277
Catholicism, 175–7 *(see also* Christianity)
cats
  abuse of, 2, 14–15, 18–19, 29 n.41, 31–2,
    132, 144, 166–9, 225, 274, 278, 285,
    306, 322
  as companions, 120–1, 128, 133
charity, 98, 101
Chase, Richard, 165
children
  bullying, 30, 39, 48–51, 55, 146
  committing animal cruelty, 15, 18, 26,
    28–9, 46–49, 131, 146, 150–9, 166–8,
    190, 195. 198, 275, 321
  committing murder, 15, 18–19, 321–3
  committing sexual abuse, 34, 146,
    275
  culpability of, 191–2, 195
  emotional abuse of, 75–86
  exposed to animal cruelty, 51–2, 69–70,
    110–12, 131–3
  exposed to domestic violence, 69–70,
    106–12
  harmed/killed by animals, 3
  protection of, 95–103
  sexual abuse of, 19, 26–7, 75, 81, 110, 132,
    223, 277–8

  (see also abuse (human); infants/toddlers;
    neglect)
Christianity, 98–9, 102–3, 175–7, 189
cock-fighting, 241, 244–6
Coetzee, J.M., 206–15
Colam, John, 97
Cole, Carroll, 18, 165
Collins, John Norman, 165
Columbine High School massacre, 18
companion animals *(see* pets)
compassion, 7, 30, 96, 97–102, 179, 181–2,
    206–11, 214–15, 229–30, 321, 324,
    326
conduct disorder (CD), 31, 39, 42, 47–49,
    70, 106, 146, 257–8, 282
Consolo, Giuseppe, 96
Constanzo, Adolfo, 166
control (power), 28, 44–5, 47, 52, 78, 82,
    111, 118–19, 121, 123, 129, 148–9,
    168–9, 175, 177, 197, 203, 232, 283,
    286, 299, 302, 304
cross-reporting, 30, 127, 136, 222, 231, 269,
    278–9, 286–8

Dahmer, Jeffrey, 165–6
Darwin, Charles, 180
de las Casas, Bartolomé, 176–7, 179
de Salvo, Albert ('The Boston Strangler'),
    18
decapitation, 165, 225
deer-hunting, 296, 304, 317–26
dehumanizing, 43
Descartes, René, 188
desensitizing, 6–7, 25, 146, 282, 323, 325
depression, 39, 66, 75, 80–1, 83, 133–4, 136,
    204
deviance generalization, 143, 145–7, 149,
    154, 157–9, 164–5 *(see also* graduation
    hypothesis)
distress, 14, 43–4, 62, 75–86, 112, 130, 317
District of Columbia
  Animal Protection Amendment Act
    (2007), 229–34
  DC Coalition against Animal Violence,
    232
dogs
  abuse of, 2–3, 7, 18, 27, 31–2, 42, 44–5,
    83–4, 144, 166–9, 224–5, 238, 250,
    267–8, 274–5, 278, 283–4, 287, 318,
    322
  and dog-fighting, 3, 44, 222, 238–45
  exempted from other animal cruelty, 15
  experimentation on, 202–5
  hunting with, 246, 295, 302–12
  induced to violence, 18, 239
  service-dogs, 133
  value as companions, 3, 30, 69, 120,
    128–9, 132–3, 213
dolphins, 178, 329–39

domestic violence shelters, 4, 25–6, 33, 110–11, 117–18, 122, 129–31, 232–3 (*see also,* violence, domestic)
drugs and drug offences, 27, 48, 53, 147, 164, 225, 242, 255, 288

education, 30, 62, 64, 85, 100–2, 132, 137, 150, 222, 229–30, 265–9
elephants, 81
Eliot, T.S., 7
electroencephalography (EEG), 42, 68–9
empathy, 6, 16, 28, 47, 49, 63–71, 132, 146, 181, 224, 286, 297–9, 310, 321, 326
Enlightenment, The, 1, 176–8
enuresis, 19–20, 36n.27, 147, 164
ethics, 184–9
Evangelicalism, 98
farms, 8, 14, 39, 44, 78, 95, 136, 276, 304
fear, 4, 30, 45, 53, 65, 75, 78, 80–4, 118, 122, 129, 132–3, 136, 229

Federal Bureau of Investigation (FBI), 2, 17, 221, 223–7, 231
feminism/feminist perspectives, 5, 117, 119, 123, 139n.51, 293n.55, 300n.2, 310
ferrets, 135
fire (*see* arson; abuse (animal), incendiary)
fish, 178, 247, 283, 322, 329–39
foster-care, 84–5, 135–6
foxes, 214
  and fox- hunting, 302–12
France
  Declaration of the Rights of Man, 175
functional magnetic resonance imaging (fMRI), 68–9
fur, 9

Gabriel's Angels (Mesa, Arizona), 135
game-hunting, 45, 240, 244, 247, 303, 317–26
Garbarino, James, 86
garden therapy, 135
genetic factors, 39, 65, 82
graduation hypothesis, 11, 28–9, 143, 145, 147, 149, 157–9, 166, 285 (*see also* abuse (animal), theories of; deviance generalization)
Green Chimneys (Brewster, New York), 135
guinea-pigs, 14
guns, 18–19, 53, 132, 165–6, 209, 301n.26, 318–22

hare-coursing, 304
Harris, Eric (*see* Columbine High School massacre)
health visitors, 281–9
'Hillside Stranglers', 168
Hobbes, Thomas, 175
Hogarth, William, 7, 324

homosexuality, 99, 148
horses, 76, 209, 215, 239, 250, 304, 311
humancentrism (*see* anthropocentrism; speciesism)
Humane Society, 99, 278, 335
  Canada, 127
  of Illinois, 100
  of the United States (HSUS) , 5, 14, 29, 99–100, 227
  Washington (WHS), 232–3
  of Wellington County, Canada, 279
  Wisconsin (WHS), 29
  (*see also* Society for the Prevention of Cruelty to Animals)
hunting, 156, 297–300, 302–12, 316–26
Huntley, Ian, 19
Hurricane Katrina, 129

incarceration, 2, 25, 32, 106, 109, 132, 145, 214, 242–3, 250–8 (*see also* surveys of prison inmates)
  and the National Offender Management System (NOMS), 256
  and the Offender Assessment System (OASys), 255, 258
infants/toddlers
  abuse of, 6, 19, 77, 83, 84–5, 99, 275, 278, 284–5, 306
  exposure to violence, 106–7
  and parental attachment, 66, 68, 80
International Whaling Commission, 330
intimate partner violence (IPV), 106–12 (*see also* violence, domestic)

Japan
  and dolphin-hunting, 329–39

Kant, Immanuel, 1, 177–9, 185–8, 309, 324
Kemper, Edmund, 18
Kinkel, Kip, 18
Klebold, Dylan, 18
Kundera, Milan, 205

La Crosse Community Coalition Against Violence, 321
League against Cruel Sports, 9, 240, 310
Lee Lucas, Henry, 19
Levinson, Boris, 134
Links Group, The, 5, 9, 288
Locke, John, 175, 324
Ludwig I of Bavaria, 102

MacDonald, J.M., 19–20, 147, 160nn.32&34, 164
Magna Carta, 175–6
major depressive disorder (MDD), 80
Malvo, Lee (Washington sniper), 165–6
'marginal human beings', 179, 187–9
masculinity, 244–7, 299, 302, 311

Maslow, Abraham, 333–4
Massey, Jason, 225
McGinn, Colin, 203
mental health and healthcare, 17–19, 48, 55,
    64, 82, 106, 112, 116, 127, 134, 192,
    205, 225, 255–7, 268, 284–6, 289
Metternich, Chancellor of Austria, 102
mice, 14, 81
mirror neurons, 63, 67–9
monkeys, 64, 68–9, 82
Montaigne, Michel de, 324
Moors murders, 18
moral disengagement theory, 43–7
More, Sir Thomas, 324
murder, 321–3
    committed by children, 11, 17–19
    mass, and serial killing, 4, 17–19, 29, 38,
        143, 147, 158, 163–9, 223–227
    sexual homicide, 2, 33, 145–58

National Institutes of Health (NIH), 134
necrophilia, 19, 165
neglect, 14, 27, 33, 40, 44, 75–9, 81, 84–6,
    101, 137, 241, 276–8, 281, 283–7
New York, humane education in, 229
Nietzsche, Friedrich, 180
National Society for the Prevention of
    Cruelty to Children (NSPCC), 3, 5,
    30, 282, 288
National Wildlife Crime Unit (NWCU), 242

Ortega y Gasset, José, 324

Paul, St, 175–6
pets
    abuse/threat of abuse to, 8, 15, 19, 25–7,
        33, 45, 52–3, 61, 70–1, 94, 106–7,
        110–12, 117–23, 130–3, 146–8, 197,
        228–9, 231, 233, 283–9, 320, 326 (*see
        also* violence, domestic)
    value as emotional companions of, 27, 30,
        64–7, 116–23, 126–30, 224–5
Pew Research Centre, 128
philanthropy, 96–8
pigs, 44
Plato, 175
post-traumatic stress disorder, 80–2, 84
power (psychological), 45, 47, 49–50, 119,
    121, 123, 129, 168–9, 175–82, 197,
    205, 218n.47, 319, 333–4 (*see also*
    control)
psychopathology, 31, 49, 81–2, 116, 121,
    169, 195
public opinion, 75, 298, 302, 308

Rader, Dennis ('The B.T.K. Killer'), 163
rape, 2, 32, 38, 54, 81, 112, 166, 168, 203,
    223, 323
    child, 2, 132, 203, 223

rationality, 187–9
rats, 45, 81–2, 84
Rebula, Alojz, 101
reform, 97–8, 102, 196–9, 229, 303
Regan, Tom, 193–6
rehabilitation, 190, 192, 226–7, 229–30,
    247–8
resilience, 81–2
Ridgway, Gary ('The Green River Killer'),
    163, 168
rights & rights organizations
    animal, 103, 178, 197–8
    general, 99, 101, 195, 207, 257, 264,
        304–5
    human, 95, 103, 173, 175–82 309
    philosophy of, 175–82
    victims', 193
rodents, 169 (*see also* rats; mice; guinea-pigs)
Rousseau, Jean Jacques, 175
Royal College of Veterinary Surgeons
    (RCVS), 264–70
Royal Society for the Prevention of Cruelty
    to Animals (RSPCA, formerly SPCA)
    3, 5, 14–15, 27, 30, 96–7, 100, 240–1,
    244, 254, 282
Royal Society for the Protection of Birds
    (RSPB), 241

sadism (*see* violence, sadistic)
Scalia, Tina, 100
self-esteem, 41, 43–4, 79, 117, 121, 133, 169
Sepúlveda, Ginés de, 176
Shaftsbury, Lord, 3
Shaw, George Bernard, 7
Shawcross, Arthur, 166
Shortall, John, 100
Singh, Rabinder QC, 304
slavery, 179–82, 332–3, 336, 339
snakes, 169
Social Services (*see* social work & workers)
social work & workers, 29, 107, 122, 127,
    137, 159, 273, 276 (*see also* Health
    Visitors)
Società Siciliana Umanitaria Educativa e per
    la protezione degli animali, 100–1
Society for the Prevention of Cruelty to
    Animals,
    American (*see* American Society for the
        Prevention of Cruelty to Animals)
    Gorizia, 101–2
    Massachusetts, 53
    Munich, 97, 102
    Palermo, 100–1
    Paris, 97
    Scotland, 241
    Trieste, 98
    United Kingdom (*see* Royal Society for the
        Prevention of Cruelty to Animals)
    Vienna, 102

Society for the Prevention of Cruelty to
Children
American, 99
New York, 99, 274
United Kingdom (*see* National Society
for the Prevention of Cruelty to
Children)
Socrates, 331–8
Solomon, Richard, 202
speciesism, 6, 173, 175–82, 190–1,
198
Stanig, Valentin, 101–2
suicide, 39, 48
surveys
of adolescents, 32, 50–1, 107–9
of children, 15, 32, 109–11, 131, 275
of criminals/offenders, 24, 32, 287
of domestic violence sufferers, 25–7, 32–3,
130, 286
ethnic, 128
of military families, 129
national (U.S.), 48
of prison inmates, 2, 20, 25, 29 32, 109,
145
of psychiatric patients, 31
of psychologists, 126
residential, 166–7
of sex offenders, 145, 149–50
of students, 32, 108, 145, 150, 167
Sutherland, Edwin, 244
symbolic interactionism, 119–20
sympathy, 6–7, 63, 206–10

Taylor, Nicola, 311
Thompson, Emily, 273
torture (*see* violence, sadistic)
transcranial magnetic stimulation (TMS),
68–9
turtles, 278

United Kingdom
Animal Welfare Act (2006), 239, 254, 263,
269, 303
Animal Cruelty Bill (1809), 1, 239
Children Act (2004), 281
Criminal Justice Act (2003), 251
Deer Act (1991), 239
Hunting Act (2004), 304–5
Laming Report, 288
Operation Gazpacho, 240
Protection of Animals Act (1911), 254,
303
Protection of Animals (Amendment) Act
(1988), 303
Protection of Badgers Act (1992),
239
Wild Mammals (Protection) Act (1996),
239
Wildlife and Countryside Act (1981), 239

United States
Child Abuse Prevention and Treatment Act
(2005), 276
cruelty laws, 191–3
Declaration of Independence, 175
Lieber Code, 179
National Centre for the Analysis of
Organized Crime, 223
National Survey of Child and Adolescent
Well-Being Study, 136
state statues on reporting child abuse,
276–7
Universal Declaration on Human Rights, 182
utilitarianism, 5–6, 39, 194, 196–7

Vachss, Andrew, 135
veterinary care, 8, 44, 77, 83, 134–5, 231–2,
261, 263–70, 273, 276–9 (*see also*
Royal College of Veterinary Surgeons)
vermin, 45
Victoria, Australia, 53
videotaping of abuse/torture
animal, 14
human, 165
violence
domestic, 2, 4–5, 15, 25–31, 33, 46–7,
50–3, 69–70, 83, 94, 106–12, 116–23,
127–33, 136, 148, 222, 228–34, 251,
263, 275, 278–9, 286, 320
legality of, 197–9
sadistic/torture, 18–19, 28, 31, 45, 130,
144, 165–9, 207–14, 222, 225, 275, 32,
325
and sex difference, 50–1, 53–54, 108
sexual, 148–59, 252–3

Washington Snipers, The (*see* Malvo, Lee)
welfare
animal, 3–4, 99, 111, 126–37, 173–4,
179–80, 197, 222, 229, 232, 238–9,
241, 254, 261–2, 270, 273, 276–9,
281–9, 299–300, 303, 330
(*see also under* United Kingdom, Animal
Welfare Act 2006)
child, 2–3, 55, 126–37, 277–9, 281–9,
300
(*see also* United Kingdom, Children Act,
2004; United States, Child Abuse
Prevention and Treatment Act, 2005)
Wellington County, Canada
Family and Children's Services (FCS) and
Humane Society (HS), 279
Wertsch, Mary, 275–6
Wesley, John, 189
whales, 178, 336
Whitaker, Joseph Isaac (Pip), 100
Wilberforce, William, 3, 104n.14
wildlife, 238, 241–2, 303
Wilson, Mary Ellen, 99, 274

women, violence against (*see* violence,
     domestic)
Wood Green Animal Association, 5
Woodham, Luke, 18
World Association of Zoos and Aquariums,
     330

Zagler, J.J., 102
zoophilia (*see* bestiality)
zoos, 78